THE FOLK-LORE OF
HEREFORDSHIRE

THE FOLK-LORE

OF

HEREFORDSHIRE

COLLECTED FROM ORAL AND PRINTED SOURCES.

BY

ELLA MARY LEATHER

WITH AN INTRODUCTION BY

EDWIN SIDNEY HARTLAND, F.S.A.

HEREFORD :
JAKEMAN & CARVER, HIGH TOWN.

LONDON :
SIDGWICK & JACKSON, 3, ADAM STREET, ADELPHI.

—

1912.

THE FOLK-LORE OF HEREFORDSHIRE

Originally published in 1912
by Jakeman and Carver, Hereford

Reprinted 1970 and 1973

This edition © 1991 Lapridge Publications

Reprinted 1992

ISBN 0 9518589 0 4

Printed and bound by
SMITH SETTLE
Ilkley Road, Otley, West Yorkshire
for
Lapridge Publications
25 Church Street
Hereford HR1 2LR
Telephone: (0432) 357617

INTRODUCTION.

A book of county folklore makes an appeal to more than one class of readers. First and foremost it appeals to local residents, and to persons who are connected with the county by birth or descent. It recalls to them old familiar things. Reading it, they are reminded of scenes of childhood, and of friends perhaps long passed away, who surrounded them with care and affection—old playmates, or elders who led their childish steps or first brought them into touch with the external world. They know the places, they remember the customs, the tales, the sayings. They remember, too, not without amusement, their early terrors, and the awe with which they approached some spot haunted by ghost or goblin, or listened to narratives of weird and uncanny experience. They can confirm from their own recollection, or perhaps correct in details, the record. And to some it suggests new and strangely mingled thoughts to find what they now regard as trivial matters unworthy of serious attention, yet matters that are somehow enwound with their most intimate feelings and sacred memories, set coldly down and treated as subjects of sober scientific interest.

Every county museum wisely planned aims to represent the local features (not merely the local peculiarities, but also the characteristics it shares with neighbouring counties), so far as they can be enshrined in a museum. The butterflies are there, as well as the birds ; the wild flowers, as well as the fossils ; old sculptured stones from Roman sites or ruined churches, as well as the more portable but not less interesting furniture taken from the graves of the prehistoric dead ; ancient implements ; tools only recently discarded for the more summary processes of modern agriculture weaving or metallurgy ; the products of former and present industries ; the garb of gentle and simple in the days before the steam-roller of modern fashions crusht into one dead level throughout the kingdom local distinctions and those of rank and occupation together. But a museum, however wisely planned and skilfully administered, tells only half the tale, because it comprises no more than the material fabrics. The intellectual and emotional interests that stirred the life from century to century are represented only indirectly and with little suggestiveness. A county library supplies the want to some extent ; but it usually succeeds in gathering only the records of political and ecclesiastical changes and the general progress of ideas among the more cultured classes. The old county histories are little more than the story—often amazingly inaccurate—of the pomp, the pedigrees, the pretensions and the downfall of the ruling families. Of the people at large they hardly take account ; and when they refer to local customs or traditions, it is with ill-concealed contempt, or with the wonder born of ignorance that blesses itself with the thought that the writer is not as these clodhoppers. If we want to gauge aright the mind of the community, the social relations, the pleasures, the pains, the hopes and sorrows, and all the thousand details that fill and colour its life—in short, to know the people as it has been and as it is—we must turn to the oral traditions, the institutions and practices of the peasant and the labourer. These are things the law barely recognises. The church frowns on them, ignores them, or tolerates them as she tolerates Dissenters—with scorn and dislike, because she must. Yet they survive from generation to generation. Political and even ecclesiastical revolutions sweep over them, and leave them—not the same, but changing so slowly that, if not roughly interfered with by external authority, the alteration is only perceptible by comparison at rare intervals. Not until these latter days has the citadel of popular conservatism been breached, by means too obvious to need enumeration here. The approaching triumph of moderniza- tion—that right-about face in the outlook upon life—renders it necessary to hasten if the old story is to be preserved, that we and our successors may understand the long evolution that has taken place. The labours of the collector of folklore are directed to this end. The collection when formed is a museum of the thoughts, the sayings and the doings of our forefathers. It is the complement and explanation of the museum of material antiquities. Such is the collection of the folklore of Hereford- shire now before the reader.

Particular interest attaches to the traditions of a border county. A border county is the meeting-place of different peoples with different (often opposite) ideals, political, social, ecclesiastical. It is the scene of what Mary Kingsley called in an expressive phrase " the clash of cultures." In Herefordshire the English and Welsh have been face to face for forty generations. If the English have partially absorbed the Welsh, the process has involved a give-and-take of culture. The value of Offa's Dyke as a symbol of division between them may be easily overrated. The custom of carrying apples stuck with oats on a quest for New Year's gifts appears, for instance, to be, or to have been, general in the county ; but it is a Welsh rather than an English practice. There are, however, as Mrs. Leather points out in her preface, items of folklore that seem to witness to a distinction of nationality. She does not refer in this connection to the custom of Sin-eating, of which she has found relics in the south-west of the county. It was first mentioned by Aubrey more than two hundred years ago in his *Remaines of Gentilisme and Judaisme.* If " Ross highway," where dwelt a professional Sin-eater whom he knew and describes, be the road from Hereford to Ross, then the only records we have show the custom confined to the western bank of the Wye. It is a matter of personal satisfaction to me that Mrs. Leather has found vestiges of it at all. For its existence anywhere has been strenuously challenged. Some sixteen years ago when, in the simplicity of my heart, I quoted Aubrey, produced parallels and laboured to explain the meaning of the rite, I brought trouble on myself and was penalized to the extent of a lengthy correspondence in *The Times* and *The Academy*, in defence not of my induction, but of the underlying facts themselves. May Mrs. Leather's new evidence convince the sceptics !

At any rate students of folklore will read these and many other things in the following pages with interest. Agricultural customs naturally take a large place in a county like Herefordshire. Independently of the scientific interest attaching to the Harvest Home and other festivities, everybody will share the author's regret " that these merry-makings, which promoted good feelings between master and man, are being gradually discontinued." We may congratulate ourselves that she has preserved so many of the genuine old songs (tunes as well as words) sung on such occasions. They are a testimony to her undaunted perseverance and scientific method, and an additional help to our imaginations in reconstructing the kind of entertainment at social gatherings of the past in the farmhouse and the cottage.

No department of folklore strikes a more human note than that which relates to the great events in the life of the individual—birth, marriage and death. I must content myself with a brief reference to the last of these, though all three of them are well represented in the section on Ceremonial. One of the death-customs mentioned is that of telling the bees of their master's death. Comparison shows that the object of so doing is to prevent the ghost from luring them away. In Borneo, when a Dyak dies the precaution is taken of calling over the names of the children and other members of the household for the same reason. If the ghost lured the children away they would die. So the bees would die, or what would amount to the same thing, so far as the new owners were concerned, they would desert the hive and vanish—perhaps (who knows ?) into the next world. It does not appear that in Herefordshire crape is put about the hives, or the hives are turned round. But the cart-horses used to be told of the death. Otherwise their souls (for they too had souls) might be commandeered by the ghost for his use yonder. Our remote ancestors often voluntarily resigned the horse to his master by slaying him on the grave. We still lead the soldier's steed in his master's funeral procession, though we no longer actually sacrifice him to the *manes* of the deceased.

The only other custom I shall mention is the operation of turning a corpse in the grave—that is, turning it so that it will lie face downwards. This is one of many methods to prevent the restless dead from haunting the living. Mrs. Leather records a case at Capel-y-ffin. A ghastlier story, which probably belongs to Herefordshire—at all events to the diocese,—is recorded by Walter Map at the end of the twelfth century, though he speaks of the occurrence as taking place in Wales. William Laudun, an English knight, came, we learn, to Gilbert Foliot, at that time Bishop of Hereford, but afterwards of London, and told him this tale. A certain Welshman who is described by the epithet *maleficus*, by which we may infer that he was reputed to have dealings with the Powers of Darkness, had lately died without being reconciled to the Church. After four nights he came back every night to the village and called forth singly and by name his fellow-villagers. Those who were called uniformly fell sick and died within three days. The village was thus being gradually depopulated ; and Laudun consequently sought ecclesiastical counsel. The bishop directed the corpse to be dug up and its neck severed with the spade. Both the corpse and the grave were then to be asperged with holy water and replaced. It was done. But this drastic treatment, generally recommended for vampires, was no more effectual than turning the hurdle-maker at Capel-y-ffin. The horrible visitations were continued ; and soon only a few survivors were left. At last the vampire called William himself with a three-fold citation. But there he met his match. William sprang up with drawn sword and pursued the fleeing demon even to the grave. He overtook the grim visitor just as he was falling back into the earth, and clove his head down to the neck. How the vampire carried his head, seeing that it had been cut off, is not specified ; but the result was satisfactory. From that hour the persecution ceased. Map speaks as if he had some personal knowledge of the facts ; and he winds up by saying : " We know the true course of this affair : the cause we do not know."[1] He perhaps looked for the cause in a wrong direction. The belief in the possibility of corpses becoming re-animated and returning among living men, for the purpose of inflicting injury or death upon them, was widely spread in the Middle Ages. It is still current in some parts even of Europe. Its roots are to be sought in savage doctrines concerning death and the dead.

A museum is not a mere collection of what are vulgarly called " curios." It is a temple of learning. It exists for the purpose of instruction. Unless the objects are arranged in order and so as to inform those who desire to study them, unless they are provided with labels properly describing them, identifying their intention (where they are of human workmanship) and their place of origin, and containing references (if necessary) to works of authority, it is no museum, but a mere curiosity-shop. All these conditions it has been Mrs. Leather's aim to fulfil. In venturing to commend the volume to readers who are interested, whether their interest be local or scientific,

---

[1] *De Nugis Curialium* (ed. T. Wright), ii. 27. Map goes on to tell another story of a *revenant*. But as it apparently relates to the diocese of Worcester, I do not cite it here.

I may express the hope that it will be found a worthy companion to Miss Burne's learned and altogether delightful book on *Shropshire Folklore*. I would add the expression of an earnest wish that an example of these two ladies may incite others to labour. There are fields yet unreaped on the Welsh Marches. They are white unto the harvest. Nay, they are spoiling for want of reapers ; and the day is fast coming when if the crop be not already gathered it will be lost.

E. SIDNEY HARTLAND.

PREFACE.

The greater part of the present collection of Herefordshire folk-lore has been gathered since 1905, at the request of friends who were interested in a chapter on the subject contributed to *Memorials of Old Herefordshire*. It was then discovered that no systematic record had been made of the old country customs which were so rapidly dying out; I therefore attempted the task with but one qualification for it, the fact that I was born in the county, and have been all my life familiar with its folk and their ways. Perhaps my folk-lore collecting was unconsciously begun in childhood, with the stories told by old Martha B——, a tiny dark-haired olive-skinned woman, who, when I first remember her, gathered apples in a Herefordshire orchard. She ate her dinner by a little wood fire under an apple-tree, surrounded by heaps of glowing red and yellow apples,—"Sam's Crabs," "Jollyboykins," and "Jack Jones's," she called them; probably these names would not agree with those of the *Herefordshire Pomona*. Her dress was of linsey-wolsey; beneath the cotton bonnet, which will soon be obsolete, she wore an old-fashioned black net cap, with ribbon and lace frilling covering the ears, while her woollen crossover and "hurden" apron were as often as not worn wrong side out. It was not easy to see the right side on dark mornings, and she would not have "turned the luck" for the world. Martha smoked a little clay pipe, apologetically, "by doctor's orders"; her greeting was always "Good-day, missie, God bless you"; I learnt long afterwards that this latter formula was an infallible protection against witchcraft and Evil Eye. It was Martha who could tell how the big house which once stood in the wood had been pulled down because it was so badly haunted; she herself saw ghosts, and could point out the very spots where they appeared to her; I am sure she believed she saw them. Her thatched and timbered cottage stood beside an ancient yew-tree; it had an enormous stone chimney-stack at one end, with the oven for baking bread as a rounded projection at one side of it, sennagreen (house-leek) flourishing on its stone-tile roof. She made a healing salve of this, and believed it protected the "chimbley" from lightning. No visitor ever left the garden without a flower or a bunch of Martha's herbs; the recipient might protest in vain, only to be reminded that "there's an auld sayin' and a true one, the more you gives 'em away, the better they grows!"

No record in cold print can give the reader an idea of the pleasure experienced in collecting the elusive material we call folk-lore from the living brains of men and women, of whose lives it has formed an integral part. In some cases, with regard to superstitious beliefs, there is a deep reserve to be overcome ; the more real the belief, the greater the difficulty.   On the other hand, in collecting songs, customs, and sayings, the older folk realise how much of such lore is passing away, and are ready and sympathetic in trying to recall it, regretting it as they do the days of their youth.   And why not ?   We all look back with tender wistfulness to our childhood and its fancies ; shall we have none for those of the childhood of our race ?

The book has been planned with a view to a clear arrangement of the facts and facility of reference, in the hope that it may be of some practical use to the comparative folklorist.   Perhaps this is just the " dry-as-dust " method of which the local and general reader is apt to complain ; yet I trust there may be those whose love of our beautiful county may be a lamp by the light of which they may read between the lines, and who, having read, may see St. Dubricius walk by the Wye in the twilight, or catch a glimpse of fairies dancing under foxgloves in the dingles once again, or see Brownie on the cottage hearth.   Those who look for such things will yet find in reality the horse-shoe over the cottage-door, with maybe, crossed twigs of " witan and quicken-tree " (mountain-ash and hawthorn) nailed beneath it, while within a wheat-plait and a bunch of dried herbs hang above the shelf.

The county of Herefordshire is bounded on the east by the Malvern Hills, on the west by the Black Mountains ; northward, it is separated from Shropshire by the Teme, which at Ludlow runs at the foot of the Clee Hills ; at its southern extremity, the Wye flows round the Great and Little Dowards.   It forms a natural basin, the surface diversified and broken by wooded hills, everywhere well watered by the Wye and its tributaries.   A garden of orchards and pastures, it is a county of great natural beauty ; from almost every part of it one may see to the west, the great rampart of the Black Mountains, or Hatterals, with the Radnor hills rolling away beyond, and the peaks of the Brecon beacons ; southwards, the Skyrrid and Sugar Loaf break the horizon ; to the east, the peaks of the Malverns make a background to fertile valleys filled with orchards in all their glory of pink blossom in Spring, or laden with the rosy apples in Autumn ; a country of green meadows, hopyards, and waving cornfields, of grey church towers with their thatched or timbered cottages clustering round them in the hollows ; all set in a framework of undulating woodlands.

The history of Herefordshire may be said to have begun when some cataclysm of Nature heaved the plutonic rocks of the Malverns above the surface of the primeval ocean ; at this time, the geologists say, all the rest of England was still submerged. Four-fifths of the county, as we know, rest on a bed of the rock known as the Old Red Sandstone.   The limestone rocks of Colwall, Aymestrey, and Woolhope are well-known to geologists and fossil-hunters.   In the carboniferous limestone of the Great Doward are several caves; the principal ones are King Arthur's Cave, or Hall, and the Bannerman Cave. King Arthur and his men must at one time have been associated with the cave that bears his name, but so far diligent enquiry for legends has been fruitless. The cave is of great interest, and when examined some years ago was found to contain evidence of man in the form of flint flakes, beneath deposits of stalagmite and cave earth, many feet in thickness; far below, after cutting through beds of red sand, pebbles of greensand and lower Silurian rock, more cave earth was discovered, in which there was a large number of bones, teeth, and jaws, belonging to rhinoceros, horse, reindeer, elk, bison, cave lion, hyena, and mammoth. Among the traces of early man in the county may be mentioned the discovery of a cinerary urn, containing charred bones, found 17 feet down in the drift, in a gravel pit at Mathon.[1] A list of the tumuli and earthworks in which Herefordshire abounds, with illustrations of flint arrow-heads and other pre-historic weapons and vessels, will be found in the *Victoria County History, Hereford*, vol. I.

In historic times Herefordshire formed part of the country of the ancient Silures, which extended over S. Wales, Glamorgan, Brecon, Radnor, and Hereford. They were described by Roman historians as a dark and curly-haired race, fierce and very brave, and are thought to have been of non-Aryan stock, Iberian or Euskarian, ultimately Celticised in language and manners; they were probably the descendants of the men who buried their dead beneath Arthur's Stone.

Of the conquering Goidels, subdued in their turn by the Brythons, we have but few traces, unless it be in one of two place-names, such as Kilforge (near Ballingham), and Kilreague, (Llangarren). The Gaelic *kil* is equivalent to the Welsh *llan*; it originally denoted a hermit's cell, and afterwards used to mean a church. The River Lugg probably bears the name of the Gaelic river-god, " Lug." It is well known that river names are everywhere the memorials of the earliest races; the Gaelic and Erse word for water is *uisge*; the Welsh *wysg*, a current, or *gwy*, *wy*, water; thus we have the Eskley, probably Gaelic, and the Wye, Cymric. The Dore is said to be named from the Cymric *dwr*, water, but it may with equal probability be derived from the Gaelic *dur*, pronounced *doar*.

There were Roman towns or settlements at Kenchester (Magna Castra), Weston-under-Penyard (Ariconium), and at Leintwardine. Five of their roads, or " streets," intersected the county. and may yet be traced in many places, while their course is indicated by the names " Stretford," " Stretton," and " Portway." They also had many fortified camps, some of which had previously been entrenched by the Britons.

1] The fragments of the urn and bones are now in the possession of Mr. Wickham, of Upper Colwall.

Christianity was introduced into Herefordshire at a very early date by the missionaries of the ancient Celtic Church, and the present deanery of Archenfield belonged to the diocese of Llandaff until the twelfth century, when it was transferred to St. David's, in which it remained until 1856. (*See* Section xv.)

After the departure of the Romans, Herefordshire eventually became part of the Anglo-Saxon kingdom of Mercia. The most powerful Mercian king was Offa, maker of the famous Dyke, which ran through the county ; its course is here much broken, and difficult to trace. Roughly, it ran from Knill, west of Pembridge, to Lyonshall, Weobley, and by Mansel Gamage to Bridge Sollers ; thence the Wye was the " mark," as far as Hereford. The dyke left the city by the Franchise Stone on Eign Hill, and passed by Mordiford, Woolhope, Marcle Hill, and Yatton to Ross. It will be seen that a portion of the county north of the Wye was on the Welsh side of the dyke ; this part is still more Welsh than the other side of the county, though the place-names are Anglicised, and those west of the Wye are not.

From a very slight study of the place-names on a modern map, it would be possible to conclude that the part of Herefordshire bounded on the west by the Wye was never really subdued or occupied by the Saxons. To the east, nearly all the names are Saxon, with the characteristic suffixes *ton, ham, wick, hope, ley, low*, while defensible places have names ending in *bury*, A.S., *burg*,—Thornbury, Aconbury, Backbury. West of the Wye, except for a small area extending five miles south of Hereford, the names are almost all Welsh. The distinctively Cymric *tre*, a place or dwelling, abounds,—Tretire, Trebandy, Trebella, Trenant ; *Llan*, an inclosure (in later times, a Church) occurs frequently—Llancillo, Llangarren, Llanwarne, Lllangunnock are but a few instances. *Pen*, a head, or headland, is also not uncommon,— Pencoyd, Pencraig, Pen-y-lan. Pencombe is far away in the north-east, but then the neighbours all say " Pencombe's a poor place," meaning that the soil is not fertile ; possibly the Saxons agreed, and left it to its British occupiers, or disdained to give it a Saxon name.

It is a matter of historic knowledge that the people of Erging (Archenfield) made terms with the Saxons, and were allowed to retain their customs and a measure of independence. (*See* Section xii., 1.) A map of Herefordshire at the time of the Domesday Survey shows the districts of Ewyas and Erging blank, but for the Castle of Ewyas, erected in the Confessor's time by his Norman favourites.[1]

Ewyas and Richard's Castle were the first of the strong chain of castles erected by the Normans to keep the Welsh in check ; this chain ran somewhat eastward of

---

1] *See* History of Ewias Harold, by the Rev. Canon Bannister.

the Saxon Dyke.   There are traces of over forty buildings which were castles, besides defensible dwellings and church towers, many of the latter are of great strength and thickness, and were almost certainly used for defence.   Perhaps no part of England, unless it be the Scottish borderland, has been the scene of so much strife.   It was harried by the Danes early in the tenth century ;   on the church door at Pembridge, beneath the old sanctuary knocker, is a tough leathery substance, said to be the skin of a sacrilegious Dane.   In later times the county was successively the theatre of the struggles between King Stephen and Queen Maud, of innumerable petty wars between the powerful Marcher lords, of the bloodly battle of Mortimer's Cross in the Wars of the Roses.   Much of the fighting during the rebellion of Owen Glendower took place on Herefordshire soil, and of the important part it played in the struggle between Charles I. and his Parliament every schoolboy knows.

Welsh was spoken by the people in the valleys running parallel to the Black Mountain so late as a century ago.   I have talked to a centenarian born at Bredwardine, who spoke English with a strong Welsh accent, and remembered many Welsh-speaking neighbours on the hill.   In 1855 the Clerk to the Hereford Magistrates was selected on account of his knowledge of Welsh, as Welsh prisoners who could not speak English were frequently brought to the court.

I venture to think that the folk-lore of the county largely corroborates the evidence of the place-names.   It is rare to hear of fairies east of the Wye or the Dyke ;   I have never heard of phantom funerals eastward of this boundary.   The folk of the Welsh districts are more superstitious, as a rule, though an exception must be made of the people in out-of-the-way hillside hamlets, and those who live in cottages dotted round the commons.

It is not easy, at this time of day, to determine with accuracy the geographical limits of our peculiar custom, " Burning the Bush " (see Section ix).   Fosbroke says it was confined to " Herefordshire and parts of Monmouthshire."   Lees (Pictures of Nature round Malvern) makes no mention of it at Colwall, Mathon, though he observed (in 1850) the mistletoe hanging in the farm-house kitchen, and the Twelfth Night fires in the spring wheatfields.

Many curious dialect words are still in use, and glossaries of local words have been published, (see Bibliography), but not as yet analysed with a view to their ethnic significance.   An old North Hereford peasant talks with quite a different accent from that one hears South of Ross, near the Forest of Dean.

Welsh or Anglo-Saxon, the folk are everywhere kindly and hospitable; even where quite a stranger, I have found them ready to help and quick to understand. It is useless for the collector of folk-lore to ask bald leading questions; like travellers of another sort, it is well to *carry samples,* for your old countryman loves to hear a story: having heard, he longs to tell you one as good, or better. Of course it may not be of the kind that is wanted, but it is well to listen patiently. I remember hearing an old grannie at Pembridge relate the history of her large family: it seemed endless and most wearisome. Last of all, she told how her youngest daughter died, of her neighbour's admiration! (*See* p. 51.)

My grateful thanks are due, first of all, to the Herefordshire folk, who have ransacked their mental attics so often for " auld-fashioned songs " and " auld sayins " and " bits o' tales "; who sang to me in quavering voices, many of which, alas, are already silent, while their faces alternately saddened and brightened with the memories, grave and gay, the songs brought back to them; who talked of old times, always " good old times " to them, when they " burnt the bush." in the spring wheatfields, and " cried the mare " at harvest. Most enthusiastic of these was William Colcombe, who died a year ago in Weobley Workhouse. He knew upwards of thirty traditional songs and carols, and had a wonderful memory for old tales and riddles, many of which he had learnt in his youth from " Old Powell," the nailmaker, last of his trade in Weobley, with whom he lived for many years. Colcombe was the last man in Weobley to work in a smock-frock; he took a great interest in this collection, and would greet me excitedly sometimes with " Got another bit for ye, missis ! ".

It is not possible to thank individually the many kind friends who have added items of folk-lore to this collection, but there are some to whom I must specially and gratefully acknowledge my indebtedness: the Dean and Chapter of Hereford Cathedral, who have given permission to reproduce the MS. charm for toothache; the Rev. T. W. W. Trumper, Mr. R. Clarke, Mr. A. Slatter, and Mr. Alfred Watkins, who have lent photographs; the Rev. Canon Capes, the Rev. Lewis Bishop, and Mr. Langton Brown, who have contributed extracts from MSS. and translations; Mrs. Powell (wife of the late rector of Dorstone), Miss Martha Williams, the Rev. Canon Bannister, the Rev. R. H. Bird (R.H.B.), Mr. H. C. Beddoe, Mr. John Hutchinson, Mr. C. J. Lilwall, Mr. Walter Pilley, and Mr. C. G. Portman (C.G.P.), who most generously placed at my disposal their own collections of local folk-lore; Mr. Cecil Sharp, who has given me the benefit of his great experience in noting morris and country dances, and has noted the dance-tunes; Dr. Ralph Vaughan-Williams, who has noted the greater number of the folk-songs and carols in Section xiv., either directly from the singers or from phonographic records; his expert knowledge of modal music and folk-song being an invaluable help ; Miss Eleanor Andrews, Miss A. M. Webb, the Rev. Edwin King, LL.D., B.C.L., and Mr. R. H. Rowlands, who have noted the remainder of the tunes ; Mr. E. Sledmere, who has compiled the index ; and lastly, Mr. E. Sidney Hartland and Mr. Frank Sidgwick, who have read all the proofs, and have readily given most kind help and encouragement throughout.

All verbatim quotations made from printed sources are in smaller type ; where the name of a place is given in a footnote, it is the name of the place where the material was collected orally ; initials in footnotes are those of contributors of collections of folk-lore.

ELLA MARY LEATHER.

Castle House, Weobley.
April, 1912.

SKETCH MAP, SHEWING PLACES REFERRED TO IN TEXT.

CONTENTS.

Section V.—Witchcraft.

1. *Witchcraft and the Law.* The last trial for witchcraft. The case of Mary Hodges. 2. *Instances of Witchcraft.* The dread of giving offence, and fear of Evil Eye. Forms assumed by witches. Charms and antidotes.

Section VI.—Diviners, Divination, and Magic.

1. *Diviners.* Stories of a celebrated diviner. A Llandovery conjurer and his Herefordshire clients. A " clever " man at Ross. A diviner on the Skyrrid and the Ross folk. Dr. Coates and his magic. 2. *Love Divinations and others.* Use of Bible and key. Instances of crystal gazing. 3. *Dreams and Portents.*

Section VII.—Leechcraft.

1. *Charms and Charmers.* Beliefs about charming. Various word charms. Efficacy of charm to remove a spell. 2. *Superstitious Cures.*

Section VIII.—General.

Miscellaneous Superstitions. Luck and ill-luck.

Section IX.—The Year, Festivals, and Seasons.

1. New Year's Day. 2. Twelfth Night. 3. Valentine's Day. 4. Shrove Tuesday. 5. Mid-Lent Sunday. 6. Palm Sunday, Pax-Cakes. 7. Good Friday. 8. All Fools' Day. 9. Easter Day. 10. May Day and Oak Apple Day. 11. Whitsuntide. 12. St. Peter's Day and St. Swithin's. 13. Harvest and Hop-picking customs. 14. Gauging Day and Cobbler's Day. 15. Hallowe'en, All Saints' Day, and Guy Fawkes' Day. 16. St. Thomas' Day. 17. Christmas Day, Holy Innocents' Day, St. Stephen's Day.

Section X.—Ceremonial.

1. *Birth.* The new born baby. Trace of the *Couvade* in Herefordshire. Birthmarks. Our Saviour's letter. The Christening. 2. *Courtship and Marriage.* Reluctance to interfere in love affairs. Luck and ill-luck. Throwing rue. The butchers' wedding march. Ancient ceremonial. Byd-ales. Selling wives. 3. *Death.* Omens. The corpse candle. A survival of " sin-eating." Importance attached to burial. Various superstitious practices.

SECTION XI.—GAMES, SPORTS, PAGEANTS, AND PLAYS.

1. *Traditional Games*, and counting out rhymes. 2. *Dances*. The Morris Dance. Other folk dances. Country dances. 3. *Plays and Pageants*. The Boy Bishop. Corpus Christi Pageant. A mummer's play.

SECTION XII.—LOCAL CUSTOMS.

1. *Parochial and other Customs*. 2. *Tenures*. 3. *Wakes and Feasts*. 4. *Farming Customs*. 5. *Punishments*. 6. *Bells*.

SECTION XIII. FOLK TALES.

SECTION XIV.—TRADITIONAL CAROLS, BALLADS, AND SONGS.

1. The Bitter Withy. 2. The Holy Well. 3. The Seven Virgins. 4. The Carnal and the Crane. 5. Dives and Lazarus. 6. Christ made a Trance. 7. The Moon shines Bright. 8. Awake, Awake. 9. The Man that Lives. 10. The Truth sent from Above. 11. There is a Fountain. 12. There was a Lady in Merry Scotland. 13. Young Lambkin. 14. Lord Thomas and Fair Elinor. 15. Cold Blows the Wind. 16. Brangywell. 17. Dilly Dove. 18. The Milkmaid's Song. 19. A Brisk Young Sailor. 20. Marden Forfeit Song. 21. Four Seasons of the Year. 22. The Pretty Ploughboy. 23. The Frog and Mouse.

SECTION XV.—PLACE AND PERSON LEGENDS.

1. *Local Saints*. 2. *Persons and Families*. The Pauncefotes, Vaughans, Wigmores. 3. *Places*. 4. *Subterranean Passages*.

SECTION XVI.

1. *Riddles*. 2. *Healths and Toasts*. 3. *Bell-Jingles and Rhymes*.

SECTION XVII.

1. *Proverbs*. 2. *Place-rhymes and gibes*.

ADDENDA.

APPENDIX A. Life of St. Ethelbert, from Capgrave.

APPENDIX B. Legends of St. Ethelbert, from Hereford Breviary.

APPENDIX C. List of Games.

APPENDIX D. Two Hunting Songs.

LIST OF ILLUSTRATIONS.

(Photographs by the Author where not otherwise stated.)

———

LIST OF AUTHORITIES.

AUBREY, JOHN. *Miscellanies*, London, 1696.

——————— *Remains of Gentilisme and Judaisme*, ed. by J. Britten (F.L.S.), 1881.

ARCHÆOLOGIA CAMBRENSIS, the journal of the Cambrian Archæological Association.

BANNISTER. *The History of Ewias Harold*, by the Rev. A. T. Bannister, M.A., Hereford, 1902.

BARING-GOULD. *The Lives of the British Saints*, by S. Baring-Gould, M.A., and John Fisher, B.A. (Cymmrodorion Society), London, 1907 (2 vols. issued).

BLOUNT. *Fragmenta Antiquatis*, or *Ancient Tenures of Land*, and jocular customs of some Manors, by T. B., of the Inner Temple, Esquire, London, 1679. (Reprint, 1815, see Hazlitt).

BRAND. *Observations on Popular Antiquities*, by John Brand. A new edition with the additions of Sir Henry Ellis. London, 1900.

BROADWOOD. *English County Songs*, collected and edited by Lucy E. Broadwood and J. E. Fuller-Maitland, M.A., F.S.A., London, 1893.

——————. *English Traditional Songs and Carols*, collected and edited by Lucy E. Broadwood, London and New York, 1908.

BULL. *The Herefordshire Pomona*, edited by Robert Hogg and H. G. Bull, M.D.; 2 vols., Hereford, 1876-85.

BURNE. *Shropshire Folk-Lore*, by C. S. Burne, from the collections of Georgina F. Jackson, London, 1883.

CAMDEN. *Britannia*, description of England, Scotland, Ireland, and islands adjacent, by William Camden; translated and enlarged by Richard Gough; 4 vols., London, 1806.

CHAMBERS. *The Mediæval Stage*, by E. K. Chambers, London, 1903.

CHILD. *The English and Scottish Popular Ballads*, by F. J. Child, 5 vols., Boston, Mass., 1882-98.

CLARK. *General View of the Agriculture of the County of Hereford*, by John Clark, Hereford, 1794.

COOKE. *See* Duncumb.

DEVLIN. *Helps to Hereford History*, and *The Mordiford Dragon*, by J. Dacres Devlin, Hereford, 1848.

DINGLEY. *History from Marble*, by Charles Dingley, 2 vols., Camden Society, 1867-8.

DUNCUMB. *Collections towards the History and Antiquities of the County of Hereford,* vol. i., 1804 ; vol. ii., 1812 ; vol. iii. and iv., a continuation, by William Cooke, M.A., Q.C., F.S.A., 1882-92 ; vol. v., part 1, by the Rev. Morgan Watkins, Hereford, 1899.

———— *General View of the Agriculture of the County of Hereford,* by John Duncumb, Hereford, 1813.

EVANS AND RHŶS. The Text of the *Book of the Llan Dâv,* reproduced from the Gwysaney manuscript by J. G. Evans, Hon. M.A., Oxon, with the co-operation of John Rhŷs, M.A., Professor of Celtic in the University of Oxford, Oxford, 1893.

FOLK-LORE JOURNAL (Folk-Lore Society). London, 7 vols., 1883–1889.

FOLK-LORE. *The Transactions of the Folk-Lore Society,* London, 22 vols. published since 1890, still proceeding.

FOSBROKE. *Ariconensia,* or sketches of Ross and Archenfield, by T. D. Fosbroke, Ross, 1821.

FRAZER. *The Golden Bough,* by J. G. Frazer, D.C.L., LL.D., 2 vols., London, 1890.

FRYER. *Wooden Monumental Effigies,* by Albert Fryer, F.S.A., London, 1910.

GENTLEMAN'S MAGAZINE LIBRARY. *Popular Superstitions,* London, 1884.

GEROULD. *The Grateful Dead,* by G. H. Gerould (F.L.S.), London, 1908.

GIRALDUS. *The Itinerary through Wales,* by Giraldus Cambrensis (Everyman's Library), 1908.

GLANVIL. *Saducismus Triumphatus,* by J. Glanvil, London, 1726.

GOMME. *Folk-Lore as an Historical Science,* by G. Laurence Gomme, London, 1908.

GOMME. *The Traditional Games of England, Scotland and Ireland,* collected and annotated by Alice Bertha Gomme, 2 vols., London, 1894.

HARTLAND. *The Legend of Perseus,* by Edwin Sidney Hartland, F.S.A., 3 vols., London, 1894-5-6.

———— *The Science of Fairy Tales,* by the same author. Contemporary Science Series, London, 1891.

———— *Primitive Paternity,* by the same author ; 2 vols., London, 1909-10.

HAVERGAL. *Fasti Herefordensis,* and other antiquarian memorials of Hereford, by the Rev. F. T. Havergal, Hereford, 1869.

HAVERGAL. *Herefordshire Words and Phrases,* colloquial and archaic, Hereford, 1887.

HAZLITT. *Tenures of Land,* and Customs of Manors, originally collected by Thomas Blount, and re-published 1784 and 1815. A new edition, London, 1874.

HEATH. *The Excursion down the Wye from Ross to Monmouth,* by Charles Heath, printer, Monmouth. Printed and sold by him in the Market-place, 1799.

HENDERSON. *Folk-Lore of the Northern Counties,* by William Henderson, London, 1879.

HEREFORDSHIRE GATHERER. A series of chapters on local customs and folk-lore, contributed by *Antiquatis* to the *Hereford Times*, in April, May, and June, 1879.

HEREFORD JOURNAL.

HIST. MSS. *Historical Manuscripts Commission*, Thirteenth Report. Appendix, Part iv. The Manuscripts of Rye and Hereford Corporations, 1892.

HONE. *Everyday Book*, by William Hone, London, 1825-27.

HONE. *Table Book*, London, 1827.

HOWELLS. *Cambrian Superstitions*, by W. Howells, Tipton, 1831.

JOHNSON. *Ancient Customs of the City of Hereford*, by Richard Johnson, Hereford, 1868.

JOURNAL OF THE FOLK-SONG SOCIETY, No. 14, being the first part of Vol. iv. Privately printed for the Society, Taunton, 1909.

KEIGHTLEY. *Fairy Mythology*, by T. Keightley ; 2 vols., London, 1828.

LEAN. *Collectanea*, a collection of proverbs, superstitions, and folk-lore, by V. Stuckey Lean, edited by T. W. Williams, 4 vols., Bristol, 1902.

LEES. *Pictures of Nature* in the Silurian region around the Malvern Hills, by Edwin Lees, F.L.S., Malvern, 1856.

LELAND. *The Itinerary of John Leland the Antiquary*, 4 vols., London, 1879.

LEOMINSTER GUIDE, THE, 1803.

LEWIS. *A Glossary of Provincial Words used in Herefordshire.* London, 1839 (by George Cornewall Lewis).

LIBER LANDAVENSIS. *Liber Landavensis (Llyfr Teilo)*, the Ancient Register of the Cathedral Church of Llandaff, edited by the Rev. W. J. Rees, M.A., Llandovery, 1840 (see Evans and Rhŷs *ante*).[1]

MEMORIALS. *Memorials of Old Herefordshire*, edited by the Rev. Compton Reade, London, 1905.

MORGAN WATKINS. *See* Duncumb.

MURRAY-AYNSLEY. *Symbolism of the East and West*, by Mrs. Murray-Aynsley, London, 1900.

NORTHALL. *English Folk-Rhymes*, by G. F. Northall, London, 1892.

NOTES AND QUERIES.

PAGE. *A History of the County of Hereford*, edited by William Page, F.S.A., vol. i., London, 1905 (Victoria County History).

PARRY. *The History of Kington*, with an Appendix ; by a Member of the Mechanics' Institute of Kington, Kington, 1845.

PHILLIPS. *Cider*, a poem, by John Phillips, with notes by Charles Dunster. London, 1791.

1] I have quoted from this edition, the only one with an English translation.

PHILLOTT. *The History of the Diocese of Hereford*, by the Rev. Canon Phillott (Diocesan Histories Series), London, 1888.

PORTMAN. *Sacred Stones and Holy Wells of Hay*, by C. G. Portman, Hay, 1907.
———— *A Guide to Hay*, Hay, 1909.

PRICE. *History of Hereford* and *History of Leominster*, by John Price, 1 vol., Hereford, 1796.

REES. *Lives of the Cambro-British Saints*, by the Rev. W. J. Rees, M.A., F.S.A., Welsh MSS. Society, Llandovery, 1853.

RICE REES. *An Essay on the Welsh Saints, or the Primitive Christians*, usually considered to have been the founders of the Church in Wales, by the Rev. Rice Rees, M.A., London, 1836.

RHŶS. *Celtic Folklore*, by John Rhŷs, Professor of Celtic in the University of Oxford, Oxford, 1901.

ROBINSON. *The Castles of Herefordshire and their Lords*, by the Rev. Charles T. Robinson, M.A., London, 1869.
———— *Mansions and Manors of Herefordshire*, by the same author, Hereford, 1873.

ROSS GUIDE, 1827.

SCOTT. *Demonology and Witchcraft*, by Sir Walter Scott, London, 1831.

SHARP. *English Folk Carols*, edited and collected by C. J. Sharp, Taunton, 1911.
———— *Folk-Songs from Somerset*. Five Series, Taunton and London, 1904-9.

SIDGWICK. *Popular Ballads of the Olden Time*, by Frank Sidgwick, First, Second, and Third Series, London, 1903-4-6.

SIKES. *British Goblins*, Welsh folk-lore fairy mythology, legends or traditions, by Wirt Sikes, United States Consul for Wales. London, 1880.

TOWNSEND. *The Town and Borough of Leominster*, by G. Townsend, Leominster and London, n.d.

TYLOR. *Primitive Culture*, by Edward B. Tylor, D.C.L., LL.D., F.R.S., third edition, two vols., London, 1891.

WEBB. *History of the Civil War in Herefordshire*, by the late Rev. John Webb, M.A., F.S.A., F.R.S.L.; edited and completed by the Rev. T. W. Webb, M.A., F.R.S.A., London, 1879.

WOOLHOPE CLUB. The Transactions of the Woolhope Naturalists' Field Club, Hereford, 1856 to 1903-5, still proceeding.
[The Woolhope Club, started as a field club for the study of natural history and geology, has gradually become also the local archæological society.]

WRIGHT. *Walk through Hereford*, by T. P. Wright, Hereford, 1819.

SECTION I.

NATURAL AND INORGANIC OBJECTS.

(1) Hills.

Robin Hood's Butts.

Popular imagination has been busy in trying to account for the existence of two small conical wooded hills in the parishes of Canon Pyon and King's Pyon, about half a mile apart, called " Robin Hood's Butts." The first version of the story runs as follows :—In the good old times the Hereford churches, including the Cathedral, began to be built, and people went to them and said their prayers. Monasteries also began to arise and to do their charitable work. Then the Devil, hearing how far the good people of Hereford were from his way of thinking, determined to put an end to such an undesirable state of affairs. Taking two large sacks from a mill hard by he proceeded to fill them with earth from the side of Dinmore Hill; the holes he made may be seen there still. Trudging along the road towards Hereford, intending to bury the offending city beneath the contents of his sacks, he met a very holy man, an ecclesiastic, who, guessing his evil design, had resolved to try and save the place. Disguised as a traveller in worn dress and shoes, he engaged the " old 'un " in conversation, which was made to turn on the iniquities of the inhabitants of the city of Hereford, and on the corruption of the priests and monks. He quickly succeeded in convincing the sack-bearer that it was not worth his while to go further ; so the devil emptied the sacks on the spot, and these to-day form the hills known as " Robin Hood's Butts."[1]

The following version is from a native of King's Pyon :—
" The old 'un had a spite against the folks in Hereford one time, and he started off with his two big sacks of earth from Birley Hill, meaning to dam up the river just below the city and drown 'em all in the night. But he was too late. Just as he got to Pyon the cock crew and he dropped his load in two heaps; there they are to this day. They are called Robin Hood's Butts because when Robin Hood stood on one he could shoot an arrow into a tree on the top of the other."

In yet another account the Devil has become Robin Hood, aided and abetted by Little John, and the place of the " holy man " is taken by a cobbler :—

Robin Hood was bent upon the destruction of the monks at Wormesley, for which object he set out with Little John, each carrying a spadeful of mould. Upon arrival at King's Pyon they met a cobbler laden

---

1] Communicated by Mr. John Hutchinson, 1907.

with shoes upon his back, from whom they enquired the distance from Wormesley. The cobbler, suspicious of some evil design, or may be with an eye to selling some of his boots, informed them that, " If they were to wear out all the shoes he had on his back and as many more, they would not reach the place." Whereupon the two travellers abandoned their purpose, and in an evil temper emptied their spadefuls upon the spots which are now Robin Hood's Butts.[1]

It is also said that Robin Hood and Little John had a wager. Robin bet Little John he could jump right over Wormesley Hill and clear the Raven's Causeway, monastery and all. " They stood somewhere near Brinsop. Robin jumped and kicked a piece out of the hill with his heel : that's Butt-house knapp.[2] Then Little John tried. He took a much longer run and jumped better, but his foot caught the hill too, and kicked the piece out that is now Canon Pyon Butt. It is farther on than the other : he kicked harder. You can see the hole on the hillside made by their heels now."[3]

The same tale is associated with Jack o' Kent and the Devil, who threw spadefuls of earth from Burton Hill, to see who could throw further. These formed the Butts. Jack, of course, won, and Canon Pyon Butt is his spadeful.[4]

There is a similar tradition at Leinthall Earles, concerning two small conical wooded hills, between Croft Ambrey and Bolstone. These are said to be formed by the Devil, who, walking through the valley when it was very muddy, kicked them off his heels.

Cobbler's Mound, Shobdon.

Yet another variant of the cobbler story is associated with the tumulus at the entrance to the village of Shobdon. It is called the " Devil's shovelful."

Shobdon was once inhabited by a contented, happy, pious population, who could boast of having invented the finest church then known. This so annoyed his Satanic majesty, that he determined to utterly destroy the place. To this end he took a shovel and started on his journey. Being about to enter the village he met the village cobbler, who in affright let fall a bag of old shoes. Then the Devil enquired if that were Shobdon ? " No," said this lying son of St. Crispin, " I am seeking the same place, and have worn out all these shoes, but cannot find it in this direction. You had better turn back." The cobbler's lie having saved the place, the inhabitants, fearing a return of the Devil, put little faith in truthfulness, pulled down their beautiful church and plundered the poor. So the sad story goes. It is a fact that from time immemorial a cobbler has lived in the house immediately opposite the mound, at the entrance to the village.[5]

Mynydd Fyrddyn, Longtown.

To the east of the castle at Longtown is an eminence called Mynydd Fyrddyn, which means " sloping mountain," or " Merlin's mountain." Tradition says it is the burial place of Merlin.[6]

1] *Woolhope Club,* 1895-7, 234. 2] *Knapp*=a small hill in the local dialect. 3] Collected orally, 1909. 4] *See* Section xiii., *Jack o' Kent.* 5] Letter *Hereford Times,* Dec. 26., 1906. 6] Jakeman and Carver's *Herefordshire Directory,* 540. Many other places claim this honour. *See* Hartland, *Science of Fairy Tales,* 209.

Tumulus at St. Weonards.

See *infra*, Hidden treasure.

Twyn-y-beddan (mound of the graves).

This is an immense tumulus, which lies under the shadow of the Black Mountain, about two miles from Hay, near the junction of the counties of Brecon and Hereford. It has been found to contain burnt human bones, and tradition says that a great battle was fought here ; the carnage was so great that the neighbouring stream, the Dulas, ran blood for three days afterwards.[1] Mr. Portman adds that the tumulus is said to mark the spot where the Welsh made a gallant stand against Edward I., but it is probably far older than that.

Adam's Rocks.

In a cave near Adam's Rocks there formerly lived a giant, who attempted to destroy the spire of Hereford Cathedral by throwing one of the rocks at it from the top of the hill.   However, the stone fell short, and dropped into a meadow near Longworth mill, Bartestree.   The stone was pointed out to my informant, Mr. Lewis Powell, and was still in the meadow a few years ago, but has now been broken up.

It is said that Adam's rocks were rent at the Crucifixion.   There is the same tradition about the rock called the Black Darren, on the Black Mountain.

Stanner Rocks.

On the top of Stanner rocks, near Kington, according to legend, the prince of darkness in olden times reserved a piece of ground for his own particular use, which is to this day denominated the " Devil's garden."   It is said that nothing will grow upon the spot.[2]

The Wonder, Much Marcle.

On the 17th of February, 1575, a very remarkable landslip occurred here.   On the evening of that day. Marcle Hill began to move, and in its progress overthrew the chapel at Kinnaston, together with hedges and trees, and after destroying many cattle, finally rested at its present position on the 19th.   The impression made by this event on the minds of the country folk is thus quaintly echoed by Camden :—

" Near the conflux of the Lugg and the Wye, eastward, a hill which they call Marcley Hill in the year 1575 roused itself, as it were, out of sleep, and for three days together, shoving its prodigious body forwards with a horrible roaring noise and overturning all that stood in its way, advanced itself, to the astonishment of all beholders, to a higher station, by that kind of earthquake the which the naturalists call Brasmatia."[3]

Phillips, the Herefordshire poet, refers to the movement of Marcle Hill in *Cider* ; so does Butler in *Hudibras*.[4]

---

[1] Portman, *Guide to Hay*, 40.   [2] Parry, *History of Kington*, 247.   [3] Gough's *Camden*, iii., 86.   [4] Phillips' *Cider*, 11-12 and note.   *Hudibras*, p. 5, iii., Canto ii., 1128.

Palmer's Churn.

At the top of the Hill at Orleton, in a spot which was once part of the Common, is a curious cleft in the rock called Palmer's Churn ; nobody now remembers why. There is a hole in the ground six feet deep, from which a passage twelve feet long rises again to the open ground. Seventy years ago the young people of the place used, with difficulty, to creep through this hole : it was said that those who stuck in the middle or turned back would never be married.

There is also a legend that a goose once entered here, and traversing some underground passage, came out at Woofferton, four miles away. When it appeared it said " Goose out !" so the place was called " Gauset."[1]

Remains of a gigantic race are said to have been found beneath the church at Orleton during the restoration in 1865, but I can hear of no tradition which refers to them.

Blount alludes to this " deep cave or den," which he calls " Palmer's Charm," of which, he says, " the inhabitants feign no fewer stories than the Italians of old did of their Sibyl's Cave," but he has unfortunately recorded none.[2]

(2) STONES.

It is said that stones have ceased to grow ever since the rocks were rent at the Crucifixion.[3]

Aegelnoth's Stone.

Some antiquaries think that Aylestone Hill, Hereford, takes its name from Aegelnoth's stone, which formerly stood on the top of it. A road leading to the spot is still called Folly Lane, a corruption of "folk lane," by which the people went up to the Shire mote, which was held round the stone.

In Hereford Cathedral library there is a very curious and ancient Latin version of the Gospels, on the back of which is a note, written in Anglo-Saxon, in the reign of Canute, of which the following is a translation :—

Note of a Shire mote held at Aegelnoth's stone in Herefordshire, in the reign of King Cnut, at which were present the Bishop Athelstan, the Sheriff Bruning, and Aegelgeard of Frome, and Leofwine of Frome, and Godric of Stoke, and all the Thanes in Herefordshire. At which assembly, Edwine son of Enneawne (?) complained against his mother concerning certaine lands at Welintone and Cyrdesley (Wellington and Eardisley). The Bishop asked who should answer for the mother, which Thurcyl the White proffered to do if he knew the cause of accusation. Then they chose three Thanes, and sent to the mother to ask her what the cause of complaint was. She declared that she had no land that pertained in aught to her son, and was very angry with him, and calling Leoflaeda, her relative, she in presence of the Thanes, bequeathed to her after her own death all her lands, money, clothes, and property, and desired them to witness it. They did so, after

---

1] Communicated by Mrs. Hill, of Orleton Manor.   2] Blount MSS.   3] See *ante*, *Adam's Rocks*.

A HEREFORDSHIRE SPINNER.

ARTHUR'S STONE, DORSTONE.

which Thurcyl the White (who was husband to Leoflaeda) stood up and requested the Thanes to deliver free (or clean) to his wife all the lands that had been bequeathed to her, and so they did. After this Thurcyl rode to St. Ethelbert's Minster, and by leave and witness of all the folk, caused the transaction to be recorded in a book of the Gospels.[1]

This entry seems to prove that the Saxon Shire-motes kept no regular official record of their proceedings, and that the transactions thus recorded in a copy of the Gospels, deposited in the Cathedral and out of the reach of the parties interested, was deemed a sufficient recognition of the judgment given.

Arthur's Stone, Dorstone.

Arthur's Stone is the name given to a dolmen which stands on the top of Merbach Hill, between Bredwardine and Dorstone. It is surrounded by an incomplete circle of stones, the whole raised on a mound of earth. The dislodgement of some of the stones led to certain protective work being carried out in 1901, when the leaning stone, one of the tallest separate monoliths, was placed in an upright position. During the work of excavation, stone hammers, heavy mauls for dressing the stone, and chips were found, and not a single metal tool of any kind was discovered, indicating so far that the stones were erected previous to the bronze age. The mauls were heavy, unpolished, and not fixed in handles. The oldest inhabitants of Bredwardine (1908) say that " Arthur's Stone is nothing to what it used to be." The circle of stones was formerly complete, but those missing were broken and carted away for building purposes, until Velters Cornewall, then owner of the Moccas estate, put a stop to the work of destruction.[2]

According to some, Arthur's Stone is so called because " Owd Artur " fought a desperate battle there with another king, broke his back, and buried him under the stones. Others say it was a giant whom Arthur slew, and that the stones on the left approaching the dolmen from Bredwardine, under the hedge, is yet marked by the giant's fall ; the hollows now visible are called the marks of the giant's elbows, and others, again, declare that the impressions were made by the knees of Arthur himself, when he knelt on the stone to pray. This stone, which seems more important in legend than the dolmen itself, is also called the " Quoit stone," having hollows for the heels of the players.[3] " Arthur's quoits " are found in many parts of the country.[3]

Colwall Stone.

In a valley below the Malvern Hills, in the centre of a group of hamlets which make up Colwall, stands Colwall Stone. It is a square block of limestone, standing at the cross roads, and is thought to have formed part of a wayside cross. Some say it

---

1] Havergal, *Fasti*, 121. Translated more copiously in Hickes, *Thesaurus ;* also Hallam's *Hist. of the Middle Ages*, ii., 393 ; *Woolhope Club*, 1900–02, 108, has " set in a Christ's book " here. 2] *Woolhope Club*, 1900–1902, 194. For illustration and full description, see *Victoria County History, Herefordshire*, I, 158-9. 3] Portman, *Sacred Stones and Trees of Hay*, 5.

was pitched into Colwall by the devil, but an old inhabitant tells a story of how there once lived, in a cave in the Malverns, overlooking Colwall, a terrible giant, who had a beautiful wife. One day he looked out from his cave, and saw her on the green at Colwall with a man he supposed to be her lover. In a fit of jealous rage he flung Colwall Stone at her, killing her on the spot. There the stone remains to this day.

It is also said that the stone was brought from a quarry near the Wyche, by a team of oxen, and that an annual rent of a penny was paid for it ; that it was an object of idolatry prior to the erection of the church, and that the poor received doles of money upon it in former times.[1] Lastly, this wonderful stone is said to turn round in the night, when it hears the clock strike twelve.[2]

The Whetstone, Kington.

On the summit of Hergest ridge there is a large stone, with a flat surface and rough sides ; the weight of it is estimated at several tons. According to the history of Kington—

Tradition informs us that a market was held weekly in the reign of Edward III., in the year 1366, and that it was the custom to place wheat and other kinds of grain for sale around this stone, which in after years was vulgarly termed the " Whet stone " from this circumstance. This tradition receives additional confirmation from the fact that persons living on mountains and in districts very distant from a town, were always apprehensive of danger if they approached a part of the country more thickly populated than their own, when the inhabitants of the same suffered the infliction of any terrible disorder.[3]

A typical specimen of rustic wit is the saying that this stone goes down to the water to drink every morning, *as soon as it hears the cock crow.*

The Hoarstone, Tedstone Delamere.

The brook at Tedstone Delamere is connected with a story of a miracle, till lately firmly believed by some of the folk there :—

A mare and her foal having been stolen in the night from a neighbouring farmer, some centuries ago, his daughter, with whom the mare was a great favourite, prayed that she, attended by some of the servants of the family, might be able to trace the retreat of the thief by the footsteps of the stolen animals. Those footsteps were followed without difficulty, until the pursuers reached the brook, but on the opposite side no vestige whatever was discoverable. It then seemed to the damsel that the robber might have taken his booty down the rocky channel of the stream to evade detection. She had not proceeded far along its banks

---

1] It should be noted, however, that the name Arthur's Quoit is sometimes given in guide-books, and even in archæological works, improperly to dolmens and other stones. The stone on Cefn Bryn in Gower, for example, is not properly so called. It is universally known in the neighbourhood as Arthur's Stone; and so far as can be ascertained it has never had any other name.—E.S.H. 2] Lee's *Pictures of Nature round Malvern* (quoted in Colwall Parish Magazine). *Cf. Denham Tracts,* iii., 19 :—
"In Dainton Town there is a stone,
    And most strange yt is to tell—
That yt turnes ix. times round about,
    When yt hears ye clock strike twell."

3] Parry, *Hist. Kington,* 249.

THE WERGIN STONE, SUTTON.

By permission of Mr. Alfred Watkins]

THE WHITE CROSS, HEREFORD.

before she exclaimed, "My prayers are heard, for see, here are the marks of their hoofs in the solid rock." Directed by these supernatural impressions, it is understood that she and her attendants proceeded, and discovered the robber in a most romantic spot, called the "Witchery Hole"; or, some contend, in another spot equally interesting, called Hoarstone. Many pretended vestiges of the mare and foal are still pointed out in the channel of the brook.[1]

The Wergin Stone.

This stone stands in a meadow on the right hand side of the road from Hereford to Bodenham and Leominster, near the third mile-stone from the city. Properly speaking, it is one stone upon another, the lower forming a base upon which stands a shaft or pedestal, not unlike a broken road-side cross. The base has a cavity evidently tooled out, about four inches deep, sloping inwards. The whole stands six feet high. It is thought that the hollow in the base indicates that the ceremonious collection of an annual money payment took place there, and that it was intended to contain the money.[2]

The following curious custom, still practised in Warwickshire, supports this theory. At a stone at the top of Knightlow Hill, is collected annually on Martinmas Eve at sun-rising, what is called "wroth money," or "ward money," from the various parishes in the Hundred of Knightlow. In 1879 there were thirty-four persons present to witness the ceremony. The Steward of the Duke of Buccleuch, having invited the party to stand round the stone (the original custom was to walk three times round it), proceeded to read the "charter or Assembly," which opens thus: "Wroth silver collected annually at Knightlow Cross by the Duke of Buccleuch, as lord of the manor of the Hundred of Knightlow." The names of the parishes liable to the fee were then called over, with the amount from each, while each parish, through its representative, cast the required sum into the hollow of the stone. The amounts collected and the several parishes are next named, and the total of nine shillings and threepence half-penny. No one seems to know why or for what purpose the money was originally collected, nor why one parish should pay more than another.[3]

This stone is said to have been moved in the night by some supernatural agency, in the seventeenth century. Blount (in his *MSS.*) notices it is among the wonders of Herefordshire. "In the Wergins lies a stone that was so wondrously removed in the last age, and since that called the Devil's Stone." Another account of this purposeless miracle says:—

"Between Sutton and Hereford, in a common meadow called the Wergins, were placed two large stones for a water mark, one erected upright and the other laid thwart. In the late republican time, about the year 1652, they were removed two hundred and forty spaces from the place of their former position and

---

1] *Duncumb*, ii., 196. 2] *Woolhope Club*, 1898-9, 143. 3] *Woolhope Club, loc. cit.*

nobody knew how, which gave occasion to a common opinion that they were carried thither by the Devil, because it seemed above human power ; for when they were brought back to their place, one of them required nine yoke of oxen to draw it.[1]

The word "Hoar Stone" means boundary stone or landmark. We have "Hoarwithy," *i.e.*, the boundary withy tree or willow, there is a "Hoarstone" farm also near Wapley Camp.[2]

For Kent's Stone. *See* Section xiii., *Jack o' Kent.*

(3) HIDDEN TREASURE.

At Bronsil Castle, near Eastnor, tradition says that a raven, presumed to be an infernal spirit, sits over the moat to guard a chest of money buried within the island whereon the castle stands. The treasure must remain there until discovered by the rightful owner ; but he cannot attain it unless he possesses the bones of the old baron (Beauchamp), its former owner. These are said to been have brought from Italy as the only means of laying his ghost, which haunted the castle.[3]

The guardian of the treasure hidden at Penyard castle (of which few traces now remain) was a jackdaw.

Two hogsheads full of money were concealed in a subterranean vault. There a farmer undertook to draw them from their hiding place, a matter of no small difficulty, for they were protected by preternatural power. To accomplish this object he took twenty steers to drag down the iron doors of the vault in which the hogsheads were deposited. The door was partially opened, and a jackdaw was seen perched on one of the casks. The farmer was overjoyed at the prospect of success, and as soon as he saw the casks, he exclaimed : "I believe I shall have it !" The door immediately closed with a loud clang, and a voice in the air exclaimed :—

> "Had it not been
> For your quicken-tree goad,
> And your yew-tree pin,
> You and your cattle,
> Had all been drawn in ! "[4]

There is a tradition that in Snodhill Park, in the Golden Valley, a vast treasure lies buried, "no deeper than a hen could scratch."

An iron "co-fer" (coffer, chest), containing a thousand golden guineas, is buried beneath the tower of Longtown Castle, but no one will ever be able to get it out. My informant was mysterious about this, so probably the reason that the treasure is said to be immoveable has been forgotten.

1] Robinson, *Mansions and Manors*, 295. 2] See N.E.D. v. 312, *Hoar* [O.E. har] used frequently as an attribute of various objects named in ancient charters as making a boundary line : Hence in many place names *Hoarstone*, an ancient boundary stone. 3] Gough's *Camden*, i., 691 ; *Duncumb*, ii., 189 ; *Webb*, i., 17. 4] *Cf.* Section iv., 1. *The Ghost of Bronsil Castle.* 5] Northall, 175.

At St. Weonards, near the Church, is a large tumulus, "employed from time immemorial as the scene of village fêtes, and especially morris dancing."[1]   Here, according to tradition, St. Weonard lies buried in a golden coffin.   Others say he is buried on the top of a golden coffer, filled with gold, and that on the lid of it is inscribed :—

> " Where this stood,
> Is another, twice as good.
> But where that is,—no man knows."[2]

(4) BRIDGES.

See Section iv., 3, *Spirit laid under Bridge.*   Section xii., *Jack o' Kent.* Section xvi., 6, *London Bridge.*

(5) CROSSES.

The White Cross.

This beautiful fourteenth century cross stands on the Hay road, a mile from the city of Hereford.   The Welsh chronicles mention that—

Sir Ralph Baskerville slew the Lord Clifford and had a pardon for it, because Clifford had unjustly disseized him, they fought near Hereford, where afterwards a white cross was erected, which stood till Queen Elizabeth's time, and then was pulled down by one Gernoras, afterwards called " Kill Christ."[3]

Tradition, however, has two other different stories to account for its origin. The first tells how one day when Bishop Cantilupe was returning on foot to Hereford from his Palace at Sugwas, the bells of the Cathedral rang to welcome him without human agency.   The cross was erected to commemorate the miraculous event.[4]   It is also said to be a memorial of the visitation of the plague in 1347, when the markets had to be removed from the town to this spot.   The lion rampant on the shield in each niche of the cross was the armorial bearing of Bishop Charlton (1327–1343),   but there is nothing to connect his name with the cross.

For Weobley churchyard cross, *see* Section iv., *Goblindom* and *The Devil.*

(6) SITES.

Vowchurch and Turnastone are twin churches, standing quite near together, on either side of the river Dore, in the Golden Valley.   They are said to have been built in rivalry by two sisters, one saying " I *vow* I will build my *church* before you can *turn a stone* of yours."   Hence the names.

1] Robinson, *Mansions and Manors,* 294.   2] Orcop, St. Weonard's.   This tumulus was opened in 1855 ; its sepulchral character was abundantly proved by the discovery of funeral ashes, and fragments of human bones, no certain proof of period being found.   (Wright, *Arch. Camb.,* 3rd series, i., 168–74) ; St. Weonard is thought to be identical with St. Gwainerth, a British Saint (Robinson. *Op. Cit.*) 3] Duncumb, i., 398.   4] *See* Section xv., 1., *St. Katharine,* and note.   5] Duncumb, i., 398-9.

The old mansion of Garnstone, pulled down a hundred years ago, when the present Garnstone Castle was built, stood much higher up the hill, in a somewhat awkward position. Popular imagination was busy in supplying a reason for this. I have talked with old people, now dead, who firmly believed that the site was chosen because of the fairies, who when the house was first begun at the bottom of the hill, pulled down every night what the workmen had built by day, carrying the stones some distance away ; so the higher and more inconvenient spot was selected instead, and afterwards the work went on without interruption.

The inhabitants of Much Cowarne had a tradition in the seventeenth century that their church was intended to have been built on a hill north-east of its present position, but the materials that were collected there for the purpose were regularly conveyed by some invisible agent to the spot it now occupies.[1]

Kingsland Church was first begun near Lawton, but the Devil pulled down the work each night, and the site had to be abandoned. At Pencombe, old people tell how it was once proposed to rebuild the old church in a more convenient spot, in the centre of the parish. In this case the spirits of those buried in the churchyard are supposed to have interfered, and effectually prevented the progress of the work,[2] so the church had to be re-built on the old site after all.

(7) RIVERS, POOLS, WELLS.

The Wye.

Mothers living near the river, in the neighbourhood of Hay, warn their children not to go near it, lest " the spirit " drag them in.[3]

Some years ago, when a boy was drowned in the river at Ross, it was remarked that his brothers would now be careful to keep away from the bank. An old man, hearing this, remarked, " Let 'em go, let 'em go, no one else 'll be drowned this year, the river has had its due."

If a drowned body cannot be recovered, a loaf in which quicksilver has been placed is thrown into the river. It is believed that it will stop at the spot where the body is to be found.[4] It is also said that the bodies of drowned persons float on the ninth day.

For a Legend of the Lugg, see Section xii., *The Mermaid of Marden ;* Section i., 2, *Delamere Brook ;* Section vi., 4, *for the Arrows.*

1] Duncumb, ii., 105. 2] Bromyard, 1908. 3] C.G.P. 4] This superstition is mentioned by Mark Twain in *Huckleberry Finn.*

Pools and Marshes.

Old Pembridge was once upon a time swallowed up in a night by Shobdon Marshes. There was a dance at Pembridge that night, and a fiddler from Eardisland played for it. On reaching his home, he remembered that he had left behind a pair of white gloves, tied with red ribbons, so he set off to fetch them. Great was his amazement, for Pembridge had utterly disappeared. The marshes are drained now, but old Pembridge has not been found. There is still a well there, of which folk say that if a stone be dropped into it, one may hear it strike against the top of the old church steeple.

In a field near Arthur's Stone, Dorstone, there is said to be a buried town, which was engulfed in an earthquake long ago. The church steeple, so they say, is sometimes visible in the bottom of a pool in the field.

St. Anne's Well, Aconbury.

The first water taken from this well after twelve o'clock on Twelfth Night was said to be of great medicinal value, and especially good for eye troubles.[1] Aconbury folk used to compete for the first bucketful, which was bottled and carefully kept by the one who succeeded in obtaining it. At midnight the water bubbled up, and a blue smoke arose from it. My informant, a native of Aconbury residing at Eaton Bishop, (1909), assured me that he had himself seen the water do this. Beyond this well, further from the church, in a coppice on the hill, is a spring said to be haunted by two lovers, one of whom was murdered in a fit of jealous frenzy by the other, at the well which was then their trysting place. The girl, having learned too late that her lover was innocent, died of a broken heart.[2]

The Dragon's Well, Brinsop.

The church at Brinsop is dedicated to St. George, and contains a fine tympanum of eleventh century date, representing St. George mounted, in the act of slaying the dragon. The Dragon's Well is in Duck's Pool meadow, on the south side of the church, while on the other side is a field called " Lower Stanks," pointed out by the late parish clerk as the spot where St. George slew the Dragon.

St. Ethelbert's Well, Marden.[3]

The water of this well is said to have gushed up from the earth miraculously at the time of the removal of the body of the saint from Marden to Hereford. It was greatly venerated, and the water was said to retain its purity and clearness when

---

1] *Cf.* Section ix., *New Year's Day, Cream of the Well, infra.* 2] *Hereford Journal,* Aug. 11, 1907. 3] See Section xv., 1., *St. Ethelbert.*

overflowed by the muddy waters of the Lugg in flood.[4] It is now inside the church, at the west end.

St. Ethelbert's Well, Hereford.

This well, too, gushed forth when the body of the saint rested on the spot, as it was being conveyed from Marden to Hereford Cathedral. It is near the bank of the river, on the left hand side of the entrance to the Castle Green from Quay Street. There was above the well a carved head of St. Ethelbert in stone wearing a crown. This is still preserved, set in the masonry which now encloses the spring.[1] Some years ago, when the well was cleared out, a quantity of pins were found in it. The water was held especially good for ulcers and sores.[2]

St. Edith's Well, Stoke Edith.

This well yields an unfailing supply of pure water, which is said to have first sprung from the ground in answer to the prayer of St. Edith. She carried water from the brook herself to mix the mortar for building the church, but her strength became exhausted, and she knelt and prayed on the spot, until the water appeared. There are several St. Ediths, but there is little doubt that it was St. Edith, daughter of King Edgar, made abbess of Wilton at fifteen years of age, who is here commemorated. She died in her twenty-third year, September 16, 984 A.D.[3] The annual Wake which was celebrated on the Sunday succeeding September 8th, thus nearly accorded with the date of her death.[4] Up to fifty years ago the folk ascribed healing powers to the well, and washed there in the hope of being cured of various ailments.

Golden Well, Peterchurch.

In this well, once upon a time, a fisherman caught a fish with a gold chain round its neck. In commemoration of the event, a sculptured representation of the fish in stone, with its chain, was placed in the church, where it may still be seen. (*See illustration.*)

Higgins Well, Little Birch.

This spring is situated at the lowest point of the road leading from Aconbury to Little Birch. Formerly, so the story goes, it had an outlet higher up in the meadow, at the top of the bank which rises abruptly behind it. The water was pure and much sought after, and the owner of the land became annoyed at the trespass of the villagers on his land when they came to fetch it, so he had the well filled up. Shortly afterwards, as he smoked a pipe in his chimney corner, he was startled by a rush of water

---

1] Duncumb, ii., 137. 2] By Mrs. E. M. Underwood, in 1904. 3] *A Walk through Hereford*, 46 ; Havergal, *Fasti*, 115. 4] Morgan Watkins, ii., 131. 4] See Section xii., 3, *Wakes*.

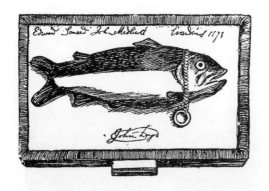

THE GOLDEN VALLEY TROUT.

ST. ETHELBERT'S WELL IN THE SEVENTEENTH CENTURY.

ST. PETER'S WELL, PETERCHURCH.

at his feet. He thought the spirit of the well had interfered, and to appease it he dug a well at the foot of his meadow. The water bubbled through the rock there, and the rush on his hearth disappeared. The well has since borne his name.[1]

Laugh Lady Well, Brampton Bryan.

In a dingle, called after it " Laugh Lady Dingle," this spring gushes out with a full rapid stream, and sometimes with a gentle gurgling noise. It is believed that if a pin be dropped in, and bubbles arise from it, the wishes then made will be granted. This is more to be relied upon if a gurgle from the spring greets the expectant lover. Above the well is an ancient oak, called " Laugh Lady Oak " ; its hollow stem is divided into three sections, all growing green.[2]

St. Peter's Wells, Peterchurch.

There were formerly three springs here. Two near together, above the large well, were good for eye troubles ; into these pins were thrown. They are now closed up. The water of the larger well flowed through a sculptured head of St. Peter into a shallow bathing place made for the use of sufferers from rheumatism. Mr. J. Powell, of Peterchurch, told me in 1905, that he could remember this chilly remedy being actually used : it was in his boyhood. The ash tree which formerly stood near the well had been cut down, and still lay above it.

In addition to the foregoing, the following Holy Wells are given in the *Archæological Survey of Herefordshire* (1897) :—Blakemere, Bodenham, Dinedor (see Section ix., 1, NewYear's Day), How Caple, Edgar's Bath (Harewood). I find many other wells to have been venerated, or at the least good for " sore eyes." Probably every ancient spring was worshipped by our pagan forefathers, and we have the last traces of this in the medicinal virtues attributed to so many even at the present day. Where references are not given in the following list, the information has been supplied by residents.

Place.		*Name (if any).*	*Cure.*
Bacton Manor	..		Skin Diseases.
Bosbury	..	Job's Well	Eye troubles.
Bredwardine	..	Guinea Well. People used to walk from Weobley (nine miles) and back again for a bottle of this water ..	Eye troubles.
Bromyard	..	Eye Well	
Crasswall	..	The Pot Well	
Clifford	..	A spring under an oak near the side of the priory ..	
Ewyas Harold	..	St. Martin's Well	

1] Letter *Hereford Times*, Apr. 4., 1900. The writer states that he heard the story 60 years ago.
2] *Woolhope Club*, 1881–2, 196.

Place.	Name (if any).	Cure.
Hereford ..	Pipe Well (St. Pippa), formerly in Pipe Lane, now Gwynne Street ..	
Hereford ..	Bridewell Fountain (see *Taylor's* map, 1757; *Duncumb,* i., 227). " Bride Well, near Castle (*Speed's* map, 1610). Gorwell (*Speed's* map) ..	
Kington ..	Crooked Well. Said to be so called because a crooked pin was a necessary offering.	
Llanveyno ..	Cae Thomas Well. The water of this well has been recently analysed, and is said to really possess medicinal virtue	Rheumatism and weak eyes.
Longtown ..	St. Martin's Well (near Cat's Back, a part of the Black Mountain range).	
Thornbury ..	Lady Well. From this well, according to tradition, an underground passage communicated with Thornbury Camp (*Woolhope Club*, 1886-9, 121).	
Snodhill Park ..	St. Mary's Well	
Stretford ..	St. Cosmos and St. Damian's Well. In a meadow near the church; still used for weak eyes by the people of the parish	Ophthalmia.
Turnastone ..	Lady Well	
Urishay ..	St. Margaret's Well	
Vowchurch ..	Heavenly Well	
Wormesley ..	Sap's Well. A woman at Dilwyn recommended water from this well mixed with a simple ointment, as " better for curing an abscess than any doctor's stuff."	
Walm's Well ..	(On the Herefordshire Beacon) was much used for skin diseases. There was on the hill a shed for the use of those who visited the spring. Both shed and spring have now disappeared (Windle, *Malvern County*).	

(8) THE SUN.

It was formerly the custom to watch an eclipse of the sun through its reflection in a bucket of water, and never to observe it directly.[1] It is not uncommon to see on the walls of old houses and barns in the county, especially in the Golden Valley, a large piece of iron in spiral shape, or two crossed, as in Figs. 2 and 3. The pieces of iron are as a rule fastened to the ends of bolts or iron pins, used to strengthen the

---

[1] Havergal, *Words and Phrases*, 47. *Cf.* Murray-Aynsley, *Symbolism*, 15, for a parallel Hindu custom.

COTTAGE AT OCLE PYCHARD WITH SWASTIKAS.

MAY-POLE AT LETTON.

building to which they are attached. I am informed by the Rev. T. Oliver Minos that when he lived at Garway some years ago he asked a blacksmith the reason of the curious shape of these irons, and was told that they were made so, to keep the house to which they were attached from being struck by lightning. This confirms the late Mrs. Murray-Aynsley's theory, that they are really forms of the *swastika*, a sun and fire symbol.[1] (*See illustration*).

For the Sun's Dance on Easter Morn, *see* Section ix., 9 ; *Three Suns*, vi., 4

(9) THE MOON.

Of moon worship we have abundant traces left among Herefordshire folk. Gardening and pig-killing operations are still regulated by the changes of the moon.

" Folks can say what they like, my father allus sowed his peas and beans in the wane of the moon, and onions, carrots and parsnips at the change ; it's right enough it is ! "

There is an old saying—

> " Sow beans when the moon is round,
> They'll pod down to the ground."[2]

Pigs must be killed during the increase of the moon, or they say the bacon will " sink in the bilin' " or waste away in the pot.[3]

> " Sow peason and beans in the wane of the moon,"
> Who soweth them sooner he soweth too soon."

Trees are cropped during the increase of the moon, as it is said that the " poles " or new branches will grow out straighter.

If nettles are well beaten with sticks on the day of the first new moon in May they will wither and not grow up again. This was done in perfect faith on a farm near Weobley, not long ago.

The moon is also thought to influence the time of child-birth, which is believed to be more likely to occur when the moon changes, or just before a new moon.

The moon is also connected with love affairs ; though, as it is the first new moon in the year that is referred to, the sun has something to do with its power in these matters. Girls who wish the time of their marriage revealed to them, watch the first new moon in the year until it " shines shadow ;" that is as soon as the light

---

1] *Symbolism*, 60 : " A Gloucester man . . . replied, ' the irons were made thus to protect the house from fire.' " 2] From MSS. of the late Rev. J. Barker, of Eardisland ; *cf*. Byard, 658 (from Tucker): 3] *Cf.* Frazer, *Golden Bough*, ii., 154 : Once a year, at the full moon, pigs were sacrificed simultaneously to the moon and to Osiris in ancient Egypt.

is strong enough, when they take a bucket of water and a new silk handkerchief, or a piece of smoked glass, through which they look at the reflection on the water.   The number of moons seen in this manner foretell the number of years before marriage.

Then we have the commoner moon superstitions firmly believed in, *e.g.*, it is unlucky to see the new moon through glass ; (on the first sight of it turn your money in your pocket without seeing it, and wish).

It is still related how the man in the moon was a wicked old labourer who would go hedging on Sunday, and how he was caught up into the moon with his bushes on his back ; you can see, if you look, how he carries them still.

When the moon changes on Sunday it brings bad luck.
" Sunday Moon
Comes too soon."[2]

As elsewhere, the moon is associated with the weather.   If the old moon lies in the new moon's lap, bad weather will follow.

" Nearer to twelve in the afternoon, the drier the moon."   " Nearer to twelve forenoon, the wetter the moon."[3]

There is a saying which shows belief in lunar influence on markets and prices." " When the harvest moon is high the price of bread will be high ; when the harvest moon is low the price of bread will be cheap."

It is unlucky to take medicine in the increase of the moon, according to *Antiquatis*, writing in 1879.   I have not heard this saying myself.[4]

There is a suggestion of reverence in the reluctance to point at the moon or at a rainbow.   A lady at Monkland, teaching her Sunday School class in the garden, pointed with her finger to show the children a beautiful rainbow. They all cried out " Oh don't, teacher, don't !"   They then explained that it was " dreadful bad luck to point at a rainbow."

Aubrey notes that " In Herefordshire the vulgar people at the time of the moon say ' It's a fine moon, God bless her ' (with ref. to Job, chap. 31, v. 26-27)."

For a well near Ross, and a holy well on Eign Hill, Hereford, *see* Section xii,, 1.

1] See Section vi., 2, for other moon divinations.   2] Weobley.   3] Havergal, *Words and Phrases*, 46.   4] *Herefordshire Gatherer*, June 4, 1879.

SECTION II.

TREES AND PLANTS.

The superstitious beliefs connected with trees and plants in this county show plain traces of primitive man's animistic theory of nature. He believed every tree and plant to be as himself, the conscious owner of an indwelling spirit, endowed with power equal to or exceeding his own.[1] He imagined so close a sympathy between plants and animals that he came to believe that injury done to a plant would react harmfully upon an animal resembling it in form or colour. For instance, it is held unlucky to bring the catkins of nut trees, called " lambs' tails," into the house, for fear of loss among the young lambs ; or the catkins of the round-leaved sallow, which are known to all as " gulls " (goslings) ; this would be fatal to the real goslings. If daffodils be brought in when hens are sitting, they say there will be no chickens ; some will allow no primroses or snowdrops either. If hawthorn blossom be brought indoors, a death in the family is said to follow. Perhaps this is on account of the injury done to the sacred tree in bloom, for hawthorn is used for the " bush " burnt on New Year's morning,[2] and is potent against witchcraft.

The Holy Thorn, said to be grown from cuttings taken from the Glastonbury thorn, grows at Wormesley, Rowlstone, Dorstone, Colwall,[3] Stoke Edith, King's Thorn, Tyberton, and other places in the county : the one at Bredwardine has died. The thorn at Wormesley is near the site of the priory which formerly stood there. It is believed that the Holy Thorn blossoms exactly at twelve o'clock on Twelfth Night, the time, so they say, at which Christ was born.[4] The blossoms are thought to open at midnight, and drop off about an hour afterwards. A piece of thorn gathered at this hour brings luck, if kept for the rest of the year. Formerly, crowds of people went to see the thorn blossom at this time. I went myself to Wormesley in 1908 ; about forty people were there, and as it was quite dark and the blossom could only be seen by candle light, it was probably the warmth of the candles which made some of the little white buds seem to expand. The tree had really been in bloom for several days, the season being extremely mild. Mr. Powell, of Peterchurch, told me he could remember that on old Christmas Eve, people came for miles round to Kingstone Grange, where a holy thorn grew in the garden ; they were liberally supplied with

---

1] Tylor, *Primitive Culture*, ii., 215 ; Burne, 240.   2] See Section ix., 1, *New Year's Day*.
3] Havergal, *Words and Phrases*, 45.   The famous thorn at Glastonbury was said by William of Malmesbury, and other writers. to have budded from the staff of Joseph of Arimathea, who there ended his wandering with the Holy Grail.   Specimens are still found about Glastonbury of *Cratægus oxycantha præcox*, a winter flowering hawthorn (see Chambers, *Med. Stage*, 1., 25).
4] *Cf.* Sidgwick, *More Ancient Carols* ;—
"At that bedside there grows a thorn
Which never so blossomed since Christ was born."

cake and cider.   At Clehonger, years ago a man was very much annoyed at the damage
done to his garden by those coming to see the thorn blossom which grew there, so he
began to cut it down.   But blood flowed from the trunk of the tree, and this so
alarmed him that he left off at once !¹

Sprays of mountain ash, elm, and witch hazel tied together and attached to the
churn are supposed to facilitate butter making and drive away the mischievous fairies,
who prevent the cream from turning into butter.   Rowan, or mountain ash, usually
called "wittan" or "witty," is held specially potent against witchcraft, and a piece
was sometimes nailed across the birch tree above the stable door on May day. ² There
is a saying still current that " the witty is the tree on which the devil hanged his
mother."   Goads made of it were formerly used by the waggoners, and collars of it
were made for the horses and cattle.³   Some still have the belief in its powers noted by
Aubrey in Herefordshire :—

> "They used, when I was a boy, to make pinnes for the yoakes of their oxen of them," (rowan trees),
> " believing it had virtue to preserve them from being forespoken, as they call it, and they used to plant one
> by their dwellinghouse, believing it to preserve them from witches and Evil Eyes."⁴

A tall birch tree, decorated with red and white rags, may still be seen occasionally, fastened near the door of the stable.   It is placed there early on May day,
and usually left up for the whole year.   (*See illustration.*)   Its purpose is to avert
ill-luck, and to prevent wicked fairies or witches from riding horses in the night, or
plaiting their manes and tails, so that the waggoners cannot comb them. ⁵ " Did you
ever see a witch's knot ?" one old waggoner asked me." " I have, many a time ; they
tie the horse's manes in knots as no man could make.   It takes half a day to undo 'em."⁶
A farmer, who once lost horses worth £160 in a year, allowed his man to put up a may-
pole twenty years ago ; he says he has had no more loss, and has therefore put up one
each year since.

Sixty years ago " witty " and birch were placed above every cottage door on
May morning, and on the pig's cot, and even stuck in the seed-beds in the garden, as
a protection against witchcraft and the Evil Eye.   Small pieces were used, one of each,
placed across each other.   This is still done at Llanveyno and Michaelchurch, where a
lady noticed the little wooden cross above the door recently, and was told it was to
counteract the influence of a malicious neighbour, whose evil eye was much feared.⁷

There are birch woods in the Orcop district, and the people still make besoms,
which are not quite ousted by the modern bass broom ; it is unlucky to make a besom

---

1] R.H.B.   2] See *infra*, Section ix., 10.   3] Fosbroke, *Ariconensia*, 74.   4] *Remaines*, 247.   5] See Section
iv., 5. *Fairies.*   6] Walterstone, ; see *infra*, iv., 6.   7] See *infra*, v., 2.

in " the Christmas " (that is, from Dec. 25th to Jan. 6th), or in May. Mrs. M——, of Orcop, *ætat* 86, told me she was most careful to get a good stock of besoms made before Christmas and May day for this reason.[1]

The Rosemary flourishes only " where the missus is master." I have heard it said that it blossoms at midnight on Twelfth Eve, " same as the Holy Thorn," and that at Orcop and Garway people sat up to see it. The tenants of the manor belonging to the Rectory at Ross had to make offerings of rosemary and marigolds to the church, as part of their rents,[2] probably for use at funerals.

The spotted laurel is said to have been spotted ever since some of the milk from the Virgin Mary's breast fell upon it, as she suckled the infant Christ.[3]

There is a trace of the widespread fear felt in cutting down a tree in the following instance of a charm to make it fall the right way. A man felling a tree near Dorstone was told that it was likely to fall in the wrong direction; he replied that it was all right, because he was doing it " according to Ezekiel."

Formerly, mistletoe was never used for decorating at Christmas, as it was considered very unlucky to bring it into the house before New Year's Day, when it was brought in and hung up in the farm-house kitchen, with the " bush," for the rest of the year.[5] An old cobbler, who died at Weobley some years ago, used to say that our Lord's Cross was made of mistletoe. But at Garway I was told that " the cross was made of quicken tree."[6]

It is unlucky to burn elder wood. Men cutting down brushwood near Weobley were allowed to take home what they liked for fuel, but they carefully sorted out the elder, one man saying that he would not carry bad luck into his house for the world.[7]

The willow brings luck if brought into the house on May day, and is potent against the Evil Eye, especially if given by a friend. It is also believed that any young animal or child struck by a willow rod, usually called " withy stick," or " sally twig," will cease to grow afterwards. A woman at Pembridge said, " I've never hit nothing with a sally twig, never, nor shouldn't like to either." This belief seems to be connected with the curse on the willow in the last verse of the ballad of the " Bitter Withy," well-known to local singers.[8]

1] See *infra*, ix., 10 and 11, for other uses of birch. 2] *Ross Guide*, 27. 3] C.G.P. 4] Mrs. Powell. The man may have meant *Ecclesiastes* xi., 3, " In the place where the tree falleth, there shall it be."
5] See *infra*, ix., 1., *New Year's Day*. 6] See Friend, *Flowers and Flower Lore*, 308. *Mistletoe :* " In Brittany it is called the *Herbe de la Croix*, because it was believed that it was from this plant that the Cross was made, though it fell from the dignity of a fine forest tree to the degradation of a parasite in consequence."
7]" Judas, the betrayer of Christ, is said to have hanged himself on an elder tree." Gutch, 62.
8] See *infra* xiv., 1. *Carols. Cf.* Burne, 248, and *Folk-lore* xxii, 18. The superstition extends to broom in Shropshire.

A large elm tree near Credenhill Court is called the " Prophet Elm " ; it is said to foretell each death in family of the Eckleys, who formerly owned the place, by flinging off a limb.

About sixty years ago a fine walnut tree at the Porch House, Eardisland, fell in several pieces in the night, though it was apparently vigorous, and there was no storm. It was thought a very bad omen, and the fears of the family were confirmed by the death of the mistress of the house shortly afterwards. If ivy growing on the wall of a house die, it is thought to be a sign of the death of one of the inmates. A bloom on an apple or pear tree after the fruit has set is also regarded as an omen of death.

It was noticed by the local peasantry that the ash trees in this county had no " keys," in the year in which Charles I. died ; they believed that Nature sympathised with their sorrow.[1] Lilacs and laburnums are said to mourn if any trees of the same kind are cut down near them, and it is believed that they do not blossom the following year.[2]

The opening of the leaves of oak and ash in spring is still carefully watched because of belief in the old rhyme :—

> " If the oak is out before the ash
> There will be a splash (*fine summer*).
> If the ash is out before the oak
> There will be a soak (*wet summer*).[3]

It is also said that if the oak be out first, there will be a good year of hops : and " Good year of black currants, good year of hops." May Dew gathered from beneath an oak tree is thought more beautifying than any other, and was formerly gathered by girls for anointing their faces.[4]

The apple is our Herefordshire tree *par excellence* ; the old labourers look upon the destruction of an orchard almost as an act of sacrilege, and they say that if an orchard be cut down to plant a hopyard, it will never pay the cost of cultivation. An apple was the badge of the old Herefordshire regiment, and it is customary to present the freedom of the city in a casket made of apple-tree wood.[5]

Holly and ivy are used for decorating at Christmas, and it is very unlucky to bring holly into the house before ; all evergreens must be taken down and burnt before Candlemas Day.

1] Webb, ii., 328.   2] C.G.P.   3] *Cf.* Northall, 474.   4] *Herefordshire Gatherer*, May 18, 1879 ; see also ix., 10, *infra.*   5] Johnson, 227.   Lord Nelson received the freedom of the city in a box of apple-tree wood. See *infra*, xii., 1, for the apple in local custom.

If the myrtle blossom it is thought to be a sign of a wedding in the family of the owner of the tree.

Parsley, being difficult to grow in some places, is said to " go to the owd 'un nine times afore it comes up." It must not be transplanted on any account. " My mon telled Mrs. J—— he didn't hold with planting parsley ; she could do it herself if she'd a mind ; she did, and she've been a cripple ever since." But as a rule it is said that a death in the family will follow.

Anything unusual in the growth of plants or flowers seems to have been sufficient to dismay our forefathers. A broad bean coming up with black leaves is an omen of death, also a Michaelmas daisy with a flattened double stalk, which is called a shroud.

Onion peelings should be immediately and carefully destroyed ; it is unlucky to keep part of an onion in the house. If all be not required, the rest is burnt or thrown away. I have had a Herefordshire cook who was most particular about this.

An old gardener at Dadnor, near Ross, used to say that blackberries were not good to eat ; " the trail of the serpent is over them," he said. My informant added that blackberries were not eaten in the district until comparatively recent times.[1]

Antiquatis records that the practice of making midsummer garlands was very common in Herefordshire in the old days. Ballads were sung while weaving the garlands, and the flowers and foliage used in their construction were for divination. Those in request were the rose, St. John's Wort, vervain, and rue, all of which were thought to have magical properties.[2]

The inclusion of rue in a midsummer garland is curious ; it is usually an emblem of sorrow :—

> " There's a herb in my father's garden,
> And some do call it rue ;
> When swallows dive and fishes fly,
> Young men they shall prove true.' [3]

Folk Names of Plants.

The late Mrs. Murray-Aynsley collected the following folk-names of plants in the Golden Valley district :—*Snappers* (Stitchwort), *Ransom* (Wild Garlic), *Jack-in-the-hedge* (Treacle Mustard), *Butcher* (Early Purple Orchis), *Whitsun Boss*, or *Queen's Cushions* (Guelder Rose).

1] *Cf.* Gutch, 61. " Blackberries are not to be eaten after Michaelmas, for by that time the devil has waved his club over the bushes." 2] *H. Gatherer*, June 28, 1879 ; see *infra*, vi., 2.
3] From a ballad, *As I walked out*, still sung in Weobley ; *cf.* also *The Loyal Lover* (*Eng. County Songs*) :—
" I'll weave my love a garland,
It shall be dressed so fine ;
I'll set it round with roses,
With lilies, pinks, and thyme."

I have not heard these in Weobley district, but we have the following :—*Old Man* (Southern wood), *Old Woman* (French Lavender), *Black Doctor* (Water Figwort), *Bee-in-a-bush* (Monkshood), *Come-and-kiss-me*, or *Two-faces-under-one-hat* (Pansy).

A native of Weobley told me that her father always grew Sweet William and Fair Margaret on either side of his door, but she could not remember the other name of the plant he called " fair Margaret," doubtless in allusion to the old ballad of the same name.

For the use of plants in charming and healing, *see* Section vii., 1 & 2 ; Trees and the Moon, 1, 9 ; Cockle, ix., 9 ; Yew Tree, I., 3 ; xiii., 1 ; Gospel Oak and Yew, xii., 1.

SECTION III.

ANIMAL LIFE.

(1) ANIMALS.

Cattle.

It is unlucky for a cow to have two calves. One would imagine that such an event would be considered rather fortunate than otherwise ; I have not been able to ascertain the particular kind of ill-luck expected to follow.

Formerly, no farmer put his lantern on the table, on account of the unfortunate effect on his cows ; the lantern must always be placed underneath the table. " The reason our cow calved a month too soon was because the master put his lantern always on the table."[1] The old-fashioned tin lanterns, for candles, with horn plates for the side, are now little used, paraffin safety lamps having superseded them.

Horses.

Horses are thought to be peculiarly susceptible to the influence of witchcraft.[2] It was at one time the custom to tell cart horses of the death of their master, but I have been unable to hear of the practice in this county to-day.[3] If you meet a white horse, cross your thumbs and wish ; the wish will certainly come true. Or bend down and make a cross on your shoe with your finger, then you will have a present.

A donkey, or more rarely a goat, may often be seen in the fields with a herd of cattle. Various reasons are given for this : that it is lucky, that it prevents mischance among the cattle, that it keeps them contented, also that it insures fertility. Others declare that it is only because donkeys and goats eat some kind of herbage that is not good for the cows.

Great importance is attached to the first sight of a lamb each spring. If the head be seen first, it is a sign of a lucky year ; if the tail, the reverse is anticipated.

It is a bad omen to meet a hare or a stoat when setting out on a journey.[4] An old farmer who lived near Longtown was once taking his cattle to market ; they had travelled some miles of the road when a stoat crossed in front of them. " Turn 'em back boys," he shouted to the drovers, " Turn 'em back, no luck to-day;" and back they all had to go.

It is believed that hedgehogs, called " urchins," suck milk from the cows, and that this is why their milk is sometimes streaked with blood. (The real reason is chill, to which good milkers are susceptible).

1] Havergal, *Words and Phrases*, 46.   2] See Section v.   3] *Byegones in Wales*, Feb. 1882.   4] *Cf.* Brand, 689.

Animals are weather wise. If a cat wash her face with her paw, it will rain. If she sit near the fire with her back towards it, it will certainly snow. The braying of a donkey is also a sign of rain.[1] The howling of a dog is here, as everywhere, an omen of death. So also is a mole-heap in the garden. A woman in the Bromyard district was found lately standing at the door surrounded by her family, all viewing with dismay the work of an " oont " (mole) in their grass plot, and hoping that it would be a very distant relative who would be " taken."

It is very lucky to have a black cat come in the house. May cats are no good and should be drowned. It is also unlucky for a child to be born in May, and a frequent taunt is " You're only a May cat."

In going to a new house, the cat should be put in through the window back-wards ; it is unlucky to let it walk in forwards. A woman complained of losing her cat, although she had buttered its feet when it came. " I always gives the new pig a bit of frizzled bacon first thing too," she said, " to make him contented, like."[2]

The church at Mordiford, which stands near the river Lugg, had until about 1811, a large green dragon painted on the west end of the church. Tradition says that it represented a dragon which lived in the woods near the village and which gave the inhabitants great trouble, destroying their cattle and even human beings. It came to the river to drink, at the spot where the Lugg joins the Wye ; its path from the wood to the river is still called " Serpent's Lane," and it is said the grass will never grow upon it. Many rewards were offered for the destruction of the dragon, but all feared to attempt it. At length a condemned malefactor was offered free pardon if he could succeed. Hiding himself in a barrel at the edge of a river, he waited till the dragon came down to drink and succeeded in slaying it, but was himself slain by its poisonous breath in the moment of victory.

There are two suggested explanations of the extraordinary painting on the church. One is that Mordiford is " The ford of Mordred," and that Mordred, an early British Chief, may have deposited a banner with a dragon on it in the church. Another —and more likely suggestion— is that it represented the arms of the Priory of St. Guthlac at Hereford. They bore in the fourteenth century this coat ;—" Gules, a Wyvern passant, Wings displayed, and tail rowed, or."

Blount (c. 1670) observed that when he was at Mordiford, a serpent was then pictured on the wall of the church. It must have been many times re-painted ; as last

---

1] Mrs. Powell. Cf. Northall, 472 :—
 " When the donkey sounds his horn,
   It is quite time to house your corn."—Lancashire.
2] Ocle Pychard.

MoRdiford Church
Dragon on West End
circa 1808

MORDIFORD CHURCH.

MORDIFORD DRAGON (FROM DINGLEY).

BRONSIL CASTLE. FROM AN OLD PRINT.

represented its body was covered with scales of green and gold. It had four legs, with webbed feet, two griffin-like wings, and a long formidable tail. Blount gives the inscription as follows :—

> " This is the true effigies of that strange
> Prodigious monster which out of the woods did range ;
> In Eastwood it was by Garson's hand slain,
> A truth which old mythologists maintaine."[1]

At Goodrich Castle, according to Silas Taylor, the cellars were floored with Irish earth, so that no toad could live there ; and the timber was also believed to be brought from Ireland, in order to avoid the annoyance of cob-webs.[2]

It is unlucky to call an animal by the name of a person ; for example, to call a horse or pet lamb by the name of a child of its owner. The animal will never thrive, and will eventually die.[3]

For reference to toads, *see* Section iv., 2 ; spirit as pig or calf, iv., 2 ; demon dogs, iv., 2 ; badger, iv., 3 ; diseases of cattle, vii., 2 ; snake in Vaughan crest, xv., 2 ; sow and pigs, xv., 1 ; King o' the cats, xiii. ; cross on donkey's back, vii., 2 ; white horses, vi., 2 ; piebald horse, vii., 2.

(2) BIRDS.

Of all the knowledge and power beyond his own attributed by primitive man to living things, birds are especially regarded as endowed with a prophetic instinct, more often bearing tidings of evil than good fortune. The screech of an owl is an omen of death, and also the fluttering of a dove or pigeon against the window of a sick room, or the flight of a crow over a house.[4]

A farmer at Longtown was ploughing, and was surprised to see a white crow come and perch on his plough ; when he came home at night the bird followed him, and hovered about near his house. He went in and told his wife, remarking " That's not for nothin' ; its all up wi' me afore long." The next night he was poisoned by a lodger in his house, who was afterwards hanged for the murder. A widow living in Weobley told me that she had a cock, which was tame, and used to eat out of her hand. When her husband was ill it used to come and crow under his window every morning. " I took it to be a sign of his death," she said, " and had it killed, that it shouldn't put him in mind of it like." It is a warning of approaching death when the cock crows before midnight; in the afternoon, he merely announces the arrival of a visitor.

1] Cooke, iii., 81, from Lipscomb & Blount *MSS.*; Delvin, *Mordiford Dragon*, v. 66. 2] Webb., ii., 260. 3] C.G.P. 4] *Cf.* Burne, 227.

> " If cocks crow when they go to bed,
>> They'll sure to come down with a watery head."

That is, it will rain next morning.

A crowing hen is most unlucky, and must be killed at once. The small yolkless eggs, called " cocks' eggs," must never be brought into the house, but carefully thrown over it to advert impending misfortune. An odd number of eggs should be set under a hen ; thirteen is the luckiest number. It is better for a man to set a hen than a woman, the chicks will hatch out better. We have the usual sayings about crows and magpies :—

> " One for sorrow,
>> Two for joy,
>> Three for a girl,
>> Four for a boy."

Or,

> " One for sorrow,
>> Two for mirth,
>> Three for a wedding,
>> Four for a birth."[1]

Jackdaws and woodpeckers are weather prophets ; it is a sign of rain when jackdaws flutter and caw round Weobley church spire. It is said that the " yekkel " (woodpecker) only utters its shrill unmusical cry before rain. An old man at Dilwyn called this bird " Nicholas' Colt." There is an old weather saying, " If the birds sing before Candlemas they will cry before May."[2]

" The Cuckoo comes to Orleton fair to buy a horse, and goes to Brom (Brampton Bryan) to sell him." He is generally first heard in Herefordshire near Wellington or Dinmore Wood, on his way to Orleton, where the fair is held on April 23rd.[3]

It is unlucky to hear the cuckoo indoors for the first time in the year, especially if in bed. The hearer's occupation at the moment will be his most frequent one till the cuckoo comes again. " If it rains when the sun shines, the cuckoos are going to heaven."[4] I have not been able to obtain any explanation of this curious saying. The cuckoo, they say, always leaves before June 19th.

> " The robin and the wren,
>> Are God Almighty's cock and hen.
>> The swallow and the swift,
>> Are God Almighty's gifts.
>> (Or " New Year's gifts.")

Their nests are respected by children and never robbed. It is lucky to have swallows' or martins' nests under the eaves, and unfortunate to destroy one even accidentally.[5]

1] Cf. Brand, 698.　2] Havergal, Words and Phrases, 49.　3] Havergal, loc. cit.　4] Cf. Burne, 222.　5] Cf. Brand, 686 ; Northall, 274, 275.

A pretty swallow story is told by Aubrey :—

At Stretton, in Herefordshire, in 1648, Charles I. was prisoner, the tenant of the manor house there sold excellent cider to the gentlemen of the neighbourhood when they met privately and could discourse freely and be merry in those days, so troublesome to the loyal party. Among those who met was old Mr. Hill, B.D., parson of the parish. . . This venerable good old man one day (after his accustomed fashion), standing up with head uncovered to drink his Majesty's health, saying " God bless our gracious Sovereign," as he was going to put the cup to his lips a swallow flew in at the window and perched on the edge of the earthenware cup (not half-a-pint), and sipt and flew out again. This was in the presence of the aforesaid Parson Hill, Major Gwillim, and two or three more that I knew very well then, my neighbours, and whose joint testimony of it I have had more than once, in that very room. The cup is preserved there still, as a rarity.[1]

Although Aubrey does not say so, it seems probable that this incident greatly encouraged the Royalists, being regarded as a good omen for the ultimate success of their cause.

The raven is usually regarded as a bird of evil omen, but an extraordinary story from Wigmore of a raven that cited Scripture references is something on the other side of the scale. The incident is thus set forth by Alexander Clogie, minister of Wigmore :

On the third of February, 1691, about three in the afternoon, this Reverend Divine, a person of the venerable age of eighty years, and forty of those a laborious teacher of God's Word in the parish of Wigmore, in the County of Hereford, being in the Hall of his own house, being with the Pious Matron, his wife, some neighbours and relations, together with two small grandchildren of his, in all to the number of eight persons Thomas Kinnersley, one of the said grandchildren of but ten years of age, starting up from the fire side, went out of the hall door and sat himself down upon a block by a wood-pile before the door, employing himself in no other childish exercise than cutting of a stick, when in less than half a quarter of an hour he returned into the Hall in great amazement, his countenance pale and affrighted, and said to his grandfather and grandmother : " Look in the third of the Colossians and the fifteenth," with infinite passion and earnestness, repeating the words no less than three times. Which deportment and speech, much surprising the whole company, they asked him what he means by those words. Who answered with great ardency of spirit, that a raven had spoken them three times from the Peak of the Steeple, and that it looked towards W.W.'s house and shook its head and wings, directing its looks and motions still towards that house. All which words he heard the Raven distinctly utter three times, and then saw it mount and fly out of sight. His grandfather hereupon taking the Bible and turning to the said text, found these words : " And let the Peace of God rule in your hearts, to the which you are also called in one body and be ye thankful." Upon recalling whereof the child was satisfied and his countenance perfectly composed again.[2]

The " pious and learned divine," as the author of this statement describes himself, goes on to moralise at great length on the significance on the event, in which he fully believed. The book is interesting as indicating the extent of popular credulity in our country during the seventeenth century.

It is still firmly believed by many that a person *in extremis* cannot die on a bed or pillow which contains even a few feathers of game or other wild birds. The turkey is held to be a " wild bird," in this connection.

1] *Miscellanies*, 99—100. 2] *Vox Corvis*, or *The Voice of a Raven* (1694), 1—4.

For crows, *see* Section xiii., "The shepherd and the crows," "Jack o' Kent;" White crow, and Devil as a crow, Section iv., 2, 4.

(3) Insects.

Bees are regarded with respect, and the general custom of telling them of a death in the family of their owner is not yet extinct ; it is believed in the Golden Valley that they would leave their hives if not told. There was a large apiary at the Moor, near Hay, and when the owner died, in 1873, no one told the bees. It was noticed shortly afterwards they all disappeared. In Weobley, it was thought they would die if not told, or that another death would follow the omission. I have heard of one case of which the bees in twelve hives died after a death, a loss attributed to neglect of the custom of announcing it to them. There is at all times a fear of offending bees ; they must not be bought or sold, or even given or received as a gift. " If any neighbour wants bees, I may give her a hive, and in course a present finds its way to me ; the luckiest thing to give is wheat or flour, in some form, such as a sack of meal."[1] When bees swarm they are " tanged " with a clatter of frying pans and tin cans. Some say this is to make them settle, others that the practice gives the owner a right to follow the bees into his neighbour's garden, or anywhere they may chance to be. Bees are lovers of peace, and will not stay with a quarrelsome family. A bee coming into the house is a sign of the coming of a stranger.

Some consider it lucky to have a cricket on the hearth, while others call its chirp an omen of death ; at Orcop they say it means a heavy storm coming. Beetles come out of their haunts before rain. I once heard a servant say " Oh, it'll be wet to-morrow, there's a black-beetle. *Please* don't kill it ; it will be wetter if you do !" Spiders are sacred ; it is very unlucky to kill one, and a sign of good fortune to find one on one's clothes or person. Spiders spin no cobwebs on Irish timber. (*See ante,* under *Animals*).

The first wasp seen in the year should be killed ; this secures good luck and freedom from enemies till the year is out. (See *Leechcraft,* v. 2, for uses of insects in folk medicine.)

1] Mrs. Powell.

SECTION IV.

SUPERNATURAL PHENOMENA.

(1) WRAITHS.

All over Herefordshire the common belief prevailed that the wraith of a dying person may be seen by friends or relatives, before or at the time of death. " When my daughter died," said Mrs. D——, " I went in next door to tell a neighbour ; she only said she knew, for she had seen my daughter standin' in the road there yesterday, as plain as you stand there now. Only she told me nothin', not to frighten me."[1] The idea seems to be that the departing spirit bids farewell to the places or persons most dear to it.

(2) EXORCISMS AND MANIFESTATIONS.

There still exists, with the belief in ghosts, faith in the power of the clergy to put an end to the wanderings of the restless spirit by exorcism. The vicar of a parish near Weobley was asked not long ago if he would " kindly come and lay a ghost."

Black Vaughan,

Perhaps the most notorious and troublesome of our Herefordshire ghosts was Black Vaughan, of Hergest Court, said to be the ghost of the Vaughan whose monument stands in Vaughan chapel of Kington Church. He was a very wicked man, so after his death he could not rest, and came back " stronger and stronger all the while." At last he came in broad daylight, and would upset the farmer's waggons, loaded with hay or corn ; he would jump up behind their wives riding to Kington market. He sometimes took the form of a fly, in order to " torment (tease) the horses !"[2] Finally, he came into the church itself, in the form of a bull.[3] It was decided that something must be done ; people went so much in fear of Black Vaughan that attendance at Kington market was affected, and the prosperity of the town suffered. " So they got twelve parsons, with twelve candles, to wait in the church to try and read him down into a silver snuff-box. For," the old man who told me the story explained, " we have all got a sperrit something like a spark inside we, and a sperrit can go large or small, or down, down, quite small, even into a snuff-box." There were present, to help to lay the spirit, a woman with a new-born baby, whose innocence and purity were perhaps held powerful in exorcism.

1] This is the Welsh *Lledrith*, or spectre, seen before death ; it never speaks, and vanishes if spoken to.— Sikes, ..215.   2] *Cf*. Section xiii., *Jack o' Kent, infra*.   3] *Cf*. Sikes, 197, for the Devil in this form.

" Well, they read, but it was no use ; they were all afraid, and all their candles went out but one.   The parson as held that candle had a stout heart, and he feared no man nor sperrit.   He called out ' Vaughan, why art thou so fierce ? '   ' I was fierce when I was a man, but fiercer now, for I am a devil ! ' was the answer.   But nothing could dismay the stout-hearted parson, though, to tell the truth, he was nearly blind, and not a pertickler sober man.   He read, and read, and read, and when Vaughan felt himself going down, and down, and down, till the snuff-box was nearly shut, he asked ' Vaughan, where wilt thou be laid ? '   The spirit answered ' Anywhere, any-where, but not in the Red Sea ! '   So they shut the box, and took him and buried him for a thousand years in the bottom of Hergest pool, in the wood, with a big stone on top of him.   But the time is nearly up ! '"[1]

Two footmarks were formerly to be seen in the grass under an oak tree near Hergest, which were pointed out as the spot where Black Vaughan was wont to stand, to watch the deer in the park.   So wicked was he that grass never after grew on the spot where he stood.   I was told by the late Mr. T. Lloyd, of Kington, that he had seen " Vaughan's footmarks " when a boy, but they have now disappeared.   The oak tree was cut down some years ago, and it was said that the man who felled it went mad afterwards, and died in an asylum.

The Thomas Vaughan whose effigy lies in the Vaughan chapel was mortally wounded at the battle of Banbury in 1469.   He and his ancestors were brave and honourable men, and history in no way corroborates the popular traditions concerning them.   Still, they have been called the " Douglases of the Welsh Border," and were probably regarded with more awe and fear than love by the folk among whom they lived.   Variants of the story of the laying of Vaughan's ghost are to be found all over the county ; sometimes it is attached to the local church, with the central figure unchanged.   Another version, which describes how the ghost of a Mr. Hoskins was laid in Hereford Cathedral, adds some picturesque details.   It was contributed to the *Hereford Times* (April 15th 1876), by " Nonagenarian."   She alludes to the fall of the West Front of Hereford Cathedral, which happened in 1786, and continues :—

It was just about the time they were laying Mr. Hoskins' ghost, and Hereford was in a great flutter about it.   Twelve parsons went at midnight into the church, everyone taking a candle.   They first drew a ring all round them.   In the middle was a table, on which they placed the twelve candles, twelve Bibles, and twelve prayer-books.   Then they sat without speaking from eleven till twelve o'clock; and while the clock was striking they each lighted their candle and called the ghost.   He was away in Ireland when they called first, and they had pretty work to make him cross the sea ; but when he did come, he looked most fierce,—not but what that was his natural look, for I remember him well.   He was a fine-looking man.   One of them said " Oh, Mr. Hoskins, why so fierce ? "   He answered " Fierce when a man, much more now a devil !"   Then they asked him where he would be laid, and he begged hard not to be laid in the Red Sea.   The old folks

---

[1] For a variant of this story *cf*. Burne, 107, 642, *The Roarin' Bull o' Bagbury*.

said they always did beg for that, but as they were obliged to lay him in running waters, they decided to lay him under Byster's Gate bridge, and there he was laid. But they had hard work, for every candle went out before it was done, but old Canon Underwood's, and I heard the servant girl say that when he came home his shirt was wringing wet. When they were pulling down Byster's Gate afterwards, I heard some of them say they hoped they would not disturb Hoskins' ghost."

Another restless spirit is laid under one of the bridges at Eardisland, for two thousand years ; but—the time is nearly up !

A ghost laid in the Haugh Pool near Yarpole was confined in a goose-quill, instead of the usual snuff-box. The Haugh Pool at Eaton Bishop was haunted by a lady on a grey horse ; but she is laid now, and no one ever sees her.

In Aconbury Church is a tomb said to be that of one Roger de Clifford. There is a legend which says that the Church was haunted by a monk, in habit and cowl, the spirit of the man who was buried beneath the monument. At last the clergy laid him, by burying him, in an empty bottle, beneath the tomb, in the church wall, " neither out of the church nor in the church." Since then nothing has been seen of him. This story was told by the parish clerk to the writer of a paper on Aconbury.[1]

The Ghost of Bronsil Castle, Eastnor.

Towards the end of the reign of Queen Elizabeth, or very early in that of James I., Bronsil was disturbed by the visits of some restless spirit, whose nocturnal perambulations effectually banished every attempt at sleep from the eyes of the troubled inmates. Mr. Gabriel Reede, the proprietor, was advised to represent the case to Master Allen, of Gloucester Hall, in Oxford, who, according to Anthony à Wood, was " The father of all learning and virtuous industry." He was not unknown in Herefordshire, where, probably, others besides the servants at Holme Lacy considered the watch that he carried to be his familiar spirit. To the University Mr. Reede repaired, and on communicating to the learned Wizard the purposes of his visit, was desired to procure " a bone of the first Lord Beauchamp," as the only effectual means of silencing the unearthly disturbance, being assured that as long as the relic of its former celebrated proprietor remained within the walls, the Castle would be free from any repetition of this spiritual infliction.

Bones were procured and taken to Bronsil, which ever afterwards remained in peace. These wonder-working bones, portions of the vertebræ, were long regarded as heirlooms in the Reede family, and escaped the destruction in which the contents of the castle were involved when it was burnt.

Mr. Reede removed to his seat at New Court in the parish of Lugwardine, and thither the cedar box containing Lord Beauchamp's bones, was carefully conveyed. New Court has within the last hundred years repeatedly changed masters, and it is not therefore surprising that this interesting proof of the credulity of the seventeenth century should have been lost from a want of information respecting its historical value ; but the box labelled " Lord Beauchamp's bones " was carefully preserved during many generations, and is known to have been in existence subsequent to the accession of King George III.

The old people of Eastnor used to say that one of the Beauchamps, Lord of Bronsil, died in Italy and could never rest until his bones were delivered to the right heir of the castle, and they were accordingly sent from Italy enclosed in a box, and were, after the demolition of the castle, long in the possession of the Redes, and afterwards of Mr. Sheldon of Abberton, in Worcestershire.[2]

1] From the collection of Mr. Walter Pilley ; a newspaper cutting, no date.   2] *Woolhope Club*, 1880—230.
    Cf. Section 1., 3. *Hidden Treasure.*

Old Taylor's Ghost.

"Nonagenarian" tells the story of another Hereford ghost,[1] who could not rest because he had moved a landmark. I have heard several similar stories, including one of a man who "wasted away like" until he died, through remorse, and afterwards could not rest until the landmark was replaced in its original position. The Nonagenarian's version is as follows :—

There was old Taylor's ghost, that used to walk about at the White Cross. He couldn't rest, because he had moved a landmark. He used to ride upon a little pony, and sometimes he would be seen sitting on a stile. I have never seen old Taylor myself, but have heard many say they had seen him. At last his ghost was laid. . . One stormy night a fellow whose name I have forgotten, walked into the bar of the Nag's Head, and said he had seen old Taylor, and had promised to meet him in the Morning Pits that night at twelve. Of course nobody believed him, and as the night wore on the others jeered him, and said "I would not go on such a night as this." He said he would not ; but as the hour drew near he was obliged to go. Something forced him to run, so that he reached the Morning Pits as the clock struck twelve. There the old man was waiting. "Follow me," said he ; the other followed him into some strange place, which they seemed to reach in a very short time. In the place were two immense stones. "Take up these stones," said Taylor. "I can't," said Denis (he was nick-named "Denis the Liar"). "You can," said Taylor, "try." He tried, and tilted them easily. "Now come with me," said Taylor, "and place them where I shall show you." He carried them, and put them down with ease. "Now," said the other, "I caution you never tell anybody what you see here this night." He promised. "And now," said he, "lie down on your face, and as you value your life, don't attempt to look either way, until you hear music, and then get away as fast as you can." He lay a long time without hearing what he earnestly desired, but at last the welcome sound was heard . . . He was a very different man after that, though he soon died from the effects of his fright.[2]

The Lady of Devereux Wootton.

Some years ago a man named Tom A—— used to walk to his work each day from Kinnersley to Devereux Wotton, a farm two miles from Weobley. Each evening, on his way home through the fields, he used to meet a lady. But one night he found her sitting on a stile, and said "Please, lady let me pass." She replied, "I have waited for years for somebody to speak to me," and proceeded to tell him that he must return with her to Devereux Wotton, which he did. When they reached

---

1] *Hereford Times*, April 15th, 1876.   2] *Hereford Times*, loc. cit.

the house, the doors flew open and the rooms were all lighted up. As they passed through the kitchen, A—— noticed the menservants had gone to bed, for they had left their boots in a row on the hearth. The lady went to the attic, where she opened an oak chest and took out a roll of papers, telling Tom A—— to throw them into the pool near the house. Afterwards he was to listen, and if he heard sweet music, she would be gone to her rest; but if he heard bad language, she would be " in the other place."[1] Her name, she added, was Lady Berington. Tom obeyed, and soon heard " the loveliest music that ever was." But he could not keep the story to himself, and talked about it; that was why he was never right afterwards.[2]

Dunwood Farm, near Weobley, was haunted by the ghost of " Old Gregg," who is said to have been poisoned by one of his own family, who gave him stewed toad for supper.[3]

A farmhouse near Bromyard was so badly haunted that its unlucky tenant could not keep a servant, until he found a girl who said she was not afraid of the Devil himself. She sat up all alone, and there came to her two ladies dressed in silk, who took her with them down to the cellar, and showed her a heavy stone. Under it the girl found a " steen " (earthenware pan), which was full of gold. The ladies told her to take it, and give her master some. This she did, putting it down on the kitchen table. The ladies disappeared, and they never heard anything after that, though before the furniture had been " clattering " and shaking every night. Those ladies had hidden the gold, and till it was found they could not rest.[4]

It is generally believed that if a person hide money, or metal, such as silver spoons, or even iron tools, his spirit will haunt the place until spoken to. In speaking to a ghost, it is held that one should say " In the name of God, who art thou ?" The ghost will then conduct the person who sees it to the place of concealment; the money or valuables must be taken and thrown in water. Few live long after this experience.

I am indebted to Mr. Portman for the following account of such beliefs in the Kington and Crasswall districts :—

" A farm labourer, from the Black Hill farm, Crasswall, while sitting by his fire in his cottage after work, noticed for several nights a white face at the window,

---

1] Some stories of this type have " the baying of hounds," instead of bad language. See *infra, Cwm Annwn,*
—the dogs of hell. 2] Told at Weobley, 1906. The Beringtons of Winsley once owned Devereux Wootton.
3] This is a very ancient method of poisoning. *Cf.,* the old ballad of " Lord Rendal," on " King Henry
my Son " (Broadwood, *Eng. Trad. Songs and Carols,* 99, and note).
" She fried me some paddocks, mother, make my bed soon,
For I'm sick to the heart, and would fain lay me down."
(*Paddocks,* O.E. for toads).
4] Told at Weobley, 1905, by a native of Bromyard.

and asked who was there ?   As the figure stood still and did not answer, he concluded
it was a ghost, and used the correct form of address.   The ghost then told him to come
away ; he was forcibly taken hold of and carried for miles over hill and dale to a wall,
where he had to remove stones and take out a box.   He was led on miles further to a
pool, into which the box was thrown.   The ghost then said he would never trouble
the man again ; he, poor wretch, was left to find his way home unaided.   He appeared
in the early morning shoeless, with his clothes in rags, and slowly faded away afterwards.   He never worked again."

"In connection with this story, people and children were warned not to put any
bits of iron in walls, for fear they should die and forget it, and therefore would be
unable to rest.   As an instance of this, only a few years ago I heard the wife of an old
workman say she had to go and search under an archway for tools her husband had left
there when working, as he was ill, and all his trouble was that he might have to haunt
the place after death."

The Ghost of Clifford Castle.

The Rev. Thomas Lewis, a nonconformist minister living on the Welsh border,
was well acquainted with a man who was employed by a perturbed spirit, and was at
the man's bedside when he died.   The ghost was, in appearance, a clergyman, dressed
in black clothes, with a white wig on.   As the man was looking out of an ale-house
window one night, he saw this ghost on horseback, and went out to him.   The ghost
bowed, and silently offered him drink, but this was declined.   Thereupon the ghost
lifted his hat, crooked his elbow, and said in a hollow tone "Attoch chwi syr," (towards
you, sir).   But others who were there could see nothing, and hear nothing.   The ghost
then said "Go to Clifford Castle, take out some money which lies hidden there, and
throw it into the river.   Do this, I charge thee, or thou shalt have no rest !"   Further
and more explicit directions were then given, and the unhappy man set out, against
his will, for Clifford Castle, which is the Castle in which was born Fair Rosamond,
King Henry II.'s beautiful favourite.   No one but himself was permitted to enter the
castle, though he was permitted to have a friend's company to the ruined gate thereof.
It was dark when he came to the castle, but he was guided to the place where the money
was, and ran with it and flung it into the river.   After that he was haunted no more.

Wormesley Grange, so the folk say, is still haunted by a beautiful lady dressed
in silk and jewels, and a gentleman in black.   It is said they have often appeared in
the house, and are to be seen walking in the drive at twelve o'clock every night, though
visible only to those born within an hour of midnight (that is, between 11 p.m. and

---

1] Sikes, 154.

1 a.m.), "that's why so many who go never see them." An indelible stain on the floor of one of the rooms is vaguely connected with these appearances.

The Homme House, Dilwyn, now taken down, was badly haunted : in fact, the story goes that it was taken down on that account ! Here, too, was a blood-stained floor, where it was thought murder was done. Often the servants heard a coach and horses come up to the front door, and even the drivers' whips would crack, but on going out nothing would be visible.

Long ago a farmer at Field's End, Weobley, committed suicide, and it was said that he " came back " in Garnstone Park in the shape of a calf. " I never seed him, myself, but I wasn't born in the night," said W—— P——, " but my sister did, as plain as I see you now." The farmhouse itself was haunted too, the chief trouble being that bedclothes were continually stripped off the occupants in the night. But at last the spirit was laid in the usual snuff-box, and now lies at the bottom of the pool in Garn-stone Park.[1]

An old woman, who would be a centenarian were she still living, told me that in the old coaching days, when she went to Hereford by coach through Burghill, she was shown an elm tree, in which there was " summat to be seen," in the form of a pig going up the tree backwards.

A man at Longtown, having heard a Baptist minister preaching against super-stitions and belief in ghosts, was heard to say : " I know what I have sin (seen), I helped myself to turn a man in his grave, up at Capel-y-fin ; he come back, and we thought to stop him, but after we turned him he come back seven times worse. He was a hurdle maker, and you could hear him tap, tap, tap, choppin' wood for his hurdles all about the place where he was used to work. No use of him (the preacher) tellin' *me* there's no ghosts ! "[2]

Aubrey has a ghost story connected with the county, illustrating the belief that " coming back " follows a violent death :—

Mr. Brown (brother-in-law to the Lord Coningsby) discovered his being murdered to several. His phantom appeared to his sister and her maid in Fleet Street, about the time he was killed in Herefordshire, which was about a year since.

The Spectre's Voyage.

There is a part of the river Wye, between the city of Hereford and the town of Ross, which was known for more than two centuries by the appellation of the " Spectre's Voyage," and across which, while it retained that appellation, neither entreaty nor remuneration could induce any boatman to convey passengers after a certain hour of the night. The superstitious notions current among the lower orders were that, at about

---

1] Told at King's Pyon, 1907. 2] From W.—P—., 1909. 3] *Miscellanies* (1696), 62.

the hour of eight on every evening, a female was seen in a small vessel, sailing from Hereford to North-brigg, a little village, then distant about three miles from the city, of which not even the site is now discernible ; that the vessel sailed with the utmost rapidity in a dead calm, and even against the wind ; that to encounter it was fatal ; that the voyager landed from it on the eastern bank of the river, a little beyond the village ; that she remained some time on the shore making the most fearful lamentations ; that she then re-entered the vessel and sailed back in the same manner, and that both boat and passenger vanished suddenly as they arrived at a certain point of the river, where the current is remarkably strong, within about half a mile of the city of Hereford.[1]

The Legend of Goodrich Castle.

The castle was besieged in 1646 by the parliamentary forces under Colonel Birch. His niece, Alice Birch, had eloped, taking refuge there. She was drowned in the Wye, with her lover, Charles Clifford, while attempting to escape from the Castle.

It is said that to this day the spirits of Alice and Clifford haunt the ruined towers of Goodrich, and are heard in every storm, shrieking on the swollen waters of the Wye. The vicinity of the fatal spot is carefully shunned on the anniversary of their catastrophe ; and a peasant more hardy than his comrades, who once ventured there on that day, is reported to have seen a horseman, with a female behind him, vainly urging his steed to cross the river.[2]

A Spirit Who Cared for the Poor.

Dr. Glanvil tells the story of a lady appearing after death to her former servant. She was the wife of Dr. Breton, minister at Pembridge during the Common-wealth. The servant was made to go out into a field, which had been wrongfully taken by the lady's father from the poor of Pembridge, and was then in possession of the woman's brother. " Observe," said the spirit, " how much of this field I measure with my feet. All this belongs to the poor, it being gotten from them by unlawful means." So the brother, who believed his sister's story, restored the land to the poor.[3]

The Guide of the Black Mountain.

A few years ago a man was driving a lady from Longtown to Llanveyno, and she, being a stranger, questioned him concerning the " Apparition of our Lady " at Llan-thony. He replied that he did not believe in it at all ; there were indeed spirits to be seen on the mountain, but they were different. He had seen, and he knew. Once he went to see friends at Llanthony, and was returning directly over the mountain to Longtown, when a fog came on suddenly and he lost his way. He was standing, quite at a loss, when a man came towards him, wearing a large broad-brimmed hat and a cloak. He did not speak but beckoned, and the man followed him, until he found himself in the right path. Turning round, he thanked his unknown friend, but received

---

1] Keele, *Romance of the History of England*, 161, which see for the supposed historical origin of the story, which seems to be embroidered upon a foundation of popular tradition ; as is also the " Legend of Good-rich Castle " below.   2] *Romance of the History of England*, 574.   3] *Saducismus Triumphatus* (1700), ii., 127.

no reply; he vanished quickly in the fog. This seemed strange, but he thought no more till, on visiting his friends at Llanthony later, they asked if he reached home in safety that evening, as they had been anxious. When the stranger in the broad-brimmed hat was described they looked at each other in surprise. " What !" they said, " tell us exactly what his face was like." He described the stranger more minutely. " It was T—— H——, for sure," they cried, " he knew the mountain well, and *he has been dead these two years*."

This story of a helpful and beneficent spirit is a pleasant contrast to those of the restless and unhappy ones it is often said to be fatal to meet.

Such are a few representative stories of " coming back." Almost any number could be collected, but they have for the most part a strong family likeness. It is generally believed that spirits cannot speak until spoken to ; that the call of a spirit must be obeyed ; that they can transport living human beings through the air, and if their secrets be revealed, insanity or death must follow. The cause of coming back is held to be violent death, hiding of property during life, moving a landmark, or the fact of having led a wicked life generally, as in the case of Vaughan, who is represented as changed into an evil spirit after death. Excessive grief of the lover, relative or friend, of the departed one is another cause of the return of the spirit.[1] A woman told me how her aunt had died shortly after her second marriage, without making a will, leaving her niece thus unprovided for, as the property went to her husband. " She came and stood by my bed three nights running, all in her widow's weeds. I saw her as plain as I see you, but I daren't speak. I hid myself under the bedclothes and left off grievin' about the money, for I was afeard I should go wrong. And she never come to me since."[2]

A curious expression for seeing a spirit is " I seed So and So's *token*."[3] If the fire burns blue, it is a sign that there is a spirit in the room."[4]

Goblin funerals are spoken of in the Golden Valley and in the neighbourhood of Hay, but I have not heard of them further east of the Welsh Border ; they are portents of death, forerunners of real funerals.[5] The old manor house of Snodhill was haunted, and an old lady, who died in 1878, used to say that in her childhood it was believed that a ghostly funeral procession, with torches seen at night, foretold a death in the Prosser family. Her name was Mrs. Powell, and she was a daughter of the Rev. F. Prosser, whose ancestors built the manor house about 1660. The rustling of silk, and tapping of high-heeled shoes, is still said to be heard in the old rooms.[6]

1] See *infra*, Section xv., *Ballads,—The Wife of Usher's Well*, and *The Unquiet Grave*. 2] King's Pyon, 1908. 3] *Herefordshire Gatherer*, June 21, 1879. 4] Mr. C. G. Portman ; *cf*. Howells, 13. 5] *Cf*. Sikes, 231 ; Howells 54, 55. 6] From Mrs. Powell.

A few years ago, a woman walking from Peterchurch to Hay met a funeral, and stepped aside to let it pass. It was " all perfect, hat bands, cloaks, and everything." On arriving at Hay she asked who had died, but there had been no death, and no one knew of any funeral. She concluded that she had seen phantoms only, and returned to Peterchurch full of gloomy foreboding.

See also Section I, 7,—St. Anne's Well, Aconbury.

(3) DEMONS AND FAMILIAR SPIRITS.

Cwn Annwn, or the Dogs of Hell.[1]

Parry (*Hist. Kington*, 205) gives an account of the superstitious beliefs of many aged persons then (1845) living in the parish.

It was the opinion of many persons then living in the out-townships that spirits in the shape of black dogs are heard in the air, previous to the dissolution of a wicked person ; they were described as being jet black, yet no one pretends to have seen them. But many believed that the king of darkness (say the gossips) sent them to terrify mankind when the soul of a human being was about to quit its earthly tenement.[2]

Parton Cross, near Eardisley, is said to be haunted by ghostly black dogs. Those who firmly believe in their existence, say that they have been seen near Pembridge within the last few years.

People at Llanveyno and Michaelchurch can still remember the terror inspired by the supposed appearance of a phantom dog in the lane about half a mile below Clodock Church. It appeared at a certain cottage, would run beside vehicles and horses for some distance, and then vanish as quickly as it appeared.[3]

Hergest Court was, or perhaps still is, haunted by a demon dog, said to have belonged to Black Vaughan, and to have accompanied him during his life. It is seen before a death in the Vaughan family. A native of Kington writes :—" In my young days I knew the people who lived at Hergest Court well, and they used to tell me strange things of the animal. How he inhabited a room at the top of the house, which no one ever ventured to enter ; how he was heard there at night, clanking his chain ; how at other times he was seen wandering about (*minus* the chain !) His favourite haunt was a pond, the " watering place," on the high road from Kington. The spot

---

1] *Cf.*, Sikes, 233. "The death portent called *Cwn Annwn*, or ' Dogs of Hell,' is a pack of hounds which howl through the air with a voice frightfully disproportionate to their size, and full of a wild sort of lamentation. . . The *Cwn Annwn* are sometimes held to be the hell-hounds which hunt through the air the soul of the wicked man the instant it quits the body." 2] *Cf.*, Howells, *Cambrian Superstitions*, 66. 3] Communicated by Mrs. Norton (Llanveyno), 1909.

was much dreaded, and if possible avoided, by late travellers. I knew many who said they had seen the " Black dog of Hergest !"[1]

A Demon in the Cathedral.

A very strange story of the appearance of a demon in the Cathedral is told by Bartholomew de Cotton. This event is supposed to have happened A.D. 1290 :—

> An unheard of and almost impossible marvel occurred in the Cathedral Church of the Hereford Canons. There a demon in the robes of a canon sat in a stall (in the choir ?) after matins had been sung. A canon came up to him, and asked his reason for sitting there, thinking the demon was a brother canon. The latter refused to answer, and said nothing. The canon was terrified, but believing the demon to be an evil spirit, put his trust in the Lord, and bade him in the name of Christ and St. Thomas de Cantilupe not to stir from that place. For a short time he bravely awaited speech. (Receiving no answer) he at last went for help, and beat the demon and put him in fetters ; he now lies in the prison of the aforesaid St. Thomas de Cantilupe.[2]

The Demon of Burton.[3]

An account of the pranks of the demon of Burton has been preserved in a letter written from Hereford, by one J. A., in 1670.

> There is a farm in Burton, a village in the parish of Weobley, which Mr. William Bridges, a linen draper of London, has in mortgage from one Thomas Tomkyns, a decayed yeoman. This farm was taken in by lease of Mrs. Elizabeth Bridges, about Michaelmas, 1669. Soon after this tenant was entered on the farm, some familiar began to act apish pranks by knocking boldly at the door in the dark of the evening, and the like early in the morning, but nobody to be seen. The stools and forms were thrown into disorder, heaps of malt and vetches mingled, loaves of bread laid on a table carried into another room, or hid in tubs covered with cloths ; cabbage plants dug up and replanted in various patterns ; a half roasted pig demolished except the bones ; the milk turned sour with vinegar, some cattle died, and among others a sow leaped and danced in strange postures, and at last fell down dead ; a mow of pulse and pease likewise.

> After these fires one John Jones, a valiant Welshman, undertook to keep watch with a sword, a mastiff dog, and a lantern. He had not long lain on the bed when he heard a knocking at the door, and as he conceived many cats came into his chamber, broke the windows, and made a hideous noise. The mastiff howled, the candle went out, the Welshman fell into a cold sweat, left the sword unused, and with much ado found the door and ran half a mile without looking behind him, protesting next day he would not be another

---

1] From Mr. John Hutchinson. In *Malvern Chase*, by the late W. S. Symonds, a tale of the time of the Wars of the Roses, which contains much local history and tradition, the hero passes a night in the haunted chamber at Hergest. The hound appears and causes the death of the hero's dog.

2] B. de Cotton, 427 :—*Tempore sub eodem quoddam inauditum et quoddamodo impossibile in ecclesia Cathedrali Canonicorum Herefordensi contigebat. Ubi quidam daemon in habitu fratris canonici in choro, post matutinas dream tatas in quodam stallo sedebat accesit adeum quidam canonicus quœreus ob quamnam caus am ibi sedebat, credens ipsum canonicum suum fore et fratrem : qui obmutescat nec vocem emisit. Idem vero canonicus ultra quam diei potuit perterritus, credens ipsum es. spin. malignum sperrans, in Do, ipsum conjura in nom Jesus Christ and S. Thomas de Cantilupe ne abeodem œcederet sed ibidem maneret : verbœ virtute remansit. Ac demum auxilio petito ibidem accessit et ipsum invenit. Tandem eum Teutonier vapulaverunt et demum in vinctis posuerunt. Qui taliti visus et ligatur ibidem coramferetro S.Thomas prœnom.*

3] See Sikes, 187, for characteristics of a Welsh familiar spirit ; the *Pwca'r Trwyn*. This demon of Burton seems to be closely related to Puck in his most malicious humour.

night in the house for a hundred pounds. These particulars I received from eye witnesses of unquestionable credit (?), and you may no more doubt the truth of them than distrust the affection of

Your humble servant,

Hereford, March, 1670.[1]   J.A.

(4) THE DEVIL.

According to Weobley folk, nothing is easier than to make the acquaintance of his Satanic Majesty, usually referred to as " Old Nick," or the " old 'un." You go to Weobley Churchyard at midnight and walk slowly round the preaching cross seven times, saying the Lord's Prayer backwards, and he will immediately appear.

But at Stoke Edith and Tarrington, it was said to be necessary to walk round the Church itself in the same manner, saying the same words, and to look through the keyhole of the door into the Church, when the Evil One would be seen. I have never heard that these irreverent experiments were actually tried.

Seventy years ago, an old inhabitant of Weobley remembers that the big boys used to frighten smaller ones by piling up their caps on a tombstone and running nine times round it. They said that would bring " Old Nick " under the bottom cap. Mr. John Hutchinson writes that in his boyhood a man offered to raise the Devil for him by placing his hat on to crossed sticks stuck in the ground, walking, as before described, seven times round it, repeating the Lord's Prayer backwards. To lay him again it was necessary to reverse the proceedings.

Perhaps this latter process was not always found easy, for it is said that once the boys at the Old Grammar School, Weobley, raised the " Old 'un " by getting the Master's books when he was out. " But they couldn't lay him again, and the noise there when the master come was terrific, things flyin' about the place. The Master soon stopped it, though." The same story is told of many places in the county, both schools and private houses, by people who believe it to be true.[2]

The old people at Longtown used to tell how travellers coming over the Black Mountain were led astray by the Devil, in the shape of a large black crow, which put out their lights and caused them to lose their way.[3]

It will be seen from the following stories that the Devil has a wife ; that he has ordered, if he has not worn, an ordinary human suit of clothing ; while he can cause the nocturnal disturbance usually attributed to ghosts, and for the purpose so often ascribed to them, of removing old deeds.[4] He can assume animal form with intent to deceive an intended victim ; he takes snuff, too, for the puff-ball (*Lycoperdon bovista*) is the " Devil's snuff-box."

1] *Arch. Camb.,* 3rd series, xv., 55, from *Harl. MSS.*
2] *Cf. infra,* Section vi., *Magic and Divination.*   3] *Cf. infra,* Section xiii., *Jack o' Kent.*   4] *Cf. ante-Lady Berington's ghost.*

The Devil and the Friar.

It was formerly not unusual in the neighbourhood of Stoke Edith, if one said "Where did you get that ?" to be answered "Where the Devil got the Friar from." It was the local equivalent for "mind your own business," but, as the story goes, the Devil really got the friar from his cell in West Hide wood. It fell out in this wise :—

The Friar was a jovial fellow, a lover of sport and of money. Badger-baiting was much in vogue in the county just then, and when one day he succeeded in trapping a badger in the wood, he put his quarry in a bag, and, throwing it over his shoulder, started to walk to the Bell Inn, at Tillington. Here he hoped to obtain a good price for his capture. But soon the bag began to get heavier, and a voice said "Mamma calls." The Friar heard, but it did not occur to him that the voice would come from inside the bag. Again he heard "Dadda calls," this time from the bag unmistakeably, and the burden had become still heavier. So he put it down in astonishment, and was opening it to see what was happening, when out came the "Old un" himself. He seized the Friar and took him away ; he was never seen afterwards.[1]

The Devil and the Tailor.

"There was a tailor at Kington who was always cursing and swearing. It was before the days of railways, and he had to go by road to Clee Hill, by Ludlow, to get a load of coal. He met a man who wanted to be measured for a suit of clothes ; measuring from his shoulders down, he came at last to two feet, cleft like cows' feet. Then he knew what his cursing had brought him to. The "auld chap" appointed a meeting place, and a certain time, at which the suit must be ready. The tailor was there in time with the suit, but he took a parson with him who stood on the other side of the hedge, praying hard all the time ; he had previously warned the tailor to take no payment from the "Old un" for his work. As soon as the suit was handed over, the Devil held out a handful of money, and tried to make him take it ; if he had it would have been selling his soul. But the parson went on praying hard till the cock crew, and the tailor held out and got safe away. He never cursed nor swore after." "And *that*," added my informant, "is as true as I'm standin' here, holding this 'ere hop-pole !"[2]

The Devil and the Hogshead.

There was a rectory near Grosmont so very badly haunted that when a new person came, long ago, he could not stay one night through. He offered a reward to anyone who would be brave enough to watch all night there and find out what was

---

1] Told by the late Lewis Powell, a native of Stoke Edith.   2] Told by a Radnorshire man in the Homme hop-yard, Weobley, 1908.

wrong. Two sailors offered to do this, and were promised five pounds each, a roast goose for supper, and as much cider as they could drink, if they could rid the house of its visitors. They made up a good fire in the kitchen, and at ten o'clock one sailor went down to the cellar to draw a jug of cider, but there was the devil himself sitting on top of the hogshutt.[1] The candle went out, the sailor fainted. As he did not come back his companion also lighted a candle, and descended to see what had happened. He was not at all dismayed by what he saw, but his candle went out. He went upstairs to the kitchen and relighted it, returning to the cellar only to have it blown out again. But the third time it kept alight, and he called out bravely, " By your leave, a jug of cider I must have." Drawing it, he took up the fainting sailor, and returning again to the kitchen succeeded in reviving him. When asked why he fainted, he said he had seen the devil, " and he was all great big eyes." Soon they wanted a faggot to roast the goose. The brave sailor going down to the cellar to get one, found the Devil sitting on the faggots. " By your leave, a faggot I must have," he said, and calmly took one, returning a second, a third, and fourth time, as the wood burnt away, till the goose was nearly done. Then came a loud noise in the chimney, and down came the Devil's wife, calling out to her husband : " Mr. Longtuth, Mr. Longtuth, the goose is nearly ready !" The undaunted sailor answered her, " Done or not done, there's none for thee !" at which his unwelcome visitor departed again up the chimney. The men ate the goose and went to bed, the timid one taking the side next the wall. They had not been asleep long when they were re-awakened by a great noise in the room. Still knowing no fear, the brave sailor, concluding that the " Owd un " and his wife were having a game of football, hurried on some clothes and kicked out in the dark, shouting that he would join the game. He soon found it much too hot for him, so he called out " Two to one's not fair, here is one for my landlord," and kicked the football straight through the window, smashing it. The devil and his wife immediately vanished like streaks of fire after the ball, which turned out to be a bundle of old deeds, torn to bits in the scrimmage. This, or something contained in them, had caused all the disturbance, for nothing has been heard or seen at that house since, and the sailor was held to have well deserved his reward.[2]

The Devil at Brampton Bryan.

The great storm at Cromwell's death wrought so much havoc that it was said the devil dragged Oliver Cromwell across Brampton Bryan Park, to spite the Harleys. Sir Edward Harley, who then owned the estate, though himself a Roundhead, quarrelled with Cromwell on the King's death, and they became bitter enemies. So after the great storm Sir Edward wrote to a friend :—" I wish the devil

---

1] *Hogshead*, an oak cask for cider, usually 100 to 112 gallons. 2] From W. Colcombe, Weobley, 1907.

had taken him any other way than through my park, for not content with doing me all the mischief he could when alive, he has knocked over some of my finest trees in his progress downwards." The tradition still remains that ever since that period, on one day in the year, the devil yet rushes across Brampton Bryan Park.[1]

For the Devil's Stone, *see* Section i., 2 ; *cf.* also Section ix., 16, Jack of France.

(5) FAIRIES.

Although there are now but few persons living in Herefordshire who believe in fairies, faith in their existence must have been common enough with the folk of the last generation. All the old people who can tell anything about fairies do not call them fairies at all, but "farîses"; the word is pronounced almost like Pharisees. Their parents have warned them earnestly to avoid fairy rings, and they believe that little people really existed once. Perhaps they think that railroads and other modern inventions have driven them away ; at any rate they are shy of admitting any belief in their existence now. A woman at Orcop had heard from her grandmother how fairies would come to the barn door, where her sons were threshing with the flail, and call them to come and play. But they did not go, having been warned that they must not answer.

William P——, of Longtown, defined "farîses" as "little people that come into folk's houses and steal things. They can fly anywhere. The king of them gets up in a apple tree maybe. He says, ' I be off !' and they says ' I be after !' and off they goes."

A clergyman at Dormington was instructing an old parishioner in the Scriptures some years ago, and was heard with little interest or intelligence until he mentioned the Pharisees. "Ah," said the old man, "I knows them farîses, the ones that makes the rings on the grass !"

Mrs. D——, of Foxley, said that her mother, now dead, so firmly believed in the existence of the little people that as long as she lived she left the door ajar, and food on the table at night. In return for which they left her money sometimes, and always silver money, too.

The author of the *History of Kington* testifies to the existence of a belief in fairies, thus :—

The notion that there are in the bowels of the earth dwarfish beings of human shape, remarkable for their riches, their activity and their malevolence, was very prevalent within the recollection of some aged

1] *Woolhope Club*, 1881-2, 198.

persons now living in this parish ; they were supposed to play tricks with the milkmaids and spoil the butter,[1] and it is said that they often appear in the form of dancing companies and looked like children leaping and frisking in the air, and were desirous of enticing people into their company and using them ill, and were quarrelsome to a proverb insomuch that it was used to be said by persons (well known to the writer) that people at Kington were like the fairies, which never agree.[2]

On the Eve of May Day at Kingstone and Thruxton, folks used to put trays of moss outside the door at night for the fairies to dance upon.[3] Perhaps the silver sixpence which was often placed in the churn to make the butter come was a protective charm against mischievous fairies, though I have not heard this definitely stated.

Fairies have been seen dancing under foxgloves in Cusop Dingle within the memory of some now living there.[4]

Not far from Hay Station on the Herefordshire side there are some rocks over-hanging a brook which flows into the Wye. Fairies, or " little people," formerly lived in these rocks, and in the haymaking time used to provide dinner for the haymakers in the adjoining fields. But once a haymaker took away a knife ; after this the fairies never came again, although the man took the knife back.[5]

One day a man was working in the fields when he heard the fairies talking over their baking ; they said they had no peel. He said " I'll find a peel." He made one and left it out in the field where they could easily get it. Next day it was gone, and in its place the fairies had given him a batch of delicious cakes. But they were invisible all the time : he never saw them, only heard them talking.[6] A peel is a flat iron shovel, with a long wooden handle, used for putting bread or loaves into the oven and taking them out.

It used to be said they danced among the ruins of the old Roman City at Kenchester (Magna Castra). Leland, *temp*. Henry viii., wrote :—" Here then yet appear ruines or buildings of the whiche foolish people caull one of the King of Fayres Chayre." But Camden says : " In a pool in this parish by the roadside abounding with fine trout, it is pretended Thomas Becket often appears. Whence the niche at Kenchester is called ' Becket's Chair.' "[7] Roman coins found near the spot were called " dwarfs money."[8]

Mrs. Cummings, an ancient housekeeper at Pontrilas Court (now dead), remem-bered in her youth an old Mary Phillips, who would relate by the hour tales of her

1] *See Ante* Section ii.   2] Parry, *Hist. Kington*, 205.   3] R.H.B., *cf*. Section ix., *May Day*.   4] *Cf*. Henderson, 228.   " Is not the proper etymology ' folks,' (*i.e.*, ' fairies ')—glove ? "   5] C.G.P., 1908 ; *cf*. the tale of a stolen drinking horn, Gervase of Tilbury, i., 980.   6] For a similar story see Rhys *Celtic Folklore*, 241.   In this Welsh version the peel is merely repaired.   I had the story from Mrs. D——, of St. Katharine's Hospital, Ledbury, who had heard her mother tell it.   7] Gough's *Camden* iii. 74. 8] Leland, *Itinerary*, vii., 152.

experience of fairies and ghosts. " I could not doubt Mary," she said ; "she knew the use of all herbs, charmed burns and cuts, and cured nearly all who went to her, but she could not cure herself. I have never heard her murmur, and she certainly possessed a great deal of knowledge. My mother would say she was suffering for her sins ; Grandmother said 'Nonsense.' She told us how to be very careful not to offend the wicked old fairies, or they would do us dreadful injury. These always accompanied the pretty bright fairies, who were always draped in white, with wands in their hands and flowers in their hair. One of her tales was that when she was going at night to nurse a sick person at Llangua, she and the man who fetched her saw something very hideous. They went on along the Kerpandys, when they heard a band of music, and saw dozens of fairies dancing in the long meadows at the back of the Llangua Church. They went over the bridge one by one, and turned into the wood. Llangua bridge was near the church then."[1] According to Mrs. Cummings, Monmouthshire Cap derived its name from a battle won opposite the Cap House. The Duke of Monmouth held up his cap, the sign of victory. The dead were buried in a meadow near the Monnow river. The spot was marked by a round mound with a bare path round it on which the grass never grew. The children were not allowed to go near : the dead lay there. A man of the name of Tom Davies undertook to mow the grass by the acre one intensely hot harvest, so he worked by night instead of by day. He said he heard music, and, looking up, saw a band of soldiers on the mound, and a great number of officers and their ladies dancing round it ; he threw down his scythe, and ran home through river without stopping. But people laughed and said it was just the fairies, who were always there at midnight.[2]

Mrs. W——, aged 75, one of the oldest inhabitants of Wigmore in 1909, told me a fairy story of her mother's. She said it happened to her mother's first cousin, and her mother remembered it well. The cousin, a girl about eighteen, was very fond of dancing : she insisted on going to all the balls for miles round : wherever there was dancing going on, there was she. Her people told her something would happen to her some day, and one night when she was coming home just by the " Dancing Gates," near Kington, she heard beautiful music. It was the music of the fairies, and she was caught into the ring. Search was made for her, and she appeared to her friends from time to time, but when they spoke to her she immediately disappeared. Her mother was told (probably by the wise man or woman), that if seen again she must be very quickly seized, without speaking, or she would never come back. So one day, a year after her disappearance, her mother saw her, and took hold of her dress before she could escape. " Why mother," she said, " where have you been since yesterday ?"

---

[1] Llangua is just over the Herefordshire border, in Monmouth.
[2] From a MS. account of an interview with Mrs. Cummings, by the late Mrs. Murray-Aynsley.

PEMBRIDGE. THE OLD MARKET HALL OPPOSITE THE NEW INN.

Photograph by Mr. T. H. Winterbourn]

CHARM FOR TOOTHACHE, FROM A MANUSCRIPT IN HEREFORD CATHEDRAL LIBRARY.

The time must have gone very merrily with her, for the year had seemed but one day. The girl was none the worse, however, and they sent her to serve at a small shop in Kington. Before long the fairies came there, and used to steal little things off the counter. Afraid she herself might be accused when the things were missed, the girl told her employer. " How can you see the fairies ?" he said, " they are invisible." She told him that when she lived with them they used a kind of ointment, and she rubbed a little of it on one eye, to try the effect. She could always see the little people with that eye since. She afterwards warned the fairies that their thefts were discovered ; they were much puzzled to find themselves visible to her. She was careful not to explain lest they might try to damage the eye with which she could see them.

The narrator of this obviously Celtic story was born at Wigmore, and had lived all her life there ; but her mother's early home was at Knighton, in Radnorshire, to which county it really belongs.[1]

An old waggoner at Haven, Pembridge, used to tell a story of how a farm hand, a waggoner, was going out of the kitchen one night when his mistress remarked that the broth for his supper was nearly ready, " Ay, ay missis," he said, " I'll be back in a minute." He was caught by a fairy ring and was lost for twenty-three years. When he came back he walked in and said, " Well, Missis, be my broth ready ?"

Some young men and women were returning from Longtown fair to their homes in the Olchon Valley one evening, when they heard lovely music, and saw the little people dancing in the fairy rings by Olchon brook. They hurried on, all but one young man, who ventured nearer. He was caught up into the ring, and never came back for a whole year ; no one could find him. At last he came home with the oranges and gingerbreads from the fair still quite fresh and in his pocket, but he did not live long after that. So people in the valley warned their children to be very careful, and never step inside the rings.[2] There were red rings there, a great many. Fairy rings were pointed out as danger spots by the old folk, within the memory of those now living, at Weobley, Orcop, and many other places in the county.

The Fairy Changeling.[3]

A woman had a baby that never grew ; it was always hungry, and never satisfied, but it lay in its cradle year after year, never walking, and nothing seemed to do it

---

1] For variants see Rhys, *Celtic Folklore*, 213. The fairy asks a woman " With what eye do you see me ?" " With this one," was the reply, and he took a bulrush and put out her eye at once.
2] Told at Longtown, 1909.
3] Possibly the origin of the belief in fairy changelings may be due to an attempt to account for cases of cretinism. In this disease, supposed to be caused by the absence of an internal secretion of the thyroid gland, development is completely arrested. An account of such a case appeared in the *Daily Mail*, Sept. 29, 1908, headed " Baby of 22, Girl who has never grown up." Other diseases have also been suggested. Probably no one disease will cover all the cases of changelings described. In fact any abnormal child might be held to be a changeling.

good. Its face was hairy and strange-looking. One day the woman's elder son, a soldier, came home from the war, and was surprised to see his brother still in the cradle. But when he looked in he said, " That's not my brother, mother." " It is, indeed," said the mother. " We'll see about that," he said. So he obtained first a fresh egg, and blew out the contents, filling the shell with malt and hops. Then he began to brew over the fire. At this a laugh came from the cradle. " I am old, old, ever so old," said the changeling, " but I never saw a soldier brewing beer in a egg shell before ! " Then he gave a terrible shriek, for the soldier went for him with a whip, chasing him round and round the room what had never left his cradle ! At last he vanished through the door, and when the soldier went out after him he met on the threshold his long lost brother. He was a man twenty-four years of age, fine and healthy. The fairies had kept him in a beautiful palace under the rocks, and fed him on the best of everything. He should never be as well off again, he said, but when his mother called he had to come home.[1]

A variant of this story from Orcop relates how a woman came home one evening to find that her two small children would not speak to her : they seemed to be struck dumb. But the " conjurer " told her to brew in an egg shell before them, then throw them into the brook, dropping them from the bridge one on either side, as they were fairy changelings. This she did, and they walked down the stream, saying, " We are old, ever so old, but never saw beer brewed in an egg shell afore." When the woman reached home her own children were in their cradles.

(6) HOBGOBLIN.

Brownie is the name now used in Herefordshire for Robin Goodfellow, the Puck of the *Midsummer Night's Dream*. We have the Welsh form of the name in the " Pwcha " farm, at Michaelchurch Eskley. Brownie, now all but forgotten, was a domestic elf, sometimes useful and hard-working, helping the maids with household tasks, more often mischievous, even evil and malicious. As elsewhere, the Brownie and the Bogie reduce themselves to different humours of the same uncanny being.[2]

Considering him first in his better humour, I can remember vaguely the talk of a nurse who was a native of Weobley marsh. She believed that tidy girls were rewarded by a fairy, who would come and sweep the hearth at night, and do a lot of work about the house.

1] From Jane Probert, of Kington. Told in the Homme hop-yard, Weobley, Sept., 1908. The woman believed the story, having had it from " a woman who knew it was true." *Cf.* Rhys, *op. cit.*, 62, and Hartland, *Science of Fairy Tales*, 118 ; also Keightley, i., 199.
2] See Sidgwick, *Sources of Midsummer Night's Dream*, 37, with reprint of chap-book, " Robin Goodfellow " (81), and Broadside (144) ; also Rhys, *Celtic Folklore*, 596 ; Sikes, 20-22.

The "sway," the iron bar over the fire on which pots and kettles were hung, was formerly made with a crook in it.   At Crasswall this was said to be the seat of the Brownie, an old lady still living there in 1908 remembered the "Brownie sway" in her old home in Cusop dingle.   If there were no curve in the sway, she said, people would hang a horse-shoe on it, upside down, that Brownie should have something to sit upon.

But Brownie sometimes took offence at what he considered slights to himself, and his favourite and chief form of revenge was to hide the household keys ; there was only one way in which they could be brought back.   The members of the household sat in a circle round the hearth, after placing a little cake on the hob, as a peace-offering to the Brownie.   The party sat in absolute silence with closed eyes, when the keys would be flung violently at the wall at the back of the sitters.   This was done at the Portway inn, Staunton-on-Wye, seventy years ago.[1]

Mr. John Hutchinson, a native of the Kington district, remembers seeing a charm hanging above stable doors to keep elves from riding the horses ; it was made of seven hairs from a grey mare's tail, twisted into the shape of a double heart.   Tangling of the manes and tails of horses is nowadays supposed to be the work of witches.[2]

In his more mischievous aspect, Puck, or the *Pwcha*, becomes confused with the will-o'-the-wisp.   For instance :—

At Aymestrey, there was formerly set apart a piece of land, the rent of which was to remunerate a man for ringing a bell in the church tower at a certain hour every night, for the benefit of any stray traveller who might be led astray by a will-o'-the-wisp in the wood just across the Lugg, called Poke-house (the abode of Puck).   The sum produced, however, was so small that in course of time no one could be found to ring the bell, and it is more than a century since it was rung.   There is still a hole in the north-east corner of the church ringing chamber, through which one of the bell-ropes was brought down into the porch for the purpose.[3]

Tradition says that the land was left by an Aymestrey man, who was tormented by Puck all night long in Pokehouse wood.   His will directed that the bell should be rung "for ever."

Will'-o'-the Wisp.

Of Kington, Parry writes in 1845 :—

The *ignis-fatuus*, or exhalation termed will-o'-the-wisp, or Jack with a lanthorn, which is sometimes seen in churchyards, or marshy places, in summer and autumn, was considered by many old inhabitants in this neighbourhood, when the author was in his infancy, to be a kind of device of the evil spirit to draw human beings from the road they were pursuing into some frightful abyss of misery ; and there leave them without any hope of regaining the enjoyment of happiness in the land of the living.[4]

1] C.G.P.   2] *Cf. Romeo and Juliet*, i., iv., 53, where Queen Mab "plats the manes of horses in the night."   See *ante* Section ii.   3] *Woolhope Club*, 1895-7, 131.   4] *Hist. Kington*, 206.

This is the belief of people still living in the Crasswall and Cusop district. At a farm between Hay and Crasswall a woman told me that there are many bogs on the Black Mountain, where the old folks said people were thus led astray.

I have not been able to hear of the " Old lady of the Black Mountain," by that name, on the Hereford side of the hills, except that a bowl of water placed at the foot of the Maypole at Crasswall was said to be for the purpose of keeping away the " Old woman of the Mountain," she being afraid of water. According to Sikes, she appears at night, or in a mist, in the form of a poor old woman, with a pot or wooden can in her hand, going before the wayfarer, causing him to lose his way, even when familiar with the road.[1]

1] Sikes, 51-52. He says people at Aberystwyth provided water for the *Gwyllion*, the female fairies, who led folks astray. But perhaps after all the water was intended for exorcism ?

SECTION V.

WITCHCRAFT.

(1) WITCHCRAFT AND THE LAW.

The last trial for witchcraft in England took place at Hereford in 1712. The name of the unfortunate woman was Jane Wenham, " Witch of Walkerne." Sir Walter Scott gives the following account of the trial :—

> Some of the country clergy were carried away by the landflood of superstition in this instance also, and not only encouraged the charge but gave their countenance to some of the ridiculous and indecent tricks resorted to as proofs of witchcraft by the lowest vulgar. But the good sense of the judge, seconded by that of other reflecting and sensible persons, saved the country from the ultimate disgrace attendant on too many of these unhallowed trials. The usual sort of evidence was brought against this poor woman, by pretences of bewitched persons vomiting fire, a trick very easy to those who choose to exhibit such a piece of jugglery, amongst such as rather desire to be taken in by it than to detect the imposture. The witchfinder practised upon her the most vulgar and ridiculous tricks, or charms ; and out of a perverted examination they drew what they called a confession, though of a forced and mutilated character. Under such proof the jury brought her in Guilty, and she was necessarily condemned to die. More fortunate, however, than many persons placed in the like circumstances, Jane Wenham was tried before a sensible judge, who reprieved the witch before he left the assize town.

There is an earlier case of one Mary Hodges ; her fate is, however, unrecorded :

> In 1662, Mary Hodges, a widow, is informed against . . . chiefly as being suspected to " fore-speak " or bewitch cattle, one horse having died suddenly and another being sick which belonged to a person whom she had cursed. This appears to be " her usual and frequent manner of witchcraft privately in her house, for at when her household is gone to bed and she is as conceived going to bed, she is observed to take the andirons out of the chimney and put them cross one another, and then she falls down upon her knees and useth some prayers of witchcraft. [1]

(2) INSTANCES OF WITCHCRAFT.

Of all superstitious beliefs, that of witchcraft and the power of the evil eye linger longest and strongest with our people. The stories given are merely representative of numbers of a similar nature that might be collected. " There must be witches," they say ; " it's in the Bible that there's witches."

Mrs. Powell observed in the Golden Valley the universal dread of " giving offence." " Thirty or more years ago," she writes, " it met one at every turn. ' I think I shall straighten that wall, repair that fence, or cut that tree,' was generally met with. ' Well, indeed, it would be a good thing, but I doubt you can't do it. It might offend A. or B.' *What* would happen if A. or B. were offended never was revealed. I believe there is, or was, some secret dread of the evil eye, or witchcraft.

1] Scott, *Demonology and Witchcraft*, 235.   2] Hist. MSS., *Heref.*, 346.

Years ago I have heard people say ' Whatever do ail the cow ? ' (or it might be a child.) ' Anyone 'd think her'd been overlooked,' or ' Someone ha surely ill-wished her.' "

Mrs. Murray-Aynsley, a few years ago, heard of a young man at Blakemere who was said to be a " dangerous person," able by supernatural power to injure anyone who offended him.[1] I find that this fear of the evil eye lingers still (1909) in the shadow of the Black Mountain.[2] It was said that a woman at Clodock was very clever with herbs and doctoring, but the neighbours were " a good bit afraid of her," and refused her nothing.

Beyond this dread of offence, there still exists the fear of excessive admiration. " I gave mother three beautiful maidenhair ferns," a young servant said lately, " but she would let folks come in and admire them all the time. They all died : I told her what it would be."[3]

A woman at Pembridge, mourning the loss of a favourite daughter, told how she was so sweet and so good, and " the best o' the bunch ; folks would allus be admirin' her so. I was afeard summat 'ud happen to her."

Gypsies are credited with having the evil eye. " They can't put a spell on you, if you don't buy anything from them " said Bessie H——, " but if you have dealings with them, that gives them power over you. A neighbour of ours offended a gypsy woman, and her little boy couldn't walk for two years. Doctors were no good. Yet at the end of two years he came right all at once. So she must have put the spell on for just that time."[4]

A farmer at Peterchurch refused to give anything to two gypsies who begged from him. That very week two colts died, worth about £60. Fearing further losses, he sent to a wise man at Llandovery.[5] The messenger was away two days ; the remedy prescribed was the burning of a bullock's heart, previously stuck all over with pins. Those that caused the trouble, said the wise man, would be obliged to come and " pother " it out of the grate as it burned. " And they did ! "[6]

Similar beliefs are recorded in the Kington district :—

The infatuation of people in this locality was so great, even so late as the middle of the eighteenth century, that when any cattle died in the parish, it was said that someone had bewitched them and thereby caused their death. And when a person had fits, or was seized with any disease not understood by the natives of Kington, it was often said that the person so afflicted was " under an evil tongue and was over-looked " ; meaning that the individual was bewitched ; and to prevent the further influence of the supposed witch and to heal the person, it would be necessary to obtain the heart of an animal and perforate it with

---

1] *Symbolism*, 159. 2] See Section ii. 3] King's Pyon. 4] Withington. 5] See Section vi., Diviners.
6] King's Pyon, 1908.

pins, taking care to let them remain until a fire of wood was kindled, when the heart and pins were cast into the flames and the person suspected of being the sorceress was compelled to come into the house and in the name of Jehovah pronounce a blessing.[1]

Witches can change themselves into the form of animals, usually bats or black cats. A man from Eardisley, going one night to see a neighbour on the Kington road, whose wife was a reputed witch, met a large black cat at the garden gate. Entering, he asked the man how his wife was. " Didn't you meet her," was the answer. " She has only this minute gone out through the door there !" " So it was certain after that," my informant added, " she was a witch, right enough."[2]

I have heard how a man at Weobley Marsh saw a strange creature come into his room one night, " something like a bat." His daughter told me he knew it was one of the witches then living on the Marsh. " But how did he know ?" I asked. " He knocked the thing down with a handkerchief, and if it had been a bat he would have killed it for certain. But he lighted a candle after, and there was nothing there at all. You can't harm them folks."

In 1909, a native of Longtown, W—— P——, told this story :—" The man at the farms along the foot of the Black Mountain used to rear greyhounds for the gentlemen when I was a boy. When they were ready to go back to their owners, it was allowed to have a day's sport with them first. One day they were a long time looking for a hare. At last they found a fine fat one under a bush on the mountain. A little boy on the hill near by shouted ' Run, grannie, run, the hounds be after thee ! ' By that they knew she was a witch. She ran straight to a little cottage and disappeared through the keyhole, but as she went through, one of the hounds bit her leg. The door was locked and they could not get in at first. When they opened it, they found a very old woman sitting by the fire doctoring a wound in her leg ! I don't hardly believe as such things could be true, meself ; but the man who told it me swore it was true."[3]

At Much Marcle, it was believed that witches became hares in order to lead the foxhounds off the right scent.[4]

At Weobley and Ledgemoor, years ago, children were taught to say, on meeting a supposed witch,—

> " If thee bist a witch, the Devil take thee ;
> If thee bain't a witch, the Almighty bless thee ! "

One old woman, if meeting anyone she suspected of witchcraft or the evil eye, would spit on the ground and say " Sattan, I defy tha !"

1] Parry, *Hist. Kington*, 206.   2] Eardisley, 1906.   3] Walterstone.   4] Ledbury.

Witches are also supposed to be afraid of a whip. The "whip" may have been originally a goad of sacred hawthorn or mountain ash.[1] Elder pith, dried and powdered, was formerly given in food to those thought to be bewitched. In addition to the horseshoe commonly used as a protective charm, a stick with nine notches in it, of elder or mountain ash, was often placed over the door.[2] Doorsteps were marked with nine crosses in chalk, for the same reason. The stone would be neatly bordered with white when washed, with a row of crosses inside the border.[3]

It was also said that a witch had no power over anyone riding a broomstick. T—— M——, of Weobley, told me how, when he was a boy, he and his schoolfellows would collect all the available besoms and ride them in procession past the house of a certain " Old Charlotte," a reputed witch, who would come out and shake her fist in impotent rage.[4]

A witch could also be detected by hammering a tenpenny nail into her footprint. If guilty of witchcraft, the woman would be obliged to retrace her steps and draw out the nail.[5]

Mrs. M——, of Orcop (86), related how " late one night the doctor from Llangarren had been to see a patient out Monmouth way, and was returning over Llanlodi Pitch at midnight. He met three witches ; they were all neighbours, and he knew them well. One rode a grindstone, another a besom, and the third a hurdle !"

It used to be said there would always be nine witches from the bottom of Orcop to the end of Garway Hill. " There will be a witch in Almeley," they say, " as long as water runs."

Forty or fifty years ago, Weobley Marsh is said to have been witch-ridden. Everything unfortunate that happened was ascribed to witchcraft and the evil eye, and a " wise man," locally celebrated, whom we will call Jenkins, living twenty miles away, between Hereford and Bromyard, was frequently consulted.[6] He used to say that from the bottom of Weobley Marsh to the top of Mainbury[7] he knew there were fifty witches, and that he had power to call them all out and make them dance.[8] At Bromyard " he was maister o' the witches. Lots of old women was going lame round Ullingswick one time ; it was Jenkins lamed them." At last Jenkins became so notorious that he was brought before the magistrates as an impostor. He said he was not, but that he had power over witches. The magistrates said they did not exist.

1] *Cf. ante* Penyard Castle, and *infra, The Mermaid of Marden* :—"If it had not been for thy wittan tree goad." 2] Dilwyn Common. 3] Dilwyn and Weobley. 4] Told 1906. 5] King's Pyon. In olden times a nail that cost 10d. must have been a large one. 6] See the next chapter. 7] The distance would be about 2 miles. There are not 50 cottages there. 8] Weobley.

He said he would convince them, and would they like to have them in a high wind or a low one ?   They declined them either way [1]

A farmer and his wife living at Bodenham suffered sadly from the evil influence of witchcraft.   Cattle bought at market broke out of the fields and returned to their former owners, in spite of locked gates.   The horses galloped about wildly and would not enter the stable when driven to water in the evening.   Jenkins was sent for. " Get thee to bed, my lad," he said, " I'll quiet them horses for thee."   About midnight the waggoner was aroused by a terrible noise : the house shook, the " furniture and plates was all movin' round and round the kitchen."   He rushed out into the garden, but was " moithered like " and could not find his way back to the house until Jenkins appeared and conducted him back to bed.   " After this there was quiet for a bit.   But then the missis began to miss things out o' the dairy.   Eggs 'ud go, and half-pounds 'o butter, and even meat, though the door was safe locked and the missis took the key to bed."   Jenkins came once more to the rescue.   He told the farmer's wife to stand that night, just before twelve o'clock, inside the locked dairy door, with a large carving knife in her hand.   When she heard a rattling of something coming rough the keyhole, she was to chop, quick !   She held the knife as directed, and brought it down sharply when the lock rattled, as foretold.   In the morning a very old woman to whom she gave milk daily appeared as usual, and " there sure enough the Missis noticed at once her little finger was clean chopped off, and there was no more goings on at *that* place ! "[2]

" George H——, a mason at King's Pyon, was ill for six months ; could not work, yet there was nothing wrong in hisself like, so the folks made sure as the witch had put a spell on him.   So they made a fire, and burnt brum " (broom), " at twelve o'clock one night and said certain words, and before long in comes old Charlotte. They all set on her and flogged her, so she was glad to get away up the chimbley ! And George was all right after.   They have to go up the chimbley, when they're *fetched !* "[3]

In the same parish a woman has told me how her grandmother was bewitched. A wise man directed that a lock of her hair should be cut off and thrown upon the fire behind a large log of wood at midnight, when the person who was the cause of the trouble would be drawn to the spot.   The instructions were carried out, and those assembled round the fire were so astonished to see a neighbour—a " wicked old man "—

---

[1] Told to the late Mrs. Murray-Aynsley by the housekeeper at Pontrilas Court, 1908.
[2] Told 1907, by an inmate of Kington Workhouse, native of Ullingswick.   I was impressed by his firm belief in every detail of the story.   He was 80 years old and "no scholar."
[3] Related 1908.

come in to the house that they let him walk up and *poke the fire.* " So it was all no good : they couldn't take the spell off when him had done that."[1]

The " hand of glory " was probably once made and used in Herefordshire. A Crasswall woman remembers among her great-uncle's " silly old tales " one of a witch who made a hand of glory, or " dead man's candle," from the hand of a corpse on the gibbet at Crasswall, in order to put a spell on some people who had ducked her in a horsepond.[2]

An inmate of Ross Workhouse remembers how he was coming over Whitney bridge, many years ago, when behind the cart he was driving came a waggoner with three horses, and no money to pay toll. He defied the old woman at the toll house, and would have driven past her, but she witched the horses so that they would not move. " I sin it meself, them 'orses 'ouldn't muv nor stir, and when I lent the mon the toll money they went on right enough. There was funny tales about that old 'ooman : folks took care they didna give her offence : er'd make their pigs dance in their cots till they fetched her to stop 'em."

This man knew a woman near Ross, too, who could make pigs dance when she whistled.[3]

" The policeman was takin' a witch's son to gaol for being drunk," said a Weobley man, " and called for help. I helped him, and didn't think. The missis said when I come home I'd be sorry for it. Sure enough, my pig died next week."[4]

In the following story, told to me at Bosbury in 1908, the narrator was not quite clear whether the black cat were the man himself, or a " familiar spirit." " Old H——, who had a brick kiln, was a very wicked old man. He put a spell on a neighbour, but she went to Jenkins (the wise man), who made him come to the door one night and say ' God bless you, my 'ooman.' The noise that night in the house was awful. She was all right after that. Everybody was afraid of offending old H——. They made him give up the brick-kiln, and he said it was no good to them, it should never get hot again. No more it did, for all they tried hard. The fire went dead and black-like—no heat in it. And as they tried to heat it, there was a black cat running backwards and forwards through the fire, putting it out. And he died an awful death in the end : an *awful* death it was."

1] 1908.   2] C.G.P. For the preparation and various supposed uses of this horrible charm, see Henderson, 239–44. It was believed that the withered hand of a man who had been hanged, with a lighted candle in it, could render those approaching incapable of motion, or prevent those asleep from being awakened, and it was therefore used by thieves and housebreakers.   3] Told at Ross, 1909. 4] Weobley, 1906.

A man at Norton's Wood listened incredulously to a ghost story I told him, remarking " Lies was used to be kep' for shoemakers and tailors ; any oaf do use 'em nowadays. The man as told you that was one."

After this crushing rebuke he thought for a little while, and then went on :— " Now I'll tell you a tale that's as true as I'm sittin' here. My grandfather lived at the Yew Tree Farm, and my grandmother had a child that was two years old, and couldna walk, nor talk, nor nothin', and it'd eat all day as much as they give it ; but nothin' did any good. So my grandfather rode off one Sunday mornin' to see a man uphill " (in Wales) " as understood such things. He could tell who had done it right enough ; it was a woman at Weobley Marsh. My grandfather was to make her come to the child, and if she refused, he could threaten to drag her by tying his mare's tail round her neck ; she would *have* to come then. My grandfather started to ride home. The man pressed him to stay all night, but he wanted to get back to the child. It dunna do to refuse those folk. He hadn't gone fur till his black mare was changed to a white un ! " (*Pause for effect*). " Yes, white with sweat she was, and all of a tremble. So there was nothing for it but to sleep at a house on the road, and the mare was turned out in a paddock. She broke out and went home in the night, a quiet mare as 'ad never broke out afore, and grandfather had to walk and carry his bridle, and saddle too. Well, he went to the marsh and made the witch come, though she wasn't willin'. My grandmother stood over her with a carvin' knife, till she said " God bless you, my child," as the wise man said she must. But grandmother had to threaten to draw blood first. And a very few minutes after . . . the child died."

Witchcraft, as this story shows, is believed powerful to prevent even the release of death. " Old Millie o' the Oont bewitched a woman," said old Mrs. S—— D—— ; " she could *neither live nor die*, she was walkin' day and night, till she was like a spirit." She was said to be cured by the famous Jenkins, who removed the spell.[1]

"Billy o' Dormee" was another clever man: "he could charm the taties out o' the stacks and nobody'd know, till they went to get 'em out ; they'd be gone, and no sign."

" You canna keep nothin' with folks o' that sort about. My daughter lived in a house at Bodenham, and she used to lock all the doors every night, but every one was allus open in the mornin' ! "[2]

1] Pembridge. 2] Pembridge, 1906.

SECTION VI.

MAGIC AND DIVINATION.

(1) DIVINERS AND CUNNING MEN.

Jenkins, the wise man, seems to have been quite as famous for his skill in divination as for his power over witches and disease. The peasantry had great faith in his quack medicine, and he must have had quite a lucrative practice; he took money for the medicines, but is said to have charmed for nothing.[1]

The story goes that Jenkins once visited the Buck Inn, Woonton, where he had a meal. When he asked what he should pay the landlady said: " Fourpence for eat, fourpence for drink, eightpence on the whole." The old farmer considered this too much, so he placed the money in the centre of the table, on a piece of paper, and drew a line round it with a piece of chalk. When the landlady tried to take it, she began to run round and round the table, unable to stop, saying: " Fourpence for eat, four-pence for drink, eightpence on the whole." The servant came in and tried to reach the money, but the spell came upon her also, and she ran round after her mistress, re-peating the same words. The ostler tried next, and met with the same fate. Another servant went out to the yard, where the wizard was just leading out his horse, and told him what was going on. He said, " You go in and take the money with a pair of tongs, that'll stop 'em." And so it did.[2]

Some sixty or seventy years ago, a farmer's wife in the parish of Bredwardine stole the Vicar's surplice out of the church, in order to spite some of the singers; at the same time she spread a report that one of them was the culprit. They were naturally much annoyed, and tried to find out the thief, but all to no purpose. At last, hearing that Jenkins was a wizard, one of their number went to consult him. When asked if he could discover the thief, the diviner said, " Would you know him if I showed him to you ?" " Certainly," was the reply, " if he belong to Bredwardine." Upon this the diviner consulted his books, and after a while the form of a woman appeared, whom his visitor at once recognised as the wife of a farmer at Bredwardine. He returned home, went to the farmer's house, and taxed the woman with the theft. She did not deny it, and going to a cupboard in the room, produced the surplice and handed it over to him, much to his satisfaction and also to that of the other singers, who were thus relieved from the unjust accusation which had been hanging over them.[3]

1] See *infra*, Section vii., *Charming*.   2] Weobley, 1904.   3] Told to the late Mrs. Murray-Aynsley.

A Withington man, owner of a brick kiln, had a barrow of coal stolen one night, barrow and all. He consulted Jenkins, who told him the barrow and coal should be restored ; when he reached home, there it was, put back exactly where he had left it.[1]

A laundress at Ullingswick lost a tablecloth ; Jenkins told her that the woman who had stolen it would come into her cottage and sit on a chair beside the chest of drawers, from which the tablecloth had been stolen ; after this visit the cloth would be found in its place. All happened exactly as he foretold.

The pig seems more frequently the victim of spite than any other animal, though this may be because it is often the only live stock the cottager possesses. One man whose pig was ailing, and thought to be overlooked, was told by the wizard to cut off its tail and throw it in the fire, by way of breaking the spell. This plan is said to have been immediately successful.

A man who went to Jenkins for some medicine fell over a grave in Much Cowarne churchyard, broke the bottle, and lost it all. So he returned and asked for more. Payment for the second bottle was refused, Jenkins saying, " I gave you the wrong stuff, that's why you had to come back."[2]

One Sunday Jenkins went to church ; during the service the wind began to roar. He " knew what was up at once, and hurried home to his farm to find that the farm lads had got out his books ; and it took him some time, yes, it did, before Somebody was quiet again." This story had just been told to me by an inmate of Bromyard Workhouse,[3] when another old man who had been listening, said, " Ay, ay, there wasn't much as *he* couldn't do. I worked with a mon oncet, as had his wife bewitched by a gypsy 'ooman ; her was all on the shiver and shake, like. Jenkins gave her a charm on a bit of paper, for her to wear stitched in her clothes, and telled the mon he'd make the gypsy come to his house, if he'd stay at home next day and wait for her, and beat her with a stick, then his wife'd be all right. She did come, and the mon put his stick about her, and his wife was all right. Jenkins took no money for that, only for medicine."

" Another mon I worked with," he went on, " lost his smock-frock. Jenkins first made him promise not to punish the one as took it. Them folks allus asks you first thing, ' What do you want done to them as done it ? ' If you be spiteful, like, they tells you nothin. Well, he promised he'd do no harm, and Jenkins says, ' Go straight home, and the first mon as comes to the house 'll be wearing your smock.' And sure enough, he come up to the house, with the smock on his back ; you see he

---

1] From Mrs. H——, at Wormesley, 1906. 2] Cowarne. 3] January, 1909.

couldn't help hisself. Ay, he was a clever mon was Jenkins, and no mistake." This story was immediately capped by one from a native of the Ross district. " I recollect," he said, " stoppin' at an inn near Llangarren, with an engine driver, and somebody stole his watch, so he went to the witch[1] at Llangarren to try and get it back. The house was full o' horrid black cats, and he wished himself out of it. But the witch says, ' You go back, its' all right.' And the next day the watch was put back on the dresser at the inn, right enough." This reminded a nonagenarian how a woman who lived at the Sheepcote, Ullingswick, once lost some cider hairs. (These are the thick hairy cloths, in which the apple pulp is placed before squeezing out the cider.) A wise woman at Leominster was consulted, and the thief came back with the hairs on his back in a bundle. But afterwards that woman's mare lost her colt ; then she lost a calf, so she declared it was unlucky to have dealings with " clever " folk, and went to Leominster for advice no more.

George L——, of Longtown, when in service as a farmer's boy, was sent by his master from Longtown to Llandovery to consult a celebrated conjurer,[2] who had at one time a great reputation. George's master had lost a ram, and he desired to know who had stolen it. George paid half-a-crown, and was told that for another half-crown he could be shown the face of the thief. So he paid again, and waited in fear while the wizard, an old man dressed in black, showed him in a large mirror a figure which he recognised as that of a neighbour of his master. He was told to go back and be at a certain place at the foot of the mountain at nine o'clock on the evening of the third day, when he would meet the man who had stolen the ram. He would say, " Here's your master's ram, I found him astray." Old George assured me that he met the man exactly at the time and place mentioned by the conjurer. The ram was returned, " and them very words did he say ! "[3]

Jenkins had a son as clever as his father, but his cleverness was not always exercised for good. He could " change hisself to anything." Once he stole a horse, and rode to Worcester and on to Gloucester, where he was caught. They took him to Hereford gaol and handcuffed him, but when the time for his trial came he was not there, " not likely ! " Once he went to a hoppicking ball ; he was the fiddler, but all at once he put down his fiddle and drew a hen and chickens on the floor in a circle with chalk. Thinking it was black magic and some evil spell might fall upon them none would step within it, and the dancing was stopped. The fiddler went on with his drawing ; he drew a sow and pigs, then a flock of geese. " There was no more dancing that night, for by the time he had done they had all gone out for fear," said the old man who told the story ; he had been one of the fearful ones himself.

1] This " witch " was a man. I have never heard " wizard."
2] See *ante*, Section v. This man seems to have been well known near the Welsh Border.
3] The same kind of story is told of sheep lost at Weobley, and restored by a wise woman of Leominster.

Another diviner was Betty L——, of Weobley Marsh. Here is an instance of her powers, as it was given to me :—" Shook had sold her little taties[1] to a neighbour for the pig for afe-a-crownd ; 'er was a sitting at tea in a neighbour's house, when the afe-crownd was took out'n her pocket." Betty was consulted, and told Shook the half-crown should be duly returned. Next Sunday morning, lying in bed, Shook heard a trembling voice below at her cottage door saying, " There thee be, Shook, there's thy afe-crownd ; I hanna had no rest night nor day, take thy afe-crownd !" Shook descended, and there was the lost coin ; it had been pushed under the door. In the evening when Shook visited Betty she said at once, " So thy afe-crownd came back this morning, Shook ; didn't I tell tha ?" " She was a mighty clever woman, she was ! "

There was a cunning man who lived on the Skyrrid years ago, and folks used to go to him from Ross, and all parts. He would take no money directly, but people used to place a fee on a certain large stone, on the Hill above Llanvihangel, and the money would mysteriously disappear, though the cunning man had not been seen to approach the spot. My informant added that he did not believe this, so one day risked a shilling to satisfy his curiosity. He laid it on the stone and sat down about two hundred yards away from it. After waiting ten minutes or so, he went to the stone, " and true enough," he said, " my shilling was gone ! " He was absolutely certain that no one had been near the stone. " But they do say as the devil it is that helps those folks, and they used to hear that wise man roaring like a bull o' nights."[2]

The expression " cunning " is one I have never heard in North Herefordshire ; they say " clever " instead, or call the diviner the " conjurer."

A charmer is still remembered in Brampton Street, Ross ; it is said that he had only to take out his little black stick,[3] and the hen and chickens would jump up on the tables. "He could do anythink,[4] he could," said my informant, with conviction.

" Nonagenarian[4]" tells us that when she was a little girl, she used sometimes to go to play with another child in the house of a Dr. Coates, of Hereford, who was supposed to be a wizard :—

He was considered to be very clever at all sorts of magic. Once when a man got into his garden to steal the cabbages, he made him sit upon a cabbage till morning ; I know it was a cold night. Dr. Coates had a room full of books and very curious machinery, at which he would let us look occasionally, when he was with us ; but when he went out he always took the key. One summer day Dr. Coates went from home, and left strict orders that neither of us children was to go out except into the garden. We played all day till evening, and running into the hall, found the servant standing at the front door. We ran past her, and were

---

2] From an inmate of Ross Workhouse.   3] *Cf. infra.*   Section xiii., 1, *Jack o' Kent.*   4] From W—— P——,
1] Potatoes.
Ross, 1908.

chasing each other up and down the causeway, when the girl screamed. Turning to look, we saw just inside the little white gate we had at that moment passed out at, an old man with hair and beard as white as snow, both hanging down to his waist, and his person covered with nothing but rags. He looked a mass of rags, as he stood there so motionless. We stood still with astonishment ; there was no creature in sight but the girl and this strange being. " I've nothing to give you," she said ; he never moved. " Go away, or I'll call the master." He took no notice. " I'll cut you with this whip," said she, reaching a large hunting whip. She aimed to cut him, and he vanished as clearly as if he had never stood there. I saw that we all saw it, and pretty frightened we were.

We told the Doctor when he came home. " I told you not to go outside the front door," said he, " I hope you will remember in future."[1]

(2) Love Divinations and Others.

These are most frequently used for the purpose of discovering the identity of the enquirer's future husband or wife ; nearly all given below are still practised, though not so firmly believed in as formerly. Girls hold out a broomstick, and jump over it by turns, believing that the one who jumps highest will be married first. The future husband may be discovered by counting a hundred white horses, each one the girl accidently meets, up to a hundred ; she will marry the first young man she meets afterwards. If a girl place a pod with nine peas in it over the door of her house, the first single man who comes in is the one she will marry. Another plan is to gather a rose on Midsummer Eve, and carry it home, walking backwards, and not speaking a word. It must be carefully preserved in clean white paper, till the following Christmas Day, and then the girl must wear it ; it will be taken from her by her future husband.[2]

In this class of charm, the lover is made to appear, willy-nilly, in his own person ; in others, he is seen in a dream or vision only. In the well-known hempseed charm, the girl must walk twelve times round the church at midnight on St. John's Eve, without stopping, repeating—

> Hemp-seed I sow,
> Hemp-seed I hoe,
> Let him that is my true love,
> Come after me and mow.

The form of her lover then appears to her. This has been done in Weobley within living memory, but with what result I was not informed.

The " dumb cake " was made on St. John's Eve by two maidens (or not more than three).

> " Two make it,
> Two bake it,
> Two break it."

1] *Hereford Times*, April 15, 1876. See *ante*, Section iv., 2, for other recollections of " Nonagenarian."
2] *Herefordshire Gatherer*, June 28, 1879.

Then at midnight, as the clock struck, each ate some, and walked to bed backwards without speaking a word. Those to be married should dream of their future husbands, hurrying after them as if to catch them.[1]

Mrs. A——, being anxious, when a young girl, to discover her future husband, once took the first egg laid by a pullet and boiled it hard. She cut it in halves, and put one half beneath her pillow. As she did so she said :—

> " I put this under my head,
> To dream of the living and not of the dead,
> To dream of the young man that I am to wed,
> Not in his apparel nor in his array,
> But in the clothes he will wear every day."[2]

Then she had to eat the other half of her egg, but before doing so, took out the yolk and filled the cavity with salt. She got into bed without speaking a word afterwards, or the charm would have had no effect. She dreamed of a young man wearing a white " apurn," and told her mother in the morning it would certainly be a trades-man. " And sure enough," she added, " first time I went to that house at the top o' this village he was standing at the door with his apurn on ; and I knew him in a minute. Then when I come in the kitchen I knew that too ; it was the very place in my dream. An' we were married not long after."[3]

Another experiment of the kind, said Mrs. A.——, was made by a young mistress of hers. She would never do such a thing herself, on account of the saying that a knife should never be used for such work : " It's sure to pierce you sometime." (I understood this in a metaphorical sense). " It brings you bad luck after," she added. The penknife must be borrowed from a young man (any young man will do), and the girl must stick the knife in the blade bone of a shoulder of lamb for nine nights in succession, each night in a different place. She must put knife and all beneath her pillow and say :—

> " 'Tis not this bone I mean to stick,
> But my true-love's heart I mean to prick,
> Hoping he may not rest nor sleep,
> Until he comes to me to speak."

She must not speak again after saying this, and should see her lover in dreams on the ninth night.

An inmate of St. Katharine's Hospital, Ledbury, had yet another method. She used to place her shoes in the form of a " T " on going to bed, saying :—

1] *Herefordshire Gatherer, loc. cit.*   2] Sometimes a faggot of rosemary and thyme would be used instead of the egg.   3] Eaton Bishop, 1909.

" I put my shoes in the form of a T,
That I in my dream my true love may see,
The shape of his body, the colour of his hair,
And the holiday clothes my true love doth wear."

But she did not remember that this was successful. Girls also used to melt lead and pour it into cold water, believing that it would take the form of the tools of the future husband. I believe all these charms were originally associated with Midsummer Eve, or All Hallows Eve, but if so this was forgotten by my informants.

It was on Midsummer Eve that a plate of flour was sometimes placed under a rosemary bush. The initials of the lover of the girl who put it there should be found traced in the flour in the morning.

If a girl sit down when she first hear the cuckoo in the spring, and take off her shoe and stocking from the left foot, she will find a hair between the big toe and the next. This will match the hair of the man she will marry.

An old lady aged eighty-six, who had told me of this, assured me she found it quite true. She had often heard her uncle (long dead) say how on Midsummer Eve his brother had gathered a little faggot of twelve different sorts of wood, which he placed under his pillow when both boys went to bed. The uncle, to tease his brother, woke him up and spoke to him in his first sleep. He answered, being hardly awake, and through speaking broke the charm ; so he had no dreams of a future bride for his pains.[1]

Rye grass is often used for divination. Girls count the ears of rye, saying :—

" Rich man, poor man, beggar man, farmer ;
Tinker, tailor, plough-boy, thief."

The word spoken to the last ear on the rye-stalk is to indicate her fate. Another way is to make a ball of cowslip blossom, and toss it, using the same words, over and over, till at the right one the ball falls to the ground. Or the ball is tossed to :—

" Tisty-tosty, tell me true,
Who shall I be married to ? "

Then the names of actual or possible lovers are recited, until the ball falls.

It is said that if a girl write a lover's name with a pin on a laurel leaf and place it in her bosom, the writing will turn red if he be true to her.

1] Orcop, 1909.

Hallowe'en affords another opportunity to those anxious to obtain a peep into the future.   If a girl go into the garden on this night, and cut a cabbage, as the clock strikes twelve, the wraith of her future husband will then appear.   Or she may pluck a sprig of yew from a churchyard where she has never been before, and sleep with it under her pillow ; he will appear to her in a dream.[1]

The following charm may be used at any time.   Dragon's blood is thrown on the fire, while the enquirer says :—

> " 'Tis this blood I mean to burn,
> Hoping ——'s heart to burn,
> That he (or she) can neither rest nor sleep,
> Till he come to me to speak."

A pigeon's heart stuck with pins was sometimes used, similar lines being repeated.

The first new moon in the year was formerly greeted by curious maidens in this fashion :—

> " All hail to thee, moon, all hail to thee,
> I prithee kind moon, reveal to me,
> Him who is my life partner to be."

The girl must then retire to bed in silence, and she will dream of her future husband.[2]

The ladybird is used for divination in the Golden Valley, where she is called " marygold," and is addressed thus :—

> " Marygold, marygold, flitter to fly,
> Tell me where doth my lady-love lie ? "[3]

The lover being found, there is yet room for anxiety and curiosity, lest he or she should not prove true.   This matter was decided on Midsummer Eve by means of a piece of orpine at one time, though I cannot hear of its use nowadays.

A piece of orpine (*sedum telephium*) was set in clay upon pieces of slate or potsherd, and placed in the house, being termed a Midsummer man.   As the stalk was found next morning to incline to the right or the left, it was held to indicate to the maiden who gathered it whether her lover would prove true or not.[4]

Then there is a way of solving the difficulty of *embarras de choix*.   An old woman was working in a green wheatfield near Pembridge with a girl who was hesitating between two sweethearts.   She took two long leaves of the wheat, folded them together crosswise, and passed them nine times round the girl's waist, repeating the name of one of her admirers.   The leaves were not sticking together after this, so the ceremony

---

1] C.G.P.   2] *Herefordshire Gatherer, loc. cit.*, also orally ; see Section i., 9.   *Cf.* Aubrey, *Miscellanies*, 105.
   3] From Mrs. Powell, *Cf.* Northall, 119.   4] *Herefordshire Gatherer, loc. cit.*

was gone through again with another name and other leaves, when they were found to adhere. " So Mrs. V—— told me I should have John, though Harry was all my fancy just then. And I did have John, sure enough !"

The following Hallowe'en charm was practised recently, to satisfy a morbid desire to know if any member of the family would die during the coming year. An ivy leaf was taken for each one and placed in a bowl of water, to remain all night. The leaves were marked, so that each person knew his or her own, and it was believed that any to die soon would have a coffin marked on the leaf in the morning.[1]

Cinders springing suddenly from the fire were formerly examined, and called either coffins or purses, according to shape. They were consequently deemed omens of either death or wealth.[2]

To ascertain if the next wheat harvest would be good or bad, the old men used to roast grains of wheat in front of the fire. As they burst they would " fly," towards the fire for a bad harvest, away from it for a good one.

Bible and Key.

This method of divination[3] is still in use. I have talked to many people who firmly believed in it, though they thought it both uncanny and irreverent, describing it as " wicked work." T—— W——, a fine old countryman of a type now unhappily becoming rare, told me he had helped to turn the key in the Bible many a time, and it had always come true. " When you sees a thing like that," he said, " you feels there's a power on earth besides the power o' human beings." " Ay, ay," said another old son of the soil, " but some says as the power as does it is a bad power."[4]

The Bible and key are used for three purposes :—(1) to discover a lover's name ; (2) the name of a thief ; (3) to remove a spell. The last is, of course, not divination, but magic.

To find a true lover, the key is placed in the Bible with the wards on the text " Whither thou goest I will go " (*Ruth* i., 15). The book is closed and bound with string ; two persons hold up Bible and key by standing on either side and placing their forefingers under the bow of the key, one on each side. The names of possible or probable lovers are then recited, the key turns when the right name is mentioned,

---

1] C.G.P., 1909. *Cf.* Brand, 776, where a similar method is described, but the leaf is put in water from New Year's Day till Twelfth Night.
2] Duncumb, i., 209.
3] *Cf.* Gutch-Peacock, 138 ; Burne, 172 ; Henderson, 138, *et. seq.*, for this practice elsewhere.
4] Ross, 1907.

and the Bible falls. To discover a thief, the verse *Psalm* i., 18, is chosen, and the names of suspected persons repeated in the same manner.

For the removal of spells, the method is different ; perhaps it was at one time a form of divination, used for the discovery of supposed witches, who had put on the spells. The key should be laid on two crossed sticks, one of *witty* (mountain ash), and one of yew, both held potent against witchcraft. These are placed on the verses in the Bible beginning " put on the whole armour " (*Ephesians* vi., 13, 14, 15). These verses are to be read aloud nine times, and at each repetition a little tear is made in a piece of white paper. To break the spell, the paper is to be folded up, and sewn in the clothing of the person thought to be bewitched, without his or her knowledge.[1]

Crystal-gazing.

A white wizard, who lived to a great age at Leominster, used to practise crystal-gazing for the benefit of his clients. He died about ten years ago, and I cannot hear of any successor. Aubrey describes and illustrates the use of a crystal, or " berill," in Herefordshire in his day.

> A clothier's widow of Pembridge, in Herefordshire, desired Dr. Shirborne (one of the canons of the church at Hereford), to look over her husband's writings after his decease ; among other things he found a call for a crystal. The clothier had his clothes ofttimes stolen from his racks, and at last obtained this trick, to discover the thieves. So, when he lost his clothes, he went out about midnight with his crystal and call, and a little boy or little maid (for they say it must be a pure virgin), to look in the crystal, to see the likeness of the person that committed the theft. The Doctor did own the call, 1671.

The call was a certain form of words to be used by the crystal-gazer before consulting it. Aubrey continues :—

> . . . I have set down the figure of a consecrated Berill, now in the possession of Sir Edward Harley, Knight of the Bath, which he keeps in his closet at Brampton Bryan, in Herefordshire, amongst his Cimelia, which I saw there. It came first from Norfolk ; a minister had it there, and a call was to be used with it. Afterwards, a miller had it, and both did work great cures with it (if curable), and in the Berill they did see either the receipt in writing or else the herb. To this minister the spirits of angels would appear openly, and because the miller (who was his familiar friend) one day happened to see them, he gave him the aforesaid Berill and call. By these angels the minister was warned of his death. This account I had from Mr. Ashmole. Afterwards this Berill came into somebodies hands in London, who did tell strange things by it, insomuch that at last he was questioned for it, and it was taken away by authority (it was about 1645). This Berill is a perfect sphere ; the diameter of it I guess to be something more than an inch. It is set in a ring or circle of silver, resembling the meridian of a globe. The stem of it is about 10 inches high, all gilt. At the four quarters of it are the names of four angels, viz., Uriel, Raphael, Michael, Gabriel ; on the top is a cross patee.[2]

1] W—— C——., Weobley, 1909.
2] Aubrey, *Miscellanies* (1696), 129-131.

(3) Dreams and Portents.

Girl has a Vision in a Trance.

Anno. 1670. A poor widow's daughter in Herefordshire went to service not far from Harwood (the seat of Sir John Hoskins, baronet, R.S.S.). She was aged near about twenty; fell very ill, even to the point of death; the mother was old and feeble, and her daughter was the comfort of her life; if she should die she knew not what to do. She besought God upon her knees in prayer, that He would be pleased to spare her daughter's life and take her to Him. At this time the daughter fell into a trance, which continued about an hour; they thought she had been dead. When she recovered out of it, she declared the vision she had in this fit, viz., That one in black habit came to her, whose face was so bright and glorious she could not behold it, and also he had such brightness upon his breast, and (if I forget not) upon his arms; and told her that her mother's prayers were heard, and that her mother should shortly die and she should suddenly recover; and she did so, and her mother dyed. She hath the character of a modest humble, vertuous Maid. Had this been in some Catholic county it would have made a great noise.[1]

The Three Suns.

Before the battle of Mortimer's Cross, the last and the most important ever fought on Herefordshire soil, the army of the Yorkists was awestruck on observing in the clear pale sky three suns, which gradually merged into one. This they took to be an omen of victory. It was really a natural phenomenon not infrequent in more northern latitudes, called a parhelion, or mock sun.[2]

Shooting the Arrow.

A quarter of a century later, when Harry of Richmond marched through Pembridge and Eardisland, on his way to Leominster and Bosworth, he crossed the Arrow at its confluence with the Lugg. He was told the river's name, and reminded of an old prophecy which promised victory, in a national strife, to him who should " shoot the arrow " first. Henry encouraged his troop by interpreting the prophecy as referring to his crossing of the stream.[3]

Aubrey, in his *Miscellanies* (71), relates how the siege of Hereford by the Scots in 1645 had been prophesied by a mysterious stranger, who appeared to a Hereford man at Carmarthen in 1639.

Lambert, a gunsmith at Hereford, was at Carmarthen to mend and put in order the ammunition of that county before the first expedition to Scotland, which was in 1639. He was then a young man, and walking on the sand by the seashore, a man comes to him (he did verily believe it was a man) and asked him if

---

1] Aubrey, *Miscellanies*, 1696, 144-5.
2] *Woolhope Club*, 1870, 3, *Mortimer's Cross*. See Shakespeare, *Hen.* vi., 3, Act. ii., 1.
3] *Woolhope Club*, 1900-02, 262.

he knew Hereford ?   " Yes," quoth he, " I am a Hereford man."   " Do you know it well ?" quoth the other.
" Perfectly well," quoth Lambert.   " That city shall be beget (he told me he did not know what the word
beget meant then) by a foreign nation, which should come and pitch their camp in the Hay Wood, and they
should come and batter such a gate (which they did, I have forgot the name of it), and shall go away, and not
take it.   The Scots came in 1645, and camped before Hereford in the Hay Wood, and stormed the gate, and
raised the siege. Lambert did well remember this discourse, but did not heed it till they came to the Hay Wood.
Many of the city had heard of this story, but when the gate was stormed Lambert went to all the city guards
of the town and encouraged them with more than ordinary confidence, and contrary to all humane expecta-
tion, when the besieged had no hope of relief, the Scots raised the siege, Sept. 2nd, 1645, and went back into Scotland, *re infecta*.   I knew this Lambert and took this account from his own mouth.   He is a modest poor
man, of a very innocent life, lives poor and cares not to be rich.

Two curious pamphlets, one published in 1649 and the other thirty years later,
bear witness to the credulous and excited state of men's minds in the troubled time
of the civil war and after.   The title pages only are given below : the pamphlets *in
extenso* are printed in Townsend's *History of Leominster*.

Vox Infantis, or the Prophetical Child,

Being a true relation of an infant that was found in a field, neere Lempster, in Herefordshire, July 16,
1649, that did declare and foretell of many strange things that shall ensue in England and Ireland within the
space of three years, concerning the crowning of Charles the Second King of England, Scotland, and Ireland ;
his great victories, with the destruction of the present Parliament and Army ; and many other passages
touching the death of our late King.

This relation is attested to bee true, as appears by the hands of severall witnesses annexed to the booke.
London, printed in the year 1649.

Strange News from Lempster, in Herefordshire,

being a true narrative, given under several persons hands there, of a most strange and prodigious opening
of the earth, in divers places therabouts, also, a true relation of several wonderful sights, viz., a hand, an
arm and a shoulder of the bigness of a man's ; and sadles of blood-colour ; which were seen to raise out
of the earth and ascend up to the skies.   Likewise, a strange and terrible noise of fighting, which was heard
during this miraculous accident.

All attested by several persons of worth and reputation, and exhibited for public information.
Licensed, May the Third.
London, printed for B. Harris, 1679.

It used to be said in Hereford that when there was a fight between boys of the
Latin (Cathedral) School and the town boys, it was a sure sign of war.   A " battle of
the boys " is minutely described by " Nonagenarian " in a letter to the *Hereford
Times* (April 29th, 1876).   She adds :—

The talk of the old people then caused me to notice that whenever the boys in the town set themselves
up for soldiers and go through for any length of time the routine of a regular army, there are sure

to happen some very dreadful wars. It was then believed that the soldiering of the boys was a sign of war. At any rate the recruiting officers soon made their appearance after the fight, which must have taken place eighty-three or four years ago.

Dreams of St. Dubricius, *see* Section xv., 1; Meaning of Dreams, x., 3; Dreams caused by love divination, vi., 2.

SECTION VII.

LEECHCRAFT.

(1) Charming and Charmers.

In 1854 the Secretary of the Diocesan Board of Education had occasion to refer in his report to the existence in Herefordshire of the belief in numerous superstitions, remedies, charms, and divinations amongst the peasantry.[1] Half a century of education has not eradicated these beliefs, and the following strange remedies are chiefly gathered from those actually believing in and practising them at the present day.

" Charming is quite right, of course," said an old man in Weobley, " there's charmin' in the Bible, and it's a good thing : it's mostly words of Scripture they do use. You knows where it says about the man that wouldn't hear the words of the Charmer, ' charm he never so wisely.' You says the words," he continued, " nine times over, as the one being charmed canna hear 'em."

Charming forms a branch of the profession of the " wise man," *i.e.*, the wizard or diviner, but many who claim no other occult powers profess to be able to charm.   The seventh son of a seventh son, however, is a charmer by nature, born with the gift of healing.   An old tailor at Almeley was heard to say of such a one : " What a pity his father couldn't make him a doctor, when even now he can charm without any trouble !"

Given faith on the part of the patient, as well as of the charmer, it is believed that almost anyone can use charms, but they must be communicated by a man to a woman, and *vice versâ*. I once asked a woman to tell me what she said when she charmed burns, but she said it would be no use at all if she told me herself, and sent me to " old Powell up above," who gave the same formula as that written in the Weobley charmer's book, quoted below.

Fifty or sixty years ago, the old folks say, they never went " runnin' off to the doctor," as their grandchildren do now, but brought their families up with herbal medicines and charms, in which many continue to have perfect faith. I know a mother of seven children who boasts of having reared her family without medical help, nursing them all unaided through scarlet fever.   The only medicine they had was made with herbs, marigold and camomile tea, and the like, and they " cut their teeth beautiful with the aid of a bag of wood-lice tied round the neck." Charms are still used for animals as well as for people, especially in the Crasswall district. I said to

---

1] *Herefordshire Gatherer,* June 14, 1879.

one believer that although charming might do good to human beings having faith in it, animals could not be expected to believe or understand it. " If your sheep is ailin'," he explained, " and you get it charmed, you that owns the sheep must ha' fayth, and that's what does it." As a rule the charmer of animals sends the owner home, telling him the animal will be well when he returns, or in so many days ; the people believe some mysterious charm or spell can be used without seeing the horse or cow affected.

Concerning charming as she knew it in the Golden Valley, Mrs. Powell writes :— " When cattle were ill in Peterchurch (1875-1887), the wise woman was sent for to charm them. Whoever fetched her must speak to no one going or returning, nor must he say, ' Will you come to our cow ? ' &c., as that would prevent the charm working. He must casually mention the cow's ailment in course of talk, as if it were of no importance. The wise woman would understand, and go and do what was required. No thanks and no reward must be offered ; by and by, a present would find its way to her, and nothing said."

An old man, aged ninety, inmate of the Bromyard Workhouse, who had been a farmer at Little Cowarne, told me how a mare of his had put its shoulder out, and nothing did her any good. So he went at last to a charmer, a butcher living at Hatfield. The man asked the mare's name, and said he thought he could cure her without seeing her, but if she were not well in a day or two, he would come to her himself. " However, she did get well in three days, and all the doctoring before had never done no good."[1]

A few years ago a gentleman staked his horse badly while hunting with the Herefordshire hounds ; the hæmorrhage was great. He said " What can I do ? " and was advised by the bystanders to send for Mr. ——, the charmer. At once a messenger galloped off, and found the charmer in his fields. " Mr. ——'s horse was badly hurt, and is dying of the blood-letting," said the messenger. The charmer told the man to leave him and went apart, remaining for a short time in an attitude of prayer ; he then returned and announced that the flow of the mare's blood was stayed. The messenger went back to the scene of the accident first carefully noting the time. He found that the mare was recovering, and that the flow of blood was stayed at the hour of the charmer's prayer.[2]

A Herefordshire girl related how when she was in service at Credenhill a charmer happened to call at the house of her mistress one night, when she was suffering from toothache. " The man offered to charm it for me," she said ; " he wrote my name on the kitchen wall with some straight lines under it, and muttered something to him-

---

1] Told 1909.   2] Kindly communicated by Col. R. Rankin.

self. I said, ' thank you very much, what shall I owe you ? ' He said, ' There, you have done it now, you should not thank nor pay, you'll have it worse than ever.' And so I have, ever since."

The form of words of which the charm consists may be used in two ways ; either written, to be worn about the person as an amulet, or for a burn or cut, muttered by the charmer while touching the injured part. It is essential that the patient, in addition to having perfect faith, shall be ignorant of the words used, and they are never spoken audibly.

I have been allowed to copy the contents of a Weobley charmer's book ;[1] it belonged to one John E———, " a very clever man he was," they say, " and he could take off spells, too. There was a man who went to him to charm his toothache ; he gave him something in a bit o' paper in a black silk bag, and told him not to look at it. He wore it till he died and never had toothache after." My informant, a Weobley woman, being curious, opened the bag after the man's death and found written on the paper within :—" For toothache. Oil " (alder) " in wood ashes, ash in wood coals." " Pull out the tooth, and put snuff in the hole."

The contents of old John's books are here given verbatim, with his quaint spelling, according to his own arrangement ; they show the character of the mysterious books of the wise man, so often spoken of with awe by the folk, many of whom in the last generation could read no books at all.

JOHN E—— HIS BOOK.

JAN 21, 1804.

To Make a Horse Follow You.

To make a horse follow his master and find him out and Challenge him amongst ever so many people, take a pound of oatmeal and put it in a quarter of a pound of honey and half a pound of lunarce (sic), and make a cake thereof and put it into bosom next your naked skin, and run or labour yourself till you swet, then rub all your swet upon your cake then keep him fasting a day and a night and give it him to eat and when he hath eaten it turn him looce and he shall not only follow you but also hunt and seek you when he hath lost you, or doth miss you and though you be envinced with ever so many yet he cometh to you.

1] The contents are similar to those in a Radnorshire farmer's book communicated to *Folk-Lore* vi., 201, by the Rev. W. E. T. Morgan.

A Charm for Burnt (*sic*).

The Virgin Mary burnt her child with a spark of fire : out fire in frost, in the name, etc. Amen.

A Screven for the Ague.

Before the gates of Jerusalem our Saviour Jesus Christ called peter unto him. Peter answered and said I am sick of an ague and cannot come Jesus said Despise the evil ague and come away. Evil Ague being dismissed Peter said Lord I beseech thee that hosoever Carrieth these words abought them that the evil ague might never hurt them. In the name &c.

A Charm to stop Teeth from Akeing.

When our Lord and Saviour was born of a Virgin an virtious maydon Baptised he was in the flowing of Jordan, the waters was mild and the child was meeke and good. So I command the waters to stand and they Stoude. And in the name of Christ I command thee, name of the person name to be wrote to Sees from payn for ever and Amen.

A Charm for Stopping Blood.

Our blessed Lord and Saviour was baptised in the River Jordan ; the waters was wild, the Child was mild the water was blest and still it stood sweet Jesus Christ in Charity stop this blood. In the name &c.

A Charm for a Spell.

Then said Jesus unto him Get thee hence Satun for it is written thou shalt worship the Lord thy God and him only shalt thou searve. Amen.

A Charm for a Thorn.

At Bethelhem our Saviour Jesus Christ was born, and at Jeruzalem was crucified with a cround of thorns and it did neither wrinkel nor swell and I trust in and through the name of our Lord and Savour this thorn it will go well. In the name &c.

From a smaller book which belonged to the same John E—— :—

To Cure the Ague.

When Jesus saw the cross whereon he was to be crucified he trembled and shook and the Jews asked him, ' Art thou afraid or hast thou the ague ?' Jesus answered and said ' I am not afraid neither have I the evil ague, whoever wears this about them shall not be afraid nor have that evil ague.'

To put up anything into the shade[1] (?).

Our Saviour Jesus Christ trod on a marble stone. He said, " Fletch to Fletch, and Bone to bone, sinnew to sinnew, Skin to skin. Blood to blood, air to air. Each one in your place. In the name, &c.

"Into the shade " may be meant for " into shape." This is a charm for a sprain or strain. Another version, from an inmate of Bromyard Workhouse, runs :— " These words was wrote on a marble stone, sinew to sinew, and bone to bone."[2]

For the Bite of a Mad Dog.

> Fuary, gary, nary,
> Gary, nary, fuary,
> Nary, fuary, gary.

Write this on a piece of cheese, and give it to the Dog.

This is the last of old John's recipes ; it is written in his shaky hand in an old pocket book, lent to me by a neighbour, who treasures a copy of Culpepper's *Herbal*, and makes practical use of it.

Mrs. Powell remembered seeing an old man (now dead) practising a charm to staunch blood. " He pressed his fingers lightly on the cut and muttered, but would not say what words he used. A bystander told me they were ' some where in Ezekiel.' "[3]

An inmate of Weobley Workhouse told me that the verses " about making dry bones live " (*Ezekiel* xxxvii., 6, 7, 8), are a charm for a sprain or a broken bone, if repeated nine times inaudibly.

Charms for Toothache.

The following written charm was given me by a woman at Dilwyn for my boy's toothache. It was on a folded half-sheet of paper marked " Charm for toothache, Not to be opened." Within was written :—

"CHARM FOR TOOTHACHE."

" As peter was standing before the gates of Jerusalem. Our Saviour Jesus Christ called peter and said come away Peter. Peter answered and said Lord my teeth

---

1] The Rev. F. Andrews has this charm in a MS. charmers' book, headed, " A charm for a beast that is lame." The book was found in a secret drawer of an old bureau at Kinnersley.

2] This is what is called a narrative charm ; many charms belong to this class. Such charms are relics of pre-Christian times, and some of them are merely adaptations by substituting the name of one divinity for another. Mr. Hartland (*Old Welsh Folk Medicine*, in *Y Cymmrodor*, ix., 240) cites examples of such charms from Grimm, *Teutonic Mythology*, iii., 1231, and Thorpe's *Northern Mythology*, i., 23, in which :—

> " Phol and Woden went to the Wood ;
> Then was of Balder's colt the foot wrenched.
> Then Sinthgunt charmed it, and Sunna her sister ;
> Then Frua charmed it, and Volla her sister ;
> Then Woden charmed it, as he well could,
> As well the bone wrench as the blood wrench,
> As the joint wrench . . .
> Bone to bone, blood to blood.
> Joint to joint, as if they were glued together."

3] This charm is given by the late Mrs. Murray-Aynsley in *Symbolism*, 160. It is *Ezekiel* xvi., 6.

does ache and therefore I cannot come. Jesus answered and said come away, away from the Evil toothache and immediately the toothache left him. Then Peter prayed and said " Good Lord might it please the that whosoever shall carry this word their teeth shall have no power to hurt or harm them. So Lord help this . . . . . who puts his trust in the, In the name, [*the invocation follows*]

Abracadabra[1]
Abracadabr
Abracadab
Abracada
Abracad
Abraca
Abrac
Abra
Abr
Ab
A."

Yet another version of this very common toothache charm was given in 1886 in the parish of Crasswall, written on a small piece of paper and sealed with pitch.

" Christ met peter and said unto him Peter what is the matter with the. Peter saide lorde I am tormented with the paine in the tooth the worme shal die and thou shalt live and thou that shalt have this in wrightin or in memory shall never have the paine in the tooth the Worme shall die and thou shalt live and thou shall have this in memory or wrightin shall never have the Paine in the tooth. Therefore believe in the Lorde youre God."[2]

An interesting mediæval charm for toothache is preserved in a volume in the Cathedral Library, entitled *Officiæ Ecclesiæ* (*see illustration*). It contains numerous notes in English, Welsh, and Latin ; the date is thought to be about 1400. It evidently belonged to some Welsh Church, possibly to Kilpeck ; Welsh would be the language spoken in that part of the country in those days. A Welsh Bible was preserved in the church at Rowlstone until recent times. The fourth word in the charm is undecipherable. It is as follows :—

Maria sedebat super . . . Jhesus venit
Ad eam et valdé tristis mater mea quare hic

1] This word was used as an amulet for ague, when written triangularly (Aubrey, *Miscellanies*, 105-6). *Abra*, here twice repeated, is composed of the first letters of the Hebrew words signifying Father, Son, and Holy Spirit, viz., *Ab, Ben, Ruach, Acadosch* (Lean, *Collectanea*, vol. ii., pt. ii., 1).
2] Havergal, *Words and Phrases*, 46.

Sedes, illa tamen dic fili me dentes mei dolent quod non possum dormire nec vigilare
Dicit ei Jhesus surge et vade et amplius non nocet
Te nec alicui homini qui ista verba super se portaverit.

$$+ O + E + C + G + R +$$
$$A + W + A + T + C + N +^{[1]}$$

Perhaps it was old John's charm for a spell that was used by the patient referred to in the following story, told to Miss Burne (March 25th, 1884), by an old farmer.

" There was a young man as worked for me when I was living in Herefordshire, as always wore a charm from a child. Couldn't do without it. When he was a little lad he was sent for a can of milk, and he came running and slopped some of the milk over a doorstone in passing, and the woman came out and abused him ; and it was always supposed she bewitched him, for he always seemed to pine afterwards. Nothing ailded him only he didn't grow or thrive. Never complained, never said he was ill, only couldn't eat, and in the night he'd get out of bed and go into the garden, and lay him down among the potatoes. And then his father or his mother would go and fetch him back, and he never knew where he was, or how he come there, and they would get him back and cover him up in the bed again."

" And there was a man that worked with his father, and he says to him one day, he says ' Tell thee what, if I was thee I'd take Jack over to the Marsh Farm.' ' Ay,' says he, ' dost tha think as the oud man'd do him any good ? ' ' To be sure,' he says, ' it's plain,' he says, ' what ails the lad, and doctor's stuff won't do nothing for him.' Well, the father said no more, but on the Sunday morning he got up and dressed himself, and he says ' I think as I'll take Jack over to the Marsh farm to-day.' So they went ; and as soon as ever they had come in, the old farmer says ' What, thou'st brought Jack, hast thou ? ' (knowed what they comed for, you see, afore ever they said a word). ' Well,' he says, ' why didstna thou come afore ? thoust like to ha' bin too late. Thou hadst ought to ha' come afore. Howsoever,' he says, ' I'll see what I can do.' So he wrote him a charm. I don't know what it was ; but it would very likely be something the same as you have showed me." (The old Toothache charm about St. Peter). " And he fastened it in a bit of green silk, and the boy was to wear it round his neck just in the centre of his chest, and never to part with it. Every time as he changed his clothes he was to be sure and keep the charm about him, never to part with it. Well, and he got all right, and quite hearty after that ; only he never durst part with the charm."

1] Havergal. *Fasti*, 192.

"Only once he'd been changing his clothes and he slipped it off somehow. It was in the harvest, and he was leading the waggon. His father was pitching at the top of the field and all of a sudden he saw the boy making straight for a dingle at the bottom, and he shouted at him. But he took no notice; it was like as if he was silly. And his father run, and he did but just get to him in time, and a good job as he did, else the waggon and horses and all would have been right over the steep side of the dingle. And they couldn't make out what ailed the lad, but they took him home and put him to bed, and when they come to examine him, of course they found he hadn't got the charm on. So they put it on again, and he was all right after. He was grown a young man when I knew him; he worked for me twelve years, but he always wore the charm.[1]

(2) SUPERSTITIOUS CURES.

Adder Bite.

Mr. John Hutchinson, an old Herefordian, has kindly communicated the following account of a cure given to him by a friend many years ago. Riding across Eywas Harold Common in his younger days (that is, somewhere about the third or fourth decade of the last century), he came on a group of people surrounding something on the ground. At first he took it to be a dead sheep, but on closer inspection he found it was but the skin of one, inside of which was the body of a child, carefully wrapped up therein, only its head visible. On enquiring what was the matter, he was informed that a little one had been bitten by an adder. A "nadder" they called it, explaining that the best cure was the one they had applied, the pelt warm and reeking from the body of a sheep.[2]

Thomas Whittington, of Walford, suffered from an abscess in his arm, which would not heal. A gypsy woman told him how to cure it by wearing the leg of a toad. "One day when I was a hedgin'," he said, "I found un and put un in a wheelbarra and looked at un a good while, and thinking how I cud cut a leg off the poor creetur, so as un cud walk, 'uthout it." In the end he decided that the toad could dispense with a hind leg, and proceeded to "whittle the corner of a spittle to make un sharp like"; with this the leg was speedily severed. A turf was next cut from under the hedge, and carefully replaced, with the unfortunate toad, still living, beneath it.

"And what did you do with the leg?" I asked. "I was to wear that round me neck, in a silk bag, and I hadna got a bit of silk but me best silk handkercher, and I wore un in that just here (touching his chest), till I lost un. And I was to look next morning if the toad was gone, and a was, and me arm was well in three wiks, and

1] *Folk-Lore Journal*, iv., 165.
2] See N.E.D., i., 102,—*Adder* [O.E. *naedre*]. . . . The initial was lost in M.E., 1300-1500, through the erroneous division of a *naddre*, as an *addre*.

kept well for ten or twelve year too, a did." The idea seemed to be that the toad carried away the disease ; if it had not disappeared no cure was to be expected.

Whittington said " un " for " it " ; a North Herefordshire man would call an inanimate object " him " or " her " ; " un " as a pronoun, is unknown.

Birth Marks.

A mother complained that her baby had a large birthmark that threatened to be permanent ; " I have licked it all over for nine mornings, too," she said.[1]

Chilblains.

If a baby is taken out of doors when the first fall of snow which occurs after its birth is on the ground, and its feet well rubbed therewith, it will never have chilblains.

Cramp.

An eelskin garter worn below the knee will prevent cramp. A ring made from the hinge of a coffin was formerly supposed to have the virtue of preventing this complaint, but I have not heard of its being used at the present day.

Convulsions.—*See* Teething.

Diseases of Cattle.

It is not now possible to find any trace of the belief, noted by *Antiquatis*, that " water blessed by a priest " (*i.e.*, holy water), is a potent medicine for diseases of cattle.[2]

Foul.

A very common cure for foul in the feet of cattle is to take a turf, with an impression of the animal's foot in the centre, and hang it up ; as the grass in the turf dries and withers, so will the foul disappear. At Almeley the same thing is done to prevent mischance among the cows.

Good Friday Bread.[3]

It was formerly quite a general custom to bake on Good Friday, in order to have some of the bread, marked with the cross, to keep for the rest of the year as a medicine, chiefly for intestinal troubles, in " dumb animals or Christians." I have known

---

1] Tarrington.   2] *Herefordshire Gatherer*, June 14, 1879.   3] An interesting article entitled *Hot Cross Buns* appeared in the *Tablet*, April 19, 1908.

many people in Weobley who did this ; now-a-days they are content to keep a baker's hot cross bun.   It is believed that bread baked on this day will never go mouldy.   It is ground up when required, and mixed with hot water as a medicine.   Mrs. Murray-Aynsley observed these practices among the folk at Bredwardine some years ago. The legend which they connect with it is a curious and interesting one.   It runs thus :—

" As our Blessed Lord was carrying His cross on his way to His crucifixion, a woman who had been washing came out of the house and threw her dirty water over the Saviour ; another woman who was standing near with some freshly baked bread said to her, " Why do you treat that poor man like that, One who never did you any harm ? " and she gave our Blessed Lord a loaf, which He ate, and said " From henceforth blessed be the baker, and cursed be the washer."[1]

It is considered most unlucky to wash on Good Friday.   The only instance of the external application of Good Friday bread I have met with is that of its use for the cure of a wen, given below.

Fits.

A ring made of a sacrament shilling given at the sacrament offertory is held a certain cure for fits.   The Rev. G. F. Bulmer, Vicar of Canon Pyon, has been asked for one for this purpose more than once, and the late Vicar of Hampton Bishop three times in two years.   Mistletoe tea made from mistletoe growing on the hawthorn tree is believed to prevent fits.   Old people near Weobley used to say of an epileptic boy " What a pity it was his mother did not get him mistletoe tea."   A roasted mouse is another remedy for fits ; it must be given in food, so that the patient will not know what he is eating.   A woman at Orcop used to tie rue to the hands, wrists, and ankles of her children, in order to prevent " fits " ; possibly convulsions were what she meant to avoid

Hair (falling).

A cap of ivy leaves, worn on the head, is supposed to make the hair grow, when it has come off after fever or other illness.[2]

Headache.

A halter with which a person has been hanged is said to cure headache, if tied round the head.[3]   Fortunately opportunities for trying this gruesome remedy are rare. I have never heard of its use.

1] *Symbolism*, 162.   2] R. H. B., Kingstone.   3] *Herefordshire Gatherer, loc. cit.*

Jaundice.

The inner rind of the bark of an elder tree, or " ellum," as my informant called it, boiled with milk, is taken as remedy for jaundice. This would at first sight seem to be a simple herbal remedy, and not superstitious ; but the bark used is yellow, and therefore suggests the idea of sympathetic magic.

Pneumonia.

The lung of a sheep still warm was formerly applied to the soles of the feet of a child suffering from pneumonia. It was spoken of as the best possible remedy by those using it ; the idea seems to be that the healthy lung of the sheep could draw the disease from the lungs of the patient.

Rheumatism.

A lady attending a confirmation service at Dilwyn about forty years ago was surprised to see a white haired, apparently aged woman, being confirmed. She made a remark about this afterwards, and was told, " Oh she is *always* confirmed ; it's good for her complaint !" But it was so long ago that although she was told at the time, my informant could not recollect what the complaint was. Probably it was rheumatism, for Mr. Portman writes :—" My Grandmother knew an old woman who was confirmed three times, in three different churches, as a cure for her rheumatism. The excuse she made to the clergyman was that certain girls would not be confirmed without her." A piece of brimstone, or a potato, are sometimes carried in the pocket for rheumatism.

Rupture.

The common cure of passing the child through a split tree was described to me, by an inmate of Weobley Workhouse, as carried out most successfully (so he said) at Broxwood. A maiden ash was split and a child passed through it, from the father's hands into another man's, nine times. The father said " The Lord giveth," the other man replied, " The Lord receiveth." The tree was then carefully bound up, and if it grew together again, the patient would recover. A willow tree, with a large hole in it, growing near the Lynch Farm, Eardisland, has been frequently used for the same purpose ; the tree was not split, the child was passed through the existing hole.

At Walterstone, an ash-tree has been used in the same manner until recently ; an old man there assured me the cure had been most successful, as he had carried it out. He said the tree must be without blemish, and two men must split it ; they then go in silence to fetch the child and one parent ; it is most essential that no word be spoken. The parent and one man then pass the child through the tree nine times, and it is taken home, still in silence. The parent must not speak till the child is at home again, and while he returns the men bind up the tree carefully with nine " nut-tree withies." My informant added that he had cured one case that had been given up as quite hopeless by the doctor, who heard of the cure, and came to enquire about it in astonishment. " I gev him this answer, ' You said he'd never be no better, and I shanna tell you no more about it !' "

At Thruxton, Ann P—— told the Vicar that she had cured many children in this way ; she said the Lord's Prayer during the operation, and bound the tree with a " sling of withy " (willow).

Sore Throat.

Tie a stocking which has been worn on the *left* foot round the patient's throat on going to bed ; his throat will be well in the morning. This cure is commonly practised in the Weobley district.

Stye in the Eye.

This may be cured by touching it with a wedding ring, or by taking a cat and crossing the stye nine times with the tip of her tail.

Teething.

A woman at Ledgemoor (King's Pyon), used to catch seven or nine woodlice, and place them, while still alive, in a little bag to hang round her babies' necks to help them cut their teeth. At Kingstone, a woman used twenty-one woodlice, sewn up alive in black ribbon, for the same purpose.

The Rev. Hyett Warner found that one of his parishioners believed in the efficacy of hairs from the cross on a donkey's back ; she hung them round the child's neck, sewn up in a little silk bag.[1] At Staunton-on-Wye a necklace of hair from the donkey's cross was worn during the whole period of teething. The mother explained that " it must be someone else's donkey." It is believed that the cross has been marked on all donkeys since our Lord's entry into Jerusalem, riding on an ass.

Thorn.

The folk at Westhope search for the cast adder-skins on Birley Hill in the spring, and preserve them for the purpose of drawing out thorns. They say, " If you have a thorn in your hand, apply the adder-skin to the other side, and the thorn will come out."

1] Almeley.

Toothache.

A gall of the wild rose is frequently carried in the pocket, as a preventive of toothache. A little bag of mole's feet is sometimes kept hanging over the mantelpiece, to be worn round the neck, if required, as a cure.[1]

Thrush.

It is believed that everyone has " thrush " once in his life, either soon after birth, or shortly before death ; if an adult has it during illness, recovery is thought impossible. A Pembridge woman used to think that she cured her baby of thrush by holding the head of a live frog in its mouth. " Not to touch, mind," she said, " but to get the breath. I mind one time as I done it, the frog drawed a breath and puffed hisself out ever so, and the youngster was well the day after."

Whooping Cough.

The same woman cured her grandson of whooping cough by holding him up to inhale the breath of a piebald horse. The boy's sister had the cough very badly, but when she got it there was no piebald horse about Pembridge, so they passed her under a bramble-bush rooted at both ends, for nine mornings. She got better, but did not seem much better at the time, and the old lady seemed to think the horse's breath far the superior remedy. The bramble-bush was supposed to be quite effectual in a recent case at Weobley, but the child was passed under nine times on one morning only, and an offering of bread and butter was placed beneath the bramble arch. " She left her cough there with the bread and butter," said my informant. At Thruxton and Kingstone they say the Lord's Prayer, while passing the patient nine times under the briar arch ; he must be eating bread and butter meanwhile. On returning, the bread and butter must be given to some bird or other creature (" not a Christian ") ; the bird will die, and the cough will be cured. Ann P——, of Kingstone, said she once got into trouble for causing the death of somebody's duck in this way.[2]

An old man at Almeley, a woodman, firmly believed that to feed a child from a bowl made of ivy wood was a cure for this complaint ; he had made such bowls for the purpose. A repulsive remedy formerly practised at Orcop was to give the child a piece of bread and butter that had been placed in a dead man's hand.

In Oaker Coppice, Eyton, is a curious ash tree growing out of the stump of an oak. Its trunk is covered with hairs, small locks of human hair placed in notches made in the bark. Eyton folk believe that an offering of child's hair to this tree will

---

1] Havergal, *Words and Phrases*, 46. 2] R.H.B.

cure the cough, and an old keeper stated that people from Eyton living in London had sent him locks of hair, requesting him to fasten them in the bark of the tree, which he had done.

Another way of curing the cough is to take a spider alive and hold it to the child's mouth, saying :—

> " Spider as you pine away
> Whooping cough no longer stay."

Then let it go and it will take the cough with it.

A woman in Almeley parish, in order to cure her child's cough, took two black hairs from a donkey (probably from the cross), and placed them under the bark of a " sally " tree.[1] The donkey hairs were used at King's Pyon, but they were fastened with clay to an oak tree beneath the bark, and the piece of bark was then replaced over them.

Once when there was an epidemic of whooping cough at Blakemere, an old woman said to the Rector " Lor bless you, Sir, when I was a girl we thought nothing of it, we never troubled the doctor. The child was taken to the mill, the miller set the mill going and said, ' In the name of the Father, Son, and Holy Ghost grind away this disease,' and it went, always." A girl who is a native of Withington told me how her grandmother hung a string of berries round her neck to cure her cough.

A so-called infallible remedy is a piece of bread, received from a woman who has successively married two men of the same name, being of different families.[2]

Vaccination.

A man in the Golden Valley recently refused to have his child vaccinated in the " dog days," because it might go mad.

Warts.

There are many different cures. One is to get a stick of elder wood, cut nine notches in it, and rub the warts on the notches : seal the stick up in an envelope, and drop it at the first cross road you come to ; the person who picks it up will get the warts. Or count them and make a packet of as many grains of wheat as there are warts. These are to be thrown over the shoulder without looking round, where four roads meet, in the hope of transferring them to the finder of the packet.

1] Rev. Hyett Warner. 2] Weobley. Also *Herefordshire Gatherer*, June 14, 1879.

At Eardisley an old man who charmed warts used pebbles in the same way ; he told me he had done it over and over again with success, and he was especially proud of curing a large wart on his niece's nose by these means. " And when I saw her next time the wart was gone," he said ; " I says, ' Where's your wart Emly ? ' She'd never missed it ! "

Another prescription is " Take a live snail, rub the warts with it, bury it alive, or stick it on the black thorn ; this must be done secretly, and as the snail shrivels up the warts will disappear. Or steal some beef from a butcher's shop, rub the warts with it and bury it, and as it decays they will disappear."

A woman at Weobley Marsh says her warts were cured by a man who crossed them with a piece of thread, each one separately and carefully ; then he placed his hand on hers, afterwards folding the thread in a piece of paper, taking it away with him.

Another plan is to steal a piece of beef from a butcher's shop or a bit of your neighbour's fat bacon, and rub the warts with it nine times. Then bury it under a stone, or, better still, in an ant heap (*Heref.* " oonty tump ") ; as it decays the warts disappear ; perfect secrecy must be observed. Pieces of bread from a newly-baked loaf, equal in number to the warts, are also supposed to cure if buried secretly.

Wens.

Wens in the neck are said to be cured by the application of a dead man's hand. I have been assured of the efficacy of this remedy, in actual use at Weobley Marsh within living memory. Duncumb says it should be the hand of a malefactor, imme-diately after execution.[1] A number of persons, he says, attended the gallows on this occasion, in order to make trial of this strange experiment, which suggests sympathetic magic, the neck being the affected part in the case of the one executed, and of the patient.

At Weobley, even nowadays, they catch a live mole, make its nose bleed, and cross the wen nine times with a finger dipped in the blood ; then the mole is allowed to go, and should take the wen away with it. Or the mole may be cut in halves, applied to the wen all night, and buried afterwards ; as it decays the wen should disappear. A woman at King's Pyon, when doctor's ointment and mole's blood had failed, cured her wen thus :—" You get somebody to give you nine hairs from a stallion's tail ; you must not say ' thank you,' nor pay. Fasten them in a little bag in a little plait and wear it round your neck till the bag wears out."

---

[1] i., 208.

An inmate of Leominster Workhouse was equally successful in the use of a Good Friday bun. He cut it in halves, dipped them in hot water, and applied them as a poultice, tied round his neck; he afterwards buried the bun carefully, and as it mouldered the wen disappeared.

SECTION VIII.

GENERAL SUPERSTITIOUS BELIEFS AND PRACTICES.

There are little sayings about good and bad luck in almost everything that happens fortuitously, and these, however foolish, are still firmly believed in. The dropping of a knife is a sign of a visitor ; a coming stranger may also be announced by a smoky film hanging on the bar of the grate, or by the lid of the teapot being left open, or by a bumble-bee coming in though the window. If you go to see a neighbour and find that she is poking the fire as you enter, it is a sign that you are not welcome. She may pretend to be glad to see you, " but that's no difference."[1] If, when dressing, a woman put her stocking on wrong side out it is for luck ; but if she turn it the luck will change. If her petticoat be accidentally put on wrong side out, she will get a letter. A present must not be returned to the giver, it causes quarrelling. If a rhyme be made in talking, without intention, it is a sign that the speaker will have a present before the end of the month. It is very unlucky to say " thank you " for a pin.

With regard to service, it is unlucky to go to a new place on a Saturday. It was the custom to place a broom on the floor if a maid servant came to seek a situation ; if she picked it up, she would be engaged ; if not, she was sent going promptly. It is said that if the handle come off the broom when sweeping, the servant will not get her wages.

There are several traces of reverence for fire and salt ; a box of coal and a plate of salt should be the first things taken into an empty house, before moving any furniture.[2] At Eastnor, people leaving a house were warned that they must leave bread and salt behind them ; if this were not done it would mean ill-luck for those leaving, and for the next tenants. In addition to the common belief that it is unluckly to spill salt, and that evil may be prevented by throwing a little over one's left shoulder, it is held unlucky to borrow salt. It may be begged, or if a neighbour will not give it she may come to the borrower's house and fetch the quantity borrowed ; but the borrower must not return it.[3] The same prohibition applies to fire, only it must not be transferred at all, not even from room to room.[4] One must on no account help a person to salt. " Help me to salt, help me to sorrow " is the old saying. Less than a hundred years ago, in Herefordshire farmhouses, it was still customary to have one large salt-cellar on the table ; the master and his family sat above the salt, the maidservants and

---

1] Withington. 2] King's Pyon. 3] Weobley and Bromyard. 4] *See* Section ix., *infra.*

SIR EDWARD HARLEY'S "BERILL."

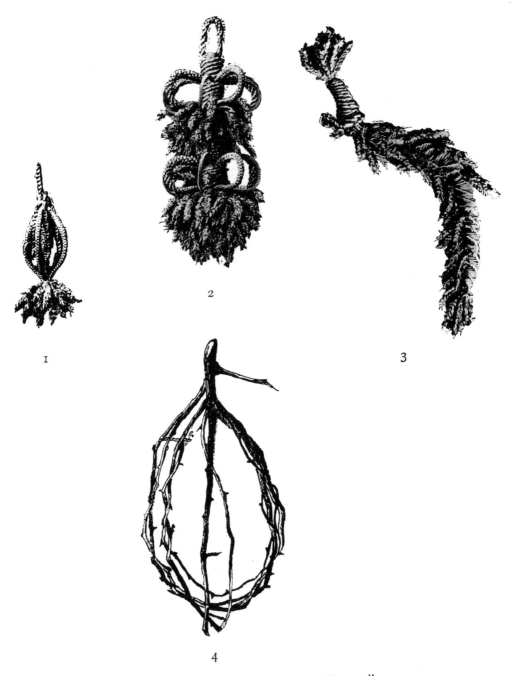

I, 2 AND 3, WHEAT-PLAITS, MADE FROM THE "MARE."
(*See page* 104.)
4, "A BUSH," BURNT ON NEW YEAR'S MORNING.

men below it.   There were formerly several young men living indoors at each farm, a system now practically abolished.

If the fire burn on the one side of the grate only, it is a sign of a wedding.   If a servant be trying to light a fire and it will not burn, she will frequently say " Oh dear, my young man's in a temper !"   If by chance the fireirons are all at one end of the fender it is a sign of a quarrel.   Crossed knives also foreshadow quarrelling, or a " row in the house."   It is unlucky to burn three candles in a room ; four, or two, but not three.   If a pair of scissors be dropped on the floor they should be closed before picking them up.   When a comb has been dropped I have seen girls carefully tread on it before picking it up, but they could give no reason, except that it would be unlucky not to do so.   It is " dreadful bad luck, " Weobley folk say, to put a pair of bellows on the table, or a pair of boots.   It seems strange that anyone would think of the table as a place for boots, but the superstition has often been mentioned to me, and some even say that it is a sign of death.   If two people wash in the same water they will quarrel unless a cross be made on the water beforehand ; this is done with the finger. Two persons, more especially if they are sisters, must not pass soap from hand to hand ; it should be put down by the first, so that the other can take it up.   It is unlucky for two persons to get over a stile together ; perhaps merely because Herefordshire stiles are ill-adapted for trying this experiment.   It is equally undesirable to meet or pass a person on the stairs.   If starting on a journey it is very unlucky to turn back ; should anything be forgotten it is better to sit down and try and think of it ; if it be something left behind, one may be gravely told still that it would be better to go on without it if possible, to avoid retracing one's steps.   It is very unlucky to stand and watch out of sight a person who is going away from home.   At Hay they say it is unlucky to pay the whole amount of a doctor's bill ; anyone who does so is likely to require his services again soon, and therefore a small sum, if only a shilling, is sometimes left unpaid.   Gypsies, on the contrary, believe that medicine does no good until paid for. In the Kington district there is great reluctance to enter a new house, as the first person to live in it will probably soon die.[1]   Certain houses and shops are held to be lucky, and unlucky.   It is very unlucky to point at a rainbow.[2]

Although at Weobley and at Pembridge they say it is a sign of a stranger coming if the lid of the teapot be accidentally left open, at Orcop it is held very unlucky to forget to close it.   In addition to the usual saying that there will be seven years bad luck for the breaker of a looking-glass, it is held unlucky to place a mirror in water. When servants break glass or china I have frequently seen them carry out two broken pieces and smash them.   They think if they break one thing they must break three,

1] C.G.P.   2] Monkland and Leominster. *See ante* i., 9.

so in this way they hope to avert further disaster. The ill-luck supposed to follow a passage beneath a ladder may be averted by crossing the fingers and thumbs.

Of superstitious beliefs concerning the person, we have the usual rhymes about " gifts " on the fingers nails, and sneezing. Also Duncumb says " nails are supposed to be cut with greater propriety on Monday than any other day.[1] Near Weobley they say " Never cut your nails on a Sunday, for that is the day on which the devil cuts his." In the Golden Valley it is just " bad luck " :—

> " He that on the Sabbath Morn
> Cutteth either hair or horn
> Will rue the day that he was born."[2]

Hair should never be left lying about, but carefully and immediately burnt, lest the birds take it to line their nests ; this will give the original owner a headache. It is very unlucky to cut off human hair after death to keep. In burning hair, they say, if it smoulders, the owner's life will be short, but if it blaze brightly it will be long. An old lady, ninety-six years of age, living in Ledbury Workhouse, used to say she expected a visitor when her eyebrows itched. Irritation of the soles of the feet is said to mean that their owner will soon tread strange ground. When babies smile in their sleep it is said that they see angels. There is a saying about the rearing of infants :—

> " Keep the feet warm and the head cold,
> They'll live to grow old."

It is said that if a maid kneading up bread rub her " doughy" hand over a boy's face, he will never have any whiskers. The belief seems to have been general in the county, for it is still known at Withington, and at Blakemere, in quite another district. Bread must not be cut with a knife while the next baking is in the oven, though it may be broken. No exact reason is given, it is " unlucky."

If a girl have toothache they say " she don't love true."

I am informed by Mr. T. Galliers, of Kings Pyon, that he remembers in his boyhood seeing that the older farm labourers always poured a little cider on the ground when drinking in the fields. He asked why, and was told " That is a donation for the gods." I thought the word an unlikely one for ignorant labourers of that day to use, but my informant assured me that was exactly what they said, and spoke of the love of the peasantry for long words of which they could scarcely understand the meaning ; " libation " was probably the word they meant to use.

1] i., 208. 2] Communicated by Mrs. Powell.

Aubrey relates how " in Herefordshire and other parts they do put a cold iron bar across their barrels to preserve their beer from being soured by thunder."[1] I cannot hear of this having been done in our own time, but there is very little home-brewed ale made now.

" No murderer can sail the sea, for the ship will sink," said an old man at Walterstone. " That's the auld sayin', but I dunna believe it meself ! "

An old inhabitant of Norton Canon, who had been ill-treated by his children, said he would curse them, but he did not like to do such a thing. " I believe," he said, " as anyone can put a blessing or a curse on when they are dying, especially a father on his children."

If visitors come on Monday it is said the house will be full all the week. It is lucky to receive money on a Monday morning, and means money coming in all the week.

A very curious practice, savouring of superstition, was described to me by the Vicar of Almeley, the Rev. Hyett Warner. In 1908 some London children were visiting Almeley for a summer holiday ; they were sent by a charity organisation and boarded out under the vicar's superintendence. When he asked a woman who had taken charge of two children if they seemed happy and comfortable, she said, " Oh yes, sir, and they ought to be ; I put a prayer book under their pillows every night, and holds the lantern over their heads while they say their prayers."

The poor will not say " thank you " for clothes which belonged to anyone that has died. They believe that they will soon become rotten.[2]

Aubrey has a casual reference to the " winnowers of Herefordshire," which seems to mean that they believed they could summon a wind by whistling to blow the chaff out of the wheat.

By whistling they call for winds. Sc. [scilicet, to wit], the winnowers in Herefordshire.[3]

In the counties of Brecon and Hereford it is thought most lucky to find " frog-stones," rough yellowish stones usually found near lakes, resembling frogs in colour and shape. I am indebted to Mr. Portman for this information ; he has three such stones in his possession ; in one the likeness to a frog is wonderfully good.

1] *Miscellanies*, 1696, p. 111. *Remaines*, 22. 2] Thruxton, Kingstone.—R.H.B. 3] *Remaines*, 195. *Cf.*, Lees, *Pictures of Nature*, 296. " In several places, particularly on Malverne Hills, in *Worcestershire*, when people fan their corn, and want wind, they cry, ' Youl ! Youl ! Youl !' to invoke it." Lees suggests that as " Yule-tide " means the turn of the year, so " Youl " referred to a turn or change from calm to breeze.

SECTION IX.

THE YEAR: FESTIVALS AND SEASONS.

(1) New Year's Day and Plough Monday.

Letting the New Year in.

As the clock struck twelve, it was customary to open the back door first, to let the old year out; then, the front door was opened, to let the New Year in.[1] At Bromyard, they said a funeral service over "Old Tom."[2] It was, and is, considered very unlucky for a woman to enter the house first on New Year's Day. This prejudice is mentioned by Fosbroke, who says that on New Year's Day a woman would not enter a house without first enquiring if a man had been there that day.[3]

The New Year Quête.

Fosbroke[4] says that on this day "the peasantry send about a small pyramid, made of leaves, apples, nuts, &c., "gilt."" There is no trace of this custom at the present time, except that the oldest people remember carrying round apples, or turnips, stuck with oats, and then floured, "to make them look pretty." These were used to decorate the houses, and also carried round when carol singing, or, as it is called, "New Year's giftin'," and they were supposed to bring luck. The custom is mentioned in Bull's *Herefordshire Pomona*, i., 58.

The following ditty is usually sung by the children in search of pence:—

I wish you a merry Christmas
  And a happy New Year,
A pocket full of money,
  And a cellar full of beer;
A good fat pig
  That will last you all the year;
I wish you a merry Christmas
  And a happy New Year.

The cock flew up in the yew tree,
  The hen came chuckling by;
If you haven't got any money,
  Please to give me a mince pie—
A mince-pie this New Year.

The roads are very dirty,
  My shoes are very thin,
I've got a little pocket
  I can pop a penny in.
May God bless all friends dear.

I wish you a merry Christmas,
  And a happy New Year.
A lump of cake
  And a barrel of beer.
Christmas comes but once a year;
  When it comes it brings good cheer.
Cheer up, cheer up, this New Year.

1] Ledbury. 2] *Antiquary*, 1873, iii., 7. 3] *Ariconensia* 73; *cf*. Christmas Day, *infra*. 4] *Loc. cit.* This is the Welsh "apple gift," *cf*. Sikes, 253. Writing in 1880, he says :—"In every town or village you will encounter children on New Year's Day. . . bearing an apple or an orange curiously tricked out. Three sticks in the form of a tripod are thrust into it to serve as a nest; its sides are smeared with flour or meal and stuck over with oats or wheat." See the drawing of one in *Report of International Folk-Lore Congress*, 1891.

Cream of the Well.

It was formerly the custom in Herefordshire farmhouses for the servants to sit up to see the New Year in, and at midnight to rush for the " cream o' the well," the first water drawn from the well in the year, which was thought to be beautifying and lucky. The maid who succeeded in getting it would take it to the bedroom of her mistress, who would give a present for it. " My missus always had the cream o' the well to wash in on New Year's morning," said Mrs. M——, " and she always put a shilling under the basin for me, too."[1]

The water of holy wells was held to possess additional virtues if drawn at this time. Duncumb says of one at Dinedor :—

A well in this parish excites much emulation on New Year's Day, in a contest for the first pailful of water, which is termed the cream of the well, and is presented to some neighbour as a mark of respect, and a pledge of good fortune ; a pecuniary compliment is expected in return.[2]

Antiquatis describes the same custom at Bromyard :—

A rush is made at twelve o'clock to the nearest spring of water, and whoever is fortunate enough to bring in the cream of the well, as it is termed, and those who first taste of it, have prospect of good luck during the coming year.[3]

No work was done on New Year's Day, and if a man were found working, he would be placed on a ladder and carried round the parish by the holiday makers, who would call with their burden at the farmhouses, where cider would be given to them. It was, and indeed still is, held very unlucky to " gear " the horses on this day. A resident in the parish of Monkland tried a few years ago to hire a horse and cart. The first farmer applied to said he would not put a horse in a cart on that day for anything ; his neighbours did not give any superstitious reason, but made other excuses, and a cart could not be obtained, although urgently needed.

For superstitions concerning boots and leather, *see* Christmas Day, *infra*.

Burning the Bush.

This custom was generally kept up all over Herefordshire until about forty years ago, and survives here and there, in the Leominster and Kington districts. The " Bush " (*see illustration*) is a globe made of hawthorn, which is hung up in the kitchen of the farmhouse, with the mistletoe, after the bush-burning ceremony each New Year's morning ; it hangs there till the day comes round again, when it is taken

---

1] Weobley. 2] Duncumb, i., 206. 3] *Herefordshire Gatherer*, 1879.

out to be burnt, and a new one is made.[1] Mistletoe is never brought into the house before New Year's Day ; to do so would be most unlucky.

At five o'clock in the morning the workmen fetch the old " bush." At Birley Court, near Leominster, the servants, being strangers, objected to the early hour, and suggested that the men should fetch the bush overnight ; this plan was evidently not at all acceptable, though the men did not explain what might happen if the kitchen were left a night without a bush. It is carried to the earliest sown wheat field, where a large fire is lighted, of straw and bushes, in which it is burnt. While it is burning, a new one is made ; in making it, the ends of the branches are scorched in the fire. An old man, who had lived all his life in the Pembridge district, told me that at Shobdon, in his time, they poured cider over it afterwards, " to varnish and darken the bush like," he said ; but the practice strongly suggests a survival of primitive ritual.

At Birley Court, there is a difference I have not heard of elsewhere. They make two globes of bushes, " one for the Master, and one for the eldest born " (child ?) ; sometimes one globe is quite small, and placed inside the other and larger one. One of the men, taking some of the burning straw on a fork, runs with it across twelve ridges, dropping a little on each ridge.

At Brinsop, the old bush was filled with straw, and carried burning over the ridges ; it was said that evil spirits could be caught in it and destroyed thus between 12 p.m. on December 31st and 6 a.m. on New Year's morning. This method would seem to be the older and original one. If the fire should go out before the twelfth ridge is reached, it is considered a bad omen for the crop. Another way is to take a bundle of straw, light a handful in the fire, another handful from this, and so on to the twelfth ridge. Then the men stand in a ring round the fire and " holloa auld cider." They sing on one very deep note, very slowly, holding each syllable as long as possible, " Auld—Ci—der." The " der " becomes a sort of growl at the end, and is an octave below the first two notes ; it has a weird dirge-like effect. This is repeated thrice, bowing low as possible as each note is sung, nine bows altogether.[2] Then follows cheering and drinking, cider and cake being provided for the purpose. At Birley the men afterwards march round the fire singing a Christmas carol. They say the bush represents our Lord's crown of thorns, and that when they run across the ridges with the fire, they are driving away the " old

---

1] *See Folk-Lore*, xi., 489 ; xii., 349 (from *Chambers' Med. Stage*, i., 251). *Cf.* Section ii. For parallel customs, *see Frazer*, i., 225 and ii., 6.
2] At Hill Court, Ross, in 1860, they sang " Auld cider for ever, as plenty as water ! "

un." It was formerly firmly believed that without this ceremony there could be no crops ; its object would thus seem to be both fertilising and purificatory. They say at Brinsop that it prevents the wheel getting the " smut," which is a disease that eats away the ears of corn, and derives its name from the black smutty appearance it gives to the wheat.

The globular shape of the thorn, and the fact that the house was not to be left at night without it, suggest that it was a sun charm, and a protection from fire and from lightning.

(2) TWELFTH NIGHT.

On this night it was customary in all parts of the county to light fires in the wheat-fields. The custom, called locally " wassailing," was thus described in the *Gentleman's Magazine* (1791) :—

At the approach of evening, on the vigil of Twelfth Day, the farmers, with their friends and servants, meet together, and about six o'clock walk out to a field where wheat is growing. In the highest part of the ground, twelve small fires and one large one, are lighted up. The attendants, headed by the master of the family, pledge the company freely in old cider, which circulates freely on these occasions. A circle is formed round the large fire, when a general shout and hallooing takes place, which you hear answered from all the adjacent villages and fields. Sometimes fifty or sixty of these fires may be all seen at once. This being finished, the company return home, where the housewife and her maids are preparing a good supper. A large cake is always provided, with a hole in the middle. After supper, the company all attend the bailiff (or head of the oxen), to the wainhouse, where the following particulars are observed. The master, at the head of his friends, fills the cup (generally of strong ale), and stands opposite the first or finest of the oxen. He then pledges him in a curious toast ; the company follow his example with all the other oxen, addressing each by his name. This being finished, a large cake is produced, and with much ceremony put on the horn of the first ox, through the hole above mentioned. The ox is then tickled to make him toss his head. If he throw the cake behind, it is then the mistress's perquisite ; if before (in what is termed the boosy) the bailiff himself claimed the prize. The company then return to the house, the doors of which they find locked, nor will they be opened till some joyous songs are sung. On their gaining admittance a scene of mirth and jollity ensues, and which lasts the greater part of the night.

The above was contributed by one J—— W——, possibly the same correspondent who wrote a fuller and more particular account of the ceremony for the *Gentleman's Magazine,* over the same initials in 1820 :—

As I have many years been an attendant of these social and hospitable meetings, permit me to offer to your readers some particulars of this ceremony as I have seen it kept up, with all due form, on the farm of Huntington, two miles west from Hereford, that for many years was occupied by my respectable friend and neighbour, Mr. Samuel Tully. . . . On the eve of Twelfth Day (the Epiphany), Mr. Tully and his numerous visitors near, the hour of six o'clock in the evening, walked to a field where wheat was growing, and on the highest parts of the land one large and twelve smaller fires were lighted up. While burning, the master and some of his company formed in a circle round the large fire, and after pledging each other in good Herefordshire cider, all the attendants joined in shouting and rejoicing. On the fires being extinguished, the company all returned to the hospitable mansion, where an excellent and plentiful supper was provided for the family, and all ranks of visitors. After the glass had circulated, and some songs had been sung, and happiness diffused through all the numerous company near the hour of nine or ten o'clock, a second procession was formed by all who joined in the concluding and more interesting ceremony. On coming to the outhouse where the oxen and cows were in their stalls, the bailiff attended with a large plum cake, which, when made, had a hole in the middle. Previous to its being placed on the horn of the ox, the master and his friends each took a small cup filled with ale, and drank a toast to each ox, in nearly the following words (each of the twenty-four oxen having a name). The master began the first :—

> " Here's to thee Benbow, and to thy white horn,
> God send thy master a good crop of corn ;
> Oh wheat, rye, and barley, and all sorts of grain ;
> You eat your oats, I'll drink my beer,
> May the Lord send us a happy new year."

After the last ox was toasted, the bailiff placed the cake on the horn of the first ox, the boy touching him with a pointed goad. This induced the ox to shake his head, when the cake was tossed on either side ; if on one side, it was to be the perquisite of the bailiff, who divided it amongst the company. On returning to the house, mirth and feasting prevailed till a late, or rather an early hour. The Harvest Supper is frequently celebrated at this time. Much of the ceremony is now omitted. The twelve fires are frequently made, and concluded by a social evening. I have lately, near six o'clock in the evening of Wassailing, from our public walk, seen numerous fires on the hills around, particularly on the camps of Aconbury, Dynedor, Credenhill, &c.[1]

The above accounts of the custom are correct in every detail, as it has been frequently described to me by those still living who took part in it ; it was believed to have had a beneficial effect on the crops.[2]

Fosbroke supplies additional details of the Twelfth Night merry-making :— "The ceremony being finished, the door of the beast-house is fastened, and every spectator obliged to sing before he is allowed to depart. Upon quitting the beast-house, which must be done without the assistance of a candle, the ingenuity of the maids asserts itself in devising how to put tricks on the company, such as setting pails of water to tumble into, together with many other feats of equal pleasantry."[3]

At Kingstone, the central fire was made of straw tied round a pole, and was called " Old Meg."[4]

There are several different explanations of the meaning of the fires. One writer says " The fire representing Judas Iscariot, after being allowed to burn for a brief time, was kicked about and put out." Another says : " On Twelfth Day they make twelve fires of straw and one large one to burn the old witch ; they sing, drink,

---

1] *Gentleman's Magazine Library, Popular Superstitions,* 19.   2] For other descriptions of the custom, see Havergal, *Words and Phrases,* 48 ; *Herefordshire Gatherer,* May, 1879 ; Blount, *Ancient Tenures,* 1815 ed.   3] The Wye Tour.   4] R.H.B.

and dance round it ; without this festival they think they should have no crop."[1]
Yet another account agrees with that of those now living who remember the custom :—
" The fires were made in a circle ; one, round a pole, they call the Virgin Mary ; the
others, the Twelve Apostles. Cider was dashed on the ox to make him throw off the
cake. If it fell forward it was a good omen for the harvest ; if backward, the reverse."[2]
Antiquatis, writing in 1879, says that a number of flat cakes were made, each with
a hole in the middle, only one was used for each ox first, all the cows being toasted
afterwards. If the majority of the animals threw the cakes forward, it was an augury
of a good harvest ; if backward, a bad one.[3] I have never heard of more than one
cake being made. *Antiquatis* gives no authority, but the more elaborate custom
may have been the original one. Or, as one old man said about variations in the
method of burning the bush, " Different folk has their own ways."

A special toast for this occasion, given by a farmer's wife, was printed some
years ago in *Notes and Queries* (*2nd Series*, viii., 488) :—

> Fill your cups my merry men all,
> For here's the best ox in the stall,
> Oh, he is the best ox, of that there's no mistake,
> And so let us crown him with the Twelfth cake.

Sometimes the cake was placed on a heifer's horn, and then the verse ran :—

> Here's health to the heifer, (or Darling),
> And to the white teat,
> Wishing the Mistress a house full of meat.
> With cruds (*sic*), milk, and butter, fresh every day,
> And God grant the young men keep out'n her way.[4]

The oxen were used in those days for working in the fields ; every one had a
name, which was called as each was toasted. This night, say the old folks, was the
" real Christmas." " My grandfather always kept up Christmas on old Christmas
day," said W—— P——, of Peterchurch, " none of your new Christmas for him ;
it must be the real Christmas, too, for the Holy Thorn blossoms, and the cattle go
down on their knees at twelve o'clock in remembrance." I have talked to many
people who firmly believed this ; though they have not seen it, their parents or grand-
parents have. Mrs. H——, of Eardisley, said that her father, who used to live at Peterchurch, had seen it, and the cattle did not only kneel down, but the tears ran down
their cheeks. In Weobley they say that it is only three-year-old oxen that kneel,

1] *Notes and Queries, Second Series*, viii., 488 ; Fosbroke, *Ariconensia*, 74.   2] A newspaper cutting (no date),
from the collection of Mr. H. C. Beddoe.   3] *Herefordshire Gatherer, loc. cit.*   4] Havergal, *loc. cit.*

not those only two years old ; but at Kingstone the Vicar was told that it was done only by the seven-year-old oxen, the same age as those in the stable at Bethlehem when Christ was born.[1]

(3) ST. VALENTINE'S DAY.

The custom of sending valentines is dying, but not yet extinct. I can find no trace to-day of the pretty practice described by Hone thus :—

Children go about in procession, dressed up in wreaths and ribbons given them at the principal house in the parish, saying :—

"Good morrow to you, Valentine,
Curl your locks as I do mine,
Two before and three behind,
Good morrow to you, Valentine."

This was said to the leader more gaily dressed than the others, and repeated under the houses of the people as they passed, the inhabitants seldom refusing a mite.[2]

The first man a woman sees on St. Valentine's Day is her Valentine. In 1678 a Mrs. Jeffries, of Hereford, made this entry in her diary :—

"Gave Tom Aston for being my Valentine, 2s."
"Gave Mr. Dick Gravel for coming to be my Valentine, 1s."[3]

Mr. Dick Gravel seems to have been too late, but received a consolation prize.

(4) SHROVE TUESDAY.

At Leominster a bell called the pancake bell was rung as a signal for the folk to commence frying their pancakes.[4] "Pancake bell" is also remembered at Ross.

At Kington the day was observed by the practice of the cruel sport of cock-fighting, described as formerly one of the chief amusements of the tradespeople of the town :—

At this period, and at Easter Monday, in company with the lower orders of the people, they assembled in great numbers in the fields in the forenoon, to witness the barbarous practice ; in the evenings, according to an old author, "men ate and drank or abandoned themselves to every kind of sportive foolery." Men paraded the town on this day with fire engines, the water going into the dwellings and on the heads of the passers by. In the evening the boys assembled in large parties, paying rude visits to the houses of the townspeople, demanding ale and cider.[5]

(5) MID-LENT OR MOTHERING SUNDAY.

The pretty custom of going a-mothering on Mid-Lent Sunday was generally kept up until a few years ago by the country people, and is now by no means forgotten,

1] R.H.B. 2] Hone, *Year Book* (1838), 201 ; *Herefordshire Gatherer*, Aug. 2, 1879. 3] *Herefordshire Gatherer loc. cit.*, from *Archæologia*, xxxviii. 4] It was originally a bell to announce that the priest was ready to shrive his flock, in preparation for Lent ; see Tyack, 166. 5] Parry, *Hist. Kington*, 199.

but declining. The confectioners' shops in Hereford are well stocked with Simnel cakes during Lent ; they have an inscription in sugar icing, " For my dear Mother," or " Mother." Formerly these cakes were always made by the donors.[1]

(6) Palm Sunday.

Palm Sunday has been until lately observed at Hentland, as it still is at Sellack, by the distribution of Pax Cakes or buns in Church, after the morning service.

The minister and congregation receive from the churchwardens a cake or bun, and formerly a cup of beer was added also. This is consumed within the church, and is supposed to imply a desire on the part of those who partake of it to forgive and forget all animosities, and thus prepare themselves for the festival of Easter.

A description of the ceremony from the *Hereford Journal*, March 30th, 1907, is given below ; the writer seems to have gathered his information from the people of the parish. Since all documentary evidence of the foundation of the charity has perished, his " probably five hundred years " of age ascribed to it must be a mere guess. I would suggest that, as in the case of the Simnel Cakes provided by David de Aquablanca, the donor only provided means for the perpetuation of a custom of great antiquity.

The simple Sunday morning service had just closed with the Benediction in the little church of St. Teseliachus, in the scattered but picturesque village of Sellack, which lies in the Wye Valley just above the point where the beauties of the English Rhine begin to unfold themselves at an ever-increasing rate. Though only early spring, the sun was shining with noontide summer glory, casting shafts of light through the mullioned windows athwart the reading desk, where half an hour before the Vicar had made what to the stranger seemed a curious announcement : " The Pax cakes will be distributed at the end of the service." A strange silence pervaded the congregation, which numbered perhaps seventy-five souls, a silence pregnant with expectant curiosity as to the ceremony immediately to follow.

Then the churchwardens, who had just taken up a collection (without which no religious service seems complete nowadays), produced from some corner unknown to the writer two baskets of cakes, daintily covered with immaculate white cloths. From these baskets they distributed to each member of the congregation a cake, the advent of which among the juveniles created not a little excitement, leading to a quick partial disappearance of some of the toothsome morsels. It was a strange sight to see everyone in church with a bun, and still more curious to see the ladies filing out with their Prayer Books surmounted by one of these confections. The male members of the congregation, missing the humour or solemnity of the occasion, pocketed their buns and walked out with the utmost *sang froid*. . . .

A comparatively few years ago the ceremony would not have ended here. The congregation would have been regaled with beer in accordance with the wishes of their unknown benefactor, a proceeding which seems to us in these days to flavour of desecration. But eventually the time came when the money was

---

1] For a full account of this custom see *Folk-Lore* iv., 167 ; *Notes and Queries*, 4th Series, v., 239. *Cf.* also *Archives of Hereford Cathedral*, edited by the Rev. Canon Capes ; Bishop Ffoliot (*circa* 1174) confirms a gift of tithes by David de Aquablanca, canon, to provide Simnel Cakes for yearly distribution.

insufficient—through the fall in the value of the coin of the realm—to provide the ale ; then the farmers of the district each brought a bottle of home-brewed beer or cider so as to keep up the custom ! These little touches of life in bygone days are still preserved in the folk-lore of the locality.

For the origin of this extraordinary custom of giving away Pax cakes we have to go back to practically the Middle Ages, for it is perhaps the oldest of the many quaint ceremonies now practised in Herefordshire, or indeed in the West Country. For probably five hundred years it has been observed annually on Palm Sunday, and though its age shrouds its establishment in a charming mysticism, its meaning has been pre-served unimpaired through the ages.

Pax cakes, as their name implies, are an emblem of peace, and were instituted by their author as a means of reconciliation between personal enemies. Friends who have become estranged by a petty quarrel or otherwise are invited to share their cakes and let bygones be bygones. How many old sores have been healed in the locality these hundreds of years it is impossible to tell, for history fails to record them, but well within living memory of the inhabitants of Sellack they have been the means of settling bitter feuds, notably between two sisters just before one of them passed away. Palm Sunday, the first day of Holy Week, seems a particularly appropriate time for the settlement of disputes in this quaint way, for a few days hence the friendly covenant between the erstwhile enemies may be ratified at what is regarded as the holiest of all Church observances, the Easter-morn Communion. The date of the origin of the Pax cakes is unknown.

Those who remember the custom at Hentland say that the clergyman broke his cake with two or three principal parishioners, and the rest of the congregation with each other, saying as they did so, " Peace and good neighbourhood," or " Peace and good will."[1] This feature of the ceremony is not mentioned by the correspondent of the *Hereford Journal*, and is probably now forgotten at Sellack.

For a survival of the mediæval *Fête de l'âne* at Hereford, *see* Section xi., 3.

The branches of the round leaved sallow are still called " palm " in Hereford-shire, in remembrance of the time when it was carried in the churches instead of real palm, representing the branches strewed before Christ.

(7) GOOD FRIDAY.

To work a team of horses on Good Friday brings " terrible bad luck."[2]

For Good Friday bread, *see Leechcraft, ante*, Section vii.

(8) APRIL. ALL FOOLS' DAY.

Anyone may be made an April fool before noon. If successful in making a " fool " the children say :—

> " April fool
> Go to school
> And learn better manners."

1] *See* Section xii., 6. This was a favourite inscription on Herefordshire bells.   2] C.G.P.

A boy would often be told to go to a chemist and ask for " strap oil," or to a farm house for " a penn'orth of pigeons' milk."

(9) EASTER.

In April, 1906, a correspondent of the *Hereford Times*, signing herself " L.T.," wrote saying that in her opinion the sun had actually danced on Easter Sunday morning that year. She had heard it would do so as it rose, but had not believed until she had " really seen it."

Some new article of dress, however small, should be provided for Easter Sunday. It is unlucky to forget about this. The proper dishes for the day are roast lamb or veal and cheesecakes, also mince-pies made with the last of the mince-meat, carefully reserved for the purpose at Christmas time. The church at Kington was formerly decorated with box at this season instead of the spring flowers now generally used. Graves are decorated with spring flowers for Easter Sunday, in most parts of Herefordshire; but in Ewyas Harold and Newton-in-Clodock this is done on Palm Sunday.

Corn-Showing.

The last surviving custom connected with Easter Day was corn-showing; it was kept up at Henwood and Dilwyn until about twenty years ago. On the afternoon of Easter Sunday the bailiff, the men, and their families went to the wheat field, armed, as in all these ceremonies in Herefordshire, with plum cake and old cider. This was eaten in the field, and then the party joined hands and marched across it repeating :

" Every step a reap, every reap a sheaf,
    And God send the master a good harvest."

The custom was not general in the Weobley district within living memory. But nearer to the Welsh border, in the Golden Valley, it is well remembered, and Mr. H. H. Wood, of the White House, has kindly described it for me, as he knew it :—

" It was the custom at Lulham, in the parish of Madley, and also at White House, St. Margaret's, for the bailiff to proceed on the afternoon of Easter Sunday to a wheat field on the farm. Plum cake was provided, and cider in wooden bottles, and consumed by the families of the workmen, and any neighbours who chose to attend. A small piece of cake was buried in the nearest part of the field, and then, a little cider being poured on it, they wished the master a good crop. The custom was discontinued about thirty years ago, when owing to the importation of the wheat from abroad, the crop had no longer so much importance, and also it gave rise to a noisy assemblage on Easter Sunday."

The custom was not confined to wheatfields, however. The late Rector of Dorstone, the Rev. T. P. Powell, who had lived all his life in the district, remembered that when he was a boy he saw cake and cider buried in the orchards. A native of Peterchurch has told me how she remembered seeing it done fifty years ago in an orchard there. The burying of the cake is not remembered now in any part of the county except in the Golden Valley.

According to Fosbroke the object of corn-showing was to weed cockle from the wheat. One hears nothing of this nowadays :—" At Easter," he says, " the rustics have a custom called corn-showing. Parties are made to pick out cockle from the wheat. Before they set out they take with them cake and cider, and, says my informant, *a yard of toasted cheese.* The first person who picks the first cockle from the wheat has the first kiss of the maid and the first slice of the cake.''[1] At Kington, Easter Sunday was called " cake Sunday." Parties of young girls went about to the houses and were regaled with cake, hence the name. My informant remembered this about forty years ago.

Hoving.

Easter Monday and Tuesday were called heaving Monday and Tuesday because on those days they would go round hoving. On Monday they would hove the women. A party would go round to the farm houses and cottages, the youngest wench carrying a bunch of flowers ; entering the house a party would sing " Jesus Christ is risen again." They would then seize the women one by one, and putting them in chairs, turn them round while the girl with flowers would dip the latter in a basin of water and sprinkle with them the women's feet. On Tuesday the men were hove. The custom, however, degenerated. into wickedness, and is now discontinued.[2]

(10) MAY DAY AND OAK APPLE DAY.

Maypoles are so generally recollected that I think they were probably erected on every village green, but not always on May 1st (*see* May 29). Sixty years ago, in Weobley, the children made a sort of bower or arch of marsh marigolds and other flowers, which they carried between them. They went round the village singing, accompanied by a fiddle and a drum and any other musical instruments available. They sang :—

> " May day, pay day,
>   Pack your rags away
>   Bu——oys ! " (boys).

The bower was often dropped and forgotten in a scramble for pence.

At Kingsland the children still go round with a may-pole ; it is a birch tree decked with ribbons, and they sing or shout :—

1] *Ariconensia*, 73.

2] Havergal, *Words and Phrases*, 47. Locality not given. For a full account of the custom in Shropshire, *see* Burne, 336–340.

A HEREFORDSHIRE CARTER IN HIS SMOCK.

THE FUNERAL STONE, BRILLEY.

" Hip-pip-hoo-ray,
It is May Day."

They expect coppers from each house visited.

At Bromyard the first of May was the " Mop," or " hiring Fair " ; there was birch over each house door, and the lads and lasses went about with it in their hats. The old inhabitants say " but May 29 was the *real* May Day in Bromyard."

" Nonagenarian," writing about May-day in 1879, states that her memory is fresh about events which happened 87 years before :—

" Ah, they may say Hereford is an altered place, there is nothing going on now like there was when I was little. We used to go every May-day to Broomy Hill, and dance round the May-pole, and play at stool-ball and have cake and cider, and the milk women used to dance with the milk pails on their heads. They used to dress the pails with all sorts of beautiful silver things which they borrowed, and they used to shine in the sun as the women danced. So the spoons, the cream jugs, and all these things used to make music along with the fiddle. Oh, there was some pleasure then for young and old, rich and poor, for every one who could used to go a-maying."[1]

Mrs. H——, an inmate of Trinity Almshouses, Hereford, remembered a sweeps' holiday, on May-day. They had sports on " Sweeps' Green," Broomy Hill. " They took their brooms and made merry," she said. She also remembered the Butchers' holiday, on Widemarsh Common, but could not tell what day it was.[2]

Duncumb thus describes May-day in Herefordshire a hundred years ago :—

On the first of May, the juvenile part of both sexes rise early in the morning, and supply themselves with green branches of trees ; returning, the boughs are placed against the doors and houses and are kept there during the remainder of the day. The birch tree, being early in vegetation, is invariably chosen in this county for the first of May, and on Ascension Day the elm.[3]

May fairs are still kept up, and generally well attended, but they are not the landmarks in country life that they used to be. Formerly, all farmers' servants of all sexes stood to be hired at the fairs. Each man had to carry his clean Sunday smock on his arm, to show that he possessed one, or no good master would engage him. It was usual to give a shilling as " earnest money." This engagement, in the case of indoor servants, lasted till the next May, and there existed on both sides a great aversion to " breaking the twelvemonth " ; mistress and maid would always try to endure

---

1] *Hereford Times*, April 15, 1876.
2] *Cf.* Section xi., 3, *Corpus Christi.* Mr. Chambers, (*Med. Stage,* i., 125), conjectures that the curious tradition which makes May-day the sweep's holiday may be connected with fire or heat charms.
3] Duncumb, i., 209 ; *cf.* Section ii., *ante.*

each other for that time, and although I have never heard it expressly stated, I think it must have been considered unlucky to change, so strong is the prejudice against it still in the minds of old-fashioned folk.

For the May-pole at the stable door, *see* Section ii.

At Kingsland, Bosbury, and Bromyard, the folk speak of May 29 as a more important festival than May-day itself.

" The twenty-ninth was our real May-day in Bromyard," said one. " You'd see Maypoles all the way down Sheep Street, decorated with oak boughs and flowers, and people dancing round them, all wearing oak leaves."

Mrs. K——, the oldest inhabitant of Bosbury (1908), remembered every house with its spray of oak over the door on May 29. At Kingsland, an octogenarian told me, " there were great doings that day ; we used to climb up and put a great bough of oak on the church tower."

The custom is now all but extinct, and was on the wane when *Antiquatis* wrote in 1879 :—

" In memory of the escape of the merry monarch, it was formerly usual in Herefordshire to carry out the customary wearing of oak leaves or oak apples on Royal Oak day, to a much greater extent than is the case at present. Every person, young or old, male or female, wore a sprig of oak about the dress or person, and in the event of anyone being discovered not conforming to the custom, he or she was considered as having an aversion to royalty, and received rough treatment at the hands of the people. The lads of the rural districts used to be (and in some parts of the county still are) very busy, for weeks before Royal Oak Day came round, collecting eggs of small birds; blackbirds and thrushes particularly, and with these they pelted mercilessly any person they chanced to see who had neglected to obtain the conventional oak leaf."

" Small branches of oak were fastened by the rustic waggoners to the head-gear of their horses in almost every part of Herefordshire, and in many places, early in the morning, ropes were stretched across the village streets, on which were hung garlands composed of all the flowers in bloom at the time, besides large boughs of oak and a multitude of gay-coloured ribbons. The country children were wont to rise early on the morning of this day and proceed to the woods to gather twigs of oak with the gall adhering, which they would place in their hats, carrying in their hands leaves and branches of trees, when they would call on a number of well-disposed inhabitants of the neighbourhood, and solicit small contributions towards keeping up their juvenile festivities. In some parts this custom was termed " Shig-Shagging," the name taking its rise from some doggerel, repeated in the event of a non-successful application for alms, of which the following is one version :—

> ' Shig-shag, penny-a-rag,
> (Bang his head with Cromwell's bag),
> All up in a bundle ! '[1]

Rogation Tide.

See Section xii., 1, *Beating the Bounds.*

(11) WHITSUNTIDE.

On Whit-Sunday, 1868, a correspondent of *Notes and Queries*[2] noticed that the church at King's Pyon was decorated in every available niche with leaves and small branches, and twigs of birch. "Each pew corner and point of vantage was so ornamented, and the light green leaves formed a pretty contrast with the woodwork." This custom is now obsolete. A Mrs. D——, aged 80, of Ledbury, remembered seeing the church there so decorated in her youth. At Kington, yew was used to decorate the church at Whitsuntide, being fastened, as the birch at King's Pyon was, to the tops of the pews.[3] The appropriate dish for the day was held to be the first green gooseberry tart of the year.

Whitsuntide seems to have been a great festival in the Ross district. T—— W——, of Walford, told me he remembered how there was a feast on each day of the week at different parishes in the neighbourhood, and there was a party of Morris dancers, who danced every day in Whitsun week, making a tour of the feasts. They wore " ruggles," (little bells), at the knees.

Corpus Christi, *June 14th.*

See Section ix., 3, *Corpus Christi Pageant.*

(12) MIDSUMMER, ST. PETER'S DAY (JUNE 29).

Aubrey describes a Midsummer Eve custom now totally disused, of which I have seen no mention elsewhere :—

1] *Antiquatis, Herefordshire Gatherer,* 1879. It is now believed that Oak-Apple Day is one of the primitive agricultural festivals, which, as its real significance was forgotten, attached itself to the anniversary of an historical event. *See* Chambers, *Med. Stage,* i., 115 ; *Folk-Lore,* xii, 394 ; Burne, 365 ; and *Guy Fawkes' Day, infra.*

2] *Fourth Series,* i., 551.

3] *Hist. Kington,* 202, *cf.* Herrick :—
> " When yew is out, then birch comes in,
> And many flowers beside,
> Both of a fresh and fragrant kind,
> To honour Whitsuntide."

In Herefordshire, and also in Somersetshire, on Midsummer Eve, they made fires in the fields in the waies; Sc., to blesse the apples. I have seen the same custom in Somerset, 1635, but there they do it for custom sake.

It must be another form of the same custom which is alluded to in a letter written to Miss Burne from Elton, in North Herefordshire, in 1880 :—

" Unless the orchards are christened on St. Peter's Day, the crop will not be good ; and there ought to be a shower of rain when the people go through the orchards, but no one seems to know for what purpose exactly."[1]

The sole trace of this I can find now is that a lady living in Eardisland remembers being told by an old inhabitant, since dead, that when the people blessed the apples they poured a glass of cider on the trunk of each tree, tapped it three times, and said a blessing.

Apples are now connected with St. Swithin ; they are said to be unfit for food until after this Saint's Day (July 15th), when they are blessed. We also have the common saying that if it rains on this day it will rain for forty days after.

St. James' Day.
See Sections xvii., 1.

(13) HARVEST AND HOP-PICKING CUSTOMS AND FESTIVALS.

Crying the Mare.

At the conclusion of the harvest, before the days of reaping machines, the reapers left a small patch of corn standing. This was tied up into four bunches, " the four legs of a mare like," my informant explained. These were again tied together at the top. Then the reapers tried to cut off the ears of corn by standing at a certain distance and then throwing their sickles at the " mare," holding them by the point to throw. In some places the men stood with their backs to the mare, but this required great skill in throwing the sickle. It sometimes took two hours to accomplish the feat ; the man who succeeded sat at one end of the table, opposite to the master, at the harvest supper.[2] As for the mare, or last sheaf, it was carefully plaited in a variety of ways (see illustration), and hung up in a farm-house kitchen with the " bush " and the mistletoe, to be kept till next harvest for luck. The sickles were carefully covered with straw plait before hanging up in the kitchen for their winter rest.

On those farms where no hops were grown the harvest supper would be given after crying the mare and " holloain' " old cider ; the latter ceremony was performed in the harvest field in the same manner as when burning the bush on New Year's Day.[3]

1] Folk-Lore, iv., 167.   2] Cf. Brand, 304.   3] See 1, ante, New Year's Day.

An old farmer at Dilwyn gave me a wooden cup, which he called a " wassail "
cup : it was goblet-shaped, and had been hollowed out of a solid piece of oak.   Unfortunately there was a hole in it, where the stem had been broken off.   It would have
held half a pint.   This cup, the owner said, belonged to his old master, and it was
kept for the harvest home and only used in the field, when crying the mare, and in the
farmhouse at the harvest supper.   On the latter occasion it was filled once for each man
with gin and cider (a most intoxicating mixture), each in turn had to give a toast,
or ask a *ridlass* (riddle), sing a song, or contribute in some way to the amusement
of the company before drinking from the cup.   The master would " tell his health "
and drink first, and then the cup was filled and refilled from a six quart jug, till all
had been served.   It does seem a pity that these merry-makings which promoted
good feelings between master and man are being gradually discontinued.   The feast
consisted principally of roast goose, and if one of the men had upset a load of corn when
driving home he was not supposed to have any ; I have never heard that this threat
was actually carried out.

Scottering.

This is a custom described by Havergal (*Words and Phrases*, 45), of which I can
now find no trace at all, nor have I heard the word used by the old people.

At the termination of harvest it was customary to carry lighted wisps of straw or pessum round the
ricks.   This was done by one, four, or six lads (unmarried only), who danced round the ricks crossing each
other on right and left sides alternately, accompanied by singing.   This seems to point to some ancient rite.

Cribbing.

It was until quite recently customary to " crib " any stranger visiting the
hop-yard during picking, unless he consented to " pay his footing."   The victim would
be seized by the pickers, and thrown into one of the " cribs " into which the hops
are gathered, and he would be covered with hops, and often one or two of the oldest
and fattest women would be thrown in too.   He would have to kiss them as the price
of release.   The custom was much objected to by the farmers, on account of the
damage to their cribs.[1]

The Hop-pickers' Feast.

At the conclusion of the hop-picking, which is also the end of the harvest, on
farms where hops are grown, it was formerly the custom to choose a King and Queen
of the Hop-pickers.   The head pole-puller, gaily bedecked with ribbons and sprays

---

1] *Cf.* Frazer, *Golden Bough*, ii., 232 :—All over Germany it is customary for the reapers and threshers to lay
hold of passing strangers, and bind them with a rope made of corn-stalks, till they pay a forfeit.

of hops, walked in front of the last load of hops from the hop-yard.   Behind this
came the two hop-pickers, who were chosen to be King and Queen ; the woman
wore male clothing, and the man a woman's dress.   They, like the pole-puller, were
adorned with hops and ribbons and streams of coloured paper ; all three carried poles
of hops decorated in a similar fashion, the finest poles being reserved for the purpose.
This procession went from the hopyard to the homestead, followed by all the other
hop-pickers and labourers, singing and making merry.   The King, Queen, and pole-
puller removed their decorations at the barn door, while the poles they carried adorned
the barn or granary until after the ball, which usually took place the same evening.
Afterwards the hops would be carefully dried and hung up in the farm-house kitchen.
The custom was kept within living memory at Hatfield, near Leominster, at Blakemere, Ullingswick, and other places.   There does not seem to have been any special
method in the choice of the King and Queen.   They were expected to make fun for
the others.   W—— R—— (age 70 in 1908), who had often been present at these
gatherings, said :—" The man had to be a smock-faced un.[1]   We chose a young mon
that 'ud make a nice gal like, and a smart woman as ud make a smart boy.   It was
all a bit o' fun, you understand, and the King and Queen opened the ball together."
The custom has now dwindled to dressing one or two hop-poles with ribbons, paper,
or flowers ; these are carried in procession to the homestead.   This was done on most
of the farms until about twenty years ago.   I saw the hop-pickers from Fields-
place (Dilwyn), carrying a " dressed " pole through the village in 1907.

(14) Gauging Day.

The game " follow my leader " appears to have had a special significance in
Herefordshire at one time, according to the following account of a custom now
obsolete and forgotten :—

The 11th of October stood prominent for Autumn sports in the county of Hereford, where an ancient
custom prevailed for the young men to assemble in the fields and choose a leader, whom they followed
wherever he might think proper to lead them, over hedges and ditches this might be. This only occurred
once in seven years, when they did the business with a hearty good will. Every publican gave a gallon of
beer and a large plum loaf which went by the name of gauging cake, which title was also transferred to the
day. Any person they might happen to meet was instantly seized upon and thumped without further
ceremony unless they preferred paying a fine to the leader.[2]

(15) Cobblers' Day, October 25th.

An old shoemaker at Ross told me that October 25th used to be cobbler's day.
All the cobblers had a holiday, and the boys used to sing :—

1] *i.e.*, clean-shaven.
2] *Cambridge Independent*, Jan. 1, 1887 ; quoted in *Folk-Lore Journal*, v., 75.   *See also* A. B. Gomme,
    Trad. Games, i., 132.

" The twenty-fifth of October,
Cursed be the Cobbler
That goes to bed sober."

October 25th is St. Crispin's Day, but the old cobbler had apparently never heard of the patron saint of shoemakers—an example of the way a dying custom is sometimes kept up, while its real significance is forgotten.

(16) ALL SOULS' DAY.

Brand mentions a custom connected with this day, now quite extinct :—

In the *Festa Anglo-Romana* we read : "The custom of *Soul Mass Cakes*, which are a kind of *Oat Cakes* that some of the richer sorts of persons in Lancashire and Herefordshire (among the Papists there), use still to give the poor on this day : and they in retribution of their charity, hold themselves obliged to say this old couplet :—

' God have your Saul
Beens and all.' "[1]

Antiquatis (*Herefordshire Gatherer*, July 19, 1897), recalls how " Soul mass " cakes were offered each visitor on this day by mistresses of many Herefordshire houses.

Jack of France.

There once lived in Dorstone a man called Jack of France, an evil doer, and a terror to all peaceable folk. One night, the Eve of all Souls, he was passing through the churchyard, and saw a light shining in all the windows of the church. He looked in, and saw a large congregation assembled, listening apparently to the preaching of a man in a monk's habit, who was declaiming from the pulpit the names of all those who were to die during the coming year. The preacher lifted his head, and Jack saw under the cowl the features of the Prince of Darkness himself, and to his horror heard his own name given out among the list of those death should claim. He went home, and repenting too late of his evil deeds, took to his bed and died.[2]

See also Section vi., 2, *Magic and Divination.*

(17) GUY FAWKES' DAY.

This day is still regularly observed, with bonfires and fireworks. A straw effigy is sometimes made and burnt. The boys go about shouting :—

1] Brand, 212. *Cf.* Chambers, *Med. Stage*, 253.
2] Communicated by Mrs. Powell to myself, and also to Prof. Rhys, who has printed the story in *Celtic Folk-Lore. Cf.* Section iv., 4 *The Devil.*

"Remember, remember
The Fifth of November,
Gunpowder, treason, and plot.
Remember, remember,
The fifth of November
Shall never be forgot."[1]

(18) St. Thomas' Day (December 21).

This was called "gooding day"; a sack of wheat was placed at the door of each farmhouse, and from it a quartern measure of wheat was given to every woman who called for it, to be added to what she had gleaned after harvest. More would be given to those who had families; it was usually ground by the miller free of charge.[2]

There are charities distributed on St. Thomas' Day at Norton Canon still.

(19) Christmas Day.

The resentment of the common people at the change of the calendar which took place in 1752, has lasted in Herefordshire almost into this century. W—— P——, of Peterchurch, talking of Christmas, as kept by his uncle, who lived at Kingstone Grange, told me how the old farmer kept Christmas in fine style, "but he always said old Christmas day was the *real* Christmas." My informant added that during the twelve days from Dec. 25th to Jan. 6th, it was, and is, considered very unlucky to borrow fire. This idea of wanting to borrow fire seems strange nowadays, but before matches came into use it was often convenient to borrow a shovelful of coals from a neighbour's cottage. Ill luck might be averted by giving some trifle in return for the fire, such as a pin.[3] Some of the folk consider it very unlucky to borrow fire at any time, or even to carry it from one room to another. I once suggested to a servant as she was lighting a fire in a hurry she might bring coals from another room. "Grandmother won't let us do that," she said, "it brings awful bad luck."

It is also most unlucky for a woman to enter a house on Christmas Day, unless she has slept there the night before. Farmers' wives of the last generation usually paid a dark-haired man to be "first foot," and to bring in the luck. He entered by the

---

1] *See* Brand, 216. *Cf.* Chambers, *Med. Stage*, 248-9. "In the seventeenth century . . . we find the winter festival fires turned to new account in the celebration of the escape of the King and Parliament, from the nefarious machinations of Guy Fawkes. All the folk-customs of the winter half of the year, from Michaelmas to Plough Monday, must be regarded as the flotsam and jetsam of a single original feast. This was a New Year's feast, held by the German and Keltic tribes at the beginning of the central European winter, when the first snows fell about the middle of November, and subsequently dislocated and dispersed by the successive clash of German-Keltic civilisation with the rival scheme of Rome and of Christianity."
2] See also *Ariconensia*, 73-4, where Fosbroke mentions the custom.   3] Fosbroke, *loc. cit.*

front door, and went out through the back, after going through each room in the house, and usually received a shilling for his trouble.

Fosbroke says that on " new " Christmas Day, and the first Monday in the year, a woman must not come first to the house, or there will be no luck through the year.[1] But I find at Blakemere, and at several places in the Weobley district, no woman was allowed to enter *all* day, and women or girls who came singing carols were not welcome, and received nothing.

At one farm, Mrs. S—— told me, she had to go into a house to sleep on Christmas Eve when she was wanted to help on Christmas Day. She could go home if she liked, and re-enter the house, but only those who had slept there the previous night might do so. " You see," she added, " they were extra particular because an uncle who had had a woman in one Christmas died soon after. She had brought him a present, and so he had brought her into the house, and gave her a mince-pie, not liking to turn her away, like."

It is unlucky to receive new shoes, or untanned leather, into the house on Christmas Day, or some say during Christmas week.[2]

The feast itself lasted for twelve days, and no work was done. All houses were, and are now, decorated with sprigs of holly and ivy, which must not be brought in until Christmas Eve. A yule log, as large as the open hearth could accommodate, was brought into the kitchen of each farmhouse, and smaller ones were used in the cottages. W—— P—— said he had seen a tree drawn into the kitchen at Kingstone Grange years ago by two cart horses ; when it had been consumed a small portion was carefully kept to be used for lighting next year's log. " Mother always kept it very carefully ; she said it was lucky, and kept the house from fire and from lightning."[3] It seems to have been the general practice to light it on Christmas Eve, but Miss Burne has noted an instance of the log being kindled on Christmas morning.

Carol-singing was formerly a great feature of the Christmas season. The singers received mince-pies, cake, and money. They sang long and ancient carols to folk-melodies, and they were sure of a warm welcome. The practice is now almost confined to children, and rewards are scanty compared with those given in the good old times.[4]

The season was further enlivened by companies of wassailers, Morris dancers, and mummers. The wassailers flourished in the neighbourhood of Bromyard and

---

1] *Ariconensia, loc. cit.*   2] This was recorded some years ago in *Notes and Queries, 5th Series*, iii., 7. The belief still survives.   3] Mrs. P——, Dilwyn.   4] *See* Section xiv., 1., *Ancient Carols*.

on the Worcester side of the county. " We used to go *wassileing*, said W—— R——,
when I was a boy, at Ullingswick. We had a captain who kept the punch-bowl, or
wass-ill bowl. It was a great big one made o' beech wood, and would hold a large
quantity, perhaps two gallons. They took it round at night, decorated with ribbons
and coloured streamers, beginning some little time before Christmas, and visiting
all the houses in the neighbourhood. They sang songs and carols, and one special carol
beginning :—

> " Wassail, wassail, round the town,
> Your bread is white, your ale is brown."[1]

At each house the bowl was filled with punch, made of hot cider, gin, nutmeg, and
sugar. They had toast with it, and money was also given.

(20) HOLY INNOCENTS' DAY.

It is considered unlucky to commence any undertaking on this day.   I am informed by Mr. G. H. Phillott that the late Vicar of Bredwardine, the Rev. R. F. Kilvert,
used to say that some of his parishioners whipped their children on Holy Innocents'
Day.

Muffled Peal on Holy Innocents' Day, *See* Section xii., 6.

Boy Bishop, *See* Section xi., 4.

(21) ST. STEPHEN'S DAY.

The old inhabitant of Peterchurch before mentioned told me he could remember
how his uncle at Kingstone used to bleed his cart horses on this day, also the oxen
used for ploughing. They were not worked at all until after Twelfth Day.

---

[1] This is given by Brand, 4.   I have collected words and tune at Pembridge, but traced both to a Gloucestershire source.

SECTION X.

CEREMONIAL.

(1) BIRTH.

A new-born child should be wrapped in something old, preferably an old flannel petticoat. An old-fashioned nurse told me she never liked to dress babies in new clothes for the first time, if she could avoid it. She always took an old flannel petticoat with her, to be the first garment worn by each baby she nursed. It is still quite generally believed, among the older folk, that the father frequently suffers as much as, or more than the mother, before and at the time of the first child's birth, and sometimes, but more rarely, on account of the birth of the later ones. It is also said that when the husband is ill the wife's sufferings are proportionately lessened. It may be even possible, they say, that the pain naturally borne by the woman may be transferred to her husband altogether. Any toothache or other ache affecting the husband at the time of his wife's illness is ascribed to this cause.[1] As this superstition appears to have hitherto escaped the notice of collectors of English folk-lore, it may be desirable to give details of it. Mrs. G——, of King's Pyon, *ætat* 75, expressed her firm belief in it thus : " When my first babby was born I suffered nothin' at all scarcely, but my poor first husband was walking the boards night after night. He suffered summat cruel, with aches and pains all over him. ' I shall be glad when that babby's born,' says he."

Mrs. T——, a midwife, living in South Herefordshire, on hearing of this, said she knew it was quite true. She had one case of a woman whose sufferings were very slight, and she went to tell the happy father—" pitching poles in the hopyard, he was "— that mother and child were doing well. " Oh ! Mrs. T——," says he, " was it about one o'clock ? " " Yes," says I, " how did you know ?" " Knowt ! " says he, " why I thought as my poor back was being sawed in two all the morning."

Mrs. T——, further related that, while " picking stone " in the fields with an old crone, she remarked that her husband was sick and ailing. The woman said : " Then I know what's the matter with you." " And," added Mrs. T.——, " she was right enough, she was : T—— seemed to take all off me with that one ; it was my third baby."

Others, however, believe that it is only during the first half of the period of pregnancy that the husband is affected. An ancient woman at Garway explained,

---

1] Weobley, King's Pyon, Withington, and other places.

with reverent simplicity, " I allus thought as the Almighty appinted that very well, so the poor woman 'ud ha' more strength when the time came." This belief seems to be founded on the idea of sympathy and unity between husband and wife. I have not been able to trace anything of the kind as between father and child.

This is a particularly interesting item, as it seems to be a last trace, surviving in the higher culture, of the strange custom found among savages in many parts of the world, which has been called the *Couvade*,[1] which implies a mysterious and magical connection between father and child very similar to that here believed to exist between husband and wife.

The first food given to the baby, as in Shropshire, is usually butter and sugar. But, at Ledbury, a woman said her mother always gave her babies a little rue, pounded fine with sugar—" only a little of it." Let us hope so !

It is a sign of luck through life to be born with a caul,[2] which was formerly supposed to be worth a considerable sum, as a charm which would prevent its owner being drowned. Birth marks are supposed to be caused by something seen by the mother before the birth of the child,[3] and they are usually thought to bear a fancied resemblance to a fish, a hare, a strawberry, or even a pancake. They are also supposed to be caused by witchcraft and the evil eye.[4]

An old inhabitant of the city of Hereford remembers that seventy years ago a charm in the form of a broadside was purchased by poor women to hang above their beds, for greater ease and safety in child-birth. It was of a sacred character, and was called " Our Saviour's letter."[5]

(For the Moon in relation to child-birth, *see* Section i., 9.)

1] *See* Tylor, *Early History of Mankind,* 291 ; *Primitive Culture,* i., 84 ; Hartland, *Perseus,* ii., 401, where other references are given. In Guiana, the mother, shortly after a birth, resumes her ordinary work, while the father goes to bed, and abstains from all work and all food, except weak gruel and cassava meal.   2] David Copperfield was born with a caul.   3] *Cf. ante,* vii., 2, for cure of birthmarks.   4] *Cf. ante.,* v., 2, *Witchcraft.*

5] For the text of this letter, *see* Gutch-Peacock, *Lincolnshire,* 126. *Cf.* also L.S., *Untravelled Berkshire,* 172, Henderson, 194, who says :—" Mrs. Wilkins . . . brought out to show me something that she laid great store by—two old broadsides. They were kept carefully in the family Bible, and were both copies of the Apocryphal Letter of Agbarus of Edessa ; she called them Saviour's letters. They had been used as charms against illness, especially in childbirth, by her mother and grandmother, who pinned them inside their dresses upon these occasions. L.S. adds in a note that :—The letter was said to be a copy of one written by our Blessed Lord and Saviour Jesus Christ, and found eighteen miles from Iconium fifty-three years after our Blessed Saviour's crucifixion. It had been found originally under a stone, round and large, at the foot of the Cross. Upon the stone was en· graven, 'Blessed is he that shall turn me over.' All people that saw it prayed to God earnestly, and desired that He would make the writing known unto them, and that they might not attempt in vain to turn it over. In the meantime there came out a little child, about six or seven years of age, and turned it over without assistance, to the admiration of every person who was standing by. It was carried to the city of Iconium, and there published by a person belonging to Lady Cuba. The letter was also pasted on cottage walls as a protection against witchcraft."

It is unlucky to buy a new cradle, and bring it into the house before the birth of the child. There is a great prejudice against weighing : " babies do not thrive afterwards." A baby's hands should not be washed for the first year, though it may wash itself by dabbling in water. Its hair must not be cut, nor its nails, or it may be a thief. Nor must baby see its own face in the glass : it is most unlucky. The mother does not go out of the house at all after the baby's birth until she goes to church. The name of the baby is decided by the father, and is never told to anyone outside the family. I have often asked " What is baby's name to be ? " and, if the parents are really country folk, the reply is always evasive, " We don't know yet," or " We haven't thought about it."

A married woman living at Eardisland refused to be godmother to her sister's child, because she had been told that if she did so, she would have no children herself.[1]

There is a very pretty notion that any baby girl born after the ninth of the month will be endowed with the virtues corresponding to those described in the verse of the 31st chapter of Proverbs, having the same number as her own birthday. If this happened to fall on the 26th, her verse would be :—" She openeth her mouth with wisdom, and in her tongue is the law of kindness." What better motto could she have ?

Mr. G. H. Phillott remembers that his father, Canon Phillott, the late rector of Staunton-on-Wye, was sometimes asked for the water used in private baptism. It was to be preserved for the baby's benefit, either as a medicine, or to wash it ; he could not clearly remember which, but it had special value as a remedy.

If the baby cries loudly at the christening, they say it will be a good singer.

It is lucky for the child if the initials of its full name spell a word, and the baptismal name or names are sometimes chosen with regard to this point. On the other hand, it is unlucky to bestow the name of any animal ; a farmer near Cusop called his little girl " Chloe," after his favourite mare. Believers in this superstition were of course confirmed in their faith when, at the age of three, the child was burnt to death in the rickyard, and the mare fell and broke her back shortly afterwards, at the same spot.[2]

(2) COURTSHIP AND MARRIAGE.

Among the typical Herefordshire peasantry of the older generation, there exists the greatest reluctance to interfere with the love affairs of their children. However

---

1] MS. notes of the late Vicar of Eardisland, the Rev. H. Barker.   2] Communicated by Mr. Portman.

unsuitably matched a couple may seem to be, a parent will say something like this : " Yes, yes, she is too old for him, maybe, but I don't hold with interferin' with them things, no good comes on it."

It is very unlucky for either man or woman to be present in church to hear their own banns published. It is even said that if both hear them, the first child of the couple will be born an idiot.[1]

It is held a lucky circumstance if the bride has never entered her future home at all before marriage. It was formerly considered unlucky to mark any of the linen or clothing with the bride's future name before the wedding. The maiden name was therefore used for clothes and house-linen ; the latter was always provided by the parents of the bride.

There are numerous small sayings and superstitions relating to marriage. If a village dressmaker accidentally pin a dress to a girl's underclothing when fitting she will say, " There now, you won't be married this year." If by chance a girl have two teaspoons in her saucer, it is said to be a sign that she will have two husbands. Briers catching accidentally in the skirt are called " sweethearts." As a child, I remember seeing my Herefordshire nurse walk a very long way, with a bramble trailing behind her, to see how long " he " might be expected to be faithful. If in the end she had to pull the brier off herself, he was " all right for certain." If a girl's apron string or shoe-string come untied, it is said to be a sure sign that her lover is thinking about her. It is unlucky to turn beds or mattresses on a Sunday or Friday ; the maids say " We shall turn away our sweethearts if we do."

If a girl about to be married has toothache, she will sometimes be told " Ah, it's a sign you don't love true." It is unlucky to marry in May, Lent, or Easter week. The first to turn away from the altar after the marriage ceremony will be the first to die.

Some people say it is very unlucky to wear new shoes at a wedding, while others believe it is lucky to do so. These contradictory beliefs I found at Orcop, and other parts of the Ross district, side by side.

It is very unlucky for the bride and bridegroom to leave the bride's home by the back door after the wedding. This was done near Hereford recently, by a couple wishing to escape showers of rice ; the old people present shook their heads, and thought it a very bad omen. It is also held unlucky to have an odd number of guests at a wedding breakfast.[3] The old saying about the bride's clothing, "Something old

---

1] Communicated by Mr. W. Pilley.   2] Perhaps this is a faint trace of bride-capture.   3] Weobley.

and something new, something borrowed and something blue," is still remembered and acted upon.

Arches of evergreens are erected for village weddings, bearing bright coloured mottoes, expressing good wishes, such as "Happy be the bridegroom and the bride," or "God bless the happy pair," and there is usually much bell-ringing. Some years ago, the ringers at Peterchurch, not having received any recompense for their services on the occasion of a wedding, repaired to the belfry and rang the bells backwards in revenge. The idea seemed to be that ringing in the ordinary way brought good fortune, and ringing the reverse way the contrary.[1]

Flowers are often strewn before the couple as they come out of church. It is only a few years ago since a young girl went to Cusop, to the wedding of a young man who had jilted her; waiting in the church porch till the bridegroom came out, she threw a handful of rue at him, saying "May you rue this day as long as you live!" My informant said this caused a good deal of talk at the time, and he was told that the curse would come true, because the rue was taken direct from the plant to the church-yard, and thrown "between holy and unholy ground," that is, between the church and churchyard. No consecration of the churchyard suffices to make it holy ground in the eyes of the superstitious, who are afraid to enter it after dark, and believe it the haunt of evil and restless spirits. Rue is very common in cottage gardens, but if there were any difficulty in obtaining it for this spiteful purpose, rue-fern, the leaves of which resemble it, might be used; it must be found growing on the churchyard wall, and be gathered directly from thence.

The only other instance of this practice I know is mentioned by Fosbroke, who describes it as a malicious caricature of the custom of strewing flowers :—" Nosegays of rue, enclosing a piece of half-eaten bread and butter, were dropt in the church porch by a deserted female, to denote an unhappy wedding."[2]

At Hereford and Ross, when a butcher married, it was the custom for all the butcher boys in the town to come to the bride's home, and play a tune with marrow-bones, upon their cleavers; they expected to be invited to drink the health of the bride.

Passing to the ceremony itself, we have a trace of the ancient custom of marrying at the church door; for in the record of the marriage contract between Grimbald Pauncefote, of Cowarne, and Constantia, daughter of John Lingayn, it is stated that her dower or settlement was to be fixed by her husband at the door of the church, as soon as the ceremony was completed.[3]

1] Told by a woman aged 80, a native of Peterchurch.   2] Fosbroke, *Ariconensia*, 74.   3] Duncumb, ii. 97.

The custom of drinking wine in the church at a marriage is enjoined by the *Hereford Missal*. It also directs that at a particular prayer, the married couple shall prostrate themselves, while four clerks hold the pall over them. This pall was a veil or square piece of cloth, held up at each corner and called a care-cloth.[1]

The form of betrothal in the Missal is as follows :—

I, N., undersynge the N. for my wedded wyf, for betere for worse, for richer for porer, yn sekeness & yn helthe, tyl deth us departe, as holy church hath ordeyned, & thereto y plygth the my trowthe.

The woman replies :—

I, N., undersynge the N . . . to be boxum to the tyl deth us departe. . . .[2]

There is in the Hereford Cathedral library a MS. volume, entitled *Officiæ Ecclesiæ* (*circa* 1400), containing another old English form of betrothal in the marriage service, which accompanied the giving of the ring (rubric within brackets) :—

Wyth this gold ring y ye wedde, gold *and* silver ich ye zene, *and* with my bodi ich ye worshep, *and* with al my wordelych catel I ey honnoure (*ad primum digitum*), In nomine patris (*ad secundum digitum*), et filii (*ad trinum digitum*), et spiritus sancti (*ad quartum digitum*), Amen.

Havergal (*Fasti*, 192) notes that this form does not agree with either the Sarum, York, or Hereford Uses, and thinks it may be a copy of the Bangor Use. It is not connected with this county except through its preservation in the Cathedral library.

The same remark applies to the form of marriage in the Welsh manual in the library, which is as follows :—

Ich N. take the N.
to my wedid wyf,
for fayroure for foulore,
for richere for porer,
for betere for wers,
in sicknesse and in helthe,
forte deth us departe,
and only to the holde,
and tharto ich plygtte my treuthe.

This is quoted by Sir Laurence Gomme (*Folk-lore as an Historical Science*, 91), who says " it preserves in the vernacular the ancient rhythmical formula of the marriage laws, and the antiquity of the church ritual is proved from the fact that it is accompanied and enforced by the old rhythmical verse, which is indicative of early legal or ceremonious usage."

For myrtle and weddings, *see* Section ii. ; love divinations, Section i., 1 & 7 ; ii., iii., 1 ; and vi., 2 ; *see* also xi., 1 (games).

1] *Hereford Missal*, 441. *See* Brand, 380.   2] *Hereford Missal*, 438.

Commorth.

This was a contribution customarily collected at Welsh weddings, on behalf of the persons married.[1] It was forbidden by Statute, 26 Henry VIII., cap. 6. We have evidence of the prevalence of this custom in Hereford, in the following order :—

1534. Aug. 26. 26 Hen. viii., Salop. Order in the King's name from the Commissioner for the Marches, to the Mayor and Aldermen of Hereford, and that whereas they are credibly informed " that by means of gadering of commortheas and other like exactions, and for affrayes and estries used in those partyes, our pour subjects be not only greatlye impoverished and endamaged, but also put in grete feair and jeperdye of their lyves by means of mis-ruled persons (contrary to our laws and peas), vsing to weyr cotes of diffence and demand silver of our pour subjects by thretnyng wordes, so that for drad thereof they dare not applye thair busynes, nor attende thair merketts, as our true lyege people ought to do, whiche we ne wold shuld contynue, but that the same shuld be redressed with spede : therefore we and our said Counsailours and Commyssioners woll and charge you, and everyone of you that frome hensforthe ye mak open proclamacions in fayres, merketts, sessions, courtes and churches, where ye shall seme most expedient, that no maner person or persones shall from hensforth gadre any commertha within our said cytye of money, corne, catell, or other unlawful colleccion, nor assemble nor gadre any of our subjectes to any love-ales, or bydden ales, nor suffer any person or persones to weyve any cotes of diffence, or any other harnes, contrary to our statutes in such case provided ; " persons offending to be committed to ward pending the Commissioners' further order.[2]

It appears, however, from the ensuing letter, that permission to give these entertainments could be occasionally obtained from persons in authority.

To my well beloved friend the Mayor of Hereford be this delivered.

Maister Mayor,—In my moste heartyest manner I commend me unto you, and all the aldermen your brethren of the city, praying you with the whole commonaltie there to be good and favourable to thys berer Henry Wenston. So it is he determined to make within the citie a Game or Geve-aill after the custome of the contrie by your license. And in that behalf he hath made labour unto me to the entente that I wold wrytt unto you for your good-wyll, and the favour of your brethren and citizens to be had.

So according to hys suytt made to me as is aforesaid, I do desire you and all other above named to be favourable and good masters unto hym, as in gyvyng hym leave to kepe the said game or geve-aill, and that it may be asmoche to hys profyt as you may cause. And in this doynge at my instant, and for my sake, I shall be at all times as good lord and as friendly to any lover or friend of yours at your request, in that shall ly in me. No more to you at this tyme, but Heven have you in hys keepyne. Wreten at Rychemond, the 8th day of May, by your assured—W. DEVEREUX.[3]

Selling Wives.

There can be no doubt that the horrible custom of a man's selling his wife, in the open market, with a halter round her neck, was kept up at Hereford into the nineteenth century. In 1802, a butcher sold his wife by public auction, in Hereford market. The lot realised one pound, four shillings, and a bowl of punch.[4] " Nonagenarian," an old lady whose reminiscences of old-time Hereford have been before referred to, witnessed a similar scene more than once. Here is a description of it in her own words :—

1] Howells, *Cambrian Superstitions*, 167-8.   2] *Hist. MSS*, xiii., 311-12.   3] Johnson, 151.
4] Andrews, *Bygone England*, 201-2.

I must recall to your memory my statement as to my being playfellow to Mona Delnotte Coates, for it was while walking with her that I first saw a man selling his wife. We were going from the Barton to the other side of the town, and necessarily had to pass the bottom of the pig market. Here we saw a crowd. The girl was desirous of knowing what was the matter, so she elbowed her way through the people, and was followed by the children to the open space in the centre. There stood a woman with her hat in her hand. . . This woman's hat was a very smart one. She stood looking down. At first I thought she was admiring her own red cloak, but as she stood so still my eyes wandered over to see what was amiss, and I shall never forget how surprised I felt when I observed she had a rope about her neck, and that a man was holding one end of it. "What has she done?" we both cried out, for I believed she was going to be hanged. "Oh," said a bystander, "she has done no good, depend upon it, or else he wouldn't want to sell her." Just then there was a loud laugh, and a man shouted "Well done, Jack, that is elevenpence more than I would give. It's too much, boy, too much." But Jack stood firm. "No," said he, "I'll give a shilling, and he ought to be thankful to get rid of her at that price." "Well," said the man, "I'll take it, though her good looks ought to be worth more than that." "Keep her master, keep her for her good looks," shouted the laughing bystanders. "No," said he, "good looks won't put the victuals on the table without willing hands." "Well," said Jack, "here's the shilling, and I war'nt I'll make her put the victuals on the table for me, and help to get it first. Be you willing Missis to have me, and take me for better for worse?" "I be willing," says she. "And be you willing to sell her for what I bid maister?" "I be," said he, "and will give you the rope into the bargain." So Jack gave the man his shilling.[1]

(3) DEATH.

In addition to the "death tokens" before given,[2] the following are said to be omens of death :—

To dream of a wedding (" dreams go by contraries.")

If the clock strike between the hours, or stop altogether.

If the tablecloth be folded with the middle doubled up, so that the octagonal crease resembles the shape of a coffin, in the centre, when it is opened.

If a pair of bellows or boots be accidentally placed on the table.[3]

If a " reeve " or ridge be missed when sowing the corn ; this sometimes happened before the introduction of machine drills, as when sowing by hand the workman might easily overlook a ridge.

If a row of garden produce fail to come up, or if the seed be accidentally mixed.

To take three loaves of bread from the oven at once is a sign of death within the year ;[4] or dropping a loaf in taking it from the oven. If the door be closed, after a funeral, before the return of the mourners, there will be another death in the family before the end of the year.

1] *Hereford Times*, May 20th, 1876 ; see also April 15th, 1876. "The authorities must have considered it lawful, for they did not send the woman so purchased away to their parishes to be confined, as they did those in that condition unlawfully." 2] See *ante*, ii. ; *Trees and plants*, iii., 2 ; *Birds*, iv., 1 & 3. 3] Weobley. Sometimes just bad luck. *See* Section viii. General. 4] Dilwyn.

If the parish clerk be asked for change by the undertaker or other person paying the funeral fees, it is believed that there will be a second death in the family of the deceased within the year.[1] If there be a funeral on New Year's Day, there will be twelve in the parish during the year.[2]

It is very unlucky to look at a funeral through the glass of a window, i.e., to watch it from the house.[3]

If a man come into the house with a shovel or any edged tool on his shoulder it is "terrible bad luck," or a sign of a death.[4] If the earth sink more rapidly than usual on a new-made grave, it is a sign that one of the same family will soon die.[5]

I was told at Orcop that an adder coming to the door was a sign of death. A doorstep seemed an unlikely place for an adder ; but my informant assured me she had known this "come true," and it had happened so often that one would think adders must have been mysteriously attracted to the doorsteps of the cottagers on the hillside ; possibly they sought warmth and sunshine.

If several people are sitting in a room and the door opens of itself, the one who first closes it will be the first to die.[6]

A mother whose baby was ill told me she was quite sure it would die, as she had been nursing it, and its natural food supply had suddenly failed, which was "a sure sign." The real cause was of course the mother's anxiety of mind, while the poor baby, being weaned in the midst of a serious illness, had not a very good chance. But it recovered, in spite of its mother's fears and predictions.[7]

Another death omen is the appearance of the wraith of the person about to die ;[8] or of a light, "where no real light is."[9] This is really the corpse candle, which is still believed in near the Welsh Border, in the Hay and Kington districts.[10] Parry alludes to it, thus :—

Among the peasantry, it was, and is, to the present time (1845), believed that a corpse candle precedes the death of persons in the neighbourhood, and marks the route of the funeral from the house of the deceased to the churchyard, and to the very spot where the body will be laid in the grave. This opinion is not confined to the lower orders of persons living on the Commons and in the villages exclusively ; there are many persons from whom better things might be expected, who entertain the like superstitious belief.[11]

If after death the eyes of a corpse are open, it is gruesomely said to be looking for the next member of the family to die, i.e., another death will soon follow. The common superstition, that a person cannot die on a bed or pillow containing wild

1] Havergal, *Words and Phrases*, 46.   2] Norton Canon.   3] Leominster.   4] "I've seen mother sit down and cry over it." (Orcop).   5] Weobley and C.G.P.   6] C.G.P.   7] Weobley, 1909.   8] *See* Section iv. Wraiths.   9] Ocle Pychard.   10] C.G.P.   11] *Hist. Kington*, 205.   This writer has noticed, as I have done, that the most superstitious folk live on and near commons.

birds' feathers, is still believed in here and there. Turkeys' feathers are considered to be included, as " wild birds," in this connection.

At Llanveyno and Michaelchurch, it was customary, until a few years ago, for the household to sit up all night when a death had occurred. They did not sit in the same room with the corpse, but elsewhere, the idea being that the spirit of the dead person was still in and about the house, and the people said " It was for the last time, it was the last night " ; so no one went to bed.[1]

But at Orcop and Garway, the watch is still kept, so Martha S——,[2] who lived on Garway Hill, assured me. " Only if it was somebody you cared about," she added, " not for strangers." I have not heard of the practice elsewhere at the present time. But usually, among the country folk, a light is kept burning in the room where a corpse lies every night until burial ; a pewter plate of salt is placed on the body ; according to Martha S——, the candle should be stuck in the middle of the salt, heaped up in the centre of the plate. Sometimes a green turf, wrapped in a piece of paper, is used instead of the salt, or a pail of salt and water is placed under the bed. The reason given for the use of these things at the present day is that they prevent the body from swelling.

In each case, however, the original idea was to keep away evil spirits.[3] A bucket of soil has been seen placed under the bed in the Kington district. Anyone visiting a house where a body lies is, or till recently was, usually asked to see it, and expected to touch it, in order that he or she may not dream of it afterwards. I remember hearing of a doctor's indignation when a child had died of diphtheria at King's Pyon some years ago, and he learned that practically all the neighbours had been to the house and had touched the body.

The country folk of the last generation seem to have attached even more importance to funerals than to weddings. Old people, asked about events they may remember, will talk of an elaborate funeral of one of the " gentry," and what a fine sight it was. A woman in the Trinity Almshouses, Hereford, told me the " longest thing " she could remember was the glare of the torches, when the funeral procession of Sir Robert Price passed through Hereford on its way to Foxley. All the poor in a country parish, a few years ago, would flock to a funeral, as a spectacle.

1] Letter from Mrs. Norton, Llanveyno, June, 1909.
2] This woman told me that she was staying with her sister at a colliery village in S. Wales, where some people next door took a corpse out of the coffin, stuck it up in a corner with 12 candles in front of it, and drank and sang in the room all night. " Folks said they was Irish : it was dreadful ! " she added. This happened several years ago.
3] Cf. Brand, 440 ; Burne, 299, 131. " In old legends and sagas, corpses taken possessed by demons are invariably found *swollen.*"

With regard to the refreshments partaken of at funerals, great importance was attached to these by old fashioned people within my own recollection. Near Hay they are still called " funeral meats ";[1] a substantial meal was provided with cold meat and other viands. A woman who can remember Weobley customs fifty years ago said " Funerals is thought nothin' of now to what these used to be. There was always as much cake and cider, even at poor folk's funerals, as anybody had a mind to take." There is no special kind of cake made ; but at Clodock, the people of Longtown, who have some distance to come to the church, bring with them a cake, which is eaten after the funeral, with drinks obtained at the inn.

In corroboration of Aubrey's oft-quoted account of the sin-eater in Hereford-shire,[2] is the incident communicated to me by a resident in the neighbourhood of Hay. He was invited to attend the funeral of a sister of a farmer, near Crasswall, and to his surprise, was invited to go upstairs to the room where the body was lying. He went, with the brother and four bearers. At the bottom of the bed, at the foot of the coffin, was a little box, with a white cloth covering it. On it were placed a bottle of port wine, opened, and six glasses arranged around it. The glasses were filled, and my informant was asked to drink. This he refused, saying that he never took wine. " But you must drink, sir," said the old farmer, " It is like the Sacrament. It is to *kill the sins of my sister.*"

Traces of this custom are to be found at Walterstone, and near the Welsh Border, from Hay to Longtown, port wine is drunk, exactly as described, by the bearers, in the room where the body lies. Finger biscuits are provided. I told the story of the Crasswall funeral to a woman at Walterstone, who said " We did that at mother's funeral, because mother always did it. I never knew the meaning of it."

Among the humbler folk it is noticeable that some who have left relatives to be maintained " by the parish " during life, will yet come forward after death and arrange for a funeral at their own expense. There is also a curious dread, among the

---

1] *Cf. Hamlet*, Act i., Scene ii. :—

> "The funeral bak'd meats
> Did coldly furnish forth the marriage tables."

2] Aubrey, *Remaines*, 375 ; (F.L.S.) " In the county of Hereford was an old custom at funeralls to hire poor people who were to take upon them the sins of the party deceased. One of them I remember, lived in a cottage on Ross highway (he was a long lean ugly lamentable poor rascal). The manner was that when a corpse was brought out and laid on the bier, a loaf of bread was brought out and delivered to the sin-eater over the corpse, as also a mazar-bowl of maple, full of beer, which he was to drink up, and sixpence in money, in consideration whereof he took upon him *ipso facto*, all the sins of the defunct, and freed him or her from walking after they were dead. This custom alludes, methinks, something to the scapegoat in the old Law [Quoting Leviticus xvi,, 21, 22. Aubrey goes on :—]The like was done at the city of Hereford in these times when a woman kept, many years before her death, a mazard- bowl for the sin-eater." *See* also Sikes, 340 ; Hartland, *Perseus* ii., 292-294, *et. seq.*

very poor, that they may not leave enough money for burial. One poor old woman, who died at Weobley, would, during her last illness, be often fingering a little bag of money beneath the pillow, and would ask everyone who went to see her if it would be sufficient for her burial. It is possible that the origin of this anxiety may be found in the fact that, at one time, the bodies of those who died in debt were actually left unburied.[1] Or it may go farther back, to the widespread belief in the necessity of proper burial, since without it the soul, when separated from the body, could find no repose.[2] It was customary, until a few years ago, to give black hat-bands and gloves to mourners ; if it were the funeral of a child, these would be white. A baby's coffin was carried by little girls dressed in white, at a funeral in Weobley a few years ago,

People formerly chose their bearers beforehand. The wife of one old man, when one of her husband's chosen bearers died before him, actually seemed rather to resent the event. " If he had only known," she said, " there was for every one of them a pair of black gloves and half-a-crown in the palm of the hand."[3]

I am informed by Mr. Portman that in the neighbourhood of Hay, it is the rule that the horses drawing a hearse must always be taken out and put in the stable for a time, before the funeral procession starts from the house. Time is therefore allowed for this, which was called " an old custom " by the driver who practised it. It is carried out at the present day in the three counties which meet at Hay—Herefordshire, Radnor, and Brecon.

The custom of singing psalms and hymns on the way to the grave has now died out.[4] "Ay, ay," said an old woman who had lived her eighty years of life in Pembridge : " it's all so different now. There was always lovely singing at funerals when I was young, psalms and hymns all the way to the church. There's nought left in Pembridge now but pride : and that's poor stuff !"

An inmate of the Trinity Almshouses (Hereford) spoke of her father's funeral, at which they sang psalms all the way from Dinedor to a church six miles off. I asked her about the tunes. " We sang 'em plain, the way they did go," she explained.

On the Welsh side of the county, in the Golden Valley, in the Kington district, and Pembridge, two curious funeral customs prevailed within living memory. The coffin was taken by a roundabout way to the church, and it was put down for a few moments at every cross road, the mourners standing still.[5]

A doctor living at Pembridge, in 1838, seems to have been not a little shocked by the customs practised there. He writes to the local paper : —

1] Gerould, *The Grateful Dead*, 165.   2] Gerould, *op. cit.*, 162–3. *Cf.* Vergil *Æneid*, 6 (the story of Palinurus) and Sophocles, *Antigone.*   3] MS. of the late Rev. H. A. Barker, Eardisland.   4] This is mentioned by Fosbroke, *Ariconensia*, 73, as general.   5] Parry, *Hist. Kington*, 203.

> I attended the funeral of a young man, who was very unexpectedly removed to an eternal world, . . . when I was eye witness to a most foolish custom. I had assembled the mourners together in a room, and prayed with them, and on the way to the parish church we sang the 90th psalm. When we reached the walls of the churchyard, we were led all the way round it, it being the custom to carry the corpse round the churchyard the way of the sun. The clergyman, a very young man, was about to enter the burial ground in another direction, it being the nearest, and he being the head of the procession, when someone cried out, "Sir, you are going the wrong way: it is the other." He immediately altered his course.

The doctor goes on to describe contemptuously the halt at a cross road, and announcement of the death to the bees, "for they foolishly affirm that if they do not, the bees will all be sure to die."[1]

At Peterchurch, where there are two chancels with a terminal apse, and an altar fixed in the latter, the coffin was always carried round both chancels, and deposited in the most westerly one before the service. Mrs. Powell, my informant, says :—" This was in 1875—1887. The practice seems to have prevailed hereabouts ; several years ago the incumbent of Newton tried to discontinue it, thinking it unseemly ; but the people clung to the custom, and prevailed in continuing it." It seems probable, however, that it was at least modified. For a man about eighty years of age, born at Peterchurch, told me he remembered the funerals always went round the churchyard, as described above at Pembridge.

At Brilley, (see *illustration*), the coffin was taken three times round the " Funeral stone," which stood in the open space outside the churchyard. It was believed that this ceremony prevented the devil from obtaining the soul of the deceased.[2] It seems not improbable that the folk held a similar belief with regard to the perambulation of the church or churchyard.

At Dulas, the mourners all kneel round the open grave, even in snow or bad weather, for the whole of that portion of the service which is read there.[3] The custom of throwing boughs or small branches of evergreens into the grave has now died out. An old inhabitant of Bromyard[4] could remember sprigs of rosemary carried by mourners and thrown into the grave.

At the funeral of Velters Cornewall, of Moccas, who died April 3, 1768, twelve women walked in the funeral procession, carrying apple-tree boughs.[5] Probably the apple-tree was chosen on this occasion, because Velters Cornewall, who was Member of Parliament for Herefordshire, obtained by his strenuous exertions, the repeal of a tax on cider and perry. This tax had been very unpopular in Herefordshire.[6]

1] *Hereford Times*, March 20, 1838 ; *Ariconensia*, 74.   2] I am indebted for this information to the kindness of Mr. John Hutchinson, who thinks that the stone now removed, was the base of a cross. 3] Kindly communicated by the Rev. Canon Bannister, when incumbent.   4] 1909.   5] Communicated by the late Rev. Sir G. H. Cornewall.   6] Reade, *House of Cornewall*, 107.   See *Memorials of Old Hereford-shire*, for the song written on this occasion.

WOODEN EFFIGY, CLIFFORD CHURCH.   WOODEN EFFIGY, MUCH MARCLE CHURCH.

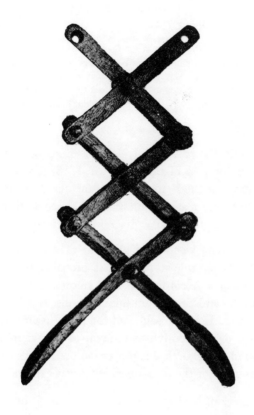

DOG TONGS—FROM CLODOCK CHURCH (OPEN).

DOG TONGS (CLOSED).

The following entry in the Hereford municipal records, 1723, alludes to a custom at funerals now long disused :—

That Thomas Davies, one of the porters of the City, having undertaken to clean the market house and Tolsey, as usual, to make fires at common council meetings, to take up vagrants and sturdy beggars and cause them to be whipped ; to make bonfires, impound pigs, to *sweep before funerals*, and do such other work as the master of the house of correction and bedels used to do ; ordered, that upon his performance of the same, he be paid ten pounds yearly . . . and that he provide brooms, spades, &c., at his own expense.[1]

For clothes of the dead, *see* Section viii.

At Much Marcle, in the parish church, is an unique wooden cross-legged effigy (c. 1350). Until the restoration of the church in 1878, it was the custom to carry this effigy into the church at the head of every funeral. I am informed by the Rev. T. Oliver Minos that some years ago he questioned old people then living in the parish concerning this practice, but they could give no reason for it.[2]

At Clifford is another wooden effigy, that of a priest. Mr. Albert Fryer (*Wooden Monumental Effigies*, 10), states that it probably represents a rector of the parish about 1270 to 1280. According to local tradition, this effigy also was carried into the church before funerals, but I am unable to discover how long it is since the practice was discontinued. It is also said that the figure represents the founder of the Priory, and that at the dissolution it was brought to the church for preservation ; that it was borne round the church in procession on Founder's Day, and that the holes in the shoulders were for the poles on which it was carried.[3]

The ancient family of Walwyn held lands both in Clifford and Much Marcle ; it is possible that some family tradition, now lost, may have originated this curious custom of the perpetual use of the effigies at funerals.[4]

1] Johnson, 223. He says the practice " was probably one of those ancient superstitious ceremonies, the origin of which is involved in obscurity, but which appears to have been quite a local observance."

2] Paper by Rev. T. Oliver Minos, *Woolhope Club*, 1898, 103. For a full account of the effigy, *see* Fryer, *Wooden Monumental Effigies*, 12. " The figure has a close fitting tunic a little over five feet in length, buttoned in front, reaching to the knees, and possessing tight-fitting sleeves buttoned from the elbows to the wrists. The hood is worn about the neck and part of the breast, but is not drawn over the head. Over the hips is a leathern girdle with a long pendant, and a small purse is buckled to it. The legs are in close-fitting pantaloons, the right is crossed over the left, and the shoes are pointed. Cross-legged effigies in the dress of a civilian are very rare. . . . . Mr. James G. Wood . . has come to the conclusion that in all probability the effigy at Much Marcle was removed from Ashperton to the new chantry chapel about 1414, and that it represents Sir Hugh Helyon."

3] *See* Morgan-Watkins, i., 31, and Fryer, *op. cit,* 10 :—" The oldest effigy is that of a priest, at Clifford, Herefordshire. . . . He is tonsured and robed in Eucharistic vestments, and the long chasuble (3 feet 10 inches) is depicted in elegant folds."

4] *Cf.* Fryer, 4 :—" The exposure of the dead at the funeral was followed towards the close of the fourteenth century by the practice of bearing in the funeral procession the hastily made ' lively effigy ' of the dead person, ' in his very robes of estate.' . . . These ' lively figures ' were closely allied to wooden effigies, and may have been suggested by them, as their foundations were of wood, while the face and hands were of wax or fine plaster tinted to life. These figures, dressed in gorgeous robes, and with tinsel crowns and ornaments, presented a lifelike appearance."

It is still believed that the corpse of a murdered man will bleed, if the murderer touches it.

At Longtown, until recently, it was not unusual to read the will of a deceased person over the body, before the funeral procession started from the house. It was sometimes done outside, after placing the coffin on the bier, notably in the case of a person who died near Longtown, leaving a little property. There were three claimants for the small house he possessed—the next-of-kin, the person named in a will made by the deceased, and the possessor of a note-of-hand or bill of some kind, which he alleged was equal in value to the whole of the property. So they agreed to state their claims in the presence of the corpse, before the funeral, believing firmly that it would bleed or make some sign if a false claim were made. This was done before the funeral procession started, but with no result. My informant could not remember how the dispute was settled, only the stir caused by the appeal to such a strange tribunal.

An old lady who had refused to pay to Orcop charities the rent of an acre of land, which had been left as a charge on her farm, died and was buried at Orcop. In those days it was the custom to use a fine shroud, with an embroidered edge, which was left hanging out under the lid of the coffin, which was carried round the chancel before setting it down. At this old lady's funeral, as the coffin reached the communion rails, " the shroud ripped from *end to end*," so old people say, " and hung down round the coffin. That was because she had robbed the poor."

It is said that people used to come from far and near to be buried in Orleton churchyard, because of a belief that the resurrection would begin there, and that those buried there would rise first. There is also a tradition that in a neighbouring parish a man left money for charity, on condition that he should be buried near the church-yard gate, with his feet towards it, that he might get out first.

About 1904 a lady visited a widow at Sarnesfield, who was living alone after the death of her husband, and was surprised to see the table laid for two. " You are expecting a visitor to tea," she said. " No, no," the woman replied, " I always lay the place for my husband."[1] This seemed strange, as the couple had been notoriously quarrelsome during the husband's lifetime. But it would seem that it is in such cases that the custom prevails. An inmate of the Trinity Almshouses related that in her girlhood, at Kinnersley, she knew an old Ann S——, who always laid a place at table for her husband as long as she lived ; " and they was bad friends in life, too," she added.

1] Communicated by Mrs. George Marshall.

Mouzend is the word used for the month's end after a funeral.[1] In North Herefordshire they talk of the twelve months succeeding a death in the family as the *Deathzear*.[2]

In September, 1911, the child of some gypsies named Price, picking hops at Dormington, was accidently burnt, and died in Hospital at Hereford. A touching rite was performed after the parents heard of the death of the child, for in accordance with superstition prevalent among the gypsies and van dwellers, the members of the family took their living van, which cost £80 to build, into the centre of a field, and there, amid much grief, they broke it to pieces with axes, and making a funeral pyre with the parts of the vehicle, set it alight and burnt it to ashes. A representative of the *Hereford Journal* asked the father at the inquest why he took such action; he replied that if the family had not done so the spirit of the boy would return in a short time and haunt the van. It was customary, he continued, to do this, and it was done by all gypsies and van dwellers.[3] Families of Welsh gypsies, named Price or Jones, are frequent and regular visitors to this county, especially at hop-picking time.

1] Rowlstone.
2] Havergal, *Words and Phrases*, 23. Month's mind and year's mind—the days on which the soul of the dead were had in remembrance and obits were sung.—Brand, 489.
3] *Hereford Journal*, Sept. 20, 1911.

SECTION XI.
GAMES, SPORTS, PAGEANTS AND PLAYS.
(1) TRADITIONAL GAMES.

Children's Games.

The old traditional games still hold first place in the affections of the children in our Herefordshire schools. I have collected particulars of upwards of sixty, in schools as far apart as Bosbury and Longtown, Eardisley and Ross. These include many of those which modern research has shown to be most interesting and ancient, enshrining something of the past history of our race, and giving us pictures of the mental habits of our forefathers. But for a few exceptions, given below, our local versions do not vary essentially from those collected in other parts of England, and recently published in Lady Gomme's exhaustive work, *The Traditional Games of England, Scotland,* and *Ireland.* Therefore it seemed unnecessary to re-describe them ; a list of the games now played in the county, with references to Lady Gomme's book, will be found in Appendix C, at the end of this volume.

Counting-out Rhymes.

These are formulas used at the commencement of a game, in which it is necessary that one of the players shall be in some way the butt or slave of the majority. The children stand in a row or ring, and the teller repeats the formula, pointing at each word to each child in succession, working round the ring from east to west. The child on whom the last word falls is " out," and the process is repeated until only one is left, who has to be *it, i.e.,* Blind Man in " Blind Man's Buff," the Hare in " Hare and Hounds," and so on. The practice is thought to be a survival of divination by lot. (*See* Northall, 341, *et. seq.*)

> 1. Ena, mena, mona, mi,
> Startle, story, story, sti,
> Ef, wef, rose knee,
> E, tot, P. and P.
>
> *Kingsland.*

> 2. Iggledy, piggledy, my black hen
> She lays eggs for gentlemen ;
> Sometimes one, sometimes two,
> Iggledy piggledy, out goes you.
>
> *Moccas.*

3.   Ena, mena, mona, mi,
       Artle, startle, story, sti,
       Ect, ot, ect, oh,
           Pop.

4.   Inky, pinky, zulu, da,
       Ick, stick, solomon, ah,
       Inky, pinky, zulu, za,
           France.

The one upon whom " France " falls has to count out twenty-one, in the same way as the formula is repeated, pointing to a child at each number ; the one upon whom twenty-one falls has to chase the others. The one caught begins the game again, by counting out as before.

Leominster.

5.   Ena, dena, dina, doe,
        Catta, wela, wila, woe,
       It's pits, pear, plum,
        Out goes Tom Thumb.

Clehonger.

Hop-scotch.

Hop-scotch has been defined as " a game, the object of which is to eject a stone, slate, or ' dump ' out of a form linearly marked on the ground in different directions, by hopping without touching any of the lines."[1]

The game is still popular in Herefordshire, and is played in practically every village. The method of play varies considerably, and in some places is different from any yet recorded ; as also is the diagram used.

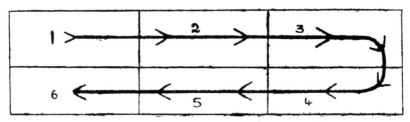

At Leominster, the diagram above, called a " Hops-bed," is drawn on the road or pavement ; a piece of flat stone or tile is placed in the square marked 1, and

---

1] Halliwell's Dictionary, quoted Gomme, *Games* i., 223.

the player hops on one foot through the squares in numerical order, pushing the stone along as he hops. If the stone rest on a line he will be out, but he may put both feet down in bed 4. The first round is called " Ones." For subsequent rounds, the player commences by throwing the stone into the bed marked 2, for Twos, 3 for Threes, and so on to Sixes, where the stone is merely thrown in. If the player be successful, and the stone has not fallen on a line, he may go on to execute the following figures :—

(1) Double Rounders : the same as " Ones," only twice round.

(2) Miss Bed : same as Double Rounders, but hop over beds 2 and 5 and miss them out altogether in each round.

(3) Cross Keys : thus, twice round :—

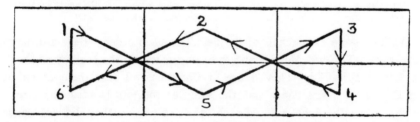

(4) Postman's Knock : once round, stamping with the disengaged foot after each hop ; otherwise the same as " Double Rounders."

(5) Change Feet : twice round, hopping on each foot alternately.

(6) Blind Man's Buff : " Ones " done blindfold.

Sports.

For Bull-baiting and Cock-fighting, *see* Section xii., *Wakes and Feasts.*

Follow my Leader, *see* Section ix., *Gauging Day.*

(2) DANCES.[1]

The Morris Dance.

" The courts of kings for stately measures : the city for light heeles and nimble footing : the country for shuffling dances : western men for gambols :

1] [BIBLIOGRAPHICAL NOTE.—For accounts of the Morris dance, see Douce, *Illustrations to Shakespeare* ; Brand, *Pop. Antiquities ;* Burne, *Shropshire Folk-Lore ;* Strutt, *Sports and Pastimes.* See also Chambers, *Med. Stage*, i., ch. 9. (Mr. Chambers thinks the Sword Dance and the Morris dance are variants of the same performance.) Those wishing to learn the dances described in this chapter will find Mr. Cecil Sharp's *Morris Book*, Parts I., II., III., and IV., and *The Country Dance Book*, Parts I. and II., an invaluable help. I have followed Mr. Sharp's plan in describing the dances and in making diagrams, hoping this may prove convenient to those who are already familiar with his books on the subject. Where tunes are not given for the dances below, they are obtainable in modern publications, such as Mr. Sharp's *Country Dance Tunes* (Novello), or Kerr's *Merry Melodies* for the violin (published in Glasgow).]

Middlesex men for tricks above grounde : Essex men for the hay : Lancashire for horn-pipes : Worcestershire for bagpipes : but Herefordshire for a Morris dance puts down, not only all Kent but very near (if one had line enough to measure it), three quarters of Christendom." So says the author of an old pamphlet, describing the famous Morris dance which took place on the racecourse at Hereford in 1609. The pamphlet is entitled, *Old Meg of Herefordshire for a Maid Marian, Hereford Towne for a Morris Daunce, or Twelve Morris Dauncers in Herefordshire of Twelve Hundred years old.* The author is chiefly concerned with the ages and descriptions of the dancers, rather than the dance itself. The dresses worn are thus described :—

"The musicians and the twelve dancers had long coats of the old fashion, high sleeves gathered at the elbows, and hanging sleeves behind, the stuff, red buffin, striped with white girdles, with white stockings, white and red roses to their shoes ; the one six, a white jew's cap with a jewel, and a long red feather ; the other, a scarlet jew's cap, with a jewel and a white feather ; so the hobby-horse, and so the Mayd-Marian was attired in colours ; the whifflers had long staves, white and red."

Whifflers were "marshals of the field," to keep order. Bells are mentioned, but not staves. The only Morris dancers I can discover in the country at the present time are from Brimfield. They dance at Christmas. I saw them at Orleton on Boxing Day, 1909. The dance was the same as the four-handed reel (*see below*), except that when the dancers faced each other, in part 2, they did not dance, but tapped their staves together to the music. Apparently this is but a fragmentary survival of the original Morris. The men say that they remember when the dancers wore smock frocks, breeches, white stockings and gaiters, with soft felt hats, and there was formerly a fool. Those I saw had their faces blacked, with white patches, and wore diagonal coloured sashes, but no bells or streamers.

An old fiddler at Dilwyn who danced with Morris men there and at Leominster, said they always had a fool, with a bell tied on behind ; they all wore bells, and carried sticks. They danced at Christmas, when they were out of work owing to prolonged frost, and they wore shirts decorated profusely with streamers and coloured rosettes ; the music was a fiddle. The dance was quite different from that of the Orleton dancers, being distinguishable from a country dance by the "stick rapping" only. (*See description below.*)

An old man in the Workhouse at Ross (1907), a native of Walford, remembered Morris dancers. They danced at Whitsuntide in the Ross district ; there were parish wakes, or feasts, every day in Whitsun week, which they attended. They wore shirts with coloured ribbons, and had "ruggles" (little bells) at the knees.

It was also customary in North Herefordshire for men to go Morris dancing during a hard frost, when masons and others could not work, in order to raise money.

THE MORRIS DANCE.

(WHOLE SET DANCE FOR EIGHT.)

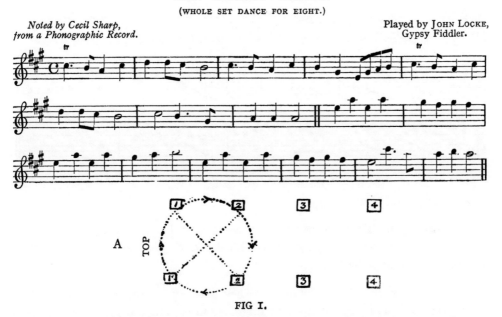

*Noted by Cecil Sharp,
from a Phonographic Record.*

Played by JOHN LOCKE,
Gypsy Fiddler.

FIG I.

(1) Dancers stand facing each other, and knock their sticks together crosswise, on the 1st and 3rd beats of each bar (16 bars: first strain of tune twice).

(2) Dancers turn to face A, and cross over behind each other and change places (4 bars), and back again (4 bars). Repeat once. During this movement the second strain is played twice.

(3) First and second couples "hands-across," holding up their sticks in the disengaged hand. Third and fourth do the same. They go round to the right (Fig. 1), 8 bars; then to the left, 8 bars. Repeat No 2 and re-commence at No. 1.

THREE JOLLY BLACK SHEEP-SKINS.

FIRST TUNE.

Noted by Alice J. Ovens.
A (Play 4 times)

From W. PREECE,
Fiddler, 1908.

B (Play twice)

Noted by Cecil Sharp.   SECOND TUNE.   From JOHN LOCKE, 1909.

Three Jolly Black Sheepskins.

"Three Jolly Black Sheepskins" was much danced in ale-houses, when the first dancer making a mistake in it, had to pay for drinks for the rest. It was therefore as much a game as a dance.

The dancers are three in number. They place their caps on the floor about 4 to 5 feet apart. Possibly the caps were originally sheepskins, but there is no tradition to this effect.

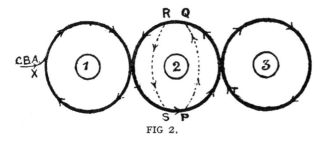

FIG 2.

1, 2, and 3 are the 3 Caps.

The three dancers A, B, and C, stand in single file, headed by A. Starting from X they dance the Hey, along the track shown in the diagram.

At P, the last dancer C, breaks the file, turns to the left along dotted line P Q, and rejoins the file at Q, as leader. The dancers are now in the following order, CAB.

Similarly, on the return journey, the last dancer, B, breaks off at R, turns to the left along dotted line R S, and rejoins his mates at S, as head of the file. The dancers are now therefore in the order B C A. The rule is a simple one. Whenever the dancers pass 2, the hindmost breaks off, turns to his left, and rejoins the file as leader. That is, he takes a short cut from P to Q while the other two dancers are dancing round 3 ; or a short cut from R to S while his mates are dancing round 1.

Dancing the Broom Stick.

Tune—" Pop goes the Weasel."

For this each dancer is provided with an ordinary broom, which is laid on the floor before him, the handle just between his toes. First,

(1) The broom is placed on the floor, thus :—

FIG. 3.

(2) When the music begins, walk round the broom as it lies on the floor, twice (16 bars).

(3) Take the broom at end of handle in both hands and rock the broom from side to side, knocking each end alternately on the floor, in time with the music. The left hand end touches the floor at the beginning, and the right end at the middle of each bar. Make as much noise as possible, while turning the broom from side to side smoothly.

(4) Take broom in left hand, at end of handle. Stand on left toe, raise right leg and hop on left foot, at the same time passing the broom under the right leg into the right hand. Then hop on right foot, pass broom under left leg into left hand again. The legs should be thrown over the broom handle as high as possible, while the hands pass it under. The hops come on the first and middle beats of each bar, so the single or half movement is executed in one bar of the music. Continue this for 16 bars.

(5) Lay the broom on the floor and hop from side to side, two hops, or rather a step and a hop, on either foot, still on the first and middle beats of each bar, crossing the feet, thus[1] :—

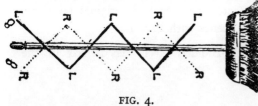

FIG. 4.

Turn at either end of the broom (16 bars).

Repeat from 3 *ad libitum.* The music is accelerated in conclusion. Either strain of time is used for the different movements.

Three-handed Reel.

Any hornpipe, in common time, will do for this dance, or for the Six-Handed Reel.

1] This is the same as the Swing-Step (*see The Morris Book,* Part III., p. 27).

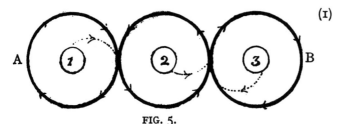

FIG. 5.

(1) Three dancers stand in single file, about three feet apart. They move as in Fig. 5, by passing each other alternately to right and left and turning back at A and B (16 bars). That is they dance the Hey, Nos. 1 and 2 first passing by the right (*see Country Dance Book*, II., 47).

(2) Dancers 1 and 2 stand and face each other, and dance a step dance, or a reel step may be used, though I have not seen this done in Herefordshire (8 bars). No. 2 then turns to face No. 3, who has danced the first eight bars alone, and dances 8 bars.

Repeat (1), and so on, *ad libitum.*

The Four-Handed Reel is danced in the same way, but as there are two dancers in the centre, Nos. 1 and 2 and Nos. 3 and 4 dance 16 bars together, facing each other in the second part.

Six-handed Reel.

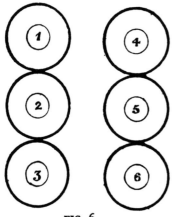

FIG. 6.

This is exactly the same dance, but it is danced in two parallel lines, thus :—

(3) While at the conclusion of Part 2, a third movement is introduced ; the lines 1, 2, 3, and 4, 5, 6, cross over, and change places, and go back again to their original positions, to re-commence with Part 1.

The "Eight-Handed Reel" is danced in the same manner.

Country Dances.

The country dance is performed by an equal number of men and women, standing facing each other in parallel lines, or, as Playford's *Dancing Master* expresses it, "longwayes for as many as will." The "top" of the dance is that end which is nearest the music, and is on the right of the women's line. There must not be less than six dancers, partners opposite each other. "Sir Roger de Coverley" is a familiar example of this formation. This is what is called a whole-set dance, because all the dancers are occupied from the beginning to the end of the dance. The following country dances are described as " duple " or " triple minor set " dances, because any figure that they contain can be performed by either two or three couples only. Every country dance contains a progressive figure by means of which an alteration in the relative position of the couples is effected, some couples moving down, others up the dance.

This progressive movement will be found fully described, with diagrams, in Mr. Cecil Sharp's *Country Dance Book, I.* At the conclusion of a figure, the couples engaged in it usually " swing," that is, they meet, engage waltz fashion, and dance round in a small circle between the lines of the set, usually to a waltz step; they bow to each other in returning to places.

Figure Eight.

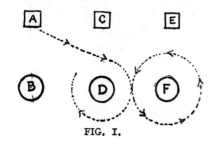

FIG. I.

TRIPLE MINOR SET.

Tune—" Jack's the Lad."

(1) First woman (8 bars) (Fig. 1).

First man, simultaneously, woman crossing in front of him (Fig. 2).

(2) They dance down the middle and up again (8 bars).

(3) First and second couples " swing " and cast one (8 bars). *See* " Haste to the Wedding," Fig. 5.

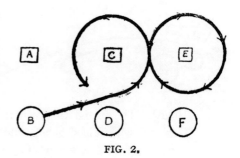

FIG. 2.

Figure Seven.

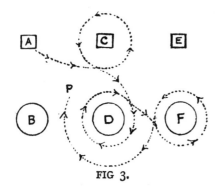

FIG 3.

TRIPLE MINOR SET.

Same tune as "Figure Eight," on any Country Dance tune, in 6-8 time.

(1) First woman, 8 bars.

First man, simultaneously.

It will be seen that at the end they are following each other round, and finish at the same point (P).

(2) As in "Figure Eight," 2 and 3.

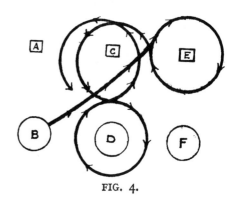

FIG. 4.

Haste to the Wedding.

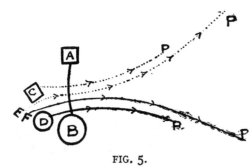

FIG. 5.

TRIPLE MINOR SET.

Tune—" Haste to the Wedding."

(1) The first three couples take hands and dance round in a ring, half way to right (4 bars), and half way to left (4 bars).

(2) They separate into couples, and gallop round once to the right (8 bars). The second time round (the same way), the top couple stand and form an arch with joined hands, under which the second and third couples pass to their original places at P (Fig. 5).

(3) A and B lead down the middle and up again, while the second couple move up one place (Fig. 6). At the top A and B release hands, cast off, pass round and outside C and D to the second place, at P (8 bars); that is, they " cast one."

(4) First and second couples swing (8 bars).

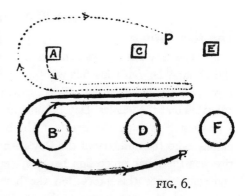

FIG. 6.

Handkerchief Dance.

DUPLE MINOR SET.

Noted by Cecil Sharp. GREENSLEEVES. From JOHN LOCKE, Gypsy Fiddler, 1909.

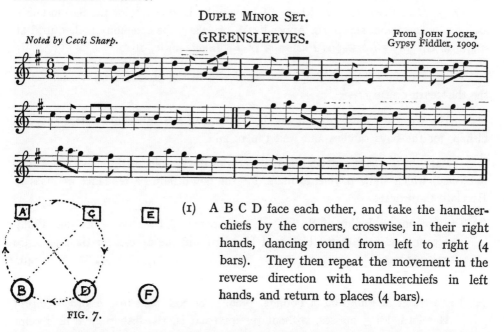

FIG. 7.

(1) A B C D face each other, and take the handkerchiefs by the corners, crosswise, in their right hands, dancing round from left to right (4 bars). They then repeat the movement in the reverse direction with handkerchiefs in left hands, and return to places (4 bars).

(2) The second couple take a handkerchief between them, holding their right arms up to form an arch : they advance up four steps, and at the same time the first couple go down and under the arch, holding their handkerchiefs loosely between them (4 steps, 2 bars). The first couple now move up four steps, making an arch, under which the second couple return (2 bars). The first movement is now repeated ; this leaves the second couple at the top (2 bars). Pause of two bars to end of strain.

(3) Plays and Pageants.

The Boy Bishop.

The Boy Bishop was chosen from among the choir boys of each cathedral or church, and he, with his fellows, took possession of the church on Holy Innocents' Day, performing the usual offices instead of the regular clergy.   In some places he officiated on St. Nicholas' Day.   Sometimes there was a quête, and the bishop headed a procession through the streets.   The Sarum Breviary and Processional give ample details as to the ministry of the Boy Bishop and his fellows in England.   The central rite was the great procession between vespers and compline on the eve of the Holy Innocents.   For this procession the boys were entitled to assign the functions of carrying the book, the censer, the candles, and so forth, to the canons, though this was forbidden in the statutes of St. Paul's.   For a full account of the custom, *see* Chambers, *Med. Stage*, ch. xv., where a bibliography is given.   For the Sarum Office used on this occasion, *see op. cit.* Appendix M., ii., 282 ; the ceremony is described at length in Gregory's *Episcopus Puerorum in die Innocentium*, 1649.

The Hereford " boy bishop "[1] is mentioned in the Hereford *Consuetudines* of the thirteenth century :—

The treasurer must present on the Festival of the Innocents before the boy bishop, for the boys candles and wax tapers 2d.[1]

Early in the next century there are entries in the rolls of the mass pence (unpublished) which show payments made for the boy bishop's attendance at Mass in Hereford Cathedral :—

(1) The account of Philip of Witley for mass pence, A.D. 1306.   The said Philip accounts as paid to the bishop of Hereford and the canons for their presence at one mass   .   .   .   .   .   . 4d.
The same Philip to the bishop on Innocents' Day   .   .   . 4d.[2]

(2) The account of Philip de la Pounde, 1309.   For 20d. paid to the lord bishop of Hereford, for 5 masses, without receipt (that is, the bishop gave no receipt for the money) ; and for 4 pence paid to the boy bishop on the day of the Holy Innocents for mass pence.[3]

1] *Thesaurius debet invenire* . . *in festo Innocencium pueris candelas et ijos cereos, coram parvo episcopo.* Lincoln Statutes ii., 6, 7 (from *Chambers*), *op. cit.*

2] *Idem Phillippus computat liberatos episcopo Herefordensi pro presencia suam ad missam* . . iiijd.   *Item episcopo die Innocencium* . . iiijd.

3] *Compotus Philippi de la Pounde, MCCCIX.   De xxd. liberatis domino episcopo Herefordensi pro v missis sine tallia.   Et de iiijd. liberatis parvo episcopo die Sanctorum Innocencium pro denariis missalibus.* I am indebted to the kindness of the Rev. R. Hyett Warner for the translations.

These entries were kindly copied from the rolls for me by the Rev. Canon Capes, who says that they continue for more than a century after 1309 ; the Boy bishop is alluded to as the " little bishop " throughout. The entries following are those of payments to canons for attendance at mass.

Mediaeval Miracle Plays. The Corpus Christi Pageant.

Bishop Trilleck, bishop of Hereford, 1344–1361, prohibited all plays and interludes in the churches of his diocese, because by them " the hearts of the faithful are drawn aside to vanities."[1]

The religious plays thus banished from the churches were probably distinct from those in the vulgar tongue, which long survived, as part of the Corpus Christi pageant. On April, 30, 1440, John Hauler and John Pewte sued Thomas Sporyour in the Hereford City Court, " de placito detencionis unius libri de lusionibus prec. iis. iiijd."[2] There is no direct evidence that these lusiones formed a Corpus Christi play, though it seems probable that they may have done so. An entry in the municipal archives for 1503, gives the order of the pageants for that year : it seems to concern a dumb show only.

The feast of Corpus Christi is in honour of the mystery of the transubstantiated sacrament. It originated locally in an alleged revelation to Juliana, a Cistercian religious of Liege, in the thirteenth century, and was finally confirmed by Clement V. in 1311. Corpus Christi day was the Thursday after Trinity Sunday. The leading ceremony was a great procession, in which the host, escorted by local dignitaries, religious bodies and guilds, was borne through the streets and displayed successively at out-of-door stations. When the plays were transferred to Corpus Christi Day they became more or less attached to this procession. The domus loci, or sedes, were set upon wheels, and known as " pageants," and the performance was gone through during the procession. There is nothing to show that the pageants at Hereford in 1503 were more than tableaux-vivants.[3] They were as follows :—

THE PAIANTS FOR THE PROCESSION OF CORPUS CHRISTI :—

Furst, Glovers	.	.	Adam, Eve. *Cayne and Abell* (erased).
Eldest seriant	.	.	Cayne, Abell, and Moysey, Aron.
Carpenters	.	.	Noye ship.
Chaundelers	.	.	Abram, Isack, Moysey, cum iiii ᵒʳ pueris.
Skynners	.	.	Jesse.

1] Havergal *Fasti*, 22. 2] *Hist. MSS.*, xiii., 4, 300.
3] Chambers, *Med. Stage*, ii., 95. ; Johnson, 116.

Flacchers	Salutacõn of our Lady.
Vynteners . . .	Nativite of our Lord.
Taillours	The iii Kings of Colen.
The belman . . .	The purificacõn of our Lady with Symyon.
Drapers	The —— (*blank*) deitours goyng with the good Lord.
Sadlers . . .	Fleme Jordan.
Cardeners	The castell of Israell.
Walkers[1] . . .	The good Lord ridyng on an asse with xii Appostelles.
The Tanners . . .	The story of Shore Thursday.[2]
Bochours	The takyng of our Lord.
The eldest seriant . .	The Tormentyng of our Lord with iiii tormentoures, with the lamentacõn of our Lady [and Seynt John the evaungelist : *faintly added by another hand.*]
[Cappers . .	Portacio crucis usque montem Oliverii, *added by the second hand*].
Dyers	Jesus pendens in cruce [*altered by the second hand from* Portacio crucis et Johanne evangelista postante Mariam.]
Smythes . . .	Longys with his knyghtes.
The eldest sariant . .	Maria and Johannes evangelista (*interlined*).
Barbours	Joseth Abarmarthia.
Dyers . . .	Sepultura Christi.
The eldest seriant . .	Tres Mariæ.
Porters	Milites armati custodes sepulcri.
Mercers	Pilate, Cayfes, Annas, and Mahounde. [*This last name has been partly erased.*]
Bakers	Knyghtes in harnes.
Journeymen cappers .	Seynt Keterina with tres (?) tormentors.[3]

The cordwainers are not represented, but there still exists among the Hereford MSS. a petition from the members of this guild to the Mayor, relative to their part in the procession on Corpus Christi day, and its profits (1500–1520 ?) They were bound to bring forth " certen torches in the procession " and received " xiiid. for the mayntenaunce of the sayd torches and for the relyeffe of the pore bretherne of the seyd occupacion." Their complaint is that " the wardens of the sayd occupacion,

1] Fullers of cloth. 2] Shere Thursday is the Thursday before Easter, and is so called, says an old homily, "for that in old Fathers' days the people would that day shere theyr hedes and clypp theyr herdes and pool theyr heedes, and so make them honest ayenst Easter day."—Brand, 75.
3] *Hist. MSS. Hereford*, v., xiii., 288. An ordinance made in Dec., 1549, with regard to the substitution of annual payments for the pageants is printed from a copy in the Black Book (f. 25) at p. 119 of Johnson's Customs of Hereford.

and certen other frowarde persons in a cedule hereunto annexted named, of theyre perverse mynd dyd dystribute and geve away the torches," and refused to give a proper account of the moneys received.[1]

It is thought that " Cob's Cross " at Ross is a corruption of " Corpus Christi Cross," and that the name is derived from the performance of a Corpus Christi pageant there.[2]

The pageant in many places survived the religious ceremony to which it had been attached before the Reformation, but was wholly discontinued at Hereford before the middle of the sixteenth century.

At a law day held on December 10, 1548, it was agreed that the crafts which were " bound by the grantes of their corporacions yerely to bring forthe and set forward dyvers pageaunttes of ancient history in the processions of the cytey upon the day and fest of Corpus Christi, which now is rare omitted and surceased," should instead make an annual payment towards the expense of repairing walls, causeways, etc.[3]

A notice of an interesting survival of another pre-Reformation custom has been preserved among the municipal archives of Hereford :—

In 1706 a labourer went through the city in the week before Easter, being Passion Week, clothed in a long coat, with a large periwig, with a great multitude following him, sitting upon an ass, to the derision of our Saviour Jesus Christ's riding into Jerusalem, to the great scandal of the Christian religion, to the contempt of our Lord and his doctrine, and to the ill and pernicious example of others.[4]

It seems possible that this may be a fragment of the festival called in France the *fete de l'âne*, or Feast of Fools. It was there held at the New Year, by the inferior clergy, in the mediæval cathedrals. An ass was sometimes taken into the church.[5] The ass may have been associated with Palm Sunday in later times, in an ecclesiastical attempt to sanctify what was originally a Pagan feast.

The Mummer's Play.

CHARACTERS.

PART I.

Father Christmas.

St. George.

King of Egypt.

1] *Hist. MSS.*, Hereford, v., xiii., 305. 2] Fosbroke, *Ariconensia*, 83. 3] *Hist. MSS.*, *loc. cit.*
4] *Hist. MSS.*, xiii., 4, 352. There was a procession in Continental churches on Palm Sunday, in which an ass formed part (Chambers, i., 333). But Mr. Chambers does not think it was ever an English custom, this " Hereford riding " being the only known example, and that not in the Church. Brand, (64), quotes from a rare work (1551 ?) entitled *A Dialoge, &c.—the Pylgremage of pure Devotyon, newly translatyd into Englishe.* " Upon Palme Sundaye they play the foles sadely, *drawynge after them an asse in a rope.* When they be not moche distante from the Woden asse that they drawe." For the Hereford Palm Sunday procession, see *Hereford Missal*, 79–81.
5] Chambers, i., 331. At Beauvais, in the thirteenth century, and at Prague in the fourteenth.

Turkey Snipe.

Captain Rover.

Bonaparte.

Little John.

Sambo the Minstrel.

Prince Valentine.

The Doctor.

PART II.

Beelzebub.

Farmer Toddy.

Head Per Nip.

Dicky Hissum.

PART I.

Prologue.

Ladies and Gentlemen all, if you wish to see,

We are come this night to act a royal comedy.

We are but actors young—

We never acted before—

But we'll do the best we can,

And the best can do no more.

If you don't believe what I say,—

Walk in, old Father Christmas, and boldly lead the way.

Enter Father Christmas with besom.

Then in comes I old Father Christmas :

Christmas or Christmas not,

I hope old Father Christmas

'll never be forgot.

For when he does appear

It's like the rising sun in three score year.

Room, room, galliant room! Give me room to reign.

Your activity, my activity, such activities you never saw before.

'Tis I that leads the King of Egypt up to the door.

Enter King of Egypt. (*Exit Father Christmas.*)

In comes I the King of Egypt, who plainly doth appear,

Likewise St. George, my only son and heir.

Walk in St. George and act thy part
That all the people in this house
May see thy wondrous works with all their heart.

Enter St. George.

Then in comes I St. George who did from England spring,
Oft-times do my wondrous works do four-fold to begin.
Girt in a closet I was kept,
And then upon a cabin set,
And then upon a rock of stone,
When Satan made my body moan ;
I slew the fiery dragon ; I beat him to a slaughter,
And by those means I won the King of Egypt's daughter.
I fought him off most manfully,
But still came on the victory.
Where is man that will against me stand ?
I will cut him down with my courage in hand.

Enter Prince Valentine.

In comes I Prince Valentine ; if there's anyone so old,
That will give to me his lofty courage bold,
If his blood's hot, I will soon fetch it cold.
St. George and Prince Valentine fight. St. George kills him.

Enter bold Captain Rover.

In comes I bold Captain Rover,
Come to view old England over.
France I conquered, Spain I beat,
And before St. George I will repeat.
(They fight. St. George kills him.)

Enter Turkey Snipe.

In comes I bold Turkey Snipe,
Who's lately come from Turkey to fight ;
To fight St. George and all his kin,
Perhaps he's a coward and won't come in.

St. George.

Stand off, stand off, thou proud Turkey dog,
Else by my sword thou shalt die ;

I'll cut thy jacket all in holes,
And I'll make thy buttons fly.
(*They fight. St. George kills Turkey Snipe.*)

Enter Little John.

In comes I, Little John, with a sword drawn in my hand ;
If any man offend me, I will bid him stand :
I'll cut him, I'll slay him as small as a fly,
And I'll send him to Yorkshire to make mince pie.

St. George.

Mince pie I do not like,
So theè and I'll go to fight.
(*St. George kills him.*)

Enter Bonaparte.

In comes I bold Bonaparte,
To cut and slay and do my part,
I have conquered many heroes, with this long and famous sword,
And now I come to see
If I can't fight St. George and win the Victory.

St. George.

There's nothing like the victory,
So I'll try as well as thee,
And if by chance thou cut me down,
I'll rise again and take my ground.
(*They fight. St. George falls on knee. St. George knocks
Boney over. Boney shouts :*)
Sambo, Sambo, help me Sambo !
Boney dies.

Enter Sambo.

Yes, my massa's words I do obey,
Wid my long sword and spear I hope to win de day ;
And does that spill my massa's blood,
I'll send dere body down de ocean flood.
(*St. George shoots Sambo and kills him.*)

St. George.

Is there any doctor to be found,
To cure these men, that lies [*sic*] bleeding on the ground.

Enter Doctor.
    Yes, I am a fancy doctor.

St. George.
    Well, my fancy doctor, where did you come from ?

Doctor.
    I come from France and Spain,
    To cure the sick, the wounded, and the lame,
    And those that lie in pain.
    I can use my skill and bid them away,
    That they might fight another day.
    I can cure the hip, the pip, the palsy and the gout,
    If old Nick's in, I can fetch him out.

St. George.
    Well, my fancy doctor, let me see a little of your skill !

Doctor goes round with flat bottle and says to each in turn :—
    Jack, take a little of my nick nack, and rise !
                                        They all get up.

St. George.
    Well, my fancy doctor, what's your fee ?

Doctor.
    Ten pounds is my fee,
    Ten guineas I'll have of thee.

St. George.
    No ten guineas you'll have of me,
    We'll fight it out most manfully.

                *St. George and the Doctor fight. The doctor kills St George
                and he is carried out.*

PART II.

Enter Beelzebub with frying pan and club.
    In comes I old Beelzebub
    And on my shoulder I carry a club,
    And in my hand a dripping pan :
    Don't you think I'm a smart young man ?
                                        Exit.

Enter Farmer Toddy.

> In comes I Farmer Toddy,
> All back and big body,
> All hips and no toes,
> If you don't give me victuals and drink, off I goes.

Exit.

Enter Head Per Nip.

> In comes I, Head Per Nip,
> With big head and little wit.
> Although my body is so small,
> I'm the biggest rogue among them all.

Exit.

Enter Dicky Hissum.

> In comes I Dicky Hissum,
> With a new second-handed old bissum ;
> Christmas comes but once a year,
> I should like to beg a few coppers
> And a jug of your best Christmas beer.

Exit.

Sambo goes in with tambourine.

> Ladies and Gentlemen, sit at your ease,
> Put your hand in your pocket and give what you please.

(Songs and music from any of the troupe.)

Finis.

This play was written out by William Powell, Brampton Street, Ross, in November, 1908 ; he said the mumming had been discontinued of late years. He had taken all the parts at different times ; the dresses worn were various and fantastic. I am not sure that the play has a long history in Ross, as Powell thought it was " brought from Cheltenham." This may be an error, as a lady who had lived near Ross all her life can remember the mummers when she was a small child. They came at Christmas ; their faces were blacked, and they rushed in without knocking at the door. In Shropshire, and Staffordshire, the guisers or mummers are also known as Morris dancers ; there would seem to be a close connection between the Morris dance, semi-dramatic in character, and this primitive drama.[1]

1] *See* Burne, 482, *et seq.* ; Chambers, *Med. Stage*, i., ch. x., where a bibliographical note, and list of twenty versions of the St. George play are given. Mr. Chambers traces the affiliation of the plays to the sword dancers, showing an obvious continuity. " The central incident " (the fight, followed by the introduction of the Doctor to revive the slain) " symbolizes the *renouveau*, the annual death of the year, or the fertilization spirit and its annual resurrection in spring. To this have become attached some of those heroic *cantilenæ*, which as the early Mediæval chroniclers tell us, existed in the mouths of the *chori juvenum*, side by side with the *cantilenæ* of the minstrels. The symbolism of the *renouveau* is preserved unmistakably enough in the episode of the Doctor, but the *cantilenæ* have been to some extent modified by the comparatively late literary element, due perhaps to that universal go-between of literature and the folk, the village school-master."

SECTION XII.

LOCAL CUSTOMS.

(1) PAROCHIAL CUSTOMS.

Clodock.

A very curious pair of dog tongs, taken from Clodock Church, were exhibited in the temporary museum at Abergavenny in 1876 (*see* illustration from *Arch. Camb.*, 4th Series, viii., 213). They were used for seizing canine intruders during service. At Peterchurch, until comparatively recent times, a person was periodically elected to the use and enjoyment of a piece of land called the " Dog acre," on condition that he should whip all stray dogs out of church. An old inhabitant told me in 1906 that he could remember seeing the dog tongs in use. There were also dog-tongs at Hentland : a woman who had seen them called them " stickies." It has been said that the introduction of dogs into church was a custom of the Puritans, to show their contempt for sacred places.[1]

Eaton Bishop.

There was formerly a curious old custom by which the Rector had the right shoulder of every calf that any parishioner killed in his own house of his own breed.[2]

Hereford Cathedral, Spur Money.

Spur money was the fine paid for wearing spurs in a cathedral. It was formerly collected by the choristers. Some years ago a visitor to Hereford cathedral declined to satisfy the demands of the boys, who thereupon seized his hat and decamped with it. The indignant despiser of old customs, instead of redeeming his property, laid a complaint before the bench. But the magistrates astonished him by dismissing the case, on the grounds that the choristers were justified in keeping the hat as a lien for the customary fine. There was one way of escaping the tax, the spur wearer being held exempt if the youngest chorister present failed to repeat his gamut correctly upon being challenged to do so.[3]

Hereford City.

" Assignment of lands or tenements. First of all we say that every citizen of the city or suburbs may give and assign their tenements freely and quietly, as well in health as in sickness, when and to whomsoever they please, whether those tenements are of their inheritance or of their purchasing or getting, without any malicious detracting of their lord, *so that they be of such an age, and no less, that they know how to measure a yard of cloth, and to know and tell twelve pence.*"[4]

1] *See* Dyer, *Church Lore Gleanings,* 61. 2] Robinson, *Mansions and Manors,* 113.
3] Chambers, *Book of Days,* ii., 541. 4] *Journal of the Arch. Association,* xxvi, 471, from the *Customs circa.* 1154. I am indebted to Mr. W. J. Humfrys for this reference.

Leominster.

The Vicar of Leominster had a certain payment called " Trug corn " allowed him for officiating at the chapels-of-ease at Stoke Prior and Docklow. When these became a separate parish about the middle of the seventeenth century, the payment of corn was transferred to the incumbent.[1]

Weobley.

There were living in Weobley until recently old people who could remember the elections before the passing of the Reform Act in 1832. Weobley was represented in Parliament till then, and the borough was a pocket one of the Marquis of Bath, who used to send tenants from his Shropshire estates to vote at Weobley. They had to boil their kettle there the evening before, and would make large fires in the main street for this purpose. Hence they were called pot-wallopers. These particulars are corroborated by a lady of Church Stretton, who wrote to Miss Burne in 1885 : " I can remember hearing of them (the pot-wallopers) drinking about in Stretton (Shropshire) on the way back."[2]

Lammas Lands and Commons.

A large stretch of pasture on both sides of the road between Hereford and Lugwardine, called Lugg-meadows, and covering some hundreds of acres, is held in common from Lammas Day (August 2nd) in each year until Candlemas. But during the other six months it is held in severalty, and stones mark the boundaries of the several properties. This is a survival from the time when the land was cultivated on a kind of co-operative system. There never was in Lugwardine an inclosure of commonable lands, which are not to be confounded with waste lands, or " commons." The difference is clearly explained by Mr. W. J. Humfrys, in his paper on *Lammas Lands* (*Woolhope Club*, 1898-9, 165).[3] Mr. Humfrys remembers Lammas Lands at Pembridge which are now enclosed. A writer on the agriculture of the county in 1794 describes the method of cultivating the arable common fields[4]:—

> The invariable rotation of crops in all the common fields is, first year, a fallow ; second year, wheat ; a third year, peas, or oats ; then begin again with a fallow.

Bewailing this practice and pitying the farmer because some of the best land in England is allowed to lie idle every third year, he adds :—

1] Townsend, *Leominster*, 260. A trug was a twelfth part of a horse load :—*Charters of Hereford Cathedral*, ed. by the Rev. Canon Capes, 130.
2] *Folk-Lore Journal*, xiv., 168. See Stephens, *Commentaries*, ii., 362—*Pot-Wallers* (*i.e.*, such as cook their diet in a fireplace of their own).
3] *See* also Morgan-Watkins, 96.   4] These were usually three fields for a three-year rotation of crops. Each field was divided into strips of half an acre, apportioned among the tenants of the manor.

He follows this course of husbandry not through choice, but by compulsion, because it is the custom of the parish; for by a remarkable feature which is interwoven with the constitution of this country and which has obtained a priority to any of its laws, old customs must not be broken.[1]

Broken they were, however, and we have only John Clarke's protest to testify the strength of them at this date. For by 1813, Duncumb, in his report on the agriculture of the country, remarks with satisfaction that many commons are already enclosed, and others " gradually converting from their natural state to that which proves more productive and beneficial to society."[2] The numerous Inclosure Acts dealt principally with the common fields, and to some extent with commons also. Clarke mentions that he estimates the waste lands of the county in 1794 at twenty thousand acres.

There was a custom that if a man wanted to enclose a piece of common land he must plant an apple tree on it. Then the lord of the manor, to preserve his rights, exacted an annual tribute of the fruit.[3]

On Ruckhall Common, in the Parish of Eaton Bishop, people used to come in the night and put up a hut of the roughest kind in which they could light a fire from which smoke would rise before daybreak. This was sufficient to establish a right to the site, and the squatters would build a better house on the same plot of ground at their leisure. " But that's done away with now," added my informant, who had lived many years at Ruckhall, " folk can't take land off the common nowadays."

Perambulations, and Beating the Bounds.

The old custom of beating the bounds of each parish at Rogationtide is not kept up in the county, as far as I have been able to ascertain, though many remember it. We have a trace of it in the " gospel " trees, under which the clergyman read the gospel for the day, and gave his benediction. There is a Gospel Oak on the spot where the parishes of Kingsland, Lucton, Aymestrey, and Shobdon meet, and a Gospel Yew at the junction of Bosbury, Castle Frome, and Canon Frome. Fosbroke (*Ariconensia*, 155), describes the perambulation of the parishes of Ross and Weston, which commenced at the stool of an oak which grew over a spring in the bottom of a little meadow called the " Flaxridge," in Penyard. This spring, he says, was venerated of old.[4]

The bounds of the city of Hereford were last perambulated in 1890. There are also accounts of this ceremony in the *Hereford Times* for May 14th, 1870, and October 7th, 1882. The *Hereford Times* of May 7th, 1870, announced that the procession would start at 10 o'clock, and proceeding down the Wye in boats, would land opposite

---

1] Clarke, *Agriculture of the County of Hereford*; Appendix 69. 2] Duncumb, *Agriculture of the County of Hereford*, 97. 3] *Hereford Times*, Dec., 1879. 4] For other Holy Wells, *see* Section i.

the Franchise Stone ; thence they would cross the fields to " The Stone" [which seems to have had no name], from there along Holy Well Gutter Lane to the " Cock," at Tupsley. Thence to Baynton Wood, and over Lugg Meadows to Lugg Bridge. From the Bridge to Holmer and Three Elms, to the cottage at Stretton Sugwas (by omnibus). The first day's perambulations concluded at the brink of the river, opposite the stone on the Hunderton side. The second day the party started from the stone near the river to a stone near the Hunderton fold-yard ; on to St. John's parish boundary stone, concluding the ceremony at the point near the Wye opposite to Whalebone Inn at Eign, their starting point. The length of the boundary is 17¼ miles.

The ornamental part of the procession consisted of about half-a-dozen rustic wands with many coloured ribbons at the top ; with these wands they tapped the boundary stones. The route taken included, as at Ross, the site of a Holy Well, which was on Eign Hill ; the place where it was is still known, but it has been filled up. Other points reached by way of Holy Well Gutter Lane were Holy Well meadow and Holy Well Coppice.

In 1882 the use of the boundary stones was explained to the boys, who were not ducked or cuffed, but allowed to race for coins placed on the stones, or rewarded for discovering them in advance of the party. The stones are called " liberty stones."

The Court Leet and Court Baron for the manor of Eardisley is still held, and the boundaries of the manor are perambulated every five years. The proceedings are fully described in the *Hereford Times*, Oct. 7th, 1893 :—

On the rising of the court the jury, accompanied by a number of the inhabitants, walked to Woodseaves, and, having hoisted a lad into an oak, duly smoked him by burning a bolting of straw underneath him, and having painted some of the other lads, to mark the starting point in the memories of the rising generation, the company started on the perambulation of the manor boundaries. This continued with an hour's rest for luncheon till 3-30 p.m., when the crier adjourned the assemblage till the next morning at Gipsy Hall Bridge. Here the court reassembled at ten next morning, when the course was continued, until the oak at Woodseaves was again reached. Here cheers were given for the lady of the manor (Mrs. Perry Herrick), who provided a dinner at the Tram Inn that evening, when the bailiff took the chair.

We have in the Cathedral archives a record of a perambulation in the county six hundred years ago, when a dispute arose concerning the boundaries of the royal forest of Haye. These were therefore perambulated on Feb. 24, 1300, and again on June 22nd, of the same year.[1]

---

(1) *Registrum Ricarde de Swinfield*, ed. Rev. Canon Capes (Cantilupe Society), 373.

Earliest of all the precedents for the custom so lately disused in the county is the account in the *Liber Landavensis* of the perambulation of the boundary of " Bolgros," thought to be Preston-on-Wye, a parish eight miles from Hereford. The Bishop Ufelwy, who took part in the ceremony was suffragan bishop of Ergyng (Archenfield), at the end of the sixth century, and a disciple of St. Dubricius.[1]

> Be it well known to all who dwell in the southern part of Britain, that Gwrfodw, King of Ergyng, having gained a victory in battle over the Saxon nation, and giving thanks to God and for the prayers of Ufelwy, and his clergy, granted in alms to him, and all his successors, under the refuge of St. Dubricius and St. Teilo, for ever, the land called Bolgros, on the banks of the Wye, at some distance from Mochros [Moccas], the quantity of three uncias [about 324 acres]. And the land having been given as an endow-ment, Bishop Ufelwy, with his clergy, went round the whole on its boundary, sprinkling holy water, the holy cross with the holy relics being carried before ; and in the presence of the King, with his wit-nesses, built a church in the middle thereof, in honour of the Holy Trinity, and St. Peter, and of St. Dubricius, and St. Teilo ; and he also granted the land free of all fiscal tribute, to God and to the Bishop who was present, and all his successors at Llandaff, and with all commonage in field and in woods, in water, and in pastures.[2]

Here follow the names of the witnesses, which include those of Ufelwy, the Bishop, and Gwrfodw, the King of Ergyng.

(2) TENURES AND MANORIAL CUSTOMS.

Borough English.

The custom of Borough English[3] prevails in the copyholds of the following Herefordshire manors :—

1. Barton and Tupsley.
2. Hampton Bishop.
3. Holmer and Shelwick.
4. Ledbury.

All these manors formerly belonged to the Bishop of Hereford and the Ecclesiastical Commissioners are still lords of all except Ledbury, which has been at some time alienated. The law of descent is as follows :—The youngest son is the customary heir, and in default of issue male, the youngest brother might become the heir, or, in default of brothers, the youngest sister. There is no co-heiress-ship. Duncumb, writing in 1813, of Borough English at Hampton Bishop, adds:—

1] *Lib. Land.* (*see* Section XV., 1). 2] *Lib. Landavensis,* 406-7.
3] " Borough English " is the custom by which the youngest son inherits his father's estate. *See* Elton, *Origins of Eng. Hist.,* 179 ; Stephens, *Commentaries,* i., 211-13 ; and Pollock and Maitland, *Hist, of Eng. Law before the time of Edward I.,* ii., 277, where the origin of the name is explained thus :— "A mere accident, for we think that it was no better, was given the name of ' Borough English ' to the custom of ultimogeniture. In the Norman days a new French borough grew up beside the old English borough of Nottingham. A famous case of 1327 drew the attention of lawyers to the fact that while the burgages of the ' burgh Francoys ' descended to the eldest son, those of the ' burgh Engloys ' descended to the youngest. . . . The true home of ultimogeniture is the villein tene-ment."

" It will be imagined that this tenure is not often acted upon, but one instance at least has occurred here within a very short period of the present time."

Gavelkind (Archenfield).

Here the tenure was that of gavelkind, according to which all lands on the decease of the parent were divided equally among the children, who might dispose thereof at the age of 15, being then deemed of age, without the consent of the lord. Felony in the parent did not forfeit the estate, which descended nevertheless to the children.[1] The best beast, however, the best bed and furniture, and the best table were heirlooms, called principals, and passed to the eldest son.

There is also a custom to devise lands in Archenfield: at all events land purchased. The better opinion seems to be indeed that the right of devise was one of the incidents of gavelkind. (*See* Robinson, *Of Gavelkind*, ii., chap. 5.)

Another distinction between Gavelkind and land held according to the ordinary law is that in Gavelkind, the widow is entitled to half the land for her dower, instead of a third as by the common law, but only so long as she is chaste and unmarried. The husband takes only a half of his wife's land, by the custom, but he is entitled whether issue has been born alive or not, and he only holds it so long as he remains unmarried.[2]

Archenfield (Irchinfield, Ergyng, or Urging in old MSS.)[3]

The men of Archenfield, according to Domesday, had the honour of forming the vanguard, when the king's army went against the enemy, and on its return the rearguard. " In Archenfelde the King has three churches. The priests of these churches bear the King's embassies into Wales, and each of them chants two masses each week for the King." From this entry in *Domesday* it would appear that Welsh was the language spoken, and that the priests were interpreters. At Rowlstone, in the deanery of Archenfield, there is still preserved a Welsh Bible that was used in the church.[4]

In the *Beauties of England and Wales* (1802), under *Herefordshire*, is the following account of a custom connected with the Wye Salmon Fishing in the district that

---

1] Grose, ii., 237. *See infra*, Archenfield. 2] I am indebted to Mr. W. J. Humfrys for this note.
3] This was an ancient British kingdom, governed at first by independent sovereigns, and retaining its
   customs and privileges under Norman kings. These lasted, with some modifications, for two centuries
   or more after the Norman Conquest. Archenfield extended from the western edge of the Forest
   of Dean to Madley and Moccas. The name is now preserved in the Deanery of Archenfield, in which
   many of the churches are dedicated to Welsh Saints. (*See* Section xv., I.). *Cf.* Rev. Canon
   Bannister, *Hist. Ewias Harold*, 102; Cooke, *Top. of Great Britain*, 87. Grose, ii., 237. *See* also
   Gavelkind, ante.
4] For the remaining customs of Archenfield from *Domesday*, see Hazlitt, 173-5.

was once Archenfield :—" The land holders or brinkers on that part of the Wye within the liberty of Irchenfield possess the right of fishing in the " free water," as the stretch of river lying between Holm Lacy and Strangford is called, provided that they expose the salmon and other fish that are called for sale upon the board fixed up in the Hereford turnpike road between Llanfrother and Horewith.[1] This custom was enforced by the manor court of Wormelow, and the fishermen ordered to carry their fish to this board, in order that any woman with child, or poor person, might have as small a piece as a pound. The order was probably made merely to give emphasis to the ancient condition which all the fishers were bound to observe. The board on which the fish were sold on the high road, as above detailed, was taken down shortly before the commencement of the present century."

I am informed by Mr. Walter Pilley that before the custom was finally discontinued the fish was thus exposed for sale on one day in the year only ; he has seen the old table used for the purpose, now lost or destroyed.

An old Court roll of the manor of Wormelow gives an account of a great Court Leet held there in the fourteenth year of the reign of Charles I. It gives the following particulars of the fishing rights of the tenants :—

Inter Alia—We find that the tenants of the said manor have free fishing within the rivers of Wye and Garron for themselves, and for their own household servants only, of every parish and every township within the said manor, that is, adjoining unto the said rivers, except exempted places where the other subjects have free fishing by the King's grant. We find that every tenant within the said manor, that hath free fishing within the River of Wye, if he take any salmon or salmons within the said river, and have a purpose of the same to sell, that they ought to bring them to the Fish Board at Horewithy, and offer the same to be sold (by quarters or otherwise), as the buyer and seller can agree, and if the buyer will bestow 4d. or 6d., the seller is to furnish him accordingly, by the space of two hours before they bring the same to any market town. . . . A true copy compared with the original, 18th day of March, A.D. 1639, by me, Richard Fisher.[2]

Chabnor (Chadnor, in Dilwyn).

At the inquest P.M. of Ralph de Thorny (5 Edw., 1), it appears that he died seized of the manor of Chabnor. Thomas de Chabbenour held under him, by the

---

[1] Now Hoarwithy, *i.e.*, the boundary willow.

[2] Reprinted from the *Hereford Journal*, Jan. 2nd, 1875. The right of free fishing has recently been the subject of litigation. The action was brought by the Earl of Chesterfield and Mrs. Madeleine Foster, as Brinkers, against George Harris and Frank Bailey, two fishermen and freeholders in King's Caple, and Hentland, parishes adjoining the River Wye, in the Manor or hundred of Wormelow. The case was decided in 1907 in favour of the right of the fishermen to fish as freeholders from boats on the seven miles known as " Free Water." This decision was reversed by the Court of Appeal in 1908. The case was taken to the House of Lords, and on July 17, 1911, a majority of one decided it in favour of the Earl of Chesterfield and Mrs. Foster.

serjeantry of doing service with one man for fifteen days with bow and arrows at the bridge of Clifford.[1]

Hereford.

A lease, dated 24th of March, 22 Henry VIII., was granted by Thomas Gebons, of Hereford, mercer, to Isabella Gardiner, prioress, and to the convent of Aconbury, of a stable situate in the street called *Wroughthall*, for ninety-nine years, under an annual rent of a red rose, to be delivered, if lawfully demanded, on the feast of St. John the Baptist.—Duncumb, *Hist. Herefordshire*, i., 390.

Kingsland.

There are heriots payable in the manor of Kingsland ; they consist of the two best beasts, or the best jewel or chattel of which the tenant dies seized. There is an entry in the court rolls in 1716 as follows :—" The bailiff of the lord of the manor aforesaid seized one black and one brindled bull." The heriots are now generally satisfied by a money payment.[2]

Kingston.

In the Domesday Survey the only service of the tenants of the manor of Kingston is to carry the game to Hereford. This would be the game from the King's forest of Treville, containing 2,014 acres, and extending from Kingstone to the River Dore.—Bannister, *Hist. Ewias Harold*, 75.

Ledbury.

Thomas Walwyn, of Hellens, Much Marcle, who died in 1532, held messuages in Ledbury of the Bishop of Hereford by fealty, and by the delivery of a red rose at the nativity of St. John the Baptist.—Cooke, *Hist. Hereford*, iii., 4.

Marden.

In the reigns of Edward III. and Richard II., 17 acres of land in Marden were held by the service of carrying a cord to measure the site of any castle which the Crown might think proper to rebuild in the Marches of Wales.—Duncumb ii., 132, from *Coningsby MSS.*

Mordiford.

The Hereford family held messuages and land in the manor of Mordiford by the annual payment of a pair of gold spurs, whenever the King should happen to ride

---

1] I am indebted for this reference to Mr. George Marshall, F.S.A., who suggests that the " bridge of Clifford " may be the drawbridge of Clifford Castle.
2] Kindly communicated by Mr. C. E. Moore, Steward of the Manor.

over Mordiford Bridge, according to Blount, who adds : " I have seen no record of it." (Blount, *MSS.*)   The manor was actually held in 1304 by the payment of a pair of gilt spurs of the value of six pennies annually at Michaelmas, in lieu of all other services.   In 1387 the value of the spurs was mentioned as being increased to 3s. 4d. (Cooke, iii., 70).

Orleton.

In the manor of Orleton the heriot is the best chattel, within or without the manor.

Pencomb.

The lord of the manor of Pencomb, by ancient custom, claims a pair of gilt spurs as an heriot from every Mayor of Hereford who dies during his term of office.

Tupsley.

" Some of the customary tenants were bound heretofore to do two days' work every week for the lord, and to weed his corn and to make hay to mow for him, and carry one day, for which they had by custom of the Bishop a halfpenny farthing. Tupsley forms part of the episcopal manor of Hampton Bishop.—Robinson, *Mansions and Manors*, 129 (from *Phillipps' MSS.*, now in the library at Belmont).

It has not been possible to make an exhaustive search for curious manorial customs of the County.   Nor is there space here for those of the following manors, collected by Blount, *Antient Tenures* (1679), and reprinted with additions by W. Carew Hazlitt, *Tenures of Land and Customs of Manors* :—Ayleneton, Bosbury, Clehungre, (Clehonger), Dylew (or Dylwin), Hampton (Hampton Bishop), Hereford (City), Kingston, Lauton, La Oke, Lastres, (Laysters), Marden, King's Stanford, Marston, Morden, Orleton, Stanford.

(3) WAKES AND FEASTS.

The parish wakes, associated in later times with the dedication of the Parish Church to some particular saint, were, in Pagan times, the local festivals of each little community, held annually at some sacred spot, a well, a hill-top, a cromlech, an ancient and sacred tree, or even perhaps a temple.[1]   (*Cf.* Section xvi., *St. Weonard*).

1] *See* Burne, 435 :—" We have evidence of this in the oft-quoted letter of Pope Gregory the Great to Mellitus, for the guidance of Augustine, in which he directs that the heathen temples should by no means be destroyed ; but, if solidly built, should be cleansed and hallowed for Christian worship. . . . And in place of their old sacrificial feasts and revelry he ordained that on the anniversary of the dedication of each church or on the festivals of those saints whose relics were preserved there, they should erect tabernacles of green boughs around the transformed temples, and there kill oxen as they had been wont, though no longer in sacrifice to devils."

In addition to the church wakes of every parish, usually held in the Church-yard on Sundays (*see* Duncumb i., 212) there were feasts at little outlying hamlets and townships, where no church was ever known to exist, even in ancient times, such as Broxwood in Pembridge parish, and the Marsh, near Weobley.

There were merry-makings within living memory at the Cromlech called Arthur's Stone, and much dancing. My informant, a native of Peterchurch, remembered " great does," but not when they took place. He was only a boy then, he said. It would be sixty years ago.[1]

At Leominster the folk held a festival, early on May morning, on Eaton Hill, of which Leland remarks " the people of Leominster and thereabouts came once a year to sport and playe."[2]

May Hill (Aston Ingham) is said to derive its name from the games played there ; these may have been hill wakes, held at the time of the spring festival. Capel Tump, near Ross, was the scene of similar merry-makings in Whitsun week.[3] I have not been able to hear of any well-wakes in Herefordshire.

The day of the church wakes was the first Sunday after the day of the particular saint to whom the church was dedicated. Thus at Kington :—" The church was dedicated to the Virgin Mary by Bishop Orleton, in 1325, the day of the assumption of the Virgin Mary being August 15th. On the following Sunday the wake or feast was invariably kept in the churchyard until the year 1795, when the Vicar interfered, and prohibited it within the limits of consecrated ground, but at the same time tolerated its continuance on Kingswood Common, where it remains, and the evening of the Sunday is spent in sport, pastime, and fighting."[4]

On the evening of the feast it was usual to settle by fighting all the quarrels of the past year. " If a man were beaten in one fight, no one else went against him ; one beating wiped off the score," said an old man at Peterchurch. He could remember badger-baiting and cock-fighting in a meadow behind the Boughton Arms, where there was a cock-pit. The latter cruel sport was a favourite one in the Golden Valley. On a tombstone in Peterchurch churchyard is the epitaph of one John Andrews, a noted cock-fighter, who died in 1799. He had a cock named " Captain," which was never beaten, and he was nicknamed after his famous bird.

1] *See* Section i., 2.

2] *Leominster Guide*, 1803 ; Leland, *Itinerary*, iv., 94. " The common fame of the People about Leominster is that King Merwald and some of his successors had a castle or palace on an Hill-syde by the Towne of Lemster. . . . The place is now called Comfort Castle, where now be some tokens of Ditches, where buildings have been." 3] *Ariconensia*, 73

4] Parry, *Hist. Kington* (1845), 58.

" Alas poor Captain winged by cruel death,
He pek'd in vain, o'ermatched, resigns his breath ;
Lov'd social mirth, none dare his word distrust,
Sincere in friendship, and was truly just."

There were bear-baiting and bull-baiting at some of the larger feasts. There is still a Bull Ring, called by that name, at Kington, where the sport was continued until 1815. The last bull was chained to a tree near the Crooked Well foot-bridge. It was usual to sell the flesh of the slaughtered bull at a cheap rate to the poor. At Orcop, an ox or ram was roasted whole for the feast under a yew tree near the church-yard, in which the people sat to eat of it. This comes very near to the words of Pope Gregory, " and there kill oxen as they had been wont." The badger-baiting at Bredwardine is still remembered by those living on the hill. There was also much boxing and wrestling at feasts, the fighting in earnest being apparently reserved for the evening as a sort of climax. The amusements were catching pigs with greasy tails, and grinning through horse collars, the ugliest face winning a prize.

There were stalls for the sale of fruit and sweets ; my informant at Peterchurch could remember the cherries spread out for sale on the tombstones in the churchyard. At Llanveyno, Crasswall, and Garway, one may still see a stone shelf or seat running along the outside of the church wall for the use of the people who watched sports in the churchyard, formerly used for this purpose on any Sunday, not only the feast day. Each feast had a special dainty associated with it, varying with the season at which it was held. At Ross it was pork and turnips ; at Peterchurch, rice pudding with currants, the farmers giving their labourers new milk for the purpose, in place of the usual " skim." Blakemere had a cherry feast ; the people of the parish also had their first roast duck and green peas that day.

At Clodock on feast day the people were allowed to course hares on the Black Mountain. They kept greyhounds on purpose for this occasion ; the privilege belonged at other times, as usual, to the owners, or occupiers of the land. For other customs connected with this feast, *see* Section xv., 1. At wakes in the Golden Valley it was usual for folk to pelt each other with crab-apples. The Rev. J. Davies, writing in 1877, mentions that traces of the custom were then still to be found at Urishay, Dorstone, and Lowmind feasts.[1]

1] *Woolhope Club*, 1897, 25. Some Shropshire wakes were called Crab Wakes ; *cf*. Burne :—" License to pelt defenceless persons seems dear to the hearts of the populace ; witness continental carnival sports, and the modern pelting at weddings."

(4) Farming Customs, Weights and Measures.

Formerly, the waggoners were given a whole holiday annually that they might cut staves for goads.[1] These were probably made of hawthorn, or mountain ash, both sacred trees.[2]

An old inhabitant of Weobley, aged 95, could remember how, when she was a girl in service, the farmer, who then usually took his meals with his men, would get up and say :—

> " Bill, Tom and Jack,
> Do you hear my knife smack ? "

" He would shut his big clasp knife, and out they would have to go, finished or not," she said.

Hone mentions an apple custom called " griggling," now extinct ; it seems to have been analogous to gleaning in the corn fields :—

> The small apples are called griggles. These the farmer leaves pretty abundantly on the trees, and after the orchard is cleared, the village climbing boys go with poles and bags and commence griggling. If the owner requests it, which is often the case, before they depart, the head boy stands before the house and recites the well-known fable in the Universal spelling book, " A rude boy stealing apples." Then the hostess, or her daughter, brings a large jug of cider and a slice of bread and cheese, to the great pleasure of the laughing recipients."[3]

Duncumb (*Agriculture*, 159) gives a list of peculiar weights and measures still in use in the country in 1813 :—

A pound of fresh butter .	Eighteen ounces
A stone . .	Twelve pounds
A customary acre .	Two-thirds of a statute acre
A hop acre .	That piece of ground which contains 1,000 plants, viz., about half a statute acre
A lugg . .	Forty-nine square yards of coppice wood
A wood acre .	Three-eighths larger than a statute [acre].
A day's math .	About a statute acre of meadow or grass land, being the quantity usually mown by one man in a day
A perch of fencing .	Seven yards
A perch of walling	Sixteen feet and a half
A perch of land .	Five yards and a half (as statute)
A bushel of grain .	Ten gallons
A bushel of malt .	Eight gallons and a half

1] Fosbroke, *Ariconensia*, 73.   2] *See ante*, Section ii., and Section xiii., *Mermaid of Marden* :—" If it had not been for thy wittan-tree goad."   3] Hone, *Every-Day Book*, iii., 635, from a letter written in 1826.

(5) PUNISHMENTS.

Denunciation and Penance.

In A.D. 1305, during a night at Whitsuntide, a party of sixteen men felled and carried away trees from the wood of Ross Foreign, in disregard of the remonstrances of the Bishop's servants. These persons were denounced by name in the churches of Walford, Ruardean, Weston, Hope, Maloysel, and Castle Goderich, until they made satisfaction in damages, giving a pledge on oath not to repeat the offence. They were ob'iged also to repeat the penance of walking once round the church of Ross, wearing only their shirts, on one Sunday, and once round the market on one market day. Thomas and John Clarkson, the ringleaders in the transaction, were required in addition to bring into the church of Ross all trees carried away on the feast day of St. Mary Magdalen, and to perform the processionary penance, in their shirts on two Sundays and two market days.[1]

Some years ago Mr. Walter Pilley copied from the fly leaf of a large Bible, formerly in Madley Church, an account of the last act of public penance performed there, by a woman named N. Gardiner, for slander :—

" She had a white sheet placed upon her, and she walked up and down the ailes (*sic*) of the church, and recanted all that she had said. Upon leaving the church she swore that she would never enter it again, and never did ; she was over 90 when she died. Madley Church Book ; Arnold Rogers, his book, 1821."

Doing the Churches.

A man had finished a year's imprisonment for manslaughter. When he came out of gaol, he went the round of all the churches, probably eight or ten within a few miles of his own parish, and it is said to the chapels also. This would seem to have been meant as a kind of public expiation, or to publish the fact that he had finished his year's imprisonment.[2]

The Ducking Stool.

In Leominster priory church is preserved an ancient ducking-stool. The latest recorded example of its use occurred in 1809, when a woman named Jenny Pipes was paraded round the town in it, and actually ducked in the water near Kenwater Bridge, by order of the Magistrates. In 1817 a woman named Sarah Leeke was wheeled round the town in a chair, but was not ducked, as the water was too low.

The punishment was inflicted, not only on scolds, but on butchers, bakers, and brewers, and all who gave short measure or adulterated food. That it was much used in the fifteenth and sixteenth centuries at Leominster, the documents of the borough show. In the rolls of the Court Leet, the jury presented the " Chamberleynes of this borough " in 1563 for not having made the " Cookyng-Stole " ; in 1564, for that they did not make a " Cokyngstole " ; in 1638, for not repairing the "tumbrel

---

1] Cooke, iii., 102.
2] Havergal, *Words and Phrases*, 45. Unfortunately the name of the parish is not recorded, nor the date of the occurrence.

ANCIENT CELTIC BELLS.

THE MARDEN BELL.   THE BOSBURY BELL.

THE LEOMINSTER DUCKING STOOL.

or Cucking Stoole "; in 1650, for not having a " Gumstole " for scolding women.
It is curious that at the same time the Chamberlain's yearly accounts show charges
for repairing the Gomstole, or Cucking-Stoole in 1571, 1577, and 1595.   A new one was
made in 1634, which was repaired in 1671 ; probably it would be roughly handled
whenever used, by the crowd present at the ducking.   *See* also Johnson, *Ancient
Customs of Hereford,* 42-3, for the use of the gouge-stool there.

Riding the Stang.

This is a name given in other parts of England to the custom of burning the
effigies of unfaithful husbands or wives.   A figure made of straw is placed astride a long
pole and carried to the house of the offender it is meant to represent, accompanied
by a crowd with pots, pans, and tins, making as much noise as possible.   Near the
house a large bonfire is made, in which the effigy is burnt.   This was done at Leominster and at Weobley Marsh within the last twenty years.   I was told by an old man
at Llanveyno that he had seen it done a few years since at Walterstone ; he could
not remember the date.   The practice is not known here now by the name of " riding
the stang ; " there does not seem to be any special name for it.   It is probably a
very ancient custom, possibly at one time the penalty really was death, and the
execution would have been a fact and no mock ceremony.   Or it may have been, as
Miss Burne suggests, a public disgrace only, the offender being made to ride the pole
in person.[1]

For the use of the pillory, *see Hereford MSS.,* 486 ; and Johnson, 43.

(6) Bells.

Church Bells.   The Passing Bell.

The manner of tolling the passing bell varies greatly in the country parishes ;
perhaps these variations are according to the number of bells and the fancy of the
sexton, though each parish clerk of the old school is convinced that his way is the
right way, and always has been the only way in his particular parish.   At Weobley,
they toll each bell twelve hours after death, ten times for a man and nine times for a
woman, and then " tell the age " with the tenor bell.   At Lyonshall, each bell is tolled
twelve times for a man and eleven for a woman.   At Dilwyn, the tenor bell is tolled
first for half an hour, and in conclusion each bell is tolled thirteen times for a man
and eleven for a woman.   At Almeley it was formerly thirteen for a man, and fourteen
for a woman.   I am informed by Mr. Short, instructor to the Hereford Guild of
Bell-ringers, that in the majority of towers they note each bell three times for males,

---

1] *Shropshire Folk-Lore,* 295.

and five for females, tolling the age afterwards. At Madley they make a distinction for a child, tolling each bell three times only. The Hereford custom is to give three times three strokes on a tenor bell (or three times two according to sex), and then toll one bell for fifteen minutes, before sounding nine strokes on each, beginning with the treble, the last bell tolling the age. Formerly the tolling of the tenor bell for a funeral changed to a chime as the mourners came within sight of the church; the custom was discontinued some years ago at Weobley and Staunton-on-Wye, but is still kept up at Dilwyn, and is remembered in the majority of the parishes in the district. We still have, or had till recently, the bells that rung for matins for early mass centuries ago, although the services to which they summoned priest or people have long been disused and forgotten. At Weobley a bell was rung at five o'clock every morning, within the memory of one old inhabitant, who died in 1907. We still have the "quarter-to-eight" chimes on Sunday, which probably once summoned the folk of the ancient borough to mass. The five o'clock bell was formerly rung at Kington.[1] At Ross, the old Parish Clerk remembers a bell being rung every morning at six o'clock; it was discontinued in his boyhood. It is thought that these bells were continued so long because they were of practical use to the work-people, in days when clocks and watches were scarce.

The Curfew Bell.

This bell was rung at Weobley at eight o'clock every evening within living memory; the sixth bell was used at Ross, and was rung at eight o'clock from October to March only, until ten years ago. Curfew was rung at Kington in 1845, and at All Saints, Hereford, until 1860.[2] At Bromyard a bell still rings every evening at eight o'clock for 15 minutes, from November to Christmas Day; the sixth bell then tolls the day of the month.

For the Pancake Bell, *see* Section ix., 4, *Shrove Tuesday*.

The custom of ringing a muffled peal on Holy Innocents' Day is still kept up at Ross, at Weobley, and also at Hereford Cathedral.

For the better maintenance and order in belfries, rules in rhyme were frequently painted on the wall. Two examples will suffice :—

Kingsland Belfry Rhyme.

> If that to ring you do come here,
> You must ring true with hand and ear.
> And if you've either spur or hat,
> Sixpence you must pay down for that.

1] Parry, *Hist. Kington*, 202.   2] Parry, *loc. cit.*

And if you either curse or swear,
Sixpence you must pay for beer.
To curse and swear it is a sin,
This is not a place to quarrel in.

Weobley.

Rules and regulations strictly to be observed by those who visit this room.   Nov. 5, 1826.

None but ringers are permitted here
Who do not pay a shilling for beer.
Should aney (*sic*) ring with hat or spur,
Sixpence must pay before he stur (*sic*).
But should a stranger wish to ring
Sixpence must pay when he begin.
Should aney quarrel, swear, or fight
A shilling each shall spend that night.
And those who wont these lines obey,
Desired are to keep away.

These lines have unfortunately been recently whitewashed over ; they were painted on the wall.   Those at Kingsland met with a similar fate.   For similar rhymes in the tower of Leominster Church, *see* Townsend, 245.[1]

A letter written about 1583 or 1584 to Bishop Storey, apparently by one of the canons at Hereford Cathedral, relates incidentally how in the dark days of Queen Mary, the Mayor, Alderman, and freemen of the city were summoned to church by St. Thomas' bell.

And every Sabbath Day and Festival Day St. Thomas' bell should ring to procession, and the Dean would send his somners to warn the mayor to the procession.   And then, upon the somners warning, the mayor would send the sergeants to the parish churches, every man in his ward to the alderman. Then the alderman would cause the parish priest to command all the free men to attend on the mayor at the procession or lecture.[2]   For want of a sermon there should be a lecture in the chapter house, every Sabbath and holy day, notwithstanding they were at high mass in the choir.   And then by the mayor and commons it was agreed at a general law day that if the mayor did not come to procession and sermon he should pay 12d. for every default, and every alderman 8d., and every man of the election 6d., and every freeman or gild merchant 4d., if it were known they were absent and within hearing of the said bell, and did not come ; which ordinance is and was recorded in the custom book of the city.[3]

For bell legends, *see* Section i., 5, *Crosses* ; iv., 6, *Aymestrey Night Bell* ; xiii., *The Mermaid of Marden* ; xv., 1., *St. Katharine.*   For Bell-jingles, *see* Section xvi., 3.

1] *Cf.* aiso Tyack, *A Book About Bells,* 145, *et seq.*
2] That is, before high mass.—Gasquet.
3] Gasquet, *Ed. VI., and the Book of Common Prayer,* 12, from *Egerton MS.,* 1693, p. 81 (B.M.)

SECTION XIII.

FOLK TALES.[1]

(1) JACK O' KENT.

" Jack o' Kent " is the name given by the folk to a mysterious personage who formerly lived in the neighbourhood of Kentchurch and Grosmont. He has been supposed by some to be Owen Glendower in hiding, or his bard, while others are sure that he was Sir John Oldcastle, who was long a fugitive upon the Welsh Border. He is also, with more probability, thought to be identical with Sion Cent, the Welsh poet whose works are preserved in the *Iolo MSS.* (*See* Coxe, *loc. cit.*) There certainly was a real John Kent, whose Welsh name was Sion Cent, vicar of Kentchurch in the reign of Henry V. But the question of identity is more a matter for historical research than for folk-lore ; the stories told of Jack are as old as the beginning of human thought, and only locally attached to his name.

Jack o' Kent's Funeral.

Jack was a wizard in league with the Devil, and when still a boy he sold his body and soul to the " old un " in exchange for supernatural power in this world, whether he were buried in the church or out of the church, that was the bargain. He was therefore buried at Kentchurch, or some say at Grosmont, in the wall of the church, so that he should be " neither in nor out." This part of the story is very generally known in Herefordshire, but an aged woman at Wigmore (1908), added that her mother used to relate how during the funeral ceremony a voice was heard saying :—

> " False David Sir Ivan,
>
> False alive, false dead."

She could not explain the name " David Sir Ivan," but supposed it was a Welsh name for the renowned Jack o' Kent.[2]

The Crows in the Barn.

Jack was set by his master to mind the crows from the wheat, while he was away at Hereford fair. Later in the day, the farmer was much surprised and annoyed to meet Jack in the fair, and asked him sharply why he had left his work. " Ay, ay," said Jack, " ay ay maister, the crows be all right, they be all in the barn." When

1] BIBLIOGRAPHICAL REFERENCES :—Coxe, *Monmouthshire*, 336-339 (with portrait) ; Evans and Britton, *Topographical Description of Monmouthshire*, 73 ; *Iolo MSS.*, 304, 387 ; *Cambro-Briton*, ii., 61 ; Wilkins, *History of the Literature of Wales* ; Williams, *Eminent Welshmen*, 268, 269 ; Rees, *Welsh Saints*, 153, 340 ; Sikes, *British Goblins*, 203.
2] For parallels, *see* Gutch-Peacock, 323, *William of Lindholme.*

the farmer reached home, there were the crows as Jack had said, sitting in an old barn with no roof on it. Their master, the " old un," was sitting on a cross-beam keeping them in order till Jack came back. " He was like a big old crow, was their master, and every now and then he said ' crawk, crawk.' "[1]

The Bridge at Kentchurch.

Jack and the Devil built the bridge over the Monnow between Kentchurch and Grosmont in a single night. What they built by night fell down by day, as long as the bridge remained incomplete ; hence the need for haste. The first passenger to pass over the bridge was to belong to the Devil, so Jack threw a bone across and a poor dog ran after it. That dog was all the Devil had for his pains.[2]

The White Rocks, Garway.

The Devil was helping Jack to stop up the weir, at Orcop Hill, in order to flood the valley, and make a fishpool. But as the Devil was coming over Garway Hill his apron strings broke, and down fell all the stones he was carrying. Then the cock crew, and he had to go home, so there are the stones to this day.[3]

That is an Orcop version ; but an old inhabitant of Grosmont said, " Jacky was the Devil's master. When they were breaking stone up at Garway, the old un said he wouldn't leave off till cock-crow. But that made no difference to Jack, him could make the cocks crow when he liked, him could ! "

Jack and the Mince-Pie.

Jack once went from Kentchurch to London with a mince-pie for the King. He started at daybreak, and was there in time for breakfast ; the pie was still quite hot. He lost a garter on the way : it was found on the top of a church spire, having caught in the weathercock as he flew over.[4]

The Christmas Block.

Once Jack was going to put a Christmas block (a Yule-log) on the fire. It was a very large one, and folks said that he would never get it into the house. " Wait a bit," said Jack. He went and fetched four goslings, and fastened them to the log ; at his bidding they drew it into the house as easily as if they had been horses.[5]

1] *Cf*. Section iv., *The Devil.* A similar story is told of St. Illtyd, for which see *Liber Landavensis,* 291. This Welsh chronicle was finished before 1132.
2] For another version, *see Folklore,* xv., 86. *Cf.* Tylor, *Primitive Culture,* i., 106.
3] *Cf.* Section i., 1, *Robin Hood's Butts.*   4] Told at Grosmont, 1908.
5] Told by Mrs. M.——, of Orcop, *ætat* 86, in 1909.

Jack and the Pigs.

Jack and the Devil agreed that Jack should go to market and buy some pigs. Which will you have," said Jack, " the curly-tailed pigs, or the straight-tailed pigs ?" " Straight tails," said the Devil. So on the way home Jack gave them all a feed of beans, and their tails all curled, every one of them ; they were as curly as pigs' tails could be. Next time Jack went to the market, the Devil said he would have all the curly-tailed pigs. That time Jack drove them through a pool of water, by the roadside, on the way home ; all their tails became straight then, because they were so wet and cold.[1]

Jack as Thresherman.

The Devil was always putting Jack to do hard tasks, trying to find something he couldn't do, but he never succeeded. Once he had to thresh a bay of corn in the barn in a day, and this is how he managed it. He took off his boot, and put it on the top of the stack of corn, and it threw down the sheaves to him, of itself, one by one. He took his flail and set it on the floor, and it threshed the corn by itself, while he sat down and just played his fiddle, repeating continually—

" Nobble, stick, nobble,
Play, fiddle, play ! "

So he went on, over and over, and the hay was threshed long before the day was out. " But when Jack was doing anything like that he always took out his little black stick as he carried, hollow at one end. In the hollow was a thing like a fly ; one o' the Devil's imps it was. He would lay the stick down near him, and then he could do anythink, like."[2]

The Tops and the Butts.

One day, Jack took the Devil into a field of wheat, when it was springing up. He said, " Which will you have, the tops or the butts ?" There was not much top to be seen, so the Devil said he'd have the butts. At harvest time, Jack accordingly had the wheat, the Devil the straw ; naturally he grumbled a good deal over such a bad bargain. Next year the field was sown with turnip seed, and Jack said " You shall have tops this time " ; the Devil agreed to this, and in due time Jack had the turnips, leaving for his partner the green tops. After that they went to mow a field of grass, each one to have all the hay he could cut : they were to begin together in the morning. Jack got up in the night and put harrow tynes in the grass, on the side

1] Told at Ashperton, also Weobley.
2] Told at Weobley by W. Colcombe, 1908. *Cf.* Section iv., *Vaughan of Hergest,* and vi., 2, *Charming at Ross.*

of the meadow where the Devil was to mow. In the morning these notched and blunted the scythe, which was continually catching in them ; but the " old un," think-ing they were only burdocks, kept muttering, " Bur-dock, Jack ! Bur-dock, Jack ! " Jack took no notice, and moving away diligently, secured nearly all the crop for him-self once more. Then they went to threshing ; Jack was to have bottoms this time, so he got the barn floor, and the Devil went on top ; he put up a hurdle for the Devil to thresh on, and as he battered away Jack collected the corn on the floor.[1]

The Dove and the Raven.

On his death-bed Jack commanded that his " liver and lights " should be placed on three iron spikes which projected from the church tower. Some say the church was Kentchurch, but at Grosmont they show the iron spikes still *in situ*. Jack prophesied that a dove and a raven would come and fight over his remains if thus exposed, and that, if his soul were saved, and the Devil successfully cheated, the dove would be victorious. This is the usual version, but some say that the dove's victory was only an omen, a sign of a good harvest. Another variant states that if birds came and devoured the remains, Jack would be proved indeed a wizard ; if they remained untouched he was not. My informant could not remember what the result of the experiment was supposed to have been.

The Pecked Stone, Trelleck (Monmouthshire).

From Monmouthshire come further accounts of Jack's wonderful exploits. " Why, one day he jumped off the Sugar Loaf mountain right on to the Skirrid, and there's his heel-mark to this day, an' when he got there he began playing quoits, he pecked (threw)[2] three stones as far as Trelleck, great big ones, as tall as three men (and there they still stand in a field), and he threw another but that did not go quite far enough, and it lay on the Trelleck road, just behind the five trees, till a little while ago, when it was moved so as the field might be ploughed, and this stone, in memory of Jack, was always called the Pecked Stone.[3]

A cellar is still shown at Kentchurch Court, which is said to have been Jack's stable, wherein he kept horses that traversed the air with the speed of Lapland witches. There one may see also Jack o' Kent's bedroom, a panelled room five hundred years old, in which a mysterious ghostly figure has been seen to issue from a recess in the wall on stormy nights. " As great as the Devil and Jack o' Kent " is still a proverb in Kentchurch.[4]

1] This story of Jack is most common of all in the county. It is a variant of the Scandinavian folk-tale, *A Farmer Tricks a Troll*, Keightley, i., 186, and is found all over Europe, as well as in Asia and Africa.
2] *i.e.*, pitched; *peck* is a variant form of *pitch*. *Cf.* the game of peck and toss (pitch and toss).
3] *Folk-Lore* xv., 86. There is a Kent's stone on the Wye near Goodrich :—Rees, *Welsh Saints*, 153, 340, *Cf.* Section i., 2.   4] *Memorials of Old Herefordshire*, 173.

(2) THE KING OF THE CATS.

Many years ago, before shooting in Scotland was a fashion, as it is now, two young men spent the autumn in the very far north, living in a lodge far from other houses, with an old woman to cook for them. Her cat and their own dogs formed all the rest of the household. One afternoon, the elder of the two young men said he would not go out, and the younger one went alone to follow the paths of the previous day's sport, looking for missing birds, and intending to return home before the early sunset. However, he did not do so, and the elder man became very uneasy, as he watched and waited in vain till long after their usual supper time. At last the young man returned wet and exhausted, nor did he explain his unusual lateness, until after supper, they were seated by the fire with their pipes, the dogs being at their feet, and the old woman's cat sitting gravely with half shut eyes on the hearth between them. Then the young man began as follows :—

" You must be wondering what made me so late ; I have had a curious adventure to-day. I hardly know what to say about it. I went, as I told you I should, along our yesterday's route. A mountain fog came on just as I was about to turn homewards, and I completely lost my way. I wandered about for a long time not knowing where I was, till at last I saw a light, and made for it, hoping to get help. As I came near it, it disappeared, and I found myself close to a large oak tree. I climbed into the branches, the better to look for the light, and behold it was beneath me, inside the hollow trunk of the tree. I seemed to be looking down into a church, where a funeral was in the act of taking place. I heard singing, and saw a coffin surrounded by torches, all carried by—— But I know you won't believe me if I tell you ! " His friend eagerly begged him to go on, and laid down his pipe to listen. The dogs were sleeping quietly, but the cat was sitting up, apparently listening as attentively as the man, and both young men involuntarily turned their eyes towards him. " Yes," proceeded the absentee, " it is perfectly true. The coffin and the torches were both borne by cats ; and upon the coffin were marked a crown and sceptre ! " He got no further ; the cat started up, and shrieking, " By Jove ! old Peter's dead ! and I'm King o' the Cats !" rushed up the chimney and was seen no more.[1]

This story was known to an old man at Honeymoor Common, Eaton Bishop, who is now dead, but in a different form. My informant could only remember fragments of it, " but old S—— used to say as he *saw* the cats rush up the chimbley ! "

---

[1] Contributed to *Folk-Lore Journal*, ii., No. ix., by Miss Burne. Told by a Herefordshire squire, 1845–6, who learnt it from an old nurse. She was living near Ross in 1882, being then upwards of ninety years of age. For parallel story see Halliwell, 167, where a Danish version is given.

(3) The Shepherd and the Crows.

The following story was told by a very old man who had been for the greater part of his life a shepherd on the Black Mountain :—

Years ago, on the Black Mountain above Longtown, there lived a hired shepherd, who managed a little farm for his master.   There were on either side of this farm two brothers, farming for their father.   I can remember, in my time, there was terrible jealousy and animosity between the shepherds on the mountain, where the sheep all run together.   I could always tell my sheep ; if I whistled they would all come running to me, every one, while the strangers took no notice.   A good shepherd knows his sheep and they know him.   Well, it was worse nor ever for this man, because the brothers were together, and they hated him.   He stuck to his master, and they to their father.   At last, one day, they got him alone on the mountain, and caught him, and said they would murder him.   They told him there was no one about, and it would never be known.   " If you kill me," he said, " the very crows will cry out and speak it."   Yet they murdered and buried him.   The body was found, after some time, but there was no evidence to show who the murderers were.   Well, not long after, the crows took to come whirling round the heads of those two brothers, " crawk, crawk, crawk," there they were, all day long—when they were together, when they were apart.   At last they could scarcely bear it, and one said to the other, " Brother, do you remember when we killed the poor shepherd on the mountain top there, he said that the very crows would cry out against us ?"   These words were overheard by a man in the next field, and the matter was looked into, so that in the end the brothers were both hanged for the murder.[1]

(4) The Mermaid of Marden.

In former times Marden Church stood close to the river, and by some mischance one of the bells was allowed to fall into it.   If was immediately seized by a mermaid, who carried it to the bottom and held it there so fast that any number of horses could not move it.   The people of the parish were told how to recover it, by wise men, according to some ; others say the bell itself gave directions from the bottom of the river.   A team of twelve white freemartins, i.e., heifers, was to be obtained and attached to the bell with yokes of the sacred yew tree, and bands of " wittern," or, in some versions, the drivers' goads were to be of witty or wittern (mountain ash).[2]

1] Told in May, 1903, by W. Parry, of Walterstone, aged 80, a native of Longtown.   There is a parallel in the classical legend of the death of the Greek poet Ibycus.   He was said to have been slain by robbers, and in dying called upon a flock of cranes to avenge him.   They hovered over the theatre at Corinth, where the murderers were ; one exclaimed involuntarily " Behold the avengers of Ibycus ! "   This led to the discovery of the murder.   *See* Dübuer's *Plutarch* (*De Garrulitate*), iv., 617.   The legend is the subject of a well-known ballad by Schiller.

2] *Cf* Section v., *Witchcraft*, and Section ii., *Trees and Plants*.

The bell was to be drawn out in perfect silence ; it was successfully raised to the edge of the river with the mermaid inside fast asleep.   In his excitement a driver, forgetting that silence was all-important, called out :—

> " In spite of all the devils in hell,
> Now we'll land Marden's great bell."

This woke the mermaid, who darted back into the river, taking the bell with her, ringing :—

> " If it had not been
> For your wittern bands (or witty goads),
> And your yew tree pin,
> I'd have had your twelve free-martins in."

So Marden folks have never had their bell back from the bottom of the river to this day, and sometimes it may still be heard ringing, echoing the bells of the church.   It lies in a deep clear pool.[1]

In 1848, in cleaning out a pond at Marden, an ancient bronze bell was discovered.   It lay at a depth of eighteen feet, beneath the accumulated mud and rubbish of centuries.   This bell, which is now in the Hereford Museum, is rectangular in shape ; the plates are riveted together on each side.   The clapper is lost, but there remains the loop inside from which it was suspended.   A similar bell of bronzed iron was ploughed up in a field at Bosbury in 1890.   There is no clapper, and the bell was suspended or carried by a wooden bar, now decayed, held by iron pins.   Its tone when struck is harsh but sonorous ; the man who found it sold it for a pint of beer, and it is now in the Horniman Museum, Forest Gate.   Sikes describes the use of these ancient bells in the Celtic Church ; his account is founded on the first chapter of Giraldus Cambrensis' *Itinerary through Wales*.   It is to the following effect :—

In all Welsh Churches before the Reformation there was a handbell similar to these, which the Clerk or Sexton took to the houses of the deceased on the day of the funeral ; it was called the Bangu.   When the procession began, a psalm was sung ; the bellman then sounded his bell in a solemn manner for some time till another psalm was concluded, and he sounded it again at intervals till the funeral arrived at the church.   The bangu was at this time deemed sacred, which accounts for the superstitious attributes given to it by Giraldus Cambrensis, who states (in his *Itinerary through Wales*) that at Elevein, in the church of Glascwm (a small village between Builth in Breconshire, and Kington, in Herefordshire), was a portable bell endowed with great virtues called Bangu, and said to have belonged to St. David. A certain woman secretly conveyed this bell to her husband, who was imprisoned in the castle of Rhayader, near Warthrenion, for the purpose of his deliverance.   The keepers of the castle refused to liberate him for this consideration, yet seized and detained the bell, and on the same night, by divine vengeance, the whole town, with the exception of the wall on which the bell was hung, was consumed by fire. These portable bells were held in such veneration in Ireland, Scotland, and Wales, that both laity and

---

1] Communicated by Mr. Galliers, of King's Pyon, and completed from other oral versions.

clergy were more afraid of swearing falsely by them than by the Gospels, because of some hidden and miraculous power with which they were gifted, and by the vengeance of the saint to whom they were particularly pleasing ; their despisers and transgressors were severely punished.[1]

Both the Marden and the Bosbury bells are of the Celtic type and have in all probability been hidden long ago by reformers, on account of the superstitious beliefs attached to them. The Marden bell was perhaps associated with St. Ethelbert ; the pond in which it was found is near the church which stands on the spot on which his body was first buried before its removal to Hereford.[2]

Kentsham Bell.

Another form of this story, given below, was collected by Miss Burne and printed in *Folklore Journal*, ii., 22. It came from the same source as the *King of the Cats*, above. Kentsham may be Kinsham, or Kentchurch ; there is no place of that name in the county.

"Great Tom of Kentsham was the greatest bell ever brought to England, but it never reached Kentsham safely nor hung in any English tower. Where Kentsham is I cannot tell you, but long, long ago, the people of the place determined to have a finer and larger bell in their steeple than any parish could boast. At that time there was a famous bell foundry abroad, where all the greatest bells were cast, and thither the Kentsham people sent to order their famous bell, and thither too sent many others, who wanted greater bells than could be cast in England. And so it came to pass at length that great Tom of Christchurch, and great Tom of Kentsham were all founded at the same time and all embarked on board the same vessel and carried safely to the shore of dear old England. Then they set about landing them, and this was anxious work ; but little by little it was done. And Tom of Lincoln, Tom of York, and Tom of Christchurch were safely laid on English ground, and then came the turn of Tom of Kentsham, which was the greatest Tom of all. Little by little they raised him and prepared to draw him on the shore ; but just in the midst of the work the captain grew so anxious and excited that he swore an oath ; that very moment the ropes that held the bell snapped in two and the great Tom of Kentsham slipped over the ship's side into the water, and rolled away to the bottom of the sea."

" Then the people went to the cunning-man and asked what they should do, and he said : ' Take six yoke of white milch kine which have never borne the yoke, and take fresh withy bands which have never been used before, and let no man speak a word neither good nor bad, until the bell is at the top of the hill.' "

1] Sikes, *British Goblins*, 340 Giraldus Cambrensis, *Itinerary*, 16.
2] *Arch. Camb.*, 1st series, vi., 253 ; Havergal, *Fasti*, 116.

FIGURE ON ALMSHOUSES, LEOMINSTER.

See page 223.

THE VAUGHAN COAT-OF-ARMS.

A GYPSY CAROL-SINGER.

(*Harriet Jones, singer of "The Seven Virgins" and "Christ made a trance."*)

"So they took six yoke of milch white kine which had never borne the yoke and harnessed them with fresh withy bands which had never been used, and bound these to the bell as it lay in shallow water, and long it was ere they could move it. But still the kine struggled and pulled and the withy bands held firm, and at last the bell was on dry ground. Slowly, slowly, they drew it up the hill, moaning and groaning with unearthly sounds as it went ; slowly, slowly, no one spoke, till they nearly reached the top of the hill. Now the captain had been wild with grief when he saw that he had caused his precious freight to be lost in the waters just as they reached the shore, and when he beheld it recovered again and so nearly placed in safety, he could not restrain his joy, but sang out merrily :—

> ' In spite of all the devils in hell
> We have to land old Kentsham Bell.'

Instantly the withy bands broke in the midst, and the bell bounded back again down the sloping hillside, rolling over and over, faster and faster, with unearthly clanging, till it sank far away in the very depths of the sea, and no man has ever seen it since ; but many have heard it tolling beneath the waters, and if you go there you may hear it too."

(5) THE MAN WITH THE HATCHET.

In the Bargates, Leominster, are four small almshouses ; these were founded by a widow named Hester Clark in 1736, and have been since rebuilt. Tradition says that the foundress spent all her money on these almshouses, and that she became in consequence so poor that she had to occupy one herself. That is why there is in the centre of the building a figure of a man, very quaint and rudely carved, holding an axe in his hand with these lines beneath :—

> " He that gives away all before he is dead,
> Let 'em take this hatchet and knock him on ye head."

The inscription on a stone on the front of the building contradicts the tradition, for it expressly states : " This Hospital was erected by Hester Clark and endowed at her death with 20 pounds per annum, to four decayed widows." This is a good example of the way in which a rhyme and folk-tale of great antiquity are as it were brought up to date and started on a new lease of life by being associated with some local hero or person of note (see ante, Jack o' Kent).

Sir Laurence Gomme (Folklore as an Historical Science, 66–78), has collected a number of parallel stories to this. He concludes that the tale has come down to us from a savage time when the mallet (in this case a hatchet) was actually used for killing off the aged. At Osnabrück, in front of a house (but sometimes at the city gate, as in several of the cities of Silesia and Saxony), there hangs a mallet with this inscription :—

> " *Wer den kindern gibt das Brodt*
> *And selber dabei leidet Noth,*
> *Den schlagt mit dieser Keule todt.*"

Which Mr. Thoms has Englished thus :—

> " Who to his children gives his bread
> And thereby himself suffers need,
> With this mallet strike him dead."

Gentleman's Magazine, 1850, 250–2.

Sir Laurence Gomme concludes that life of the folk-tale commenced when the use or formula of the mallet ceased to be a part of the social institutions. " The old customs which we have detailed as the true origin of the mallet and its hideous use in killing the aged and infirm had died out, but the symbol of them remained. To explain the symbol a myth was created, which kept sufficiently near to the original idea as to retain evidence of its close connection with the descent of property." He goes on to give reasons for his belief that this story dates from a pre-Celtic period. It clearly takes us back to practices very remote from the reverence for the parents' authority, which might perhaps have been expected from descendants of the Aryan household. In most of the stories the father takes the place given to the charitable Hester Clark at Leominster.

(6) KING HERLA.

Herla was King of the Ancient Britons, and was challenged by another king, a pigmy no larger than an ape, and of less than half human stature. He rode on a large goat ; indeed, he himself might have been compared to Pan. He had a large head, glowing face, and a long red beard, while his breast was conspicuous for a spotted fawnskin which he wore on it. The lower part of his body was rough and hairy, and his legs ended in goats' hooves. He had a private interview with Herla, in which he spoke as follows :—" I am lord over many kings and princes, over a vast and innumerable people. I am their willing messenger to you, although to you I am unknown. Yet I rejoice in the fame which has raised you above other kings, for you are of all men the best, and also closely connected with me both by position and blood. You are worthy of the honour of adorning your marriage with my presence as guest, for the King of France has given you his daughter, and indeed the embassy is arriving here to-day, although all the arrangements have been made without your knowledge. Let there be an everlasting treaty between us, because first of all, I was present at your marriage, and because you will be at mine on the same day a year hence." After this speech he turned away, and moving faster even than a tiger, disappeared from his sight. The king, therefore, returned from that spot full of surprise, received the embassy, and assented to their proposals. When the marriage was celebrated, and the king was sitting at the customary feast, suddenly, before the first course was served, the pigmy arrived, accompanied by so large a company of dwarfs like himself, that after they had filled all the seats at table, there were more dwarfs outside in tents which they had in a moment put up, than at the feast inside. Instantly there darted out from these tents servants with vessels made out of precious stones, all new and wondrously wrought. They filled the palace and the tents with furniture either made of gold or precious stones. Neither wine nor meat was served in any wooden or silver vessel. The servants were found wherever they were wanted, and served nothing out of the king's or anyone else's stores, but only from their own, which were of quality beyond anyone's thoughts. None of Herla's provisions were used, and his servants sat idle.

The pigmies won universal praise. Their raiment was gorgeous ; for lamps they provided blazing gems ; they were never far off when they were wanted, and never too close when not desired. Their king then thus addressed Herla :—" Most excellent King, God be my witness that I am here in accordance with our agreement, at your marriage. If there is anything more you desire I will supply it gladly, on the condition that when I demand a return you do not deny it." Hereupon, without waiting for an answer he returned to his tent and departed at about cock-crow with his attendants. After a year he suddenly came to Herla and demanded the observance of the treaty. Herla consented, and followed at the dwarf's bidding. They entered a cave in a very high cliff, and after some journeying through the dark, which appeared to be lighted, not by the sun or moon, but by numerous torches, they arrived at the dwarf's palace, a splendid mansion. There the marriage was celebrated, and the obligations to the dwarf fittingly paid, after which Herla returned home loaded with gifts and offerings, horses, dogs, hawks (race horses ?) and all things pertaining to hunting and falconry. The pigmy guided them down the dark passage, and there gave them a [small] blood-hound (*canem sanguinarium*) small enough to be carried, (*portabilem*) then strictly forbidding any of the king's retinue to dismount until the dog leapt from his carrier, he bade them farewell and returned home. Soon after, Herla reached the light of day, and having got back to his kingdom again, called an old shepherd and asked for news of his queen, using her name. The shepherd looked at him astonished, and said : " Lord, I scarcely understand your language, for I am a Saxon, and you a Briton. I have never heard the name of that queen, except in the case of one whom they say was Herla's wife, queen of the earliest Britons. He is fabled to have disappeared with a dwarf at this cliff, and never to have been seen on earth again. The Saxons have now held this realm for two hundred years, having driven out the original inhabitants. The king was astonished, for he imagined that he had been away for three days only. Some of his companions descended from horseback before the dog was released, forgetful of the dwarf's commands, and were instantly crumbled to dust. The king then forbade any more of his companions to descend until the dog leapt down. The dog has not leapt down yet. One legend states that Herla for ever wanders on mad journeys with his train, without home or rest. Many people, as they tell us, often see his company. However, they say that at last, in the first year of our [present] King Henry [the second] it ceased to visit our country in pomp as before. On that occasion many of the Welsh (*Wallenses*) saw it whelmed in the Wye, the Herefordshire river (*Waiam Herefordiæ flumen*). From that hour that weird roaming ceased, as though Herla had transferred his wandering (*errores*, a pun containing the idea of error) to us, and had gained rest for himself. (A hit at contemporary politics).[1]

(7) JACK THE GIANT KILLER.

Once upon a time—a very good time it was—when pigs were swine and dogs ate lime, and monkeys chewed tobacco, when houses were thatched with pancakes, streets paved with plum puddings, and roasted pigs ran up and down the streets with knives and forks on their backs crying " Come and eat me ! " That was a good time for travellers.

Then it was I went over hills, dales, and lofty mountains, far farther than I can tell you to-night, to-morrow night, or any other night in this new year. The cocks never crew, the winds never blew, and the devil has never sounded his bugle horn to this day yet.

Then I came to a giant castle ; a lady came out of the door with a nose as long as my arm. She said to me, she says, " What do you want here ? If you don't be off my door I'll take you up for a pinch of snuff." But Jack said " Will you ? " and he drew his sword and cut off her head. He went into the castle and hunted all over the place. He found a bag of money, and two or three ladies hanging by the hair of their heads. He cut them down and divided the money between them, locked the doors, and started off.

1] Walter Map, *De nugis Curialium Dist.* i., ch. 2. Kindly translated by the Rev. Lewis Bishop, *Cf.* Hartland, *Science of Fairy Tales*, 180, 234.

Then it was I went over hills and dales, &c.

Then Jack[1] came to another giant's castle, but there was a drop over the door. He slipped in as quickly as he could, but nevertheless the drop struck him on the side of the head and killed him. And the old giant came out and buried him. But in the night three little dogs named Swift, Sure, and Venture, came and dug him up. One scratched him out of the ground, one breathed breath into his nostrils and brought him to life, while the other got him up out of the grave. Then Jack put on his cloak of darkness, shoes of swiftness, and cap of knowledge. He went once more to the giant's door and knocked ; when the giant came out, of course he could see nobody, Jack being invisible. He at once drew his sword and struck the giant's head off. He plundered the house, taking all the money he could find, and went into all the rooms. He found four ladies hung up by their hair, and again dividing the money between them, turned them out and locked the door.

Then he went off again over hills and dales and lofty mountains, &c.

Then Jack came to another giant's castle. He knocked at the door, and an old lady came out ; he told her he wanted a night's lodging. She said " My husband is sorely against Englishmen, and if he comes in he will smell the house all over to find one. But never mind, I'll put you in the oven." When the woman's back was turned, Jack got out of the oven and went upstairs into a bedroom. He put a lump of wood in the bed and hid underneath. By and bye the old giant came in. He said :—

> " Fee, fi, fum,
> I smell the blood of an Englishman.
> Let him be alive or let him be dead,
> I'll have his flesh to eat for my bread
> And his blood to drink for my drink."

He then went down to supper, and after it he slept. On waking up he said to his wife, " Now I will find the man that's here." He went upstairs, club in hand, and hit the log in the bed three times. Every time Jack groaned under the bed the giant said " I think I've finished ye now." He went down again, talked to his wife for a bit, and went to bed.

At breakfast next morning he was much astonished to see Jack, and said " How d'ye feel this morning ?" Jack said " All right, only in the night a mouse gave me a slap with his tail !" Then they had breakfast ; it was a hasty pudding.

1] This is the first mention of Jack. I noted the story as related ; probably part of it was forgotten.

There was poison in Jack's, and instead of eating it he put it in a little leather bag inside his shirt. When they had breakfasted, Jack said : " I can do something more than you." The giant said " Can you ?" " Yes," said Jack, and pulling a knife out of his pocket he slit the leather bag, and loosed all the pudding out on the ground. The giant, trying to follow Jack's example, pulled out a knife, and wounding himself, fell dead immediately. Then Jack found two or three ladies hanging up, cut them down, took a bag of money that was lying on the table, and then went out and locked the doors.

> Be bow bend it,
> My tales ended.
> If you don't like it,
> You may mend it.[1]

(8) THE BOY AND THE FAIRIES.

Once there was a boy who wandered away from the right path on a journey to his home, and lost himself in a big wood ; night came on, and he lay down tired out and fell asleep. When he woke two or three hours after, he could see that a bear was lying beside him, with his head on its little bundle of clothes. It got up, and the boy was very much frightened at first, but finding the bear was quite tame and gentle, he allowed the animal to lead him out of the wood, to a spot where he could see a light. Walking towards it, he found it came from a little turf hut. In answer to his knock, a little woman opened the door, kindly inviting him to enter. There he saw another little woman, sitting by the fire. After a good supper, he was told he must share with them the only bed, and lying down he fell fast asleep, to be wakened when the clock struck twelve by his bedfellows, who sprang up, putting on little white caps which hung at the bed's head. One said "Here's off," and the other " Here's after," and they suddenly disappeared as though flying. Afraid to stay in the hut alone, and seeing another cap hanging at the bed's head, the boy seized it, saying " Here's after." He was immediately transported to the fairy ring outside the door of the hut, where the little women were dancing merrily. Then one said " Here's off to a gentleman's house," the other " Here's after," so the boy did likewise, and found himself on the top of a tall chimney. The first fairy said " Down the chimney," and the others repeating the usual formula, down they went, first to the kitchen and then to the cellar. Here they began collecting bottles of wine to take away ; they opened one and gave it to the boy, who drank so greedily that he fell asleep ; on waking, he found himself alone, and in fear and trembling went up to the kitchen,

---

1] Told by W. Colcombe (80), at Weobley, 1909. He learnt it from an old chap-book, when a small boy. For bibliography of this folk-tale *see* Gerould, *The Grateful Dead*, 24.

where he met the servants, and was taken before the master of the mansion. He could give no satisfactory account of himself, and was condemned to be hanged. On the scaffold, he saw, pushing eagerly through the crowd, a little woman carrying a white cap, and wearing a similar one. She asked the judge if the prisoner might be hanged in the cap, and he gave his consent, so she walked up to the scaffold and placed it on the lad's head, saying, " Here's off !" He quickly said " Here's after," and away they went like lightning to the turf hut. Here the fairy explained that she had been displeased by his taking her magic cap, and that if befriended by fairies he must never in future take liberties with their property. This he promised, and after a good meal, was allowed to depart to his home.[1]

(9) THE FOX AND THE MAGPIE.

Once a fox and a magpie agreed to go a-robbing together on the King's highway. They overtook a girl with a basket of eggs and butter. " We cannot manage this," said the fox. " Oh yes, we can," says the magpie, " I'll go and peck her nose while you pick up the basket." But when the fox had the basket safe he carried it off to his hole, and the magpie could get no share of the eggs and butter. " I'll serve him out for this," he thought to himself. So a little time after he went to the fox and said, " I know where to find some horse-flesh, but it's no good to tell you, you'll keep it all yourself." " No, I won't," says the fox, " I promise you it shall be all right this time." So away they went over hedges and ditches, one flying, the other jumping, till they came to a high wall. " Now," says the magpie, " you jump, I'll fly." The fox jumped, cleared the wall, and fell into the midst of a pack of hounds. As the magpie flew overhead he cried " What about eggs and butter now ? "

(10) THE INDEPENDENT BISHOP.

Once King George came to Worcester, and went to see the Bishop. Now he was a very independent man and would give way to nobody, therefore he had fixed to his door a brass plate, and on it was this :—" The Independent Bishop of Worcester." When King George saw this he stared. " I like this," he says, " this won't do at all ; I'll give him independent indeed." So he walked in. When the Bishop came in, he said : " I see you call yourself the Independent Bishop of Worcester ?" " Yes," said the Bishop, " so I am ; I am afraid of no man," says he. " Well," says King George, " you must come to me in the Tower of London in three weeks' time, and you must answer three questions. If you can answer truly you can keep that plate on the door ; if not, off it comes, and you shall not call yourself the independent Bishop

1] From W. Colcombe, 1908. For another version, see Hunt, *Popular Romances of the West of England*, 1st series, 76.

any more. You shall tell me first how soon I can travel all round the world ; secondly, to a farthing what I am worth ; thirdly, what I think at the moment we are speaking." " Very well, your Majesty," said the Bishop. And the King went off to London. Next morning the Bishop was up very early ; he had not slept a wink, and he kept walking up and down, up and down the walk in his garden. His old gardener asked him what the trouble was. " Nothing at all, nothing at all," said the Bishop. But he walked up and down faster and faster, and the gardener, an old servant, ventured to ask him again what was the matter. " Well," said the Bishop, " I'll tell you ; you've served me well these many years." " Is that all ?" said the gardener, when the Bishop had finished. Then he thought a bit. " Does the King know you well ?" he asked. " No," said the Bishop, " he saw me yesterday for the first time." " They say I am a bit like your lordship," says the gardener, " give me a suit o' your clothes and I'll answer those questions in the Tower o' London for you." It was agreed, and when the day came the King, with the courtiers all round, asked the first question : " Well, how soon can I travel all round the world ? " " You must go with the sun," said the gardener, " then it will take you exactly twenty-four hours." " Well done," said the King, and all the courtiers said " There, that's one for the Bishop." " Ah," said the King, " but you must tell me what I am worth ?" " Nothing at all ; only one man in the world has ever been worth anything, and that was our Saviour ; he was sold for thirty silver pieces, and you therefore cannot be worth one farthing." " True again," said the King." " Another to the Bishop !" they all shouted, " another to the Bishop !" " But you cannot tell me what I think ? " said King George. " You think I am the Independent Bishop of Worcester, but I am his gardener and his servant come to answer for him," said he. The King laughed, and they all said " The Independent Bishop, another for the Bishop !" So the gardener took good news home to his master, who was independent still, and he kept that plate on his door as long as he was Bishop of Worcester.[1]

  This is a prose version of the ballad of *King John and the Abbot,* and an example of the way a folk-tale is brought up to date in oral tradition. Riddles asked by a monarch of one of his dependents, and answered by the third person assuming the guise of the person questioned, form the subject of many ancient tales. *See* Sidgwick, *Popular Ballads of the Olden Time,* ii., 173.

(11) Two Riddle Stories.

  There was a man convicted of having stolen a sheep ; he was sentenced to death, but the magistrates said he could go free if he could ask a riddle they could not answer, and he was liberated for three days so that he might invent one. As he went out of prison he saw a horse's skull by the roadside. Returning to prison on the

---

1] Told by a mason at Longtown, 1909.

third day in despair he noticed that within it was a bird's nest, with six young ones, and he thought of the following riddle :—

> " As I walked out,
> As I walked in,
> From the dead I saw the living spring
> Blessed may Christ Jesu be
> For the six have set the seventh free."[1]

A young man had been sentenced to be transported for some crime, but if he could make a true riddle he should be set free. He went into the garden with his mother, and she told him to draw milk from her breast through her wedding ring, and they made up this riddle about it :—

> " A riddle, a riddle to you I'll tell,
> He drank out of a needful well ;
> Through a golden ring the stream it run, (*sic*),
> And in the garden the deed was done."[2]

Another version, from Longtown, runs thus :—
> " A riddle, a riddle to you I'll tell,
> I drank out of a needful well.
> Through a gold ring the stream did run,
> If you'll tell me the riddle I'll be hung."

1] Weobley, 1907.   2] Told at Bromyard, 1908.

SECTION XIV.

TRADITIONAL CAROLS, BALLADS, AND SONGS.

The following carols and songs are selected from a much larger number, collected in this county since 1905. They are chosen, for the most part, with regard to
the popular origin of the words ; a few, such as *The Pretty Ploughboy* and the carol
There is a Fountain, are included for the sake of the folk tunes to which they are
sung, the words having no intrinsic value for the student of folk-lore. The songs are
not " Herefordshire," in the sense that they are wholly peculiar to the county, though
the tunes are either noted for the first time, or interesting variants of those obtained
elsewhere. The only really local songs sung by the peasantry are not folk-songs at all,
but of eighteenth century date, such as the *Herefordshire Fox Chase, The Herefordshire Farmer and his Yorkshire Boy*. These are of local interest only ; both words
and tunes are inferior, when compared with the really ancient ballad, even when
corrupted, as it often is, by centuries of oral transmission. When it is remembered
that these ballads have been handed on to us by generations of illiterate folk-singers,
it is wonderful that the words are not even more imperfect thnn they are. So often
singers do not understand what they sing, and repeat what they think they hear ;
thus, a man sang to me " Lord Thomas he was a bold *fairy stern*," when he really
meant " bold forester." The true spirit of tradition yet survives from the time when
the bards transmitted history orally through their verses ; in spite of the fact that
the same song is sung to totally different tunes in different localities, or to interesting
variants of the same tune, an old country singer is nearly always certain that his
version is the only right one. He takes pains to sing exactly what he learnt at his
mother's knee, or following his father at plough. The wonderful variety and fluidity
of our English folk-song proves the creative influence of the folk, but I think it is
most often exercised unconsciously.

Carols and carol tunes seem to be especially well represented in this county ;
the fact may be partly accounted for by the popularity of the Christmas *quête*, now
rapidly declining. The songs, as distinct from carols, were not sung for profit.

The carols may be divided from a literary point of view into three classes :—
(1) Those of undoubtedly ancient popular origin, in narrative ballad form, such as
The Bitter Withy, (2) Those which are probably not so old, but of which we find
greatly varying traces and fragments worked into both popular and pious literature of the 16th and 17th centuries, if not earlier. These, such as the *Virgin Un-
spotted, God rest you merry Gentlemen, The Moon Shines Bright*, are in hymn form ;

(3) The modern carol or hymn, resembling or identical with hymns published in the 18th century and onwards, included here for the sake of the music. Of the ancient carols, Nos. 1, 2, and 5 are well known locally; No. 4 I have found only once; none of these were known to the singers of Nos. 3 and 6, who were gypsies. No. 3, *Christ made a Trance*, after its puzzling first verse, passes into the gloomiest version of the *Moon shines Bright*. In its earliest form this carol was probably a secular poem in praise of May-day, sung at the dawn of this pagan festival. A version collected by Miss Lucy Broadwood, in Hertfordshire, has retained the verses alluding to a joyful May, and asking for a bowl of sweet cream from the dairy-maid (*Eng. County Songs*, 108). For these Herefordshire singers substituted, perhaps in Puritan days, exhortations and moralizings concerning death and the grave.

It is impossible to say how much the preservation of the words of these carols and songs may be due to the vogue of the broadside ("ballet," or "ballad-sheet"), which came in with printing. When genuine popular ballads were printed on these sheets, the words were taken down from tradition for the publishers; afterwards the broadsides were taken through the country districts by pedlars and ballad chanters, who sang in the streets the ballads they had for sale. I have heard of these people often from those who remember them, but could never find one; they must have died out. One who came to Weobley fair every year cried, "A song, a song, a song for a penny! As large as a barn door and not quite so thick!" The word "broadside" is not used by the local peasantry; they say "ballet." The boys never came back from the fairs without two or three "ballets." One singer explained that "they rolled them up into balls in their pockets," which is probably the reason why so few survive. Hereford printers of broadsides were Hull & Sons, and Elliott, whose son still prints a sheet of carols at Christmas, including the *Moon shines Bright*. Broadsides were also issued by Farror, of Ross.

1.—THE BITTER WITHY; OR, THE SALLY TWIGS.

FIRST TUNE.

Noted by A. M. Webb
and R. Vaughan Williams.

Sung by the late MR. W. COLCOMBE,
Weobley, 1908 and 1909.

As it fell out on a high ho·li·day, When drops of rain did fall, did fall, Then Je·sus ask'd of His Mo-ther Ma·ry if He should go and play at the ball.

FIRST TUNE.   SECOND VERSION.

Noted by Rev. Edwin King, LL.D., B.C.L.

Sung by MRS. MARY JONES (60),
at King's Pyon, 1908.

SECOND TUNE.

Noted by Eleanor Andrews.

Sung by MR. G. T. BRIMFIELD (MASON),
Winforton, 1908.

As it fell out one high ho‑li‑day, When
drops of rain did fall, did fall, Our Sa‑viour begg'd leave of His
Mo‑ther Ma‑ry If He should go play at ball.

THIRD TUNE.

Noted by R. Vaughan Williams,
from a Phonograph rocord.

Sung by MRS. TRISTRAM,
Withington, 1909.

Our Sa‑viour built a bridge of the beams of the sun, And
o‑ver the sea went He. And the three jol‑ly jor‑dans they
fol‑low'd af‑ter Him, And drown‑èd they were all three......

Subsequent verses.

(a)

(b)

(a)   (b)

Variants.

FOURTH TUNE.

Noted by R. Vaughan Williams,
from a Phonograph Record.

Sung by MR. W. HOLDER (62),
at Withington, Jan., 1909.

(*Ver.* 1.) Our Sa·viour ask·èd leave of His mo·ther Ma·ry If He should go ...... to play at the ball, "To play at ball, my own, dear Son, Oh it's time You was gone, and com·ing, com·ing home; But pray do not let me hear of Your ill··do·ings, At night, when You do come home."

(*Ver.* 5.) So our Sa·viour made a bridge of the beams of the sun, And o·ver it went He, went He; And these three jol·ly jer·dins, they fol·low'd af·ter He, And drown·èd they were all three.

The following text was sung by Mrs. Jones (*see* first tune, 2nd version.)

As it fell out on a high holiday,
  When drops of rain did fall, did fall,
Jesus asked of His mother Mary
  If He might go and play at the ball.

"To play at the ball, my own dear Son,
  It's time You're going or gone,
But let me hear of no complaints
  At night when You come home."

Sweet Jesus went down into yonder town
  As far as the Holy Well,
And there He saw as fine children
  As any tongue can tell.

"I say God bless you every one,
  Your bodies and souls pray keep;
Little children, shall I play with you?
  And you shall play with Me."

"Oh nay, oh nay, that must not be,
  And oh nay, that must not be,
For we are all lords' and ladies' sons
  Born in our bowers all."

. . . .
"And the very meanest amongst them
  Told Me I was a poor maid's son
  Borned in an oxen's stall."[1]

Sweet Jesus turned Himself round about,
  He did neither laugh nor smile,
But the tears run trickling from His eyes
  Like water from the skies.

Sweet Jesus went home to His mother Mary;
  "I've been down, I've been down to yonder town,
As far as the Holy Well,
  And there I found as fine children
As any tongue could tell.

I said 'God bless you every one,
  Your bodies and souls pray keep,
Little children, shall I play with you?
  And you shall play with Me.'"

"Go You down, go You down to yonder town,
  As far as the Holy Well,
And take away those sinful souls
  And dip them deep in Hell!"

1] The division of verses 4—6 is uncertain.

" Oh nay, oh nay, that must not be,
    And oh nay, that must not be !
There's many thousand sinful souls
    Crying out for the help of Me !"

Jesus made a bridge of the beams of the sun,
    And over Jordan went He,
And there followed after the three jolly jordans,
    And drowned the three all three.

And it's upling corns and downling corns
    The mothers of them did whoop and call :
" Oh Mary mild, call home your child,
    For ours are drownded all !"

Then Mary mild called home her child,
    And laid it across her knee,
And with a rod of bitter withy
    She gave Him thrashes three.

" Oh the withy, the withy, the bitter withy
    Which caused My back to smart !
The withy shall be the very first tree
    To perish at the heart !"

The following version of words was sung by Mr. G. T. Brimfield (*see* 2nd tune).

As it fell out one high holiday,
    When drops of rain did fall, did fall,
Our Saviour begged leave of His mother Mary
    If He should go play at ball.

" Go play at ball, my own dear Son,
    It's time You were going or gone ;
But don't You let me hear of any complaint
    To-night when You comes home."

Then it's upling call and downling call,
    Our Saviour He did whoop and call,
Until He met with three jolly jordins,
    And He asked them to play at ball.

They said they was lords' and ladies' sons,
    Born in power, all in all,
" And you are but a poor maiden's child
    Born in an oxen-stall."

" If I am but a poor maiden's child,
    Born in an oxen-stall
I will let you know at the very latter end
    That I am above you all !"

So our Saviour built a bridge of the sun,
    And over the sea, the sea went He,
And after did follow the three jolly jordins,
    And they were all drownded three.

Then it's upling call, and downling call
    Their mothers, they did whoop and call,
Saying, " Mary mild, call home your child,
    For ours are drownded all !"

Then Mary mild, she called home her child,
    And laid it across her tender knee,
And with a handful of bitter withy
    She gave Him the slashes three.

" Oh ! the withy, the withy, the bitter withy !
    That is causing me to ache and to smart !
Oh ! the withy shall be the very first tree
    That shall perish and die at the heart !"

The singer of the first tune above called this carol " The Sally Twigs," but it is usually called the " Bitter Withy " in the county, although a willow wand is a " sally twig " in local dialect. Though often confused and mixed with the Holy Well, as in Mrs. Jones' version, each is also found complete, in quite distinct forms, with different tunes ; there seems no reason to suppose any real connection between them. Country singers frequently introduce a verse or verses of one ballad into another. (*See* the lines " Oh hell is dark," &c., common to *Christ made a Trance.* and *Dives and Lazarus*). A solitary verse of *The Bitter Withy* appeared in *Notes and Queries*, 1868 ; the whole carol was first printed by Mr. Frank Sidgwick in *Notes and Queries*, 1905, and has been accepted by Professor F. B. Gummere (*The Popular Ballad*, 1907), as the first genuine popular ballad discovered since the publication of Child's great work, *English and Scottish Popular Ballads.* Professor G. H. Gerould (*Publications of the Modern Language Association of America*, vol. xxiii., i., 141–167), has investigated and confirmed its genuineness ; Mr. Frank Sidgwick subsequently contributed to

Folk-Lore (June, 1908, 190–200), a number of texts of the ballad collected by himself, chiefly from Herefordshire, since Prof. Gerould's paper was published. *See* also notes by Miss Broadwood, Miss Gilchrist, and Mr. Sidgwick in the *Folk-Song Society's Journal IV.*, 29–47, where the above texts and tunes are printed.[1]

I have collected versions of the ballad frequently ; it is known in many parts of the county ; but no later texts shed light on the corrupt or obsolete words. These are variously sung as (*a*) " Upling scorn and downling scorn," " Upling call and downling call," " Uplane call and down lane call," &c., while (*b*) " jolly jordans " may be either " jerdins " or " jorrans." Mr. Sidgwick (*Folk-Lore, loc. cit.*) suggests that as " Linkum " is a stock ballad locality (*see* Child's *Ballads*, v. 354), (*a*) might be a corruption of " Up Linkum and down Linkum." Miss Broadwood and Miss Gilchrist (*F.S.S. Journal, loc. cit*), trace a connection in both tunes and words between the *Bitter Withy* and *Sir Hugh of Lincoln*. Herd's MS. version of " Sir Hugh " in Child's *Ballads* gives " merry Linkine " for Lincoln ; it seems possible that " Up Lincoln or down Lincoln " may be the right solution. The singers make no attempt to explain these words, or " jordans " either, except that they say the latter signifies the children. One version has " vergins " here, but, as Prof. Gerould observes, it is unlikely that a common word would be changed into a rare one, and the children were " lords and ladies *sons*." With regard to the source of the legend, Prof. Gerould traces it to three tales in the Apocryphal Gospel of *Pseudo-Matthew*, which was probably written soon after the middle of the fifth century : these are—(1) the story of how Jesus played with children on a sunbeam : one child, Zeno, was thrown down and killed, but restored to life by Jesus ; (2) Jesus went with some children to the well to draw water ; one child struck Him and caused Him to break the jar, but He gathered the spilled water in His mantle ; (3) Jesus sat on the sunbeams—others tried to follow His example, and fell down, and broke their limbs, but He healed them all. We find these three legends were expanded into six by the thirteenth century, the result of the " common process of fictional embroidery," and were afterwards spread by vernacular versions in England and on the Continent. All six miracles occur in *MS. Additional*, 31042, British Museum ; they are as follows :—(1) Jesus leaps from hill to hill, followed by his companions, with fatal results,—a variant of the story of Zeno ; (2) a broken jug miraculously repaired ; (3) the jug suspended on the sunbeam ; (4) Jesus sits on a sunbeam ; (5) the story of Zeno ; (6) the spilled water collected in a mantle.[2]

To these possible sources Miss Gilchrist adds a seventh legend from the Greek *Gospel of Thomas*. Christ goes out to play after rain showers, and gathers the fallen water into pools—maliciously broken down by the son of Annas, who is cursed by

---

1] For another version, from Gloucestershire, *see* Sharp, *English Folk-Carols*, 5, and note.
2] Other vernacular versions are *MS. Harl.* 2399, and *MS. Harl.* 3954 (from Gerould, *loc. cit.*)

Christ and made to wither like the willow branch in his hand, with which he has destroyed the pools (Harris Cowper, *Apocryphal Gospels*, 1897).[1]

The commonness of the sunbeam stories in mediæval legend points to a pagan source. This Prof. Gerould finds in an Oriental story of a robber, who was carried into the houses he plundered on a ray of the moon. But Miss Broadwood has called attention (*Journal, loc. cit.*) to the closer parallels to be found in Celtic traditional story, referring to an incident in the life of Fionn, a child of miraculous birth, who is struck with a bundle of hawthorn twigs. This child drowns the children of his father's enemies. (*Campbell, Waifs & Strays of Celtic Tradition*, 16–19, and 24–26.)

Both Prof. Gerould and Prof. Gummere regard the curse on the willow in the last verse as " an afterthought and a tag." It may not have formed part of the story radical originally, but is probably as old or older, since it is ætiological, an attempted explanation of the hollow interior of the willow. For another superstition connected with willow *see* Section ii., p. 19, *ante.*

2.—THE HOLY WELL.

Noted by R. Vaughan Williams, from a Phonograph Record.
ÆOLIAN.

Sung by MR. J. HANCOCKS (70), MONNINGTON, OCT., 1908.

As it fell out up - on a day, On a bright and a ho - ly day, Sweet Je - sus asked of His dear mo-ther. If He might go to play.

SECOND TUNE.

Noted by R. Vaughan Williams, from a Phonograph Record.

Sung by MRS. E. GOODWIN (60), at King's Pyon, March, 1909.

" To play, to play sweet Jesus shall go,
To play now get You gone,
And let me hear of no complaints
To-night when You come home."

Sweet Jesus went down to yonder town
As far as the Holy Well
And there did He see as fine children
As any town[2] can tell.

He bid God bless them every one
And Christ their portion be.
" Little children, shall I play with you ?
And you shall play with Me."

But they jointly answered Him " No "
They were lords' and ladies' sons,
And He, the meanest of them all,
Was born in an ox's stall.

1] St. Bridget hung her cloak on a sunbeam: *see* Baring-Gould, *Lives of the Saints*, ii., 19 ; St. Aldhem suspended his chasuble in this way at Malmesbury, during Mass ; so did St. Omer with his gloves, at Cambray. *See Golden Legend*, iii., 192, and vii., 201 (Temple Classics). 2] ? Tongue.

Sweet Jesus turned Himself around, |
   And neither did laugh nor smile,
But the tears came trickling from His eyes,
   As the rain falls from the skies.

Sweet Jesus turned himself around,
   To His mother home went He,
He says, " I have been down to yonder_town
   As far as you can see.

I have been down to yonder town
   As far as the Holy Well,
And there did see as fine children
   As any town can tell.

I bid God bless them every one,
   And Christ their bodies hear[1] and see ;
" Little children, shall I play with you,
   And you shall play with Me ?'

But they jointly answerèd me ' No '
   For they were lords' and ladies' sons,
And I, the meanest of them all,
   Was born in an ox's stall."

" Sweet Jesus, go down to yonder town
   As far as the Holy Well,
And take away those sinful souls
   And dip them deep in Hell !"

" Nay, nay," sweet Jesus smiled and said,
   " Nay, nay, that must not be,
For there are too many sinful souls,
   Crying out for the help of Me."

Then up and spoke the angel Gabriel
   Upon our good St. Stephen,
" Although Thou art but a maiden's child,
   Thou art the King of Heaven."

"Upon our good St. Stephen" is "Upon a good set steven," or "Upon one sure set steven," in some versions. Husk says "set steven" means an appointed time. A MS. note in the British Museum copy of this *Songs of the Nativity* corrects this solution to "with a sure, set voice" (O.E. "stemm" or "stefn"—"voice"). Since the *Carnal and the Crane* was printed on broadsides as a carol "For St. Stephen's Day," it seems possible that the allusion is to St. Stephen's Day here. It was the custom to add a verse to the end of a carol to make it suit the season, whether Christmas, New Year, or May Day ; it is not unlikely that, at least in pre-reformation days, carols for this saint's day, December 26, were distinguished from those of the Nativity by a final verse such as this.

3.—THE SEVEN VIRGINS, OR, UNDER THE LEAVES.

Noted by R. Vaughan Williams,
DORIAN INFLUENCE. from a Phonograph Record.

Sung by ANGELINA WHATTON (Gypsy),
Near Weobley, Oct., 1908.

Un - der the leaves, the leaves of life, There I saw maid-éns*[to]seven, And one of those was Ma - ry mild, Was our King's mo-ther from Heaven.

* *Variants.* (a) *verses 2 and 3 have*

    (b) *verse 2 has*   *verses 3, 4 and 5 have*

    (c) *verse 2 has* C♮ *here.*

    (d) *verses 2 and 3 have* C♮ *here.*

1] ? Save.   * Usually " of."

Under the leaves, the leaves of life,
  I saw the maidens seven,
And one of them was Mary mild
  As was our King's mother from Heaven.

They asked me what I was looking for,
  All under the leaves of life :
" I am looking for sweet Jesus Christ,
(a) { With His body nailed to the tree." }
(b) { To be our heavenly guide."   }

" Go you down, go you down to yonder town,
(b) { As far as the Hol-i-well, }
(ab) { As far as you can see,   }
And there you'll find sweet Jesus Christ,
  With His body nailed to a tree."

" Dear Mother, do not weep for me,
  Your weeping does me some harm,
That I (? John) may be a comfort to you,
  When I am dead and gone.

Dear mother, dear mother, you must love John,
  For John is an angel so bright,
That he may be a comfort to you
(a.) { When I am dead and gone."   }
(b.) { Dear Mother what have I been." }

" Oh no, dear Son, that never can be,
  That I should love John
As well as my own Son Jesus,
  That I bore from my own body."

Oh the rose, the rose, the gentle rose,
  The { fern[1] } that grows so green,
      { laurel }
May the Lord give us grace in every place,
  To pray till our ending day.

The lines marked (a) and (b) were sung respectively by (a) Mrs. Whatton, and (b) Mrs. Loveridge, gypsies hop-picking at the Homme, near Weobley. Mr. Frank Sidgwick printed this carol (from Sylvester), in *More Ancient Carols*, Shakespeare Head Press booklets, 1906, the last lines run :—

God give us grace in every place
To pray for our King and Queen.

Furthermore for our enemies all
Our prayers they shall be strong ;
Amen, good Lord. Your charity
Is the ending of my song.

Later, Mr. Sidgwick discovered two additional verses, in a unique chap-book of 1847, now printed in *Popular Carols* (Watergate Booklets). " One of these," he says, is " extremely interesting, as it occurs word for word in a lyric of the 15th century." For other references, *see* Burne, *Shropshire Folk-Lore*, 566, *F.S.S. Journal*, iv., 50.

4.—THE CARNAL AND THE CRANE.

Noted by R. Vaughan Williams.
ÆOLIAN.

Sung by Mr. Hirons (60),
at Haven, July, 1909.

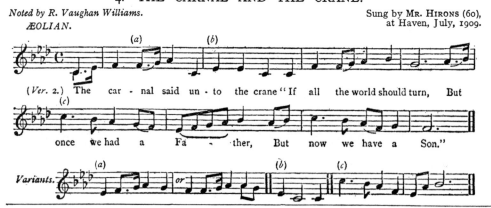

(*Ver. 2.*) The car - nal said un - to the crane "If all the world should turn, But once we had a Fa - ther, But now we have a Son."

Variants.

1] " Fennel " in some versions.

As I walked out one morning,
  A little before it was day,[1]
I heard a conversation
  Between a carnal and a crane.

The carnal said unto the crane
  " If all the world should turn,
But once we had a Father,
  But now we have a Son."

There was a star in all the East
  Shone out a shining throng,
And shone into King Pharaoh's chamber,
  And where King Pharaoh lay.

The wise men they soon spied it,
  And soon King Pharaoh told
That an earthly babe was born that night
  As no man on earth could destroy.

King Pharaoh sent for his armed men.
  And ready then they be,
For all children under two years old
  Shall be slainèd, they shall be.

Joseph and Mary
  Was weary of their rest,
They travelled into Egypt
  Into the Holy Land.

" God speed thy work," said Jesus,
  " Go fetch thy oxen-wain,
And carry home thy corn again
  As which this day hath sown.

If any should ask you
  Whether Jesus He has passed by,
You can tell them that Jesus He did pass by
  Just as your seeds were sown."

Then up came King Pharaoh
  With his armèd men so bold,
Enquiring of the husbandman
  Whether Jesus He has passed by.

" The truth it must be spoken,
  The truth it must be told,
I saw Jesus passing by
  Just as my seeds were sown."

King Pharaoh said to his armèd men
  " Your labour and mine's in vain,
It's full three quarters of a year
  Since these seeds were sown !"

This is part of a carol of thirty verses, printed on broadsides of the 18th century ; a copy of one of these is in the collection of Mr. Walter Pilley, of Hereford. It is probably of great antiquity, but may have been preserved and kept in the memory of the folk through the broadsides. The full version has the legend of the conversion of King Herod to the belief that Christ is born, which is the subject of another carol, *St. Stephen and King Herod.*[2] Herod says that if the news be true, the roasted cock on the dish before him shall crow,—

" And then three fences[3] crowèd he,
  In the dish where he did stand."

There follows the legend of the miraculous harvest, as in the fragment above. The word "carnal" is said to mean "crow," from French *corneille* (*F.S.S. Journal* iv., 24). " Pharaoh " is, of course, a substitute for Herod, and this peculiarity occurs also in a variant noted by Miss Broadwood in Sussex, for which see *F.S.S. Journal,* i., 183, and her *English Traditional Songs and Carols.* For further notes and references to the legends upon which the carol is founded, and which are known nearly all over Europe, see Child's *Ballads.* The *Journal of the Folk-Song Society ;* iv., 24–5, has also interesting notes on this carol.

1] Hone quotes a Worcestershire version, sung in 1823 :
  " And there as I did *reign* " (="renne" O.E. for "run.") This is internal evidence of the antiquity of the carol, as is also the obsolete word "carnal, ' not to be found in dialect dictionaries.
2] *See* Sidgwick, *Popular Ballads of the Olden Time, Second Series,* 125.   3] Fences=times. *See also* C. J. Sharp, *English Folk Carols,* 4, where the word is "senses,"

5.—DIVES AND LAZARUS.

FIRST TUNE.

Noted by E. Andrews.

Sung by Mrs. HARRIS,
at Eardisley, 1905.

As it fell out on a light dully day When Div'rus made a feast, And

he in-vi-ted all his friends, grand gen-try of the best.

SECOND TUNE.

Noted by R. Vaughan Williams,
from a Phonographic Record.

Sung by Mr. J. EVANS,
Dilwyn, January, 1907.

[As it] fell out up-on one day Rich Div-'rus made a feast, And

he in-vit-ed all his friends And gen-try of the best.

Variant.

Then Lazarus laid himself down and down
    Under Diverus's Wall
" Some meat, some drink ! brother Diverus "
    For hunger starve I shall."

" Thou wer't none of my brethren as I tell thee
    Lie begging at my Wall,
No meat nor drink will I give
    For hunger starve thou shall "

Then Diverus sent out his hungry dogs,
    To worry poor Lazarus away,
They hadn't the power to bite one bite,
    But they licked his sores away.

Then Lazarus he laid himself down and down
    And down at Diverus's gate
" Some meat ! some drink ! Brother Diverus
    For Jesus Christ His sake."

Then Diverus sent out his merry men,
    To worry poor Lazarus away,
They'd not the power to strike one stroke,
    But they flung their whips[1] away.

As it fell out, on a light dully day
    When Lazarus sickened and died,
There came two Angels out of heaven
    His soul for to guide.

" Arise ! Arise ! brother Lazarus
    And come along with me ;
There's a place provided in heaven,
    (For) To sit on an Angel's knee."

As it fell out on a dark dully day,
    When Dives sickened and died.
There came two Serpents out of hell,
    His soul for to guide.

" Arise ! Arise ! brother Diverus]
    And come along with we
There is a place provided in hell,]
    For to sit on a Serpent's knee.

There is a place provided in hell
    For wicked men like thee.

▸   •   •   •   •

Who had they as many days to live
    As there are blades of grass
I would be good, unto the poor
    As long as life would last.

1] Pronounced " weeps."

Mrs. Harris sang " Diverus," the old form of Dives, throughout; this form has obviously been influenced by Lazarus. The Dilwyn version was " Divus "; it concludes as follows :—

Then Divus lifted up his eyes,
  And saw poor Lazarus blest,
" A drop of water, brother Lazarus !
  For to quench my flaming thirst."

If I had as many years to live
  As there is blades of grass,
I would make it in my will secure
  That the Devils should have no power !

Oh, hell is dark, oh, hell is deep,
  Oh, hell is full of mice,[1]
It is a pity that any poor sinful soul
  Should depart from our Saviour Christ.

And now my carol's ended,
  No longer can I stay,
God bless you all, both great and small,
  And God send you a happy New Year.

Yet another version, kindly sent to me by Mr. H. C. Beddoe, was noted by his brother (the late Dr. John Beddoe) in this county many years ago. It concludes thus :—

If I had as many years to abide
  As there are blades of grass,
Then I should have { an ending } day,
           { unending }
But in hell for ever must last.

If I had as many years to abide
  As there are stars in the skies,

Then I should have { an ending } day,
             { unending }
But in hell for ever must lie.

At merry Christmas time,
  And among good Christians all,
This Christmas car-i-ol might be sung
  In either house or hall.

The last verse in both texts has probably been added to make it seem suitable for singing at Christmas or New Year. The carol, with these tunes, has been printed in *F.S.S. Journal*, ii., 125, and iv., 47, with notes and references. Miss Broadwood notes that in Beaumont and Fletcher's *Nice Valour*, Dives is spoken of as one of the ballads " hanging at church corners," and that in Fletcher's *Monsieur Thomas* (1639) he uses the form Diverus, while a " ballet of the Ryche man and poor Lazarus " was licensed in 1558. *Cf.* also Child, *Ballads*, and a reprint in *Popular Carols* (Watergate Booklets).

As regards the word " moss," or " mice " (*see* third verse quoted, from Dilwyn, above), Mr. Frank Sidgwick suggests that the right reading is " mist," which in Middle English would rhyme with " Christ." And " mist " in hell would be quite intelligible to a mediæval audience, as being equivalent to " thick darkness " or " mirk." (*F.S.S. Journal*, iv., 15.)

---

[1] *Cf.* " Christ made a trance," *infra*—" Hell is full of moss." Other versions give " Mist."

6.—CHRIST MADE A TRANCE.

Noted by R. Vaughan Williams,
from a Phonograph Record.

Sung by ANGELINA WHATTON (Gypsy),
at the Homme, Dilwyn, Sept., 1908.

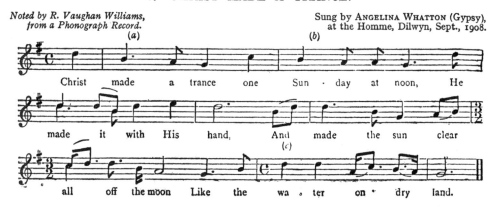

Christ made a trance one Sun - day at noon, He made it with His hand, And made the sun clear all off the moon Like the wa o ter on · dry land.

Variants. (a)   (b)   (c)

Christ made a trance one Sunday view,
  All with His own dear hands,
He made the sun clear all off the moon,
  Like the water off dry land.

Like the water off the land, man Christ,
  What died upon the Cross ;
What shall we do for our Saviour,
  As He has done for us ?

What shall we do for our Saviour, man Christ,
  What died upon the Cross ?
We'll do as much for you, dear Lord
  As you have done for us.

Oh, hell is deep and hell is dark,
  And hell is full of moss ;[1]
What shall we do for our Saviour
  That He has done for us ?

Oh, these six days in all this week,
  Are for the labouring man,
And the seventh for to serve the Lord
  Both the Father and the Son.

Come, teach your children well, dear man,
  And teach them when they're young,
The better it'll be for your own dear soul,
  When you are dead and gone.

Mrs. Whatton repeated this carol to me in a gypsy van ; her daughter sang it into the phonograph. All the gypsies who have sung for me know the carol, and the usual version had " Sunday view " in the first line ; none could explain what the first verse meant. I think the version with a similar tune, noted by Miss Burne (*Shropshire Folk-Lore*, 565), must be from the same family of gypsies. The first line is probably a corruption of something quite different in meaning ; or it may be a fragment of a legend of creation now forgotten. Miss Broadwood has discussed both possibilities fully in the *Journal of the Folk-Song Society*, iv., 14, pointing out that in some broadside versions of the *Cherry-Tree Carol*, Christ is made to say " O, the sun and the moon, mother, shall both rise with me " ; and in a Warwickshire copy, " The world shall be like the stones in the street, For the sun and the moon shall bow down at my / thy feet." Compare also a gypsy version in *Notes and Queries*, 8th Ser. ii., Dec. 24, 1892.

1] "Remorse" in some versions. *See* " Dives and Lazarus " *ante.*

THE SINGER OF "AWAKE, AWAKE."

A WEOBLEY CAROL-SINGER.

(*Singer of "The Man that Lives."*)

7.—THE MOON SHINES BRIGHT.

Noted by R. Vaughan Williams, from a Phonograph Record.
DORIAN.

Sung by G. VAUGHAN,
at Dilwyn, March, 1907.

The moon shines bright, and the stars give their light, And a lit-tle be-fore it's day Our Lord our God died on the Cross For us who He loved so dear.

SECOND VERSION.

Noted by R. Vaughan Williams.

Sung by G. LEWIS,
at Hardwick, Pembridge, July, 1909.

SECOND TUNE.

Noted by A. M. Webb.

Sung by WILLIAM COLCOMBE,
Weobley, 1905.

The moon shines bright, and the stars gave a light, A lit-tle be-fore it was day. The Lord our God He called on us, And bid us a-wake and pray.

Awake, awake, good people all ;
　Awake, and you shall hear ;
Our Lord Our God died on the cross,
　For you he loved so dear.

There is six days in every week,
　Is for the labouring man ;
And on the seventh you must serve the Lord,
　The Father and the Son.

And when you goes into the Church,
　Down on your two knees fall,
And pray unto the living Lord
　For the saving of your souls.

And for the saving of your souls,
　Christ died upon the cross ;
We never shall do for Jesus Christ
　As he has done for us.

And for the saving of your souls
　Christ died upon the tree ;
We never shall do for Jesus Christ
　As he has done for we.

Bring up your children well, dear man,
　They have but little thought ;
It's better for them to be unborn,
　Than them to be untaught.

To-day a man's alive dear man,
　With many a hundred pound ;
To-morrow morn he may be dead,
　And his corpse be underground.

With one turf at your head dear man,
　And another at your feet ;
Then your good deeds and your bad ones
　Before the Lord shall meet.

And when you are dead and in your grave
　And covered over with clay ;
The worms shall eat your flesh, dear man,
　And your bones shall mould away.

The above text is Colcombe's. He did not connect it with May Day, and the Dilwyn version has a verse for the New Year. The first verses are the same as Colcombe's above, continuing :—

Oh fair, Oh fair, Jerusalem
　When shall I come to thee ?
When will thy griefs be at an end
　Thy joys that we may see.

When fields were as green as grass could grow
　All from his glorious seat
Our Lord our God He watered us,
　With His heavenly dew so sweet.

The Life of man is but a span,
　He's cut down like a flower,
We're here to-day, we're gone to-morrow,
　We're all dead in an hour.

When there's one green turf all at his head
　Another at his feet,
His good deeds and his bad, poor man,
　Will all together meet.

My carol's done, I must be gone
I can tarry no longer here,
God bless you all, both great and small,
And send you a happy New Year.

Versions of this very popular carol are to be found in nearly every collection of traditional songs. For various tunes and words, and other references, *see Journal of the Folk-Society*, i., 180 ; ii., 131 ; and iv., 10 ; *Eng. County Songs, Sussex Songs,* Burne (*Shropshire Folk-lore*), Bramley and Stainer's *Carols*.

8.—AWAKE, AWAKE.

Noted by R. Vaughan Williams.
DORIO-MIXOLYDIAN.

Sung by Mrs. CAROLINE BRIDGES (82).
at Pembridge, July, 1909

A · wake, a wake, sweet Eng' · land, sweet Eng · land now a- wake. And do your prayers o · be · dient - ly, and to your soul par - take ; Our Lord our God is call - ing, all in . the sky so clear, So re · pent, re · pent, sweet Eng land, for dread - ful days draw near ; Let us pray, and it's to the liv · ing Lord let us pray.

It's ho,[1] unto the woman that big with child do go,
Likewise their selling[2] horses, as they give suck also ;
For there's never any man so stout, nor man nor woman looks gay,
For worms will eat your flesh, and your bones will waste away.
　Let us pray, etc.

1] " Woe."　　2] " Silly nurses."

To-day you may be alive, dear man, with many a thousand pounds,
To-morrow you may be dead and gone, and your body underground,
[With one stone] at your head, dear man, and another at your feet,
Your good deeds and your bad ones altogether will meet.
    Let us pray, etc.

God bless the ruler of this house and send him long to reign,
And all the sons and daughters, kind leaven to maintain.[1]
But we'll shake all shame and sorrow, put on your best array,
So I wish you all good morning. May God send us a happy day.
    Let us pray, etc.

This carol was printed in the *Journal of the Folk-Song Society*, iv. 7, where Miss Broadwood describes it as a very interesting survival of a late 16th or early 17th century broadside ballad, still wedded to the tune to which it was sung 330 years ago. Thomas Deloney wrote a penitential ballad after the great earthquake of 1580, when part of St. Paul's Cathedral fell. It began " Awake, Awake O England," and had a burden of " Repent," &c. Miss Broadwood refers to other versions in the Ballad Society's *Roxburghe Ballads*, part xi., 467, and part xxii., vol. vii., xix., some lines in which are identical with the Pembridge carol. Verse 3 comes into the " Moon shines bright," *q.v.*

9.—THE MAN THAT LIVES.

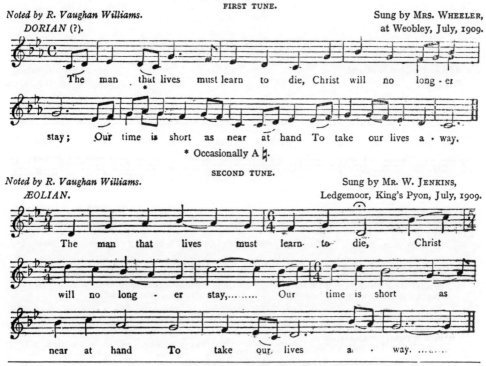

FIRST TUNE.

Noted by R. Vaughan Williams.
DORIAN (?).

Sung by MRS. WHEELER,
at Weobley, July, 1909.

The man that lives must learn to die, Christ will no long-er stay; Our time is short as near at hand To take our lives a-way.

* Occasionally A ♮.

SECOND TUNE.

Noted by R. Vaughan Williams.
ÆOLIAN.

Sung by MR. W. JENKINS,
Ledgemoor, King's Pyon, July, 1909.

The man that lives must learn to die, Christ will no long-er stay,........ Our time is short as near at hand To take our lives a-way. ....

1] ? " Heaven to obtain " or ? " leaven " meaning " good cheer."

What is our lives that we must die,
  Or what's our carcase then ?
It's food for worms to feed upon—
  Christ knows the time and when.

Our lives are like the grass, oh Lord,
  Like flowers in the field,
So welcome death ! Praise ye the Lord !
  Willing I am to yield.

New we must die and leave this world,
  As we have livèd in,
Nothing but one poor winding sheet
  To wrap our bodies in.

When shall we see that happy heaven,
  That blessed resting place ?
So we like angels there shall feed,
  Upon God's royal grace.

Happy that man that never swore,
  'Gainst the living Lord,
Nor ever took God's name in vain
  At any trifling word.

The bittery plagues, the fiery hell
  Where sinners are slain,
His beasts shall die, his sheep shall rot,
  Cold clay shall be his grave.

Besides himself no sickness shall find,
  No physic shall him cure.
When we shall live to see old age,
  Our lives shall not endure.

Mrs. Wheeler's tune was learnt in her youth at her home in the Bromyard district, near the Worcestershire border. The first tune being a variant of that to " The Carnal and the Crane " suggests that possibly morbid puritanical or evangelical words have in this instance supplanted an older legendary ballad.

10.—THE TRUTH SENT FROM ABOVE.

Noted by R. Vaughan Williams.
DORIAN.

Sung by W. JENKINS,
at King's Pyon, July, 1909.

This is the truth sent from a - bove, The truth of God, the God of love ; There-fore don't turn me from your door, But heark · en · all— both rich and poor·

The first thing which I do relate
Is that God did man create,
The next thing which to you I'll tell :
Woman was made with man to dwell.

Then after this was God's own choice,
To place them both in Paradise,
There to remain from evil free,
Except they eat of such a tree.

And they did eat, which was a sin,
And thus their ruin did begin ;
Ruined themselves, both you and me
And all of their posterity.

Thus we were as[1] (?) to endless woes,
Till God the Lord did interpose,
And so a promise soon did run
That He would redeem us by His Son.

1] Heirs ?

11.—THERE IS A FOUNTAIN.

FIRST TUNE.

Noted by A. M. Webb.

Sung by WILLIAM COLCOMBE, Weobley, 1904.

There is a foun-tain of Christ's blood, Wide o-pen stretch'd for to drown our sins, Where

Je-sus stands with o-pen arms Of mercy to............ in-vite us in.

SECOND TUNE.

Noted by R. Vaughan Williams, from a Phonograph Record.

Sung by W. HANCOCKS (aged 70), at Monnington, Oct., 1908.

There is a foun-tain of Christ's blood, Wide

o-pen stretch'd to drown our sins, Where Je-sus stands with

quicker slow again.

o pen arms Of mer-cy, to in vite us in.

Variant. (a)

SECOND VERSION.

Noted by R. Vaughan Williams, from a Phonograph Record.

Sung by MRS. ELIZA SMITH (Gypsy), at Weobley, Oct., 1908.

There is........ a fount-ain of Christ's blood, Wide

o-pen stretch'd to drown our sins, Where Je-sus stands with

o-pen arms Of mer cy, to in-vite us in.

* Sometimes a crotchet.

THIRD VERSION.

Noted by R. Vaughan Williams.

Sung by G. Lewis,
Hardwick, July, 1909.

There is a foun - tain—...... of Christ's · blood Wide
o - pen stretch'd to......... drown our sins, · ·· Where · Je - sus stands with
o - pen arms Of mer - cy, to in - · vite us in.

This carol is a great favourite with Herefordshire singers, and was formerly sung at Christmas, although the subject is the Crucifixion and not the Nativity. It is quite unconnected with Cowper's hymn, " There is a fountain filled with blood."

12.—THERE WAS A LADY IN MERRY SCOTLAND.

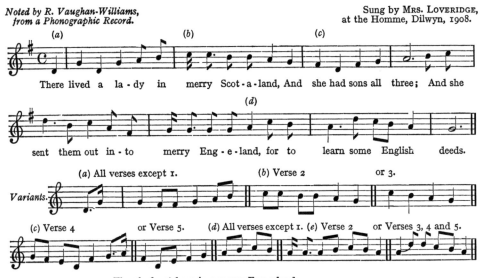

Noted by R. Vaughan-Williams,
from a Phonographic Record.

Sung by Mrs. Loveridge,
at the Homme, Dilwyn, 1908.

(a)   (b)   (c)

There lived a la - dy in merry Scot - a - land, And she had sons all three; And she

(d)

sent them out in - to merry Eng - e - land, for to learn some English deeds.

(a) All verses except 1.   (b) Verse 2   or 3.

Variants.

(c) Verse 4   or Verse 5.   (d) All verses except 1. (e) Verse 2   or Verses 3, 4 and 5.

They had not been in a-merry Eng-e-land
For twelve months and one day,
When the news came back to their own dear mother
That their bodies were in cold clay.

" I will not believe in a man," she said,
" Nor in Christ in eternity,
Till they send me back my own three sons,
And the same as they went from me."

And God put life all in their bodies,
Their bodies all in their chest, (*sic*)
And sent them back to their own dear mother,
For in heaven they could take no rest

As soon as they reached to their own mother's gates,
  So loud at the bell they ring,
There was none so ready as their own dear mother,
  For to loose the children in.

The cloth was spread, the meat put on ;
  " No meat, Lord, can we take,
Since it's so long and many a day,
  Since we have been here before."

The bed was made, the sheets put on ;
  " No bed, Lord, can we take,
It's been so long and many a day,
  Since we have been here before."

Then Christ did call for the roasted cock,
  That was feathered with His only (holy?) hands ;
He crowed three times all in the dish,
  In the place where he did stand.

" Then farewell stick and farewell stone,
  Farewell to the maidens all.
Farewell to the nurse that gave us our suck " :
  And down the tears did fall.

This is a variant of the Scotch ballad *The Wife of Usher's Well,* from Scott's *Minstrelsy of the Scottish Border.* The story has a fairly close parallel in the well-known German ballad *Das Schloss in Oesterreich* (*see* Sidgwick, *Popular Ballads,* ii., 56) ; this version is much nearer to Scott's than an unrhymed one, called *The Widow Woman,* collected for Miss Burne at Bridgnorth in 1883 (*Shropshire Folk-Lore,* 541). Verse 8 really belongs to the *Carnal and the Crane* ; the Scotch ballad has here :—

" Up then crew the red, red, cock,
  And up and crew the gray ;
The eldest to the youngest said
  " Tis time we were away."

13.—YOUNG LAMBKIN.

Noted by A. M. Webb.

Sung by WILLIAM COLCOMBE,
at Weobley, 1905.

Then up steps young Lambkin, and pulls at the string,
Saying " How shall I get in to her ? How shall I get in,
When the doors are fast bolted and the windows penned in ?"

"I'll pierce this tender baby with a silver bodkin
And call down the lady for to quiet him."
"Dear Lady, dear Lady, how can you sleep so sound
A'hearing your dear baby making such a moan."

"How can I come down this time of the night
When there's no candle burning and no fire lit (alight ?)
Then as the Lady was a'coming out of her bower so high
So ready was Young Lambkin to catch her in his arms.

"Dear Lambkin, dear Lambkin, spare my life till ten o'clock,
Then you shall have as much money as you can carry on your back.
Dear Lambkin, dear Lambkin, spare my life one half-hour,
You shall have my daughter Betsy, she's a beautiful flower."

"I don't want your daughter Betsy, nor none of the rest ;
I should rather see my naked sword through your milk white breast.
Now call down your daughter Betsy to do you some good,
To hold this silver basin to catch your heart's blood."

"Dear Betsy, Dear Betsy, stay where you be,
And see if your dear father's coming o'er the lea."
As Betsy was a'crying at her window so high,
Up came her father a-riding close by.

"Dear Father, dear Father, lay no blame on me,
It's the false nurse and Lambkin that kilt my mam-mee."
Now Lambkin is hanged on the gallows so high,
And the false nurse they burned her on the mountain close by.

The above text is very imperfect, and the singer knew he had forgotten something after verse 2. In verse 3 it is the "false nurse," Lambkin's accomplice, who is speaking. For other versions, *see* Child's *Eng. and Scottish Popular Ballads*, and *Journal of the Folk-Song Society*, ii., 111-13, for tunes, words, and notes. I have another version taken down from the singing of an Irish nurse, who believed the story to be true ; she said that Lambkin bribed the nurse, and afterwards murdered her as well as the baby and its mother, whom he had passionately loved.

14.—LORD THOMAS AND FAIR ELINOR.

Noted by A. M. Webb.

Sung by F. WHEELER,
Weobley, 1904.

Lord Thomas, he was a bold fo-res-ter, A-keep-ing of the King's deer Fair
El-i-nor she was the fair-est wo-man, Lord Thomas he lov-ed her dear

Last Verse.

And ev-er so soon they part, ... "Oh, you who dig my
grave, Pray dig it both wide and deep, ... And bu-ry fair El-i-nor
at my right hand, And the lit-tle brown girl at my feet .... That if
ev-er my moth-er she do pass by, She may sit down and weep." ...

" O riddle, O riddle, dear mother," he said,
  " O riddle it both as one,
Whether I shall marry fair Ellen, or not,
  And leave the brown girl alone.

" The brown girl she've a-got houses and land,
  Fair Ellen, she've a-got none ;
Therefore I charge thee to my blessing,
  The brown girl bring safe to home."

Lord Thomas he rode to fair Elinor's gates,
  And loud he tirled at the pin,
There was none so ready as fair Elinor,
  To let Lord Thomas in.

" What news, what news, Lord Thomas ?" she said
  " What news hast thou brought unto me ?"
" I'm come to invite thee to my wedding,
  And that is bad news for thee."

" O God forbid, Lord Thomas," she cried,
  " That any such thing should be done,
I thought to have been the bride myself,
  And you to have been the bridegroom."

" O mother, come riddle, come riddle to me,
  And riddle it all in one,
Whether I be to go to Lord Thomas' wedding,
  Or whether to stay at home ?"

" O daughter, I riddle your riddle,
  I riddle it all in one,
      (*Two lines missing*).

" There's thousands are your friends, daughter
  There's thousands are your foes,
Betide your life, betide your death,
  To Lord Thomas's wedding don't go."

" There's thousands are my friends, mother,
  There's thousands are my foes,
Betide my life, betide my death,
  To Lord Thomas's wedding I go."

She drest herself in her scarlet red,
  The merry maids drest in green,
And every town that she rode through
  They took her to be the queen.

She rode on to Lord Thomas's door,
  So loud did she pull at the ring ;
None so ready as Lord Thomas
  To let fair Elinor in.

" Is this your bride ?" fair Elinor said,
  " I think she looks wonderful brown,
You may have had as fair a woman,
  As ever the sun shone on."

" Despise her not," Lord Thomas he said,
  " Despise her not unto me,
For I love your little finger,
  Better than her whole body."

The brown girl had got a little penknife,
  Which was both keen and sharp,
Between the long ribs and the short
  She pierced to fair Elinor's heart.

" Oh, what is the matter," Lord Thomas he said,
  " I think you look wondrous wan,
You used to have as fair a colour
  As ever the sun shone on."

" Art thou blind, Lord Thomas ?" she says,
  " Or canst thou not very well see ?
Canst thou not see mine own heart's blood
  Come trickling down my knee ?"

Lord Thomas he had a long sword by his side,
  As he walked through his hall ;
Off he cut the brown girl's head,
  And dashed it against the wall.

Lord Thomas he had a long sword in his hall,
  He pointed it up to his heart ;
Was it ever so soon they met,
  Or ever so soon they did part. . . .

" Pray those that dig my grave,
  Dig it both wide and deep ;
And bury fair Elinor at my right hand,
  And the little brown girl at my feet,
That if ever my mother she do pass by,
  She may sit down and weep."

They grew and grew to a red rose-bud,
  For thousands to admire,
They grew up to the chancel wall,
  And the brown girl grew to a brier.

[Verses 2, 3, 4, 5, 6, are from a Somerset version, noted by H. E. D. Hammond.]

For other versions of the words of this favourite ballad, " Lord Thomas and Fair Ellinor, or The Nutbrown Bride," *see* Child, *English and Scottish Ballads*, ii., 179, and Percy's *Reliques* ; for both tunes and words, see *English County Songs* (from Burne, 651), *Journal of the Folk-Song Society*, ii., 105, *et. seq.*, with references there given. The ballad should be compared with " Fair Margaret and Sweet William," in Percy's *Reliques*, a variant of the same story.

15.—COLD BLOWS THE WIND; OR, THE UNQUIET GRAVE.

Noted by R. Vaughan Williams,   Sung by W. HIRONS,
from a Phonograph Record.   at Haven, Dilwyn, 1909.

Cold blows the wind o'er my true love, Cold blows the drops of rain; I
-ne - ver, ne - ver had but one true love, And in green wood he - was slain.

I'll do as as much for my true love,
  As any young girl may,
For I will sit and weep down by the grave,
  For twelve months and a day.

When twelve months and a day were gone,
  This young man he arose ;
Why do you weep down by my grave,
  That I can take no repose ?"

" O fetch me a nut from a dungeon deep,
  Or water out of a stone ?
Or white, white milk from a fair maid's breast,
  Or from me begone."

" How can I fetch a nut from a dungeon deep,
  Or water out of a stone ;
Or white, white milk from a fair maid's breast,
  When fair maid she is none ?"

" One kiss, one kiss from your lily white lips
  One kiss from you I crave."
" The cock does crow and we must part,
  I must return to my grave."

" If you have one kiss from my lily white lips,
  Your days will not be long,
My lips are as cold as any clay,
  My breath it is earthy and strong."

(Words from Mrs. Powell, singer of *The Milkmaid's Song, infra*).

For variants of words and tunes, *see Shropshire Folk-lore*, 542, with references to other texts ; Broadwood and Fuller-Maitland, *Eng. County Songs* ; Broadwood, *Eng. Traditional Songs and Carols* ; Sharp, *Folk Songs from Somerset* ; *Journal of the Folk-Song Society*, i., 119 and 192 ; ii., 6 ; also Baring-Gould, *Songs of the West*. The ballad illustrates the widespread beliefs that excessive grief can cause the return of the departed spirit to the mourner, and that such communication is fatal. *See ante*, Section iv., 2.

<h3 style="text-align:center">16.—BRANGYWELL.</h3>

Noted by R. Hughes Rowlands

Sung by Mrs. Mellor,
at Dilwyn, 1905.

" What makes thee sit so high, lady,[1]
  That no one can come nigh to thee ?"

" There is a wild bear in the wood,
  If I come down he'll suck my blood."

" If I should kill the boar," said he,
" Wilt thou come down and marry me ?"

" If thou shouldst kill the boar," said she,
" I will come down and marry thee."

---

[1] The burden is repeated for each verse.

Then Brangywell pulled out his dart,
And shot the wild boar through the heart.

The wild boar fetched out such a sound
That all the oaks and ash fell down.

Then hand in hand they went to the den,[1]
And found the bones of twenty men.

17.—DILLY DOVE.

Noted by R. Vaughan Williams
from a Phonograph Record.

Sung by Mrs. E. Goodwin,
at Weobley, 1909.

Dil - ly-dove he   went to plough, With those two hors - es   and a plough, *Collin-dame,*

Variant. Verse 3.

cum - and - go,   kil - ly - co - cum.   He said fair maid what makes you sit so high?

Variant. Refrain of verses 3, 4 and 5.   *Variant. Verses 3 and 4.*

Dilly-dove he went to plough,
And saw a fair maid on a bough,
    Collin-dame, cum and go, killy-co-cum.

He said " Fair maid what makes you sit so high "
That no young man can come anigh ?"
    Collin-dame, come and go, killy-co-cum.

"O there's a wild boar in the wood,
If I come down he'll suck my blood."
    Suck my blood, Collin-dame, come and go, killy-co-cum.

"If you'll come down and go with me,
Both you and I will go and see."
    Go and see, collin-dame, come and go, killy-co-cum.

Then he went unto the park,
And shot the wild boar through his heart.
    Through his heart, collin-dame, come and go, killy-co-cum.

Then he went unto the den,
And there were bones of forty men,
    Collin-dame, come and go, killy-co-cum.

Both " Brangywell " and " Dilly Dove " are abbreviated versions of the popular ballad " Sir Lionel "; for which *see* Child, *Ballads,* i., 208. Mrs. Goodwin sang " Dove " to rhyme with " cove." " Brangywell " has the g hard : the word may be a phonetic degradation of Egrabel (*see* Child).

1] The ballad has been traditional in Mrs. Mellor's family for generations.

WILLIAM COLCOMBE.

THE DOORWAY OF ST. CATHARINE'S CHAPEL, LEDBURY.

18.—THE MILKMAID'S SONG.

Noted by R. Vaughan Williams,
from a Phonograph Record.
DORIAN.

Sung by Mrs. Ellen Powell,
at Westhope, Canon Pyon, 1907.

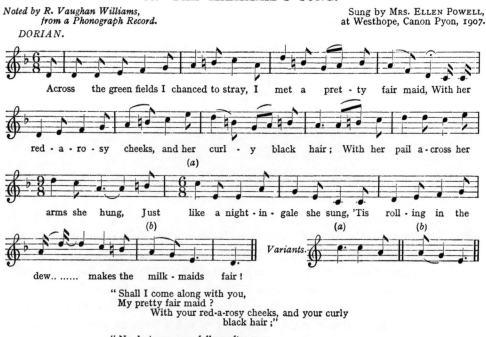

Across the green fields I chanced to stray, I met a pret - ty fair maid, With her
red - a - ro - sy cheeks, and her curl - y black hair; With her pail a - cross her
(a)
arms she hung, Just like a night - in - gale she sung, 'Tis roll - ing in the
(b)   (a)   (b)
Variants.
dew.. ...... makes the milk - maids fair!

"Shall I come along with you,
My pretty fair maid ?
With your red-a-rosy cheeks, and your curly
black hair ;"

"No, but you may follow after me,
Kind sir," she answered me,
"'Tis rolling in the dew makes the milkmaids fair."

(The remainder of the words are unsuitable for publication).

For another version of words, *see* Halliwell, *Pop. Rhymes*, 336 ; for another tune, *see Folk Songs from Somerset,* second series, 18 ; Mr. Cecil Sharp has noted the ballad several times in Somerset, and the Rev. S. Baring-Gould has found it in Cornwall and Devon. It is a ballad form of the nursery rhyme, " Where are you going to, my pretty maid ? "

19.—A BRISK YOUNG SAILOR.

Noted by R. Vaughan Williams
ÆOLIAN.

Sung by W. Colcombe,
at Weobley, 1909.

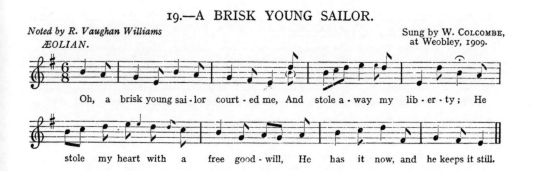

Oh, a brisk young sai - lor court - ed me, And stole a - way my lib - er - ty; He
stole my heart with a free good - will, He has it now, and he keeps it still.

Down in the meadow as I did run,
To pick the flowers as they sprung ;
At every sort I gave a pull,
Until I puck my apurn full.

And as I carried my apurn low
My true love followed, through frost and snow ;
But now a smile I canna win,
He'll pass me by and say nothin'.

Yonder is an alehouse in yon town,
He'll take a seat and sit himself down,
He'll take a strange girl on his knee,
And don't you think that's grief to me ?

Oh, how grieved I am, how grieved I am,
For she has gold and I have none ;
But gold will waste, and beauty blast,
This poor girl will come like me at last.

There is a rogue on yonder hill,
He has a heart as hard as steel ;
He has two hearts instead of one,
And he'll be a rogue, when I am gone !

For other versions of words, with tunes, *see* Miss Broadwood's *English Traditional Songs and Carols*, 92, and note ; also *Journal of the Folk-Song Society*, i., 252, " There is an Alehouse " ; ii., 158, " Died for Love " ; " In Jessie's City," ii., 159 ; " A Bold Young Sailor," ii., 168 ; and a Lincolnshire " Died for Love," iii., 188. There is a modernised version, entitled " There is a Tavern in the Town," in the *Scottish Student's Song-Book*. The words of the different versions vary considerably ; the tunes are almost always good. I have two other versions noted from gypsy singers.

20.—MARDEN FORFEIT SONG.

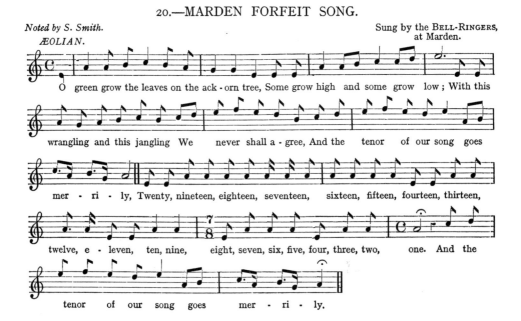

Noted by S. Smith.   Sung by the BELL-RINGERS, at Marden.
ÆOLIAN.

O green grow the leaves on the ack-orn tree, Some grow high and some grow low ; With this

wrangling and this jangling We never shall a-gree, And the tenor of our song goes

mer-ri-ly, Twenty, nineteen, eighteen, seventeen, sixteen, fifteen, fourteen, thirteen,

twelve, e-leven, ten, nine, eight, seven, six, five, four, three, two, one. And the

tenor of our song goes mer-ri-ly.

Anyone missing the right number in the above backward reckoning had to drink "a tot" of cider to most of the rustics. I should think not an unwelcome "forfeit," and rather a premium on inaccuracy.—W.D.V.D.

I am indebted to the Rev. Custos Duncombe for permission to include this song. Lady Gomme has printed two versions of *Green Grow the Leaves* in *Traditional Games*, i., 183–6; one is a ring game, the other a sort of dancing, "Follow my Leader." Two tunes are given, distinct from the one above, and there is no mention of the numbers or of forfeits.

21.—FOUR SEASONS OF THE YEAR.

Noted by R. Hughes Rowlands.
DORIAN.

Sung by JOHN MORGAN,
at the Pitch, Dilwyn, Oct., 1905.

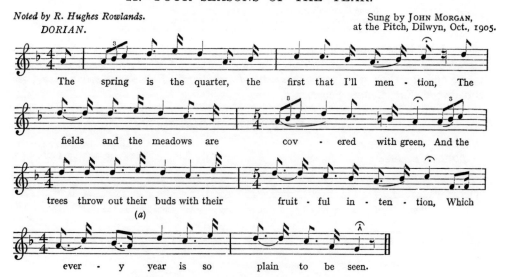

The spring is the quarter, the first that I'll men - tion, The

fields and the meadows are cov - ered with green, And the

trees throw out their buds with their fruit - ful in - ten - tion, Which

(a)

ever - y year is so plain to be seen.

Come all you lads and lasses, I pray you give attention
Unto these few lines which lately have been penned ;
The seasons of the year I'm just a-going to mention,
Which the nature of all things with us do depend.

When you are young, and in your prosperity,
Cheer up your friends, and revive like the spring.
Join yourselves together like the birds in February,
Which Valentine's day unto us do bring.

The Spring is the quarter, the first that I shall mention
The fields and the meadows are covered with green,
And the trees throw out their buds with their fruitful intention
Which every year is so plain to be seen.

You will see the little lambs, round their dams they were a-playing
The cuckoo is a-singing in every shady grove ;
Oh but Nature is reviving, long time has been decaying
Once more the drooping heart still begins for to move.

Now summer it is come, we must all be a-doing,
The reaping and the mowing the farmer will be among ;
We have cut down all his corn, and we've housed it in the barn
And to-night we'll drink his health to a merry merry song.

Now the autumn it is come, it's not so hot but pleasant ;
The sportman he goes out with his dog and his gun ;
He knocks down the birds, both partridge and the pheasant,
Some do it for profit, and others for fun.

You will see the fruitful trees, that the farmer is depending on
To fill up the old keg, that has so long been dry.
You will see the dropping leaves, they were depending,
And a more severer winter we shall have by-and-by.

Now winter is come, and it is so cold and chilly,
You will see the poor thresher preparing in his barn,
With his jacket well lined with flannel or with beaver,
He lays upon his task for to keep himself warm.

But a milder wind will blow, as the sun shines on the mountains,
The face of the earth is once more to be seen,
The days increase in length, as the sun unbinds the fountains,
Which by the long frost so long have been sealed.

Some you'll see a-laughing, others a-crying,
Some they will murmur while others do sing,
Nature is reviving, long time has been decaying,
Once more we shall rejoice at the return of the spring.

John Morgan told Mr. Rowlands that he learnt the song 50 years ago, from a travelling thatcher. I am indebted to the kindness of Mr. H. C. Beddoe for verses 1, 2, 9 and 10. For other versions, *see* the *Journal of the Folk-Song Society*, i., 77, and Broadwood, *Eng. County Songs*, 143.

22.—THE PRETTY PLOUGHBOY.

Noted by R. Hughes Rowlands.
DORIAN Influence.

Sung by JOHN MORGAN,
The Pitch, Dilwyn. (Oct., 1905).

It's of a pret-ty plough-boy was ploughing on the plain, When his horses stood under-neath the shade, This was his song, as he did walk a-long, And his chance *was* to meet a pretty maid.

2nd Verse.

" If I should fall in love, and your parents come to know, And the next *thing* they would send *me* to the sea." When their aged par-*ents* the same came to know, Pretty ploughboy was ploughing on the plain ; " The press gang they sent and they pressed my love away, And sent *him* to the wars *to* be slain."

She dressed herself out in her best,
Her pocket she well lined with gold ;
See how she trudged the streets, with the tears all in her eyes,
" I am come in search of a jolly sailor bold."

The first that she met was a jolly sailor bold
" Did you meet my pretty ploughboy ?" she cried ;
" He's just crossing the deep, and sailing for the fleet,"
And he sayed, " Pretty maid, will you ride ?"

She rode till she came to the ship her love was in,
And to the captain did complain,
" O, I am come for to see the pretty ploughboy,
That was sent in the wars to be slain."

O one hundred bright guineas, she freely put out,
And gently told them all o'er ;
" If this will not do, here's twice as much more,
O you leave me have the lad I adore."

When she had got her pretty ploughboy in her arms,
Where she'd had him many times before,
She set the bells to ring, most sweetly did she sing,
That she'd met with the lad she adored.

And blessed be the day when all true lovers meet,
And their sorrows they all are at an end.
This last cruel war called many lads away,
And their true lovers they never saw no more

Mr. Rowlands explained that all notes marked "ʌ" the old man made a special stress on ; he adds, " I distinctly remember it as it was rather peculiar that it should occur in every instance on the *weak* accent, except that of the word *love,* in second bar of second verse.   He also divided the triplet in several cases for two words, but sang it as a triplet."

23.—THE FROG AND MOUSE.[1]

There was a mouse lived in the mill
And in the mill this mouse did fill.

Stem, stim, stam, pam-ariddle faro bob-o-reg, and the rigdum bob rick-i-no ; kime, naro, kimo ; Stem, stim, stam, pam-a-riddle faro bob-a-reg, and the rigdum bob rick-i-no.

There was a frog lived in the well
And in this well this creature did dwell.

The frog and mouse went out to ride
With guns and soldiers by their side.

The cat and kittens did come in
And they did all come in to sing.

I noted this in 1906 from a native of Weobley, who learnt it from James MacCarthy, an Irishman, since dead.   He sang it, but the tune was not worth recording.

In Wedderburn's *Complaint of Scotland,* 1549, one of the songs sung by the shepherds is " The Frog came to the Myl dur " (Mill door).   In 1580 a ballad of " A

1] Traditional versions are recorded in *Notes and Queries :* First series, i., 458 ; Second Series, ii., 27, 74, 75, 110, 188 ; Third Series, 51.   *See* also First Series, ii., 136,222, Halliwell, J. O., *Nursery Rhymes* (Percy Society, 1842), No. xcii,. p. 70, A. H. Bullen, *Lyrics from Elizabethan Song-books* (1897), p. 202, from Ravenscroft's *Melismata,* 1611, in notes, also a Scottish version from C. K. Sharpe's *Ballad Book.*   (I am indebted to the kindness of Mr. Frank Sidgwick for these references.)   *See* also Baring-Gould, *A Garland of Country Song,* 31.

most strange wedding of the Frog and the Mouse" was licensed to Edward White at Stationer's Hall, and in 1611 this song was printed with music among the country pastimes in *Melismata.* "A frog he would a wooing go" is a modern version by C.E.H. (Chappell, *Pop. Music,* 88).

The following version was noted in Herefordshire from an old Irish nurse :—

THE FROG AND THE DUCK.

There was a frog lived in a brook,
    Fa la linkum larrum,
And a mouse lived in a well,
    Tay dee om dee diddle um,
    Tay dee om nom nurrum.

Mrs. Mouse, are you within ?
" Yes, kind sir, I am sitting to spin."

Mrs. Mouse, will you marry me ?
A loving husband I will be.

Uncle Rat is not at home,
And you must get his consent.

Uncle Rat knocked at the door,
Who's been here while I've been out ?

Who's been here but a nice young man,
And he'll have me if he can.

Up there came a farmer's duck,
And gobbled up the fine young frog.

Then there came a bouncing cat,
Gobbled up the mouse and rat.

So there's an end to the one, two, three ;
Their wedding-day will never be.

SECTION XV.

PLACE AND PERSON LEGENDS.

(1) LEGENDS OF LOCAL SAINTS.

The majority of the saints whose lives were spent wholly or in part in Here-fordshire belonged to the ancient Celtic church. Folk-lore is chiefly concerned with the legends and fables attached to their names, therefore only the briefest historical facts concerning them are given here. It would seem from the old Welsh chronicles that the British kingdoms of Erging (Archenfield) and Ewyas were the districts of the present county of Herefordshire earliest converted to Christianity. Their kings in the fifth and sixth centuries made extensive grants of land to the Celtic church, which, spreading from the west eastward, was eventually to meet and unite with, or be subjected by, the Anglo-Saxon church founded by St. Augustine, advancing from the east, westward. It follows that our most ancient churches are those in the deanery of Archenfield ; nearly all are situated near to springs or running water, probably because they were erected on sites hitherto reserved for the worship of the spirits of wells and streams. It is here that we find numerous churches dedicated to Welsh Saints, though in some cases the ancient dedication has been changed in later times. Many of these churches retain their Welsh names ; Llandinabo is a corruption of Lann Junabui, the church of Junapeius, a cousin of St. Dubricius[1] ; Llangarren is Lann Garan, the church in the valley of Garan, founded by St. Deiniol,[1] a British saint. Four Herefordshire churches are dedicated to St. David, or Dewi, the patron saint of Wales ; they are :—Much Dewchurch, the Lann Dewi Ros Cerion of the *Book of Llan Dâv* ; Little Dewchurch ; Kilpeck, the Lann Degui Cilpedec of the *Book of Llan Dâv* ; and Dewsall.[2] It was customary to name each church after its original founder ; Dewi was a common Welsh name, and it is very probable that these churches originally commemorated a local St. Dewi, and became associated with his more celebrated namesake by later tradition.

St. Beuno.

Llanveyno is Llanfeuno, the church of St. Beuno. About the end of the 6th century lands in Ewyas were granted to St. Beuno, by the king, Ynyr Gwent, and here he built the church which still bears his name. It is said that the king resigned

---

1] Baring Gould, *Lives of the Welsh Saints*, ii., 370.　　2] Baring Gould, ii., 317.

his royal position and became a disciple of Beuno. Hearing that his father was seriously ill, the saint left the charge of his foundation to three disciples, and departed for Powys. Many miracles are ascribed to him, and he is said to have raised six persons to life, but we have no record of his return to the little church in the Olchon valley, then an outpost, standing as it were face to face with the heathen Saxon. One legend tells how he planted an acorn by the side of his father's grave, that grew in time to be a mighty oak, of which one branch curved down to the ground, and then rose again. " And there was a part of this branch in the soil, as at present ; and if an Englishman should pass between this branch and the trunk of the tree, he would immediately die ; but should a Welshman go, he would in no way suffer."[1]

After his father's death, St. Beuno continued to dwell in Powys, and afterwards in Flintshire, where he is closely associated with the legend of St. Winefred, whom he restored to life. (*See* Rees, *Cambro-British Saints*, 199–202.) Finally, he settled at Clynnog, in Carnarvonshire, where he founded a church, and lived there till his death, about 648 A.D. Here his shrine and fountain were of great repute for many centuries. For the many Welsh legends and superstitions associated with St. Beuno, *see* Baring Gould, *op. cit.*, i., 208–221, from a life in Welsh, now in the library of Jesus College, Oxford.

St. Gwainerth (St. Weonard).

The church of St. Weonard's, Llan Sant Gwainerth of the *Book of Llan Dâv*, is so called from St. Gwainerth, a British saint, said to have been decapitated by the Anglo-Saxons. He seems to have been a holy man and a hermit, for Blount, who lived in the seventeenth century, saw in the church, in a stained glass window on the north side of the chancel, " the picture of an ancient man with a long beard, holding a book in one hand and an axe in the other, and under written in old characters, *St. Wenardus, Heremyta*. I suppose," he adds, " he was a British Saint, and the church was dedicated to him."[2] For the legend of the burial of St. Weonard in the tumulus near the church, *see* Section i., 3.

St. Catharine (Katharine, or Catherine Audley).

The story of this Saint, " Blessed Catharine of Ledbury," as she is called, affords an interesting example of the purely local cult of some holy person. Her name was Catharine Audley, said to be one of the Audleys of Dilwyn ; she lived with her maid Mabel in a hermitage near Ledbury, at the spot called the Hazel, subsisting

---

1] Baring Gould, *op. cit.*, i., 208.   2] Robinson, *Mansions and Manors*, 294 ; *Ariconensia*, 39.

on herbs and milk. The King, Edward II., in consideration of her birth, or piety, or both, granted her an annuity of £30. She died at Ledbury, and an effigy in a beautiful chapel which bears her name is pointed out by the folk as hers, antiquaries say quite erroneously.[1]

It was revealed to St. Catharine, according to legend, that she should make her home in the place where the bells should ring without hands to welcome her.[2] Coming one evening to Ledbury she sat down on a large stone to rest, and the bells of the church rang out sweetly. Her maid Mabel went to the belfry and found it all locked up, no ringers being near, so St. Catharine knew it was the place where she was to stay. Near the town are two small meadows called "Cattern's acre," and "Mabel's Furlong." In the former, old people still remember Cattern's stone, said to be the very one she sat upon when she heard the bells ring.[3] It has unfortunately been removed. Before St. Catharine died she prophesied that if the door of the chapel now dedicated to her in Ledbury church were never opened until it should do so of itself, Ledbury would become the richest town in England, but if it should be opened by human hands Ledbury would always be poor. So people were always careful to keep it closed, until one night in a drunken frolic, some of the townsmen burst it open ; since then Ledbury's hope of prosperity has vanished.[4]

The churches of Bosbury, Ledbury and Pembury, (Pembridge), have towers detached from the church in memory of St. Catharine, who passed through those places on her way to the Hazel.[4] The curious marks on the rocky bed of the brook at Upper Sapey are said by some to be the marks of the feet of the mare with a colt beside her which conveyed St. Catharine to Ledbury ; in this case, in which an earlier legend has been attached to a Saint's name in later times, the older form of the story is probably that already given. (See Section i., 1).

King Clydawg (or Clydog).

Clodock takes its name from a king of Ewyas, King Clydawg, who was murdered near the Monnow, where the church now stands, during the latter half of the sixth century. His story is thus told in the *Liber Landavensis* :—

King Clydawg son of Glydawyn, when he was in his kingdom enjoying peace and administering justice, became a martyr through his virtue, and had a crown of heavenly glory with the palm of carnal chastity.

1] Morgan Watkins, iv., 84 ; *Memorials*, 274.
2] *See* Section i., 5, *The White Cross* ; *Cf. Child Ballads*, ii, 235 ; Bells which ring without hands are common in popular tradition. *See* Sidgwick, *Ballads of the Olden Time*, ii., 111, (from Jamieson) :—
   " And a' the bells o' Merry Lincoln, without men's hands were rung."
Child also gives notes on automatic bells in an Icelandic ballad, (i., 173), and a Moravian one, (i., 231).
3] Wordsworth has a sonnet on the subject—*St. Catherine of Ledbury*.
4] Collected at Bosbury, 1908, and at Ledbury Workhouse. There are seven detached belfries in Herefordshire, the others being Holmer, Garway, Yarpole, and Richard's Castle.

A certain young woman, daughter of a wealthy man, was in love with him, and said to those that sought her that she would marry no one but the illustrious Clydawg. The answer of the girl being heard, and she refusing all persons as usual, one of the companions of the king, because he could not obtain her, was filled with an evil spirit, and an intense desire respecting her; and receiving excitement for bad conduct from the malignity of rashness, and the malice of luxury, on a certain day he killed King Clydawg, innocent as a lamb, near the river Mynwy, while he was waiting for the meeting of hunters, and meditating with great devotion on sacred subjects. On his death his acquaintance, companions and friends of noble parentage, having joined oxen to the carriage, began to take away the body from the place, and to pass the river by a ford. And in one part of the river the yokes of the oxen began to break and the oxen to stand still, for they could not move the body from the place on account of its great weight, and although often fastened with chains and ropes, yet they were broken to pieces, and although the oxen were frequently goaded on they would not move a step, as though a fiery globe opposed them. And all beholding and wondering, the body remained in the place which was divinely prepared for it; and the people immediately, on account of the excellent life which they had known the holy man to lead, and his sanctity, and his death, which obtained for him the crown of martyrdom, and the wonderful lightness of his body in the first place after his death, and secondly its very great weight, which caused it to be immoveable, rendered praises to God. And immediately by the advice of the bishop of Llandaff, and clergy, an oratory was there built, and consecrated with the sprinkling of water in honour of the martyr Clydawg; and from that time the place began to be held in veneration on account of the blessed martyr."[1]

The surrounding land was dedicated to the church," as it was better given to Clydawg the Martyr and the three hermits, Lybian, Gwrwan, and Cynwn, the first inhabitants and cultivators of the place after the martyrdom, as an island placed in the sea, free from every service and with refuge according to the will of the refugee, without limit as long as he should choose to remain."

Clodock was the scene of a miracle said to be worked by the saint after the church had been erected in honour of his so-called martyrdom :—

Ithael, son of Eddilwyrth, a certain rich man in Ewyas, proceeding one Sunday to the church of Clydawg, became suddenly paralysed in a meadow on the banks of the Mynwy (Monnow). He directed his companions to go to the sepulchre of the martyr Clydawg, " and on my behalf place on the holy altar of Clydawg that meadow, which I unjustly took away from it by force; and placing your hands joined together in suretiship, as with a given endowment, the four gospels having been placed thereon before, grant it free and quit of all laical service, from henceforward, except only daily prayer and mass for my health." This done, he was restored before all the people and returned thanks to God.[2]

The parish feast, or wake, of Clodock was held on the first Sunday after Nov. 15th, according to some of the folk now living who just remember it. On the feast day special cakes like a large currant bun were made at all the farms in Clodock, Longtown and Llanveyno, and given to all who called for them. I can hear of no name for the cakes nor is it remembered that any special words were said or sung by the recipients. "We didn't say nothin'," they say, " all the farmers wives knew what we come for." The cakes seem to have been made and given as part of the day's observance; probably they were originally in remembrance of St. Clydawg. I could discover nothing to connect them with Soul-mass cakes. (See All Saints Day, ix., 15.).

1] *Liber Landavensis,* 445. *See also* Evans-Rhŷs, 193–5, Baring-Gould, ii., 153, where references to MS. lives of St. Clydog are given. 2] *Lib. Land., loc. cit.*

St. Dubricius (Dyfrig).

St. Dubricius was born in the fifth century, probably at Madley ; he was the son of Pabiali, and grandson of Brychan, king of Brecon. His mother's name was Eurddil, daughter of Peibau king of Erging.[1] He founded a monastery at Henllan (Hentland) on the Wye, where he spent seven years, and then moved to Mochros (Moccas). According to Geoffrey of Monmouth, he officiated at the coronation of King Arthur. He retired in his old age to Bardsey island, and here he died and was buried. His remains were translated to Llandaff cathedral in 1120 by Bishop Urban of Llandaff.— (*See* Baring-Gould, *Lives of the Welsh Saints*, ii., 359–382, and Evans and Rhŷs, 78–86).

The legend of the birth of St. Dubricius tells us that his mother was Eurddil[2] daughter of a certain king of the region of Erging, (Archenfield) whose name was Pebiau. Returning from an expedition against his enemies he ordered Eurddil to wash his head. He then perceived that she was about to become a mother, and being excessively angry

"commanded that she should be put into a sack and cast headlong into the river that she might suffer whatever might befall, which however happened contrary to what was expected, for as often as she was placed in the river, so often was she through the guidance of God impelled to the bank. Her father then being indignant because he could not drown her in the river resolved to destroy her with fire. A funeral pile was therefore prepared into which his daughter was thrown alive. In the following morning the messengers who had been sent by her father to ascertain whether any bones of his daughter remained, found her holding her son in her lap, at a spot, where the stone is placed in testimony of the wonderful nativity of the boy, and the place is called *Madle*[3] because therein was born the holy man. The father, hearing this, ordered his daughter, with her son to be brought to him, and when they came, he embraced the infant with paternal affection, as is usual, and kissing him, from the restlessness of infancy he touched with his hands the face and mouth of his grandfather, and that not without divine appointment ; for by contact of the hands of the infant he was healed of the incurable disease where with he was afflicted, for he incessantly emitted foam from his mouth.

Who, when he knew that he had been healed by the touch of the infant, rejoiced greatly, like one who had come into a harbour after having suffered shipwreck."[4]

Here follows an account of the education and growth in wisdom and fame of St. Dubricius, who was made by his grandfather heir of Madley, and of an island called *Ynys Eurddil*,[5] after his mother ; scholars and doctors flocked to him for instruction.

And with these he retained two thousand clergy for seven successive years at Hentland[6] on the banks of the Wye in the literary study of divine and human wisdom ; setting forth to them in himself an

1] *See* Section xii., 2, *Archenfield*.
2] Her name is variously spelt Ebrdil, Efrddyl, and otherwise ; for her life *see* Baring-Gould, *op. cit.*, ii., 414.
3] Now Madley near Hereford, on the South side of the Wye. There is no stone there now, but a cross which stands in the centre of the village may have replaced it.
4] *Liber Landavensis*, 323, Book of Llan Dâv, 78-9.
5] The tract of land from Madley to the line of hills that encloses the Dore Valley juts into the river Wye. Between that range and the Wye was Ynys Efrddyl. Ynys did not necessarily mean an island ; the word was employed for a tongue of land, and even sometimes for a monastic possession shut off, in-sulated from the world.—(Baring-Gould, ii., 369). But it may be that in those days the land really was an island in the river. Swiftly flowing rivers often change their course, and the change begins by the formation of an island.
6] Now Hentland, near Ross, where there is a farm called Llanfrother, (*Llanfrodyr*), *i.e.*, The Church or Convent of the brethren. *Liber Landavensis* 325, note.

example of religious life and perfect charity. And during auother space of time he remained with his numerous disciples for many years directing their studies in his native district, namely, Ynys Eurrdil, having chosen a place convenient for wood and fish in a corner of that island on the banks of the Wye giving it the name of *Mochros*; that is, *Moch*, hogs, *rhos*, a place, *Mochros* in the British language signifying the place of Hogs.[1] And rightly was it so called, for during the preceding night an angel of the Lord appeared unto him in a dream, and said "See that thou on the morrow go all round the place which thou hast proposed and chosen, and where thou will see a white sow lying with her pigs, there lay a foundation, and build in the name of the Holy Trinity a habitation and an Oratory. The man of God having awoke from his sleep, and being mindful as usual of the angelic precept, immediately went round the place with his disciples, and as the voice of the angel had promised him, a white sow and her young pigs got up before them ;[2] and there he immediately founded and constructed an oratory, and a habitation, where for many years he regularly lived, preaching and giving instructions to the people.[3]

The old chronicler records with loving pride other miracles of St. Dubricius, performed both during his lifetime and by his relics after death, but these are not connected in any way with Herefordshire. When his remains were transferred from Bardsey Island to Llandaff Cathedral in 1120, " there was plenty of rain which was much wanted by the people, for it had not rained even a drop for seven weeks, or more than that throughout the district of Glamorgan. "[4]

The Churches in Herefordshire dedicated to Saint Dubricius are Hentland, St. Devereux, Ballingham and Whitchurch, all in the deanery of Archenfield. But the number of churches founded by the saint in this district was about four and twenty.— (*See* Baring-Gould, ii., 39).

There was a chantry at Woolhope dedicated to St. Dubricius, and according to tradition he worked many miracles there.[5]

St. Edith.

See Section i., 7, *St. Edith's Well.*

St. Ethelbert, King and Martyr.

Ethelbert succeeded his father Ethelred as King of the East Angles ; in 792, according to the *A. S. Chronicle*, he journeyed to the palace of Offa, King of Mercia, which stood on the spot now called Sutton Walls. The night before his intended marriage with Elfrida, Offa's daughter, he was treacherously murdered by the Queen

---

1] *Rhos* more properly signifies a moor. There is still a " Swinemoor " farm at Moccas, so the name has survived in both Welsh and English.
2] *Cf.* Vergil, viii., 42 and 45. Tiberius, the river-god, foretells the appearance of a white sow with 30 young pigs, to show the site of Alba Longa. The fulfilment of the prophecy is also narrated (viii., 80).
3] *Liber Landavensis* 323-4. This section is headed in the original Latin, *Readings from the Life of St. Dubricius,* intimating that it was publicly read in portions.
4] *Op. cit.* 330. 5] Cooke, 239.

Quendreda. Ethelbert's body was first privately buried at Marden and afterwards transferred to Hereford to the church which is now the cathedral. (*See Dict. Nat. Biography*, where full bibliography is given).

The following life of St. Ethelbert is translated from Capgrave's *Nova Legenda Angliæ*, (Vol. I., 412, *et seq.*).[1]

Ethelbert was the son of Ethelred and Leoverorina. Brought up religiously while his companions were given to games, he rejoiced in the services of the church. Having become King of East Angles, his nobles urged him to marry for the sake of an heir, to which counsel he yielded with docile heart. He rejected the suggestion that he should marry Seledrith (Seledridam), the daughter of a certain Egeon in the Southern parts who had the kingdom since her father was dead, but he was disposed to seek in marriage a daughter of Offa, King of the Mercians. Evil omens appeared at the beginning of his journey, for as he was mounting his horse the earth shook under him, presaging his imminent danger of death: the brightness of the day was suddenly withdrawn. Then the sun appeared to grow black, and to bring on the horrid darkness of dreadful night. Many of his followers being amazed, Ethelbert consoled them. And when they could not see one another, he said, " Let us do what is expedient, let us humble our minds and bodies before God, and prostrate on the ground let us ask the Lord to remove from our hearts and bodies the darkness and pour into us the light of his brightness." All bowed themselves to the earth, and while Ethelbert, the servant of God, prayed a long while, the splendour of the day suddenly shone out and the sun showed forth its rays. Coming to Mercia, the King when asleep had a vision, which he related afterwards to his people. It seemed to him that while surrounded by his councillors and courtiers, the roof of his palace tumbled down, and the corners of his bridal bed, being torn off, fell down ; his mother looked on, weeping as it were tears of blood. Then he saw a tree to which none other was to be compared in beauty, growing in his house, at whose roots certain men were standing cutting at it with all their strength, and from the cuts a torrent of blood flowed forth, hastening towards the east with great force. He saw a column of light arise, more splendid than the sun, and deeming himself a wonderful bird with gold tips to his wings, he flew to the top of the column, and soaring upwards heard voices singing with the sublime harmony of heaven, and then awoke. The others interpreted the dream to mean that he would attain to greater power and excellence than former kings ; Ethelbert answered that he would await with joyful and willing mind God's decision concerning him. In the morning he came to the court of King Offa. Alftrida, the maiden, seeing him coming, admired greatly his beauty and was delighted

---

1] For extracts from the original text, *see* Appendix A ; and for other versions of the legends, taken from the Hereford Breviary, *see* Appendix B. For the latter I am indebted to the kindness of Mr. Langton Brown.

at beholding his military train. And as she praised the magnificence of the King, and his beauty and nobility, and thought him more praiseworthy and glorious than her father, her mother, stirred by hatred, deliberated how to bring Ethelbert to death. Forthwith she went to Offa, and on the plea that Ethelbert would become more powerful, and Offa less, until the former would dominate the kingdom of Offa, advised him to have him put to death. Offa then called together his great men and offered a large sum of money to him who should betray Ethelbert. Winebert,[1] stirred by avarice accepted the commission, which he could do the better through having been brought up in the household of Ethelbert's father. He went to Ethelbert, and assured him of welcome from Offa, and that he would attain his desire. He then kissed him, and brought him to Offa, persuading him before entering the latter's presence to lay aside his belt and sword, because none might enter armed to this tyrant without stirring him to anger. Upon Ethelbert being introduced to Offa's presence, the courtiers and soldiers were not admitted, and the doors were closed. Ethelbert now understood that the darkness which had surrounded him foretold his death, and commending his soul to God awaited patiently his sentence. Offa, not enduring that he should live longer, ordered Winebert at once to slay him. Whereupon Winebert rushed on him and beheaded him with a sword (xiii. kal. Junii). Seeing this, the daughter of Offa, flinging herself on the ground, returned thanks to Christ, because Ethelbert, by his glorious death, was made a sharer of heavenly joys. And then she called, with a loud voice, to those awaiting the coming of their lord outside to return to their own country, and to tell the East Angles how their king by beheading had attained martyrdom. When they heard this, as they were not strong enough to avenge their king, they returned homewards. Then Alftrida, filled with the Holy Spirit, foretold to her mother the death of her son (the mother's son), three years after that day, and that the mother herself should die a horrible death ; she vowed herself to virginity, purposing to live the life of a solitary in the marshes of Crowland. Offa ordered the body and head of Ethelbert to be buried on the bank of the river Lugge ; those who carried the head separately, to make the more game of the matter, running in front of the others rolled it along the ground. But at night the great glory of the Lord appeared over the glorious grave of the blessed martyr Ethelbert, and the brightness of a great light shone there. There seemed to be such an immense flame that the whole region might be thought kindled by fire. For a column of light more splendid than the sun stretched from his grave to heaven ; sparks as of a flame, devouring everything around, followed it, and gleaming rays. These things being related to Offa, grievously frightened him, and brought him back to the way of humility so that he repented. He gave a tenth of all his goods to God's church ; he tithed fields also and countries, and whatever

---

1] " Gimbart " or " Ginnbert " in the Breviary.

he possessed. On the third night after his martyrdom [the saint] appeared to a simple man resting on his bed, with a great light, in shining raiment, and bade him rise quickly. " Rise," said he, " Brithfrid, arise and go to my grave, and bury my body again near the monastery built near the river Wye. I am king of the East Angles, Ethelbert, and God hath bidden thee that thou shouldst do this command." Awaked from sleep that man opened his eyes and beheld the whole house alighted with heavenly brightness. And when he would stretch forth his arms to take hold of the saint, the martyr withdrew and in splendid brightness disappeared. The man arose, and taking with him his neighbour named Egmund, together they lifted the body out of the earth, washed it, and clad it in white garments and laid it in a carriage. And a certain blind man running against it obtained the light of his eyes, by the merits of the saint, returning thanks. But they buried the holy body in the place which was anciently called Fernleigh, that is, " the forest of ferns ; " now indeed by the country people it is called Hereford. In the same season, through a long space of years, there shone every night on the holy tomb a light sent from heaven, which truly in a column of fire showed forth the saint's glorious martyrdom. At length King Milfred ordered a certain bishop of his to go to the holy place and adore the martyr with devotion. Having done so, he took care to announce to his prince the wonderful words of God which he heard, the healing of the sick, the curing of the feeble which he beheld with his eyes, and the death of the innocent king which he learnt. King Milfred therefore bequeathed vast sums to the place, and built to the honour and praise of the blessed martyr a church of wonderful foundations, and first of all the kings appointed a bishop to the same place and adorned it with possessions in land and royal ornaments.[1]

For St. Ethelbert's Wells, at Marden and in Hereford, see Section i., 7.

St. Thomas de Cantilupe.

St. Thomas de Cantilupe was born at Hambleden in the Lincolnshire diocese about 1218. He was Chancellor of Oxford, and was appointed by Henry III. Lord Chancellor of England, which office he resigned on the accession of Edward I. He became bishop of Hereford in 1275, and died in 1282, when returning from a journey to Rome, at Montefiascone in Italy. His remains were first interred, but afterwards brought to Hereford and deposited in the Lady Chapel ; in 1287 they were removed to the tomb in the north transept, in the presence of Edward I.

About the year 1300 seeing that the king and nation desired the canonization of St. Thomas, a commission was appointed to enquire into the alleged miracles ; St.

1] This King Milfred was a Mercian sub-regulus under Egbert. He rebuilt the cathedral about 825 A.D., but it fell into decay, and was again rebuilt under Edward the Confessor by Bishop Athelstan. A Bishop of Hereford is said to have been present at the meeting of the Welsh bishops with Augustine in 601 ; there was certainly an episcopal see long before Milfred's day.

Thomas was canonized in 1320 and was thus the last of the English saints.   His festival was kept on October 2nd.

For further details of his life, *see* Strange, *Life and Gests of St. Thomas Cantilupe, Bishop of Hereford* (printed at Ghent in 1674, reprint 1879) from which the following account of the miracles is taken, also an article in *Woolhope Club Transactions* (1902), by the Rev. Canon Bannister, entitled *The Hereford Miracles* ; Havergal, *Fasti*, 19 ; Webb, *Household Roll of Bishop Swinfield*, (Camden Society) ;   and the *Dictionary of National Biography*.

Folk-lore is of course only concerned with what is miraculous in connection with the life of St. Thomas de Cantilupe, and with the illustrations of popular custom and belief the story affords.

Father Strange relates how

" it happened that one night after his decease that one of his Officers, whom he had left behind him in England (his name was Robert of Gloucester, then his secretary, after chancellor of Hereford), being at that time at London, and lodging in the Bishop's own chamber, had this dream or vision, call it as you please. He thought himself to be at Lyons in France where in the great street of the city which leads to the Cathedral he seemed to behold his lord and master, going toward that church whither himself was also bound.   Both being entered, his lord he thought went into the sacristy, where putting off the upper garment which he wore, he vested himself with white pontifical Robes, and those most rich, and carrying in his hand the body of our Lord, or most Blessed Sacrament, in form of a consecrated Host, he appeared suddenly in the midst of a most solemn and stately procession, both of clergy and religious, and those likewise clad all in white.   The procession seemed to move toward the cloister of the cathedral, while others of the choir intoned and pro-secuted with delicate music the part of the Capitulum proper to the office of St. Peter and Vincula.   .   .   .   . .   . But before all had entered the gate which led to the said cloister, on a sudden it was shut, and Robert who with many others desired to enter was excluded, ... and left to consider the dream.[1]

After the death of the saint his bones, head, and heart were separated from the rest of his body, to be deposited as a most precious treasure in the Cathedral at Hereford.   The people of the city with the chapter and clergy went forth to meet them, among them Gilbert, Lord Clare, Earl of Gloucester, who had a dispute with the late Bishop on account of some lands; the Earl had been compelled to restore them to the church by force of law with both costs and penalties.

He now approaching to the sacred pledge, it was very remarkable and looked on as a miracle by all the company, that the dry bones in his presence began to bleed afresh, and in such a quantity that he and all might see the cask in which they were carried imbrued with the same.   The Earl, much amazed hereat, was struck with compunction, expiating by penance what he had rashly committed, as the only way to make the best of a ill bargain.[2]

When Bishop Swinfield, St. Thomas' successor, decided to transfer the remains from the Lady Chapel to the eastern aisle of the north transept new wonders were revealed :—

1] Strange, 126.   2] Strange, 133.

While the workmen considered how they should move the heavy slab above the tomb, and the stone coffin, two of the Bishop's pages who stood by put their hands to it as it were in sport, to try their strength, where four of the ablest men could have done nothing. And here behold a strange accident, at the slender impulse of these two alone, the massy stone yielded and gave place as far as was necessary for the present purpose, as if it had been a thin board, not what it was. All the company cried out a miracle, wrought by the saint to attest his sanctity, and show how grateful the translation was to him ; but here was not an end to their amazement, yea, it was much increased, when after the Mass of requiem and solemnity ended, trial was made in the same manner to put the same stone into its former posture, which now, though they had the advantage of the ground much more than before, not these two, but neither ten more joined with them, endeavouring with all their might and main, were scarce able to set it in its place.

From this time we are told that miracles were almost daily wrought at the tomb. The biographer next describes a remarkable cure which was wrought while the sacred relics remained yet in the Lady Chapel ;

One Edith, wife to a citizen of Hereford, in the beginning of that same Lent was seized with a furious frenzy, and all human means falling short, so she continued till the day before Palm Sunday. The recourse to St. Thomas not being as yet famed by any miracles, her husband caused her to be measured to a relic of the Holy Cross much venerated in that cathedral, at whose altar she was kept night and day, bound and attended to by two of her sex, though at the same time she was advised by a priest of the Church to have recourse to St. Thomas, and to be measured to him, giving her great hopes of of a recovery by his intercession. All this was done at his suggestion, and a candle was made of the thread that measured her, and set at her head as she lay bound hand and foot, her ordinary station being all this while at the altar of the Holy Cross. The Friday before Palm Sunday, as she was there hearing Mass, not only the candles on the altar, but all through the church, were on a sudden put out, nobody knew how, and great noise like the murmur of a great river was heard at the same time. This lasting for the space of ten *Paters* and *Aves*, visibly before them all fire came from heaven and lighted the candles standing at her head, whose wick was made from the thread that measured her to the Saint. At the lighting of this, she recovered her senses, and became well, at the same time the cords that bound her to themselves became loose, and she in their presence and hearing of them all repeating it over and over again, said aloud " Where is St. Thomas, that bids me be well ?" . . This was the first miracle the saint wrought in the church of Hereford.[1]

The meaning of this practice of " measuring to the saint " is thus explained by Father Strange :—

Truly I do not remember to have read it elsewhere, nor is it any ecclesiastical ceremony of any church, much less of the Catholic ; it seems to have been taken up by the devotion of the people thereabouts, as an innocent, harmless expression of their devotion and recourse to the saint, approved by custom ; and though frequently used, yet not so of necessity. This their recourse and application to the saint was twofold, and the miraculous effects as to both show its acceptableness to him, either by bending a piece of silver coin over the patient's head who sought redress to the honour of the saint, appropriating the party by this expression to him and his peculiar patronage for redress, or else by measuring the said client by a thread or some such thing, that is by taking his length and breadth with the same intention as in the former, and depositing them at his altar or to his honour.[2]

1] *Op. cit.*, 144.
2] *Ibid.*, 144. *See* Hartland, Perseus, ii., 225. " The practice of measurement as a method of conveying the divine effluence was a favourite one during the Middle Ages, and is still practised in Roman Catholic Countries." The practice alluded to by Mr. Hartland is however the reverse of the Hereford custom : the saint's body was measured and the string bound round the patient; thus we have two ways of performing the same piece of sympathetic magic.

The measuring to the saint was certainly not indispensable, for no mention is made of it in the cure of one Juliana, who was unable to walk. Having been a cripple for nine years, she was carried to the shrine of St. Thomas in a basket. She had no sooner touched it and said a few prayers than she found herself well, and the next day walked home without any help. The basket had been left at the shrine, but the poor neighbour from whom it had been borrowed demanded it again. So Juliana sent for it and it was no sooner taken away than she relapsed into her former state. " It seems," says Father Strange " the Saint required it for a monument of his charitable redress." Juliana was again carried to the shrine in the basket, where she remained a day and night in tears and prayers ; she then again became restored to health and presumed no more to take it away.[1]

A drowned child is said to have been restored to life, when the father, who had heard much of the miracles of St. Thomas, measured her to him with his girdle according to custom. The successor of St. Thomas, Bishop Richard Swinfield, being very ill, the chamberlain one night in his sleep seemed to hear one say to him, " Arise, take the relic thou hast of St. Thomas, wash it in the wine, which in a silver cruet stands in the window ; give thy master to drink of it and he shall be cured." The relic was the first joint of the Saint's right thumb, of which only the chamberlain knew. He fearing to lose this precious relic, if his possession of it were known, disregarded the voice, even when he heard the call a second time, but on the third night there came to him " the Blessed Lady, accompanied with many virgins, all which were clad in white, and enveloped with great brightness." He was again commanded to wash the relic with wine, to be given to the Bishop. This was done in the presence of his confessor and physician ; the Bishop drank it, and having made the sign of the cross, was immediately able to go down to the Chapel and say Mass for the first time for many weeks.[2]

A blind barber who had once been a servant of St. Thomas was measured, according to custom, to him, and sent the measure with two eyes of wax, to Hambleden, in Lincolnshire, the Saint's birthplace. Finding some glimmering of light, he was measured again, this time sending the measure to the Cantilupe Shrine at Hereford. The man's sight was said to have been restored a week afterwards. The efficacy of the miracles extended not to men and women alone, but to animals. King Edward I. sought on two occasions to obtain its benefit for sick falcons belonging to him ; on the first visit the messenger Gilatus took the bird to Hereford, and appears to have been absent from court some days, making oblations at the tomb ; on the second occasion the King first of all sent Thomelin, the son of Simon Corbet, who first made oblations to the value of 6d. ; then he caused a waxen figure of the bird to be presented, and

1] *Op. cit.*, 154.						2] *Op. cit.*, 162.

lastly despatched Thomelin with the bird itself ; with what result does not appear. Thomelin was absent eight days from court, and his oblations cost 1s. 6d.[1]

On August 30th, 1307, the Bishops appointed by the Pope to enquire into the life and miracles of St. Thomas arrived in Hereford. They stayed until November 16th. There, in the North transept, day and night, stood or lay or knelt the sick and infirm, the blind, the deaf, and the halt. The commissioners investigated and approved 17 miracles, and heard details of 204 more into which they had not time to make full enquiry. They also made a list of offerings at the shrine as follows :—

170 Ships in Silver.
 41 Ships in wax.
120 Images of men, or their limbs in silver.
1424 Images of men or their limbs in wax.
 77 Figures of animals and birds of divers species.
108 Crutches.
  3 Vehicles in wood.
  1 Vehicle in wax.
 97 Night-gowns.
116 Gold and silver rings and brooches.
 38 Garments of gold thread and silk.

There were, in addition, many lances and arrows, with which men had been wounded and miraculously cured, and some chains and anchors of ships.[2]

In 1610, the year of the plague in Hereford, the relics of St. Thomas were carried through the city, in a secret night procession, " giving a total succour to the same."[3]

See also Section i., 5.—*The White Cross.*

(2) PERSONS AND FAMILIES.

The Pauncefotes (Much Cowarne).

A pretty story of wifely devotion is told of Constantia, daughter of Sir John de Lingen, who married in 1253 Grimbald Pauncefote, of Cowarne. Her husband having been captured by the Moors, could only obtain his freedom by the production, as a ransom, of a joint of his wife, the fame of whose beauty was doubtless as widespread as that of her lord's valour. The lady made no demur to these exorbitant terms, but cutting off her arm above the wrist conveyed it to her husband and thus effected his release.

1] Phillott, *Hist. of the Diocese of Hereford*, 92. I am indebted to Mr. Harold Easton for this reference.
2] Paper by the Rev. Canon Bannister, *Woolhope Club* (1902) 378.   3] Strange, 240.

In Silas Taylor's[1] day there was in the parish church of Much Cowarne, in the east end of the south aisle, an altar tomb, with the effigies of Grimbald and Constantia. Grimbald was crossed legged, and habited after Norman fashion, while the lady, whose name Constantia was legible, exhibited her left arm couped above the wrist, in memory of her heroic conduct. Silas Taylor notes precisely that the woman's arm is somewhat elevated as if to attract notice, and the hand and wrist cut off are carved close to the man's left side, with his right hand on his armour.[2]

The Vaughans.

Parry explains the strange coat of arms of the Vaughans thus :—

The ancestor of the house of Vaughan with whom their pedigree commences . . . . was known by the name of " Moreiddig Warwyn " the first appellation, " the mighty jealous one " being undoubtedly descriptive of his mind, and the next, the " Whitenape," or " White shoulder," of some singularity or mark upon his body.

Tradition tells us that he was born with a snake round his neck, from whence the place of his nativity was called the place of horror, and from this supposed event his posterity took their arms :—*Sable, three boys' heads couped at the shoulder, each having a snake wreathed round his neck, proper.* . . (*see illustration*).

He lived in the twelfth century, but of his exploits at the time of his death history has not afforded us the smallest information.[3]

The Wigmores.

The Wigmores of Lucton, a Cavalier family who had been in possession of their property since Saxon times, and one of whom who married a daughter of Sir Jasper Croft soon after the Conquest, lost all they possessed in the struggle between King and Parliament. A curious legend is connected with this family. A great oaken post was set up at the outer gate of Lucton House, and tradition said it would stand there as long as the Wigmores were owners of Lucton. The post fell in August, 1670, and within a few days after, William Hooper took possession of the estate under a mortgage.[4]

(3) Places.

The Bacho.

I am informed by the Rev. J. C. Murray-Aynsley of a tradition among the people at Madley that a Scotch queen was once successfully hidden from her enemies on the

---

1] Silas Taylor, *alias* Domville, was a captain in the Parliamentary army under Col. Massey. He left manuscript collections for a history of Herefordshire in the library of Sir Edward Harley at Brampton Bryan ; portions are preserved in Harl. MSS.—*Dict. Nat. Biography*, under Domville.
2] *Woolhope Club*, 1902, 263.
3] Parry, *Hist. Kington*, 218. For other Vaughan legends *see ante*, Section iv., 2.
4] Price, *History of Leominster*, 143.

top of a small hill called the Bacho, (Welsh, " The little one "). According to Jones' *History of Brecknockshire*, (34), Tydyr ap Neubedd, King of Brecon, died early in the sixth century, and was succeeded by one Dyfnal, a Pictish or Caledonian prince, and an usurper. Dyfnal was subsequently defeated and driven out, in which direction history does not say. Still the fact that a Scottish prince once reigned so near the Welsh Border goes to show that the tradition may be historic fact : it may have been Dyfnal's queen herself who found a refuge in a long forgotten fortress on the Bacho.

Bosbury.

Bosbury was once a very large town, much larger than Hereford, in the days before the wars with the Saxons, but when they came they destroyed it ; their leader said " If I can take big Bosbury, I can take little Hereford." Hereford held out and became in consequence a place of importance while Bosbury was never built up again.[1]

Edvin Loach and Edvin Ralph.

Oral tradition derives the curious names of these parishes from those of two young noblemen who arranged to fight a duel with swords because they both wished to win the same lady. She heard of the fight and rushed between them ; the swords of both pierced her body, and she died. Distracted with grief her lovers fought each other so fiercely that both were killed. All three were buried together in Edvin Ralph Church.[2]

Hereford.

Hereford, say the old folks, is the maiden town of England, because it has never been taken ! It was very nearly taken once, but a little drummer boy hearing vibrations from his drum and speculating as to the cause, guessed that the enemy were undermining the Castle. So he took a pea, and placed it on the drum. It danced about every now and then, and he was certain when he saw that. The alarm was raised, and the garrison let the Wye flow in on the besiegers in the mine so that they all were drowned.

There can be no historical truth in this story, since Hereford was taken as far back as 1055 by Griffyd, prince of Wales. If this, and the historical (?) tradition above concerning Bosbury have any foundation, they must go back to 760 A.D. when there was a Welsh Invasion. " This was the year of Christ when a battle between the Britons and Saxons took place, to wit, the action of Hereford."[3]

1] From inmates of Bromyard workhouse, 1909. *Cf*. Markham, *Proverbs of Northamptonshire* (from Morton) :—
 The people there have a notable Rhime, which they make the Danes to say upon the Point of battle
   " If we can Padwell overgoe, and Horestone we can see :
    Then Lordes of England we shall be."
2] Told at Bromyard, 1909. 3] Townsend, *Leominster*, 5, (from a Welsh Chronicle).

Leominster.

Merewald, son of Penda, King of Mercia, founded the church and convent at Leominster in 658 A.D.; the following legend concerning him attempts to explain the origin of the name of the place.

Ealfrid, a priest of Northumbria, coming to the court of Merewald footsore, faint, and weary, sat himself down, and taking bread out of his wallet began to eat it. A lion appeared, which, on being offered bread, mildly took it from his hand. The lion, according to the narrative, was typical of Merewald, who on the teaching of Ealfrid, from a fierce pagan became a mild and forbearing Christian.[1]

It is possible that the builders of the Norman portion of the priory church erected in the twelfth century knew and apparently desired to spread a belief in this origin of the name of the town. On the portals of the great west door, amongst other devices, there is the figure of a lion. The legend would seem to have been an allegorical one, possibly circulated by the monks to explain the already existent name and representing the lion of heathendom overcome by Christianity; or the story may have been invented later, to explain the figure of the lion, not uncommon in Lombardic architecture. The real derivation is thought to be Leofric's Minster from Earl Leofric, who died in 1033.[2]

(4) SUBTERRANEAN PASSAGES.

We have several legends of subterranean passages, though any stories of treasure or marvels to be found therein are lost. There is said to be a passage from Longtown Castle, under the Black Mountain, to Llanthony Abbey; there is a legend of treasure buried in the castle, but this story is not connected with the tradition of the passage. (See Section i., 3). There was said to be a passage from Leominster Priory to Ivington Camp, the site of a Roman encampment three miles away.[3] Another such story is connected with Thornbury camp; where one may hear of an underground passage from the top of the camp to " Lady Well," near the Church. The upper end terminated where two yew trees now stand on the western side of the camp.[4] In the Doward Hills is a remarkable cavern called King Arthur's Hall. An underground passage was said to extend from thence to New Weir; there are traces of an ancient encampment here also. The skeleton of a giant was found in another cave there about 1695.[5] It is noteworthy that such remains were also found at Orleton, where there is a cave and a legend of a passage leading from it. (See Section i., 1).

1] Townsend, *op. cit.* 2, from Leland *Collectanea* i., 169. *Apparuerat Leo Ealfrido apud Mercios coenanti cui cum panem manu porrexisset mitis accepit. Leo autem ad Merevalem alludit, qui Paganus-ferox, adveniente Ealfrido, mitis per fidem factus est, unde locus ipse postea vertitur in Leonis Monasterium.*
2] Mr. H. Easton, in *Memorials,* 250.
3] Leominster Guide, (1803), 264.   4] *Woolhope Club,* (1886-9), 121, See Section i., 7.—*Wells.*
5] Heath, *The Wye, under* Whitchurch.

Johnson gives the following account of a real passage :—

At the beginning of the present century there was in a Meadow near Eign, eastward of the city, a wide entrance leading to a subterranean passage, called Scot's Hole ; and within the memory of persons yet living, it has been explored for some distance in the direction of Hereford.   Near this place bullets have also been dug up.   Some antiquaries have supposed the passage to be a mine made by the Scots during the siege, others that it was an underground communication from St. Guthlac's Priory to the Vineyard, where it is said a religious establishment was formerly situated.[1]

1] Johnson, 198, *Cf.* Burne, 8, and Henderson, 320.

SECTION XVI.

(1) RIDDLES.

[Those already printed by Halliwell, *Nursery Rhymes*, and Burne, *Shropshire Folklore*, are excluded.   Where no place is mentioned, the riddles are generally known.]

Once I was born in flesh and blood,
As other creatures be ;
But now am neither flesh nor blood,
But it all belongs to me.
They plucked me from my native soil
Where I was born and bred ;
But, for the use of man, indeed
They then cut off my head.
I took a draught, a hearty draught,
Of with all the skill I had,
Which made enmity between kings and kings
And made true lovers glad.
I, oft a sword, my brother's foe,
My friendship does not fail ;
I often cause the rich to weep,
The poor lament and wail.[1]

A goose quill pen (King's Pyon).

As round as a hoop,
As black as a coal,
A long tail, and
A little round hole.

Frying pan.

Long waist, brazen face, no great thing of beauty,
It stands most bright by day and night,
Performing of its duty.

Grandfather Clock.

1] *Cf.* Halliwell, 241, where a Swedish version is given.

There was a man of Adam's race
That had a certain dwelling place.
'Twas all round and covered o'er,
No man lived there since nor before,
Neither in heaven, nor in hell,
Nor on the earth, this man did dwell.

> Jonah inside the whale.

She walked on earth, she talked on earth,
She rebuked a man for sin ;
She's not on earth, she's not in heaven,
Nor likely to get in.

> Balaam's Ass.

A head like a snake, neck like a drake ;
Side like a bream, back like a beam ;
Tail like a rat, foot like a cat.

> Greyhound.

As I went down in my Pintaly Pantaly Prededy Presence,
There I saw Unicle Carnacle Carrady Currents ;
I called to my man John,
For to mortify Unicle Cornicle Carrady Currents,
That had been in my Pintaly Pantaly Prededy Presence.

> Hare eating parsley in Garden.

Four little landers,
Four stick standers,
Two rappers,
Two lookers,
Two Crookers,
And a Bowmbell
(or " And a Wagabout").

> A Cow.

There was a thing was three days old
When Adam was no more ;
The same thing was but three weeks old
When Adam was four score.

> The Moon.

Found long ago, yet made to-day,
　　And most enjoyed when others sleep,
What few would wish to give away,
　　And fewer still would wish to *keep*.

　　　　　　　　　　　Beds.

As I sat upon Spriggum Spraggum,
I looked down in the land of Wiggin Waggum ;
And there I saw a great Bum Baggum ;
Then I called to my little Tom Taggum,
To fetch this great Bum Baggum,
Out of the land of Wiggin Waggum.

This is a man sitting on a stile, (Spriggum Spraggum), looking at his field of
beans, (Wiggin Waggum) ; he sees an old sow, (Bum Baggum), and sends his little
dog to fetch her out (Tom Taggum).

How was it ?　A man rode upon the hill, Yettie walked.

　　　　　　　　　Yettie was the dog.

Ink, ank, in the bank ;
Ten a drawing four.

　　　　　　　　　Man's fingers milking.

Through the hedge, and through the hedge, and takes a long tail after it.

　　　　　　　　　A needle.

I have a cock on yonder hill
I keep him for a wonder,
And every time the cock do crow
It lightens, hails, and thunders.

　　　　　　　　　A Gun.

A cow calved it : it grew in the wood : and a smith made it.

　　　　　　　　　A pair of bellows.

Yonder stands a tree of honour,
Twelve limbs grow upon her ;
Every limb a different name,
It would take a wise man to tell you the same.

　　　　　　　　　Twelve months of the year.

As I was going to church one day, I saw an ill-formed beast ; ten heads, ten tails, forty feet, eight score nails.

A sow and pigs.

White fowl featherless came and lit upon the barn-door legless ; out came old Rolus Bolus and shot him bloodless, cooked him fireless, ate him mouthless.

A snowflake melting on barn-door.

Hoddy Toddy, all legs and no body.
Round as a hoop, and deep as a cup,
All the King's horses canna pull it up.

Draw well.

I had a little meadow,
And in this little meadow I had a grove of trees ;
Some I could cut, but none I could cleave.

Hair on the head.

I had a little meadow, and in this little meadow I had a little house. In this house I had a little bench, and how many sat on it ?

A man named " More," so to any
number guessed the answer is
— *More !*

As I was going along the road I met a little man with a blue coat, and yellow breeches on. He said, " Um, ha ! I care for no man !" Who was he ?

A wasp.

How was this ? I was going along the road and met a man, and asked him what did ailed him ? He said his father and mother *dyed* nineteen years before he was born, and he had a piece of plum cake at their burying ![1]

As I was going up Himple Dimple,
I looked down on dimples do ;
I saw Jack with a pack on his back,
And so merrily he did go.

Fox with a goose.

---

[1] *Cf.* Burial Customs, Section x., 3.

Riddle me, riddle me, rot-e-tot,
I saw a man with a red long coat,
A stick in his tail, and a stone in his throat,
Riddle me, riddle me, rote-e-tote.

Cherry.

As I was going over London Bridge,
I saw two men a hanging,
I ate their flesh, and drunk their blood,
And left their bones a hanging.

Two bottles of wine.

Round the rick, and round the rick,
There I met my Uncle Dick,
I cut off his head, and drunk his blood,
And left his body standing.

Bottle of cider.

On yonder hill there is a deer,
Reaches from here to Lancashire,
East, West, North, South,
Five thousand teeth, but ne'er a mouth.

Gorsty (Gorse) bush.

Little-hittle,
Wrapped up in a whittle
Nineteen times as high as St. Paul's Steeple.

A star.

Yellow and green,
Sharp and keen
Grows in the mene.
The king can't ride it no more than the Queen ;
The Duke of Northumberland brought it to shore,
And that's the best riddle that ever came o'er.

Gorse-bush.

Hibbledy hobbledy greasy,
When he's out, he's all about,
When he's in he's easy.

Fish out o' water.

1] *Mene*, a moor or common.

As I went over London Bridge,
I saw a little house : I looked in
Through the window, and there was
A red man making a black man sing.

> A fire making the kettle boil.

When I was young, and in my mother's lap,
She never gave me milk or pap :
She never sang me lullaby,
But left me there to live or die.
Then I sprang up, became all green,
I lookèd like some fairy queen.
Then I turned from green to yellow,
And I became a noble fellow.
A rub-a-rout came and cut me down,
And in a band my body bound.
Then they carried me to the barn,
There I thought I could take no harm.
Here comes a man with a stick cut in two,
Then he places me on the floor :
He broke my back, knocked out my brains,
And thus rewarded me for my pains ![1]

> Wheat.

The Herefordshire folk of the last generation never talked of riddles, but of " ridlasses." I have often been carefully corrected thus : " Oh, you means a rid*lass* ! " These were much in request at harvest suppers, and to pass the time in the long winter evenings. See Section ix., 13, *Harvest*.

Many of the riddles were told me by William Colcombe (*see illustration*, and *Preface*).

(2) HEALTHS AND TOASTS.

For harvest suppers and other festivals :—

Here's to the champion, to the white horn,
Here's God send the master a good crop of corn ;
Of wheat, rye, and barley, and all sorts of grain,
If we live to this time twelvemonth we'll drink his health again.

1] From a labourer at Norton Canon.

Or :—

Good health to the master, and all on his farm ;
May he live long and prosper, and grow good crops of corn ;
Wheat, oats, beans and barley, yea, and all kinds of grain,
So that he may have plenty, to treat us again.

Thee cut thy oats, and I'll drink my cider ;
And God send us all a Happy New Year.[1]

Here's a health to the heifer (or Darling), and to the white teat,
Wishing the mistress a house full of meat,
With cruds (*sic*), milk, and butter, fresh every day,
And God grant the young men out on her way ![2]

Here's to the plough, the fleece and the pail !
May the Landlord ever flourish,
And the tenant never fail.[3]

———

A health and a cheer for the bonny corn stacks,
As they're up to the sky pointing high,
For the pitching, and the raking,
And the merry hay-making ;
We've had beautiful Midsummer days.

Here behold and see my glasses full,
I'll take 'em off at such a pull ;
I'll take 'em off as you shall find,
I scarce shall leave one drop behind.
Here's a health to you my brother, Tom,
It's time that you and I were gone,
We'll drink and stand our ground . . .
And that is called the Ploughboy's round.

Here's health to me and my little barrel,
Which him and me do never quarrel,
If he don't mind his little eye,
I shall be sure to suck him dry ;
He's my friend and I'm his foe,
And down my throat this drop shall go.

1] Havergal, *Words and Phrases*, 48.   2] Havergal, *loc. cit.*   3] Havergal, *loc. cit.*

Here's health to the wheel that the world turns on,
Which death is the thing we are all sure on ;
If life was a thing that money could buy
The rich would live and the poor would die ;
Since God in His Heart has ordained it so,
There's a grave where rich and poor shall all go.

I drink my health to the leg of the bench,
That every man kisses his own wench.

Oceans of cider, rivers of wine,
Plantations of trees,[1] and a girl to your mind.

Here's to all Fortune's daughters, save the eldest.   (Misfortune).

Here's a health to my thumb and your thumb,
And all the luck that is to come ;
It comes in itches and stitches
To the young man as wears the corduroy breeches.

Here's a health to you two and we two,
And if you two loves we two as we two loves you two
Here's a health to we all four ;
And if you two don't love we two
As we two love you two,
Here's a health to we two
And to no more.

I wish you health,
I wish you wealth,
I wish you gold in store ;
I wish you heaven after death,
What could I wish you more ?

Communicated by an old inhabitant of Weobley Marsh. " This was always old Bill Hundred's toast of a New Year's morning, when we burnt the bush at Dunwood."[2]

Here's wishing you all hanged and transported ;
Hanged in the arms of love,
Transported in the bosom of Friendship.

1] Orchards.   2] See *ante*, ix., 1.

Inside of a loaf,
Outside of a gaol,
A pound of beefsteak,
And a quart of good ale.

Here's a health in water,
I wish it was wine,
You drink to your true love,
And I'll drink to mine.

He. Here's to an apple over an orange,
I drink to you in the way of marriage.

She. Sir, your ale is of the best,
I drink at your request,
But I'll marry the man I love the best,
And all the same I thank you !¹

Another version :—

He.   Here's health to you in the reign of Orange,
Here's health to you in the way of marriage ;

She. If I say Ay, you'll think me too bold,
If I say No, you'll think me too cold,
So I'll say nothing if that will do ;
I mean to get married, but not to you !

Here's to the rose that's in full bloom,
And I hope it'll never be blighted ;
Here's to the young man that's constant and true,
And I hope that he'll never be slighted.

May we all thrive together,
Like Bees in a hive,
And may we never sting each other.

May we kiss all we please,
And please all we kiss !

Health and happiness, peace and goodwill,
I always loved kissing, and so I do still.

1] There seems to be some allusion to the House of Orange in this toast, which has probably come down
from the time of William and Mary.

Here's health to the man with a ragged shirt,
And no wife to mend it ;
Here's to the one with plenty of money,
And a good wife to spend it.

Here's to poor old Thomas Tough,
Likes a drop o' good old stuff.
Likewise to Moses and Aaron,
I can drink more than you're aware on.

Or :—

Likewise to Moses and Aaron and his brother ;
When I've finished this toast,
I'm ready for another.

Here's a health to the garden that brings forth all flowers,
Bad luck and destruction to all false lovers.
May they never prosper, nor grow fat,
While they carry two faces under one hat.

Or :—

All smock frocks,
All leather apurns ;
Here's wishing the lad 'll never get fat
As carries two faces under one hat.

Long may you live,
Happy may you be,
Blest with content,
And from all misfortunes free.

Here's a health to a leg of mutton in the Workhouse,
And nobody there to eat it.

Here's a health to the bird that sits on the plough,
And if he ain't gone, he's there now.

Here's a pot o' bonny brown ale,
See how it do invite me,
I were never bit all the days o' my life,
Till the brewer's dog did bite me.

Here's wishing you all hanged, drawn, and quartered ;
Hanged in riches,
Drawn in a carriage and pair,
Quartered in heaven.

Health to your wealth,
  Money to your purse,
Heaven to your soul,
  And I wish you no worse.

Here's a health to Jack and likewise Bet ;
If Bet was afe (half) as good as Jack
I wouldn't rob her o' one drop.
This'll do ma good, more w'd do ma harm,
This'll strengthen ma to do ma work
And keep ma innards warm.

The next would seem to be appropriate for a sailor's wife ; it is obviously a woman's toast :—

Here's to the ship that's near the shore !
I love one, I canna love no more.
The world is wide and far to range,
I love my own too well to change.
As he's not here to take my part,
I'll drink his health with all my heart.

Another version :—

Here's health to you and all the rest,
Here's health to one that I love best ;
He is not here to take my part,
But I'll drink his health with all my heart.

Here's a health to him that's far away,
Wishin' he was nigh,
If drinking healths would bring him near,
I'd drink the river dry.

Here' a health to those that we love
Here's a health to those that love us,
Here's a health unto those that love them that love those
    that love those that love them that love us.

For a christening :—

> I will drink a health to the new Christian Soul,
> I'll drink his health in a full flowing bowl,
> God send that his pocket may never want chink.
> When he is dry may he never want wine (drink ?)
> Let every man put his hat on the ground,
> And keep on his knees as the health goes round.
> When I have drunk it, you may rise up and sing,
>   " God bless the New Christian,
>   And God save the King !"

Big bees fly high, little bees gather the honey ;
While the poor men do the work, the rich man pockets the money.
Here's to the tree of liberty, that grows on the globe of the world,
It's a fitting thing for every poor man to have a branch.

A toast for a guest :—

> Here's to you, and yourn !
> When you and yourn come to see us and ourn,
> Us and ourn will do for you and yourn
> What you and yourn have done for us and ourn.

(3) BELL JINGLES.

Be good to the poor,
Say the bells of Abbeydore.

Be as good as you can,
Say the bells of Bacton.

A dish and a spoon,
Say the bells of Bish. Frome.

Roast beef and old perry,
Say the bells of Bosbury.

But the largest bell says :—
Ring me well and hold me tight,
For I weigh one ton one hundredweight.

Long-tailed sow,
Whither goest thou ?
Say the bells of Bridstow.

My dog's bone !
Your dog drive
My dog home.
Say the bells of Brampton.

Sixpence and a shillin'
Say the bells o' Dillin (Dilwyn).

Hang old Morgan,
Say the bells o' Dorstone.

Bim Boum, Bim Boum,
Say the bells o' Canon Pyoum (Pyon).
(My informant added :—" The old folks allus said Canon Pyoum ").

An old man with a blue beard,
Say the bells of Bromyard.

Or :—

Come old man and shave your beard,
Say the bells of Bromyard.—H.

Hot pudding and pie,
Say the bells of Eye.

Candles and soap,
Say the bells of Hope.

Buttermilk and whey,
Say the bells of Garway.

Down in the lurch,
Say the bells of Kentchurch.

Steel and iron,
Say the bells of King's Pyon.

How dare you do so ?
Say the bells of Ludlow.

Because I've a mind,
Say the bells of Leintwardine.[1]

Up the cop and down the furrow,
Say the bells of Leominster borough.

Trip a trap a Trencher,
Say the bells of Leominster.

An old woman in a red cloak,
Say the bells of Longhope.

The bull's in the barn,
Say the bells of Llanwarne.

White bread and brown,
Say the bells of Longtown.

Up the kitchen and down the hall,
Say the bells of Lyonshall.

Here be I, and where be you?
Say the bells of Marstow.

At Staunton-on-Wye, folk declare that the bells at Norton Canon say :—

" Norton's men be hungry,
Stole a pig last Thursday !

Up the reen and down the ridge,
Say the bells at Pembridge.

Up the ridge and down the reen,
Say the bells of Presteign.

Witty-tree[2] and birch,
Say the bells of Peterchurch.

Two sticks across,
Say the bells of Ross.

Crack nuts and bannuts (walnuts),
Say the bells of St. Weonard's.

1] Burne 606. Leintwardine is in Herefordshire.   2] Mountain Ash.

Turnips and carrots,
Say the bells of St. Margot's (St. Margaret's).

Pancakes and fritters,
Say the bells of St. Peter's (Hereford).

Hang Tom Potter, and kill old Gunn,
Smith o' the wood is dead and gone.

So the bells say at Stoke Lacy ; but nobody now remembers either " Potter "
or " Gunn."

Pigs in the mire,
Say the bells of Tretire.

At Welsh Newton, the bells say :—
Erfyn, cawl erfyn.

" The church is little, having two small bells, which, when a-ringing, the neighbours report them to say :—*Erfyn, cawl erfyn* (*i.e.*, turnip and turnip-pottage). The
soil being barren, the poor people plant much of that root."—Robinson, *Mansions
and Manors*, 289.

Coffee and tea,
Say the bells of Weobley.

Roast beef and mince pie,
Say the bells of Wormesley.

Stick a goose and dress un[1]
Say the bells of Weston (under Penyard).

There is a pudding in the pot,
All stuck with plums,
All stuck with plums,
As big as my two thumbs,
Say the bells of Winforton.

Red fire and charcoal,
Say the bells of Yarpole.

1] *Cf*., p. 78, *ante*.

SECTION XVII.

PROVERBS AND SAYINGS.

(1) PROVERBS.

Weather Proverbs.

> The weather's always ill
> When the wind's not still.[1]

> A storm of hail
> Brings frost in its trail.

> If there be a cruddledy[2] sky
> It's neither long for wet nor dry.
> (*i.e.*, unsettled weather).[3]

Where the storms come from at the time of the spring equinox, that determines whether the summer will be a wet or fine one. If from the north-west, fine ; if from the south-west, wet.[4]

> A rainbow at eve,
> Sends the ploughboy home with a dripping sleeve.

> When the wind is in Weobley Hole there's sure to be rain.

If the wind blows at the end of a rainbow, it will be wet ; if right under, it is sure to be dry.

> If the oak is in leaf before the ash,
> 'Twill be dry and warm, and good wheat to thrash ;
> If the ash be in leaf before the oak
> 'Twill be cold, and of rain too great a soak.
> If the oak and the ash open their leaves together,
> Expect a summer of changeable weather.

> If the oak is out before the ash
> 'Twill be a summer of wet and splash ;
> But if the ash is out before the oak
> 'Twill be a summer of fire and smoke.[5]

1] Lees, *Pictures of Nature*, 303. 2] *i.e.*, Mackerel. 3] King's Pyon. 4] Dilwyn. 5] *Woolhope Club*, 1886, 341.
Cf. Northall, 474–5.

There is never a debt is paid so nigh
As that which the wet owes to the dry.

A windy winter, a good crop of apples.[1]

To dream of the dead is a sign of rain.[2]

If the fire blows (*i.e.*, makes a flaring noise from the escape of gas), wind will soon follow.[3]

There's always a high wind at the time of the Assizes : because the lawyers have got together, and there's hard swearing going on ![4]

When it snows they say the Welshmen are plucking their geese.[5]

If the pudding comes broken to table on Sunday, it will be wet all the week.[6]

Fine Friday, fine Sunday.[7]

Friday is a trick,[8]
The fairest or the foulest of the week.

The sun always shines on a Saturday.[9]

[This has been explained to me in this way :—" The old men says that meanin the gold and silver of their wages shinin' o' Saturday nights."]

If the moon on a Saturday be new or full,
There always *was* rain and there always *wull.*[10]

Seasons.

February.

A February spring is worth nothing.—H.

Candlemas.

If the birds sing before Candlemas, they will cry before May.

Where the wind blows on Candlemas Eve, it will continue till May Eve.

1] Dilwyn (see *Husbandry, infra*).   2] Dorstone, Mrs. Powell, *cf.* Section iv., 4, *Dreams.   See* also Section iii., *Animals, Birds.*   3] Cornewall Lewis, 122.   4] Weobley.   5] Weobley and Dilwyn.   6] Dilwyn. 7] Dorstone.   8] Mr. Hartland has heard " Friday will have its freak " in Worcestershire ; this form is probably the correct one.   9] This is also a belief of the Jewish population at Amsterdam.   Lean's *Collectanea* ii., ii., 610.   10] Lees, *op. cit.,* 304.

If Candlemas Day be clear and bright,
Winter will have another flight ;
But if Candlemas Day be thick with rain,
Winter is gone and will not come again.

Or :—

If Candlemas Day be fine and clear
There'll be two winters in the year.—H.

March.

March will search, April will try,
May will tell if you'll live or die.

A peck of March dust is worth a guinea.

May.

A May wet,
Was never kind yet.[1]

May, June, July.
(*See* Husbandry).

Easter.

Easter come soon, or Easter come late,
It's sure to make the old cow quake.

(*i.e.*, Cattle are often weakly in spring).—H.

If the sun shines on the altar during service on Easter Day, there will be a good harvest.[2]

Rain on Good Friday or Easter Day,
A good crop of hops, but a bad one of hay.—H.

June.

A dripping June,
Keeps all things in tune.

St. James' Day (July 25tth).

Till St. James's Day is past and gone,
There may be hops, and there may be none.[3]

November.

Ice in November to walk a duck,
The winter will be all rain and muck.

1] Lees, *op. cit.* 303.　2] Weobley.　3] *Notes and Queries*, 2nd Series, i., 226 ; *Cf.* Northall, 453.

Christmas.

> If Christmas Day be bright and clear
> There'll be two winters in the year.

A windy Christmas Day, a good crop of fruit.[1]

If the sun shines on Christmas Day, there will be accidents by fire all the year after.[2]

If the sun shines on the branches on Christmas Day, the fruit trees will bear well.[3]

Husbandry.

> Heart of oak is stiff and stout,
> Birch says, if you keep one dry in see it out.—H.

> Who sets an apple tree may live to see its end,
> Who sets a pear tree may set it for a friend.—H.

> If the blossom comes in March,
> For apples you may search ;
> If the blossom comes in April,
> You may gather a bag full ;
> If the blossom comes in May,
> You may gather apples every day.[4]

Or this :—

> If the apple tree blossoms in March,
> For barrels of cider you need not sarch ;
> If the apple tree blossoms in May
> You can eat apple dumplings every day.[5]

> March dust on an apple leaf
> Brings all kinds of fruit to grief.[6]

> An apple a day
> Keeps the doctor away.

> Take an apple going to bed,
> 'Twill make the doctors beg their bread.

1] Weobley.　　2] Cornewall Lewis, 122.　　3] Almeley.　　4] From MSS. of Mr. Walter Pilley.　　5] *Notes and Queries*, 6th S., iv., 55, and ix., 258.　　6] Bull, *Pomona*, 50.

Hops are a constant care, but uncertain profit.—H.

If it were not for the hops, the farmers would have to hop themselves.—H.

Hops make
Or break.

Sally tree will buy a horse, before an oak will buy a saddle.[1]

A plum year is a dumb year :
A cherry year is a merry year.—H.

If you want a parsnip good and sweet,
Sow it when you sow the wheat.

When elmen leaves are as large as a *farden*,
It's time to plant kidney beans in the garden.[2]

A woman at Orcop said :—

" It's an auld sayin' and a true one—You can't be lucky with feathers and wool." She had had the luckiest year she remembered with geese and goslings, while it was the worst her husband ever had with the sheep.

Cut thistles in May, they'll grow again some day,
Cut thistles in June, that will be too soon.
Cut thistles in July, they'll lie down and die.

Metaphors and Quaint Sayings.

A hurden mother is better than a golden father.—H.

Hurden is the coarse brown cloth of which the roughest aprons are made : hence, a rough hard-working mother.

To pay the Almighty's debts with the devil's leavings.

" Mrs. S.—— was a wicked woman : she put her husband against her step-daughter so that he should leave his property to her own daughters. But it all came back on her, it did : the husband took to drink. Then she tried to pay the Almighty's debts with the devil's leavin's. Although she looked so high, anybody in the church could have her daughters afterwards !" (Weobley.)

1] MS. of the late Rev. T. Barker, Eardisland.   2] Lees, 308.

God Almighty always pays his debts, *i.e.*, wrong doing is eventually punished.

Pride and ambition were the distinction of old Cob's dog, for before he'd give way for the cart to go by, he suffered it to crush him against the wall.

A queer quist. "Thee bist a queer quist"—you are a peculiar person.

Your head was not made to save your heels.

Your father was a bad glazier. (To one standing in the light.)

Winter and summer folks afore you know 'em—be slow to trust new friends.

I don't boil my cabbage twice in the same water.

> This is a rude reply sometimes made by school children, when asked what they have said.

To creep up a person's sleeve—to coax.

Meg's diversions—noisy merry-making.

> "There was all sorts of Meg's diversions goin' on next door last night." I think this is a reminiscence of the famous Morris dance by Old Meg of Herefordshire and her contemporaries, in 1609, on the race-course.

To talk the leg off an iron pot.

> "Talk ay ! 'Er'd talk the leg off an iron pot, give her time enough !"

A craking (creaking) gate hangs long on the hinges.

The earliest crow sometimes gets the latest breakfast.—H.

One-sided, like the Bridgnorth election.—H.

Such an one would cut big thongs out of another's leather, *i.e.*, be generous out of the poor rates or out of another's pocket. [This refers to times before the introduction of the new Poor-Law].—H.

To have a tile loose—slightly mad.

On a boy having the name of Solomon Abraham Napoleon, " There must have been a tile loose when that name was given ! "

Of a stupid person :—" She must have been behind the door when the manners was given out." " Faggots was scarce when *her* was baked."

It's all for the sieve, and none for the give, nowadays.

" To go for a ha'porth of gapes—to go out and see what is going on, in an idle way (*gape*, to yawn).—R.H.B.

Of a short stout woman—the nearest way round her is over her head.—R.H.B.

I have worked ten years for him, and never had *worse than my Christian name* from him—never had a mis-word.—R.H.B.

I'll give him Jack-alive, or I'll give him what for—a threat of angry retaliation, or punishment.—R.H.B.

Tib's Eve—never. It is said to be neither before Christmas Day nor after.—R.H.B.

To keep one's nose on the grindstone—to be always at work.

Every whipstitch—frequently, every now and then. (From the close fine stitches in " whipping," or over-sewing ?)

To turn the head—to nurse a sick person. " My wife's very bad, and not a sou to turn the head on her." (*On* is frequently used for *of* in Herefordshire).—R.H.B.

He's a king to what he was—he is much better, much stronger.

Of an enemy :—Ay, ay, there be worse folk nor him ; but—*ye mun go a long way to find 'em !*

It's half-past five with him—he will not live long. An allusion to leaving off work at six o'clock.[1]

" It's a bright night to see a sovereign," on a bright moonlight night.[1]

Similes.

A miserable as a pig in pattens.

As happy as a duck in a stocking.

As staring as a duck in thunder.

As miserable as the grave.

As long as the Oak and Ash grow.—H.

As sure as 'lection.—H.

As sure as eggs are eggs.

As useless as a midsummer gosling.—H. (Because sun makes them weak.)

1] Eaton Bishop.

As big an oaf as Bull's dog, which bayed at the moon till his tail froze to the ground.

Sharp as a needle with two points.

To dance (with rage) like a bull at a gate.

Shines like Worcester agen Glo'ster.—H.

Some amusing similes in rhyme which follow appeared in a local newspaper. I take them from Mr. Walter Pilley's collection : unfortunately the date is missing, also the name of the paper.

"*Herefordshire Similes.*—The following ' Herefordshire sayings ' are extracted from an old manuscript, dated just 100 years ago. Can anyone say whether the compilation is original ?—D.T., Leominster.

> As wet as a fish—as dry as a bone.
> As live as a bird—as dead as a stone.
> As plump as a partridge—as poor as a rat.
> As strong as a horse—as weak as a cat.
> As hard as a flint—as soft as a mole.
> As white as a lily—as black as a coal.
> As plain as a pikestaff—as rough as a bear.
> As tight as a drum—as free as the air.
> As heavy as lead—as light as a feather.
> As steady as time—as uncertain as weather.
> As hot as an oven—as cold as a frog.
> As gay as a lark—as sick as a dog.
> As slow as a tortoise—as swift as the wind.
> As true as the gospel—as false as mankind.
> As thin as a herring—as fat as a pig.
> As proud as a peacock—as blithe as a grig.
> As savage as tigers—as mild as a dove.
> As stiff as a poker—as limp as a glove.
> As blind as a bat—as deaf as a post.
> As cool as a cucumber—as warm as toast.
> As flat as a flounder—as round as a ball.
> As blunt as a hammer—as sharp as an awl.
> As red as a ferret—as safe as the stocks.
> As bold as a thief—as sly as a fox.

As grey as a badger—as green as a parrot.
As long as my arm—as short as a carrot.
As tame as a rabbit—as wild as a hare.
As sound as an acorn—as decayed as a pear.
As busy as ants—as nimble as goats.
As silly as geese—as stinking as stoats.
As fresh as a daisy—as sweet as a nut.
As bright as a ruby—as bitter as soot.
As straight as an arrow—as crooked as a bow.
As yellow as saffron—as black as a sloe.
As brittle as glass—as tough as gristle.
As neat as my nail—as clean as a whistle.
As good as a feast —as bad as a witch.
As light as the day—as dark as pitch.
As wide as a river—as deep as a well.
As still as a mouse—as sound as a bell.
As sure as a gun—as true as a clock.
As frail as a promise—as true as a rock.
As brisk as a bee—as dull as an ass.
As full as a tick—as solid as brass.
As lean as a greyhound—as rich as a Jew.
And ten thousand similes equally true."

Maxims.

A good contriver is better than an early riser.—H.

Man appints, the Almighty disappints.—H.

A thin dog for a long hunt.—H.

Mottoes and Various Rhymes.

In a book :—

Black is the crow,
  Black is the rook.
Blacker the blackguard
  That steals this book.

> Steal not this book,
> > For fear of shame ;
> For here you see,
> > The owner's name.

On giving a child a new dress :—
> Health to wear it ;
> Strength to bear it ;
> And money to buy another.

(2) PLACE RHYMES AND SAYINGS.

Herefordshire.

> Herverdschir,
> Schild and Sper.
>
> > > *MS. Harl,* 7371.
>
> Herefordshire,
> Sheeld and Speere.
>
> > *MS. Rawl,* Leland (from Lean, *Collectanea*).

The five W's of Herefordshire :—Wine (cider), Women, the Wye, Wells, and Woods.

> > Gough's *Camden.*

> So Hereford for her says, " Give me woof and warp,
> And Shropshire saith in her, that " Shins be ever sharp."
> > Drayton, *Polyolbion,* Song xxiii (1622).

Bacton.

" Miss Okkard (awkward) is come from Bacton ! " An expression used at Thruxton in reference to a clumsy action.—R.H.B.

Bosbury.

Make your will before going to Bosbury.

> A Malvern saying in reference to the badness of the roads between the two places.
> > Lean, *Collectanea,* i., 98.

Burton Hill.

> When Burton Hill puts on its cap,
> Weobley men put on their hats.

This is in reference to the white cloud on Burton Hill before rain.

Brampton Bryan.

When peas and other crops fail to come up, 'tis said " They are gone to Bron Fair."—H.

Cowarne.

> Dirty Cowarne, wooden steeple,
> Cracked bell, wicked people.—H.

Hope-under-Dinmore.

> Hope-under-Dinmore, if Dinmore should fall,
> The Devil will have Hope, Dinmore and all.

Kingswood Common.

> Kingswood Common and Molesey Mere,
> Are the two coldest places in Herefordshire.

Ladylift.

> When Ladie Lift puts on her shift,
> She fears a downright raine ;
> But when she doffs it you will find,
> The rain is o'er, and still the winde,
> And Phœbus shines again.

Not far from Weobley is a high hill, topped by a clump of trees, called Ladylift Clump. When obscured, rain is expected.

Notes and Queries, 1st s., ix., 53.

Letton.

> In summer, " Letton where is it ?"
> In winter, " From Letton, where should un ?
> From Letton, God help un."

This in allusion to the disastrous Wye floods.

Llangarren.

> Llangarren for riches, Orcop for poor,
> Buckle for witches, the Kymin for more.

Luston.

Luston short and Luston long,
At every house a tump[1] of dung ;
Some two some three,
The dirtiest place you ever did see.—H.

Orcop.

Orcop, God help us.

A saying based on the poverty of the parish. An old man used to come to the Savings Bank at Hereford, who when asked where he came from, would reply, " From Orcop, God help ! " but in summer his reply would be, " From Orcop, the Lord be präaysed ! "—H.

Pencombe.

Pencombe, God help !—H.

Sutton.

Sutton Wall and Kentchester Hill,
Are able to buy London, were it to sell.—

W. C. Hazlitt, *English Proverbs*, 361 (from Ray).[2]

Tarrington.

Lusty Tarrington, lively Stoke,
Beggars at Weston, thieves at Woolhope.

Weobley.

Poor Weobley, proud people,
Low church, and high steeple.

The Wye.

Blest is the eye
Between Severn and Wye.

Eye—A.S. *eyot*, an island (*see* Halliwell, 281).—Cornewall Lewis, 107.

When the bud of the aul (alder) is as big as a trout's eye,
Then that fish is in season in the river Wye.—Cornewall Lewis, 6.

1] Tump—a small heap.   2] This has been supposed to signify the fertility of the districts mentioned, but I think it more probably refers to a lost tradition of buried treasure.

(3) Gibes.

" Bromyard knaves."

" Herefordshire kindness ; a good turn rendered for a good turn received. .
Fuller says the people of Herefordshire drink back to him who drinks to them.' "[1]

The men of Orcop are called " Orcop idiots " at Dorstone.

" Go to Ross to be sharpened."

" Go to Weobley to see the tide come in ! "

> (An allusion to the sudden overflow of a brook which passes
> under the main street).

The following sayings current about the men of neighbouring counties are
probably not confined to this locality :—

Herefordshire Whitefaces.

> (The Hereford breed of cattle are called " Whitefaces," hence the
> nickname).

Devonshire cuckoos, " that put a fence round the cuckoo, so as he'd stop and
sing for 'em all the year round."

" Gloucester longeared uns," or Gloucester donkeys.

> There are said to be more donkeys in Gloucestershire than any
> other county.

Warwickshire, where they milk the cow by the tail !

Radnorshire sheep stealers.

" Worcestershire, where they cut a field o' beans in full blow,[2] because they'd
never look purtier."

Wiltshire men : moonrakers.

> A Wiltshire man tried to rake the moon out of the brook, thinking
> it was a cheese. " Rake again, daddy," said his little boy, " there's
> another cheese."[3]

1] Brewer, *Phrase and Fable*, 7th Edition, 400.
2] Pronounced to rhyme with *bough*.   3] Well known everywhere.

ADDENDA.

SECTION II. TREES AND PLANTS.

At the end of a little volume entitled *Pictures of Nature around the Malvern Hills*, by Edwin Lees, describing the Malvern Hills and surrounding districts, from a geological and botanical point of view, there is a short chapter on customs and superstitions collected chiefly in the parish of Colwall and Mathon, Herefordshire, about 1840–50. The author finds the Holy Thorn " much venerated by the peasantry of these parts." He went to see the thorn at Redmarley Farm, Acton Beauchamp, but was told by the farmer's wife that her husband had cut it down, because he was annoyed at the concourse of people that came to see it blossom on old Christmas Eve. This farmer broke his arm the next year, and soon afterwards his leg also ; not long after, part of the farm house was burnt down ; all these calamities were looked upon by the country-people in the light of " a judgment !"[1]

Nuts.

Lees (299) says " It is considered a rare year for children to be born if there are plenty of nuts in the copses and hedges ; and *double nuts* presage a considerable number of twins." This seems to mean that children are born in proportion to the crop of nuts. I have never heard the saying in North Herefordshire.[2]

SECTION III., 2. BIRDS.

Lapwing.

Lees notes a superstition concerning a bird happily very common still in our county, the lapwing, or plover :—

" In some of the low marshy meadows of this [Colwall] parish, the lapwing or pee wit (*vanellus cristatus*) breeds ; but I was informed that the country people regard these birds with much dislike, believing that the cry they made was—" bewitch'd— bewitch'd "—and shrank from them in consequence, fearing that some witchery and evil were connected with them. A lady resident in the parish informed me that her son caught a young lapwing in the meadows, and showing it to the wife of the parish clerk, he was earnestly advised by her not to keep it, because if he did, some accident or misfortune would be sure to happen. Mr. Custance tells me that the rustic belief is that the peewits are departed spirits, who still haunt the earth, in consequence of something that troubles them."[3]

1] *Op. cit.*, 296.   2] *See* Hartland, *Primitive Paternity*, vol i., p. 37.
3] Lees, 294. *See* Hartland, *Primitive Paternity*, i., 187-99.

SECTION IV., 2. MANIFESTATIONS.

Headless Ghost.

Lees (*op. cit.* 294) has recorded that at Colwall a haunted field was pointed out to him, where a ghost had been seen stalking about without a head !

3. DREAMS.

Eggs.

It is believed to be very unlucky to dream of eggs, especially spoiled eggs, and it is thought to be a sign of a death in the family of the dreamer.   A short time ago a Herefordshire lady sent her maid to gather eggs before breakfast, remarking that she had been dreaming that they had been forgotten and were all spoiled.   Later in the day, she had occasion to tell the same maid of the death of a relative, news of which had come by the morning's post.   " Yes, ma'am," was the unexpected reply, " cook was saying how it would be when she heard of your dream about the eggs all spoiled !"

SECTION VI., 2. LOVE DIVINATIONS (page 61, *et. seq*).

Pullet's Eggs.

According to Lees (*op. cit.* 297), the egg must be eaten walking upstairs backwards, backing into bed, in silence.   If the lover, in the dream, offer a glass of water, he will be a poor man ; if ale, a tradesman ; but if a glass of wine, a gentleman.

Crossed Shoes.

These should be placed under the pillows, crossing the left shoe over the right. Lees, *loc. cit.*

Dumb Cake.

Lees gives New Year's Eve as the day for this, and gives careful directions after the cake has been made and eaten in silence by the girls, " one of them must place a clean chemise, turned inside out, before the fire.   This must be sprinkled with water by a branch of rosemary.   All must then sit round the fire in silence till the clock strikes twelve.   If any among the party will be married during the ensuing year, the form of such foreshadowed husband will approach the fire and turn the chemise."   Lees adds :—

The observation of certain plants is here as in other parts of the country productive of superstition, such as the well-known " Midsummer Men," Livelong, or *sedum telephium,* considered to show affection in a lover, by enduring a long time alive when hung up against a wall ; the " Five-leaved grass with six leaves on "—*potentilla reptans,* which brings a lover ; and the root of the common brake-fern (*pteris aquilina*), which, cut in two obliquely, shows the initial letters of a sweetheart's name . . . . The leaves of the common ash are still looked to, under the hope of their bringing "*luck or a lover*," if the terminating leaflets are even,—the leaves generally ending in an odd leaflet . . . . . To ascertain whether a pretended lover is sincere or not the lorn damsel takes an apple-pip (or kernel) from the pericarp, and naming one of her followers, puts the pip into the fire. If it make a noise in bursting from the heat, it is a proof of love; but if it is consumed without any crack, then there is no real regard for her in the person named. The charm was thus spoken as the pip was thus thrown into the fire :—

> "If you love me, bounce and fly;
> If you hate me, lie and die."

Another charm consisted in sticking pips upon the cheek, and naming several lovers, the truest being designated by remaining longest upon the cheek.

Section VII. Leechcraft.

Bite of a Viper.

The same author describes a curious cure for the bite of a viper used by those living round the Malvern Hills. The county boundary runs along the top of the hills, and much of the folk-lore of the district is common to Herefordshire or Worcestershire.

The viper, or adder, is occasionally to be met with in bushy ground, about the southern part of the range. . . . It is a superstition among the country people of the neighbourhood, that when a viper bites anyone, if it can be killed forthwith, an ointment made from the liver will be a specific for the wound. When I resided at Malvern Wells in 1841, a boy there was bitten by a viper, and his father was out on the hills all day, seeking in vain to catch and destroy the venomous creature, with the view of making the ointment considered necessary.[1]

Section VIII. General Superstitions.

Burning Boots.

It is lucky to burn any old boots available, before starting on a journey. A Herefordshire servant told her mistress she had seen the hop-pickers, who were to leave next day, with such funny old boots laid out all round their fire. "They [are] sure to be going to burn them," she said; "Mother always does before going away any-where; she says its *such* a lucky thing to do!"[2]

White Liver.

Lees, (*op. cit.*, 307) notes that the expression "white-livered scoundrel" was in common use in the middle of last century, and adds "an impression exists that some people really *have white livers*. I knew a young woman who had refused to marry a man because she was told he had a white liver, and therefore she would be sure to die within twelve months after marriage. A gentleman, too, whom I knew some years since, I have heard people say, had a white liver, because it must be so, they thought, as he had married several wives, who had all died."

1] Lees, 71.   2] Dilwyn.

A Copy of a Letter,

WRITTEN

By Our Saviour JESUS CHRIST.

Found 18 Miles from *Iconium*, 65 Years after our blessed Saviour's Crucifixion: Transmitted from the holy City by a converted Jew, faithfully translated from the Original Hebrew Copy, now in the Possession of the Lady *Cuba's* Family at

Mesopotamia. This Letter was written by *Jesus Christ*, and found under a great Stone both round and large, at the Foot of the Cross, near a Village called *Mesopotamia.* Upon the Stone was written or engraven—*Blessed is he that shall turn me over.*

People that saw it prayed to God earnestly, and desired he would make known to them the Meaning of this Writing, that they might not attempt in vain to turn it over. In the mean Time there came a little Child about six or seven Years old, and turned it over, without any Help or Assistance, to the Admiration of all those that stood by. And under this Stone was found this Letter which was written by Jesus Christ, and was carried to the City of Iconium, and there published by a Person belonging to the Cuba Family; and in the Letter was written the Commandments of Jesus Christ, signed by the Angel Gabriel, 78 Years after our Saviour's Birth. To which are added, King Agbarus's Letter to our Saviour and our Saviour's Answer; Also his Miracles, and Lentulus's Epistle to the Senate of Rome.

A Letter of Jesus Christ.

WHOSOEVER worketh on the Sabbath-Day shall be cursed.

I command you to go to the Church, and keep the Lord's-Day holy, without doing any Manner of Work. You shall not idly spend your Time with bedecking yourself with superfluities of costly Apparel and vain Dresses, for I have ordained a Day of Rest. I will have that Day kept holy that your Sins may be forgiven you. You shall not break my Commandments, but observe and keep them, written with my own Hand and spoken with my own Mouth. You shall not only go to Church yourself, but your Men Servants and Maid Servants, and observe my Words and learn my Commandments. You shall finish your Labour every Saturday Afternoon by six o'clock, at which hour the Preparation of the Sabbath begins. I advise you to fast five Fridays in every Year, beginning with Good Friday, and to continue the four Fridays immediately following, in Remembrance of the five bloody Wounds which I received for all Mankind. You shall diligently and peaceably labour in your respective Callings, wherein it hath pleased God to call you. You shall love one another with brotherly Love, and cause them that are baptized to come to Church and receive the Sacrament of the Lord's Supper; and be made Members of the Church: In so doing I will give you a long Life, many Blessings, your Land shall flourish, and your Cattle shall bring forth in Abundance and I will give you many Blessings and Comforts in the greatest Temptations; and he that doth to the contrary shall be unprofitable. I will also send a Hardness of Heart upon them, till I see them; but especially upon the impenitent Unbelievers: He that hath given to the Poor shall not be unprofitable. Remember to keep holy the Sabbath-Day, for the Seventh Day I have taken to rest myself; and he that hath a Copy of this Letter, written with my own Hand, and spoken with my own Mouth, and keepeth it without publishing it to others, shall not prosper; but he that publisheth it to others shall be blessed of me. And though his sins be in Number as the Stars of the Sky, and he believes in this, he shall be pardoned; and if he believes not this Writing and this Commandment; I will send my Plagues upon him, and consume both him, his Children, and his Cattle. And whosoever shall have a Copy of this Letter, written with my own Hand, and keep it in their own Houses nothing shall hurt them, neither Pestilence, Lightning, nor Thunder shall do them any Hurt. And if a Woman be with Child, and in Labour, and a Copy of this Letter be about her, and she firmly puts her Trust in me, she shall be safely delivered of her Birth. You shall have no News of me but by the Holy Scriptures, until the Day of Judgment.

All Goodness and Prosperity shall be on the House where a Copy of this Letter shall be found.

Christ's *Cures and Miracles.*

HE cleansed a Leper by only touching him. He healed the Centurion's Servant that was afflicted with a Fever. Several possessed with Devils. A violent Tempest was stilled by him. A man sick of the Palsy. Raised a Maid from the Dead. He cured two blind Men. A dumb Man possessed of the Devil. He fed above five Thousand with five Loaves and two Fishes. He walked on the Sea. All the Diseases in Genesaret he healed by the Touch of his Garment. He cured a Woman vexed with a Devil, and a Multitude that were lame, blind, dumb, maimed, etc. He fed above four Thousand with four Loaves and a few little Fishes.

King Agbarus's *Letter to our* SAVIOUR.

I Have heard of thee, and of the Cures wrought by thee without Herbs or Medicines: For it is reported thou re-storest Sight unto the blind, makest the Lame to walk, cleansest the Leprous, raisest the Dead, and healest those who are tormented with Diseases of a long Continuance.

Having heard all this of thee, I was fully persuaded to believe one of these Things, either that thou art a very God, and camest down from Heaven to do such Miracles; or else thou art the Son of God, and performest them. Wherefore I have now sent these lines, entreating thee to come hither, and cure my Disease; because, having heard that the Jews murmur against thee, and contrive to do thee a Mischief, I invite thee to my City, which is a little one indeed, but beautiful, and sufficient to entertain us both.

Our SAVIOUR's *Answer.*

BLESSED art thou, Agbarus, for believing in me, whom thou hast not seen: For it is written of me, that they which have seen me should not believe on me; that they which have not seen me may believe, and be saved. But concerning the Matter thou hast written about, these are to acquaint thee, That all things for which I am sent hither must be fulfilled, and then I shall be taken up and returned to him that sent me, but after my Ascension, I will send thee one of my Disciples, who shall cure thy Distemper, and give Life to thee, and to them that are with thee.

Lentulus's *Epistle to the Senate of* Rome, *containing a Description of* Jesus Christ.

THERE appeared in these Days a Man of great Virtue called Jesus Christ, and by the People called a Prophet, but his own Disciples called him the Son of God. He raised the Dead, and cured all Manner of Diseases. A Man of Stature somewhat tall and comely, with a reverend Countenance, such as the Beholders may both fear and love. His Hair is the Colour of a Chestnut full ripe, and is plain down almost to his Ears, but from thence downwards it is somewhat curled, but more orient of Colour, waving about his Shoulders. In the midst of his Head goeth down a Seam of Hair, or parting, like the Nazarites, his Forehead very plain and smooth, his Face without Spot or Wrinkle; beautiful with a comely red, his Nose and Mouth so formed, that nothing can be reprehended, his Beard thick the Colour of the Hair on his Head; his Eyes grey, clear and quick; in reproving he is severe, in counselling courteous; he is fair spoken, and pleasant in Speech, mixed with Gravity; it cannot be remembered that any have seen him laugh, but many have seen him weep; in Proportion of Body he is well shaped and straight; his Hands and Arms very delectable to behold; in speaking very temperate, modest and wise; a Man for singular Beauty far exceeding all the Sons of Men.

FINIS.

Printed and Sold by ADAMS & SONS, 5, 6, 7, East Street, Hereford.

Charm in a Mattress.

Mrs. W———, of Pembridge, said she had been making a new cover for a feather bed, which belonged to a farmer's wife for whom she occasionally worked. In the feathers she found "two little things like pincushions." "Charms, they was," she explained mysteriously, "and that was why her never had no children." What the supposed charms contained she could not or would not tell. This woman was typically Welsh, and extremely superstitious.

SECTION X., 1. BIRTH.

Our Saviour's Letter. (*See* page 112, and illustration.)

Since this chapter was in type, Mrs. Cresswell, of Ocle Court, has found the "Saviour's Letter" in use, and still firmly believed in by the folk of South Hereford-shire. It was printed and sold in Hereford, as the illustration shows. One of Mrs. Cresswell's informants has given a copy of the letter to several members of her family, and has perfect faith in its efficacy.

The letter is of course apocryphal, a well-known mediæval forgery. *Cf. Folk-lore*, xiii., 424.

SECTION XV., 1. LOCAL SAINTS.

St. Catharine. (*See* pp. 212, and 6, *ante.*)

Lees gives a version of the story of St. Catharine's mare and colt, as follows :—

"A person, said to be a girl with a pair of pattens on, having stolen St. Catharine's mare and colt and led them down several brooks to avoid detection, the saint, upon being informed of her loss, prayed that wherever the animals and thief trod, the marks of their feet might be left ; and that in answer to this prayer, the prints of the animals' feet, and also of the patten rings, were deeply indented, not only in the earth, but also in the stones wherever they trod, and thereby they were traced to, and found at, Ledbury."

The writer goes on to explain the natural formation of these "whirl-holes" by the action of the water on the softer parts of the stone slabs, and gives several parallels to the story, including the legend of St. Degan, a Welsh saint, whose foot-marks are shown on the cliffs in Pembrokeshire. He adds that many of the stones from Sapey brook were carried off for museums.[1]

1] Lees, 140, 250.

APPENDIX A.

Legendary portions of the Life of St. Ethelbert, from Capgrave's *Nova Legenda Angliæ*, i., 412, *et. seq.*

(1) " For as he was about to mount his horse . . . . the sun showed forth his rays."

Sed in ipso profectionis exordio antequam equum ascenderet, mirabile signum, stupentibus cunctis, innotuit. Sub ipso namque ascendente terra mota est, imminens periculum mortis prefigurans ; totaque diei claritas subtracta subito disparuit, et quasi quedam columpna nebulis hinc inde oppositis obducta sub nube erupit, que aliquamdiu quadam tenui flamma eis vestigia lucis ministravit ; que columpna, diu visa, a nube demum suscepta est. Deinde visus est nigrescere sol et horidas tenebras tetre noctis ingerere. . . . . Prostratis in terram cunctis, et dei famulo Ethelberto diutius orante, splendor diei repente illuxit, et sol suos radios patefecit.

(2) " But that night . . . . and royal ornaments."

Eadem autem nocte magna gloria domini super gloriosum beati martyris Ethelberti sepulchrum apparuit, et luminis immensi claritas effulsit. Videbatur adeo flamma immensa ut tota regio igne putaretur accensa. Nam columpna lucis sole splendidior ab ejus sepulchro usque in celum tendebatur, quam velut flamime omnia devorantis scintille et radii, coruscantes sequebantur. Que regi Offe relata, eum graviter terruerunt, et ut peniteret, ad viam humilitatis reduxerunt. Qui decimam omnium rerum suarum ecclesie dei tribuit, agros etiam et rura et quecunque possedit decimavit. Tertia post illius martirium nocte apparuit [sanctus] cuidam simplici viro quiescenti in stratu suo, cum magna luce in habitu claro, et ut veiociter surgeret, imperavit. " Surge, inquit, Brithfride, surge et perge ad sepulchrum meum, et corpus meum juxta monasterium prope Waye fluvium constructum reconde. Ego sum Orientalium Anglorum rex, Ethelbertus, et ut hoc verbum facias, precepit tibi deus." Expergefactus a sompno vir ille, oculos aperuit, et illustratam celesti claritate totam domum prospexit. Cumque brachia, ut sanctum comprehenderet, extendere vellet, cum splendore claritatis martyr abscedens non comparuit. Exurgens vir ille, et assumpto secum vicino suo nomine Egmundo, corpus de terra elevatum, lotum et albis vestibus indutum, in curru posuerunt. Et occurrens cecus quidam, oculorum lumen sancti regis meritis, gratias agens, impetravit. Sepelierunt autem corpus sanctum in loco qui antiquitus Fernlega dicebatur, id est, " saltus filicis," nunc vero a provincialibus Herefordia nominatur. Eadem tempestate per plura annorum spacia unaquaque nocte super sanctum sepulchrum lux de celo emissa radiabat, que quidem in columpnia ignea gloriosum ejus martyrium revelabat. Milfridus demum rex precipit cuidam episcopo suo locum sanctum adire et martyrem cum devocione adorare. Quo facto, magnalia dei qui audivit, sanitates infirmorum, curationes languorum quas oculis perspexit, innocentis regis interitum quem didicit, principi suo nunciare curavit. Milfridus igitur rex ad eundem locum pecunias infinitas delegavit, et ecclesiam miro opere lapideo, ad laudem et honorem beati martyris a fundamentis construxit ; primusque omnium regum eidem loco episcopum substituit, et terrarum possessionibus atque regalibus ornamentibus decoravit.

APPENDIX B.

The following versions of the legends of St. Ethelbert are from the Hereford Breviary, *Breviarium secundum usum Herford*, printed at Rouen by Inglelbert Haghe, in 1505.

(1) From the lessons for St. Ethelbert's Day, if it occurred after Trinity.

Lectio V. Cum enim rex in conspectu omnium regum equum ascendit, motum dat terra, exercitum territat universum. Terre signo mox celi respondet signum ; sol enim per orbem radios spargens fulserat lucide : et ecce subito obscuratur tota curia.

Lectio VI. Rex suos confortans "Flectamus," inquit, "genua, prece polum pulsemus ut nostri misereatur Deus." Vix completa oratione, fit aura tota serena. Tum rex hylaris effectus ait, "Sit nomen Domini benedictum ex hoc nunc et usque in seculum."

(2) From the lessons for the second day of St. Ethelbert's octave.

Lectio I. Vidit namque sanctus Ethelbertus per somnium aule regie sue tectum dedisse, vestem qua induebatur, sanguine madefactam, trabem longam et latam in medio urbis erectam, in altum seipsum in navem transfiguratum, et levi volatu super-volutasse.

(3)

Lectio VIII. Rex autem Offa corpus beati martyris in paludem prope ripam fluminis Lugga proiici precepit ; in quo loco eadem nocte ad celum usque porrecta visa est splendere fulgide lucis columna.

(4) From the Responds to the lessons at Matins on St. Ethelbert's Day (May 20).

(1). Illustris regis martyrium signa stupenda precedunt, terra tremore concutitur, dies in noctem repente vertitur. Sol rutilans tetra caligine obducitur. Alleluia.

(5) Antiphons to the Psalms at Lauds, on St. Ethelbert's Day.

(1) Innocentem dolo regem manus ferit impia ; signa mortem Deo gratam testantur cælestia. Alleluya.

(2) Ut probaret quod regnaret cum Christo vir inclitus, circumfulsit corpus sanctum lux emissa celitus. Alleluya.

(3) Tangens caput venerandum cecus lumen recipit ; Ethelberto personare dignas laudes in-cipit. Alleluya.

(4) Dum trementem caput sanant martyris suffragia, regione boreali dotatur ecclesia. Alleluya.

APPENDIX C.

A list of games played in Herefordshire with references to accounts and descriptions of the same in Lady Gomme's *Traditional Games* ::—

Alligoshee	Gomme, i.,	7
Bell-horses	,, i.,	27
Bingo	,, i.,	29
Blind Man's Buff	,, i.,	37
Carry my lady to London	,, i.,	59
Cat's Cradle	,, i.,	62
Cobbler's Hornpipe	,, i.,	71
Conquerors *or* Conkers	,, i.,	77 (No. 4)
The Cushion Dance	,, i.,	87

An old fiddler at Kinnersley said he used to play " Green grow the Rushes O !" for this.

Drop Handkerchief *or* Drop the Glove	Gomme, i.,	109

This game is called " Dummy " at Wigmore.

Duckstone	,, i.,	116
Eller Tree (locally, " A bundle of rags ")	,, i.,	119
Fivestones	,, i.,	122
Follow my Leader	,, i.,	131
Forfeits	,, i.,	137
Fox and Goose	,, i.,	139
Green Gravel	,, i.,	171
Green grow the Leaves	,,	i., 185 (No. 2)

(*See Marden Forfeit Song, ante,* p. 206).

Hand-dandy, *or* Tip it	,, i.,	191
Hare and hounds	,, i.,	191
Hark the robbers	,, i.,	192
Hen and chickens	,, i.,	201
Hop-Scotch	,, i.,	223
How many miles to Babylon	,, i.,	231
Hunt the slipper	,, i.,	241
Isabella	,, i.,	247
Jack, Jack, the bread's a burning	,, i.,	259
Jenny Jones	,, i.,	260
Jolly Sailors, *or* Sailor Boys	,, i.,	294
Kiss in the Ring	,, i.,	305

    " An ancient game, of which the representation is still kept
up." (Fosbroke, *Ariconensia,* 74).

APPENDIX D.

The following hunting songs are included on account of their interest for local readers; they are of eighteenth century date.

THE HEREFORDSHIRE FOX-CHASE.

All you that love hunting
Attend to my song,
I must beg some indulgence
As 'twill be rather long.
It's concerning a huntsman,
His horse, and his dogs,
That never fear'd mountains,
Hedges, ditches, or bogs.

In the year ninety-seven (1797),
Twelfth Eve was the day,
Bright Phœbus shone forth
And the morning was gay.
Resolved on a chase,
To which Reynard gave birth,
I'm convinced such a one
Was ne'er equalled on earth.

Squire Parry well mounted,
Away he did ride,
James Carless, with dogs,
Coupled close by his side.
Off to St. Margaret's Park
Did I repair
For Reynard long time
Had been harbouring there.

No sooner arrived,
As I've since understood,
Than the drag of a fox
They soon cross'd near the wood ;
Cries James, " Hark !" to Rounder :
For that was the hound
That led the whole pack
When old Reynard was found.

Hark, hark, altogether !
" Good dogs ! " was the cry :
The next that did second
Was Bumper and Fly ;
Then they all came together,
How sweet was the sound,
For the fox now broke cover
And dashed o'er the ground.

Now Reynard's unkennel'd,
Hark forward, my boys !
Hark, hark ! Tallyho !
What can rival those joys ?
And those who have souls
Let them join in the choir,
For yonder goes Reynard
At full speed before !

O'er Snodhill Park, then
Off to Cusop Hill ran,
Through Dorstone to Moccas,
The sport thus began.
Then he took Blakemere Hill,
So pleasing a thing
For to hear the woods echo
And the valleys to ring.

Then he turned down again
And round Preston Court went,
Through Tiberton back, and
To Timberline bent ;
But before I go farther
A joke I'll unfold :
If I'm wrong, pray, forgive me,
For this I've been told.

That the first time old Reynard
Had left his abode,
Thinks he, I'll provide for
A bait on the road.
He equip'd himself off
With the wing of a goose,
But was so tightly pursued
That his prey he let loose.

The Squire fatigued was,
Long left behind.;
Spied the wing—catched it up,
And it served him to dine ;
For the next house he came to
Was Lloyd's, I declare.
So he left the sweet hounds
For to feast on it there.

So leave him I must
At this soaking place,
Since wine be preferred
To the fox-hunting chase ;
So he dined on what Reynard
Intended to lunch,
And instead of pursuing, too,
Stuck to the punch.

And now to continue
My song as before :
Through Brampton to Kingstone
And round by Blackmore,
O'er Moorhampton Park,
With what speed he did bound.
How charming the hills
Redoubled the sound.

The Golden Vale crossed,
That well-known, sweet turf,
In Chanstone great covers
'Twas said he would earth.
But the hounds press'd so hard
And the warmth of the day
Obliged him to pass it
And soon take the way.

Then up the Cwm dingle
Was Reynard's next choice :
You'd have thought that
The trees on each side had a voice,
Not Handel himself could
Such music impart.
Had Diana been there
She'd been pleased to the heart.

Once more to his own
  Native park did repair,
And sought, though in vain,
  For to find shelter there.
For the hounds, gaining ground,
  Scarce a field now behind,
Although quite at home
  Yet no safety could find.

The sun, which had shone
  So delightful all day,
Had finished his course
  And to Luna gave way.
Poor Reynard, now weakened,
  His brush sweep'd the ground,
Yet he aims for the Darren
  By way of Longtown.

The Black Mountain climb'd,
  Though scarce able to creep.
But Rounder and Brusher
  Soon made him retreat.
Close down by the Darren
  They run him in view,
Such a night of confusion
  No fox ever knew.

Then for Abergavenny
  He takes them ahead.
The old, old hounds got up,
  And the pack they soon lead ;

Thus showed that old Reynard
  Soon conquered must be,
As you, in the sequel,
  Shall certainly see.

James Carless came up
  Who had tired his nag,
And as for himself
  Was scarce able to wag ;
For in ninety-eight miles,
  All bad ground, I protest,
Thus horse, man, and dogs,
  Not one moment did rest.

Then seeing bold Reynard
  Lie dead on the ground,
The hounds, all in rapture,
  Enclosing him round.
To welcome the huntsman
  The dogs all rose up,
And each joined in Chorus
  With the joyful whoo-whoop !

Now Reynard is dead
  And my song ends at last ;
Excuse me, I'm thirsty,
  Then push round the glass.
So I'll drink with a wish
  That all men in place,
May to their Queen stick,
  As true as the hounds to the chase.

Mr. Noah Richards, of Moorhampton, who wrote out the song, believed the account of the run to be true ; he could remember James Carless, a well-known Herefordshire huntsman.

THE FOX-HUNTING CHASE.

Come all you bold sportsmen, come listen awhile,
I will sing you a ditty which will cause you to smile,
Concerning bold Reynard, bold Reynard the fox,
Which mostly doth harbour in woods or in rocks.

It was the ninth day of April, as I've heard them say,
Bright Phœbus shone clear and the morning was gay,
Squire Berington was mounted and away he did ride,
And likewise his huntsman, with his hounds by his side.

Then away for old " Badnage," so bold they did steer,
To find out bold Reynard which harboured there.
Go harking to cover Tom Hughes he did cry,
No sooner had Tom spoke but bold Reynard they spied.

Now when the fox wakened and on his legs stood,
He said, " I think now I heard some hounds in the woods ;
And I know they are swift, and they'll run like the winds,
But I will run faster and leave them behind."

Then up Brinsop's Dingle, bold Reynard made choice,
You would have thought that the trees on each side had a voice.
Up rode Squire Berington wth such music in part.
And likewise Sir Yunstall was pleased to the heart.

Then away for Minehead's Park so bold they did steer,
Such prattling music I'm sure ne'er was heard ;
Where the people ran out and they did them extal,
Saying, " I think the grey horse is the best of them all."

Now away for Church Dilwyn, bold Reynard was bent,
But the hounds followed after, so strong was their scent,
The hounds followed after, they are all in full cry.
Tom swore by his Maker bold Reynard should die.

"Now here's a fig for Squire Berington and likewise his hounds;
I'll go back now to Chance Hill and there I'll take grounds."
But the hounds followed after and their scent did embrace,
And there's few can compare to our fox-hunting chase.

It was in the Dog Wood, as I have been told,
Little Gaylass she caught him and so fast did she hold;
There was Vermer and Bumper, but the bitch did embrace,
And she soon put an end to our fox-hunting chase.

Now our day's sport is ended boys, home we'll return,
In a bowl of good liquors for the fox we will mourn;
Come fill up our glasses most sweetly we'll sing,
" Here's a health to Squire Berington, and long live the King."

This song was written, and a tune composed for it, by Richard Matthews, of Upper Hill, in the reign of George III. Squire Berington lived at Wintercott then, and kept a pack of foxhounds at Winsley. When he heard of the song he sent for Matthews, locked the door of the room, and told him to sing his song; if it should prove derogatory to the pack of hounds, he should have a flogging with the Squire's hunting crop. But after hearing the song, Squire Berington was so pleased that he gave the man two sheep, and had him in to sing the song to his guests frequently afterwards. It was noted from a descendant of Richard Matthews, by Miss Nellie Smith, to whom I am indebted for its history.

INDEX.

ERRATA.

On page 13, line 31, *read* " A spring," *not* " As pring."

On page 27, line 2, insert " *when* Charles I."

On page 3, line 3, *read* " Twyn-y-beddau," *not* " Twyn-y-beddan."

On page 33, note line 1, page 38, line 8 and line 1, in note *read* " Cwn Annuw," *not* " Cwn Annwn."

On page 180, line 16, *read* " imperfect than."

On page 196, line 9, *read* " now," *not* " new."